Journal of Semitic Studies Supplement 33

The Palmyrene Tax Tariff

by

Il'i͡a Sholeĭmovich Shifman

Translated by Svetlana Khobnya

and

Edited by John F. Healey

Published by Oxford University Press
on behalf of the University of Manchester
2014

OXFORD
UNIVERSITY PRESS

Great Clarendon Street, Oxford OX2 6DP

Oxford University Press is a department of the University of Oxford. It furthers the University's objective of excellence in research, scholarship, and education by publishing worldwide in

Oxford New York

Athens Auckland Bangkok Bogotá Buenos Aires Cape Town Chennai Dar es Salaam Delhi
Florence Hong Kong Istanbul Karachi Kolkata Kuala Lumpur Madrid Melbourne Mexico City
Mumbai Nairobi Paris São Paulo Shanghai Singapore Taipei Tokyo Toronto Warsaw

with associated companies in Berlin Ibadan

Oxford is a registered trade mark of Oxford University Press in the UK
and in certain other countries

Published in the United Kingdom
by Oxford University Press, Oxford

© The University of Manchester, 2014

The moral rights of the author have been asserted
Database right Oxford University Press (maker)

First published 2014

All rights reserved. No part of this publication may be reproduced, stored in a retrieval system, or transmitted, in any form or by any means, without the prior permission in writing of Oxford University Press, or as expressly permitted by law, or under terms agreed with the appropriate reprographics rights organization. Enquiries concerning reproduction outside the scope of the above should be sent to the Rights Department, Journals Division, Oxford University Press, at the address above

You must not circulate this book in any other binding or cover and
you must impose this same condition on any acquirer

A catalogue for this book is available from the British Library

Library of Congress Cataloguing in Publication Data
(Data available)

ISSN 0022-4480
ISBN 978-0-19-872615-9

Subscription information for the *Journal of Semitic Studies* is available at the journal website:
jss.oxfordjournals.org

Printed in Great Britain by Bell & Bain Ltd, Glasgow

Table of Contents

Foreword	v
Acknowledgments	vii
Biography of I. Sh. Shifman by Dr Alexander Grouchevoy	ix
Introduction	1
1. Preliminary Remarks	1
2. Sources on the History of Palmyra	2
3. Palmyrene History and Culture	14
4. The Circumstances Surrounding the Finding of the Palmyrene Tariff and the History of its Interpretation	37
5. Description of the Inscription	46
6. The Structure of the Text	47
7. The Particularities of the Palaeography and the Language of the Document	77
8. The Palmyrene Tariff as an Historical Source	85
Text of the Inscription	97
Translation	111
Commentary	129
Glossaries (Greek and Aramaic)	221
Abbreviations and Bibliography	291
Plates	301

Foreword

The idea of publishing a translation of Il'ĩa Sholeĭmovich Shifman's *Pal'mirskiĭ poshlinnyĭ tarif: vvedenie, perevod i kommentariĭ* (Moscow 1980)[1] had its origin in my work on Palmyrene inscriptions for my 2009 book, *Aramaic Inscriptions and Documents of the Roman Period* (Oxford University Press). I visited St Petersburg to examine the Palmyrene Tariff inscription (published as *CIS* II, 3913) in the State Hermitage Museum and only then became aware of the usefulness of Shifman's book. It is the only monograph dedicated to the Palmyrene Tariff and contains a mass of detailed commentary, as well as an edition of the Aramaic and Greek text and a Russian translation. It also contains invaluable information on the discovery of the inscription and its transfer to the Hermitage.

I wanted access to Shifman's work despite my ignorance of Russian and felt that it would be valuable to arrange for a translation of the book into English. The initial idea of having a translation made simply for my own use developed into a proposal to publish the English translation so that Shifman's work could become better known.

The aim has been to translate Shifman's work as it stands, but with the hand-written Greek and Aramaic replaced by typed text. A brief academic biography of Shifman has been added, provided by one of Shifman's own students, Dr A. Grouchevoy.

Since an effort was being made to complete as far as possible the bibliographical details cited by Shifman, I decided that it would be best to bring the book into line (more or less) with the normal style of the *Journal of Semitic Studies*. Hence, for example, the list of abbreviations has been reorganized and simplified and pagination and other details have been added, as far as possible (and not without difficulty in the case of the Russian publications), to the Bibliography.

In one or two places the inflexibility of modern technology has enforced a minor change of layout.

The transcription of Russian names presents particular problems. In general

---

1   И. Ш. Шифман, *Пальмирский пошлинный тариф. Введение, перевод и комментарий*, Москва: Наука [Главная редакция восточной литературы; Академия Наук СССР, Институт Востоковедения], 1980.

we have adhered to the American Library Association-Library of Congress system, though the established spelling of the names of well-known authors who have also published in western European languages has been retained in a few cases (e.g. Rostovtzeff). In rendering names of Semitic origin, diacritics are generally added to aid with the identification especially of consonants. These diacritics are usually omitted where the Greek text is being translated into English.

No attempt has been made to change citations of Greek, Latin, Aramaic and Hebrew texts to editions more commonly used in western Europe, though there has been some checking to ensure that the original text in question can be easily found.

Minor errors have been corrected without comment and some terminology which seems to have been current in Soviet-era Russian is adjusted to ensure the meaning is clear in English. I hope that new errors are few and ask the reader to bear in mind the fact that this is a 'practical' translation designed initially to help me understand Shifman's interpretations and comments: it is not meant to be literary or even literal at all points!

There is naturally a dilemma about how far to 'correct' a work which is now over thirty years old without misrepresenting the thought and argument of the original author. Broadly, I have let Shifman stand as it was originally published (apart from the minor changes referred to above). Very rarely and only when really necessary, I have added a comment in parentheses introduced by 'ed.', for 'editor'.

I have also reproduced the Aramaic and Greek texts which Shifman included in his book and which formed the basis of all his discussion. With regard to readings of the text of the Tariff, having worked on the Aramaic in St Petersburg in 2009, I am confident of the Aramaic readings given in my own book (above). The Greek will form a separate volume of the *Inscriptions grecques et latines de la Syrie* series, to be published in due course (though not imminently, as I understand) by J.-B. Yon. A first volume, containing the other Greek inscriptions of Palmyra (and including the Aramaic in the case of bilinguals), has already appeared (*IGLS* XVII [fascicule 1] [Bibliothèque Archéologique et Historique t. 195], Presses de l'IFPO, Beirut 2012). Professor Yon's publication will no doubt improve the readings. Meanwhile, Shifman's volume presents a comprehensive account of the inscription.

Biography of I. Sh. Shifman

The *Journal of Semitic Studies* (University of Manchester) kindly agreed to publish the translation in its supplement series. I am deeply in its debt. In addition the translation work was largely funded out of monies ultimately derived from *JSS*.

The basic translation work has been carried out by Dr Svetlana Khobnya, who began the work while she was still a Ph.D. student in New Testament Studies in Manchester. She is a graduate of the Volgograd Pedagogical State University (Faculty of Linguistics). My own contribution has been in the polishing of the English translation, the clarification (as far as is possible) of academic aspects and the insertion of sections of Aramaic and Greek text.

While the above work was in progress I obtained the formal permission to publish this translation from the Russian Academy of Sciences (heir to the Academy of the USSR) and the authorities related to the original publishers, the Nauka Publishing House. Professor Dr Serge Frantsouzoff acted as initial intermediary in the obtaining of these permissions, including the necessary contact with Mrs Svetlana Anikeyeva of the Publishing House 'Vostochnaya Literatura' in Moscow and Professor Dr Irina F. Popova, Director of the Institute of Oriental Manuscripts of the Russian Academy of Sciences (St Petersburg) who kindly agreed to the project on behalf of the Institute.

Acknowledgments

To be thanked above all is Dr Svetlana Khobnya. She proved to be a diligent and skilled translator, who brought to the project her impressive academic background in the field. Katia Kozlova, a doctoral student of Oxford University, is to be thanked for help on points of Russian when I needed urgent answers to some specific questions.

Special thanks are owed to Professor Dr Serge Frantsouzoff. He dealt with matters which would have been very difficult for me to negotiate. His help is very much appreciated.

Other Russian colleagues who are to be thanked are Dr Alexander B. Nikitin, Assistant Curator at the State Hermitage Museum, who facilitated my visit to the Museum in 2009 and first drew my attention to the book by Shifman. He himself was also the compiler and editor of the booklet *Pal'mirskiĭ Tamozhennyĭ Tarif* (The Palmyrene Trade Tariff), published in St

Petersburg in 2011. He and Elena Obukhovich, Manager of the Rights and Reproductions Office in the Hermitage, also provided me with copies of photographs originally taken in Syria by Yaʿqūb Khouri, dragoman of the Russian consulate in Jerusalem at the beginning of the twentieth century. Professor J.-B. Yon helped me to obtain excellent photographs from the archives of the Laboratoire Histoire et Sources des Mondes Antiques (HiSoMA), Lyons, and I am especially grateful for his help.

Dr Alexander Grouchevoy of the Institute of Oriental Manuscripts, a former student of Professor Shifman, gave valuable advice, checked a particular point in the Russian Academy's archives and provided a short biography of his teacher. I am extremely grateful to him: his biography gives us a much better understanding of Shifman as a scholar and as man.

My Manchester colleague, Professor David Langslow, has been kind enough to discuss the Greek text with me and has saved me from a number of errors.

The practicalities of preparing a book of this kind for publication would be a challenge for any typesetter. Fortunately the *Journal of Semitic Studies* has an Assistant Editor in Bronwen Campbell who is used to and adept at handling such challenges. She has worked tirelessly, showing her usual skill and patience, in preparing this volume for publication.

Remaining mistakes are, of course, mine — or Dr Shifman's.

John F. Healey
November 2013

Department of Middle Eastern Studies
University of Manchester
Manchester M13 9PL
john.healey@manchester.ac.uk

Il'ia Sholeĭmovich Shifman (1930–1990): his life and scientific work

by A.G. Grouchevoy

Il'ia Sholeĭmovich Shifman, the well-known Soviet specialist in the study of the Ancient Near East, Doctor of Historical Sciences, Senior Researcher in the Leningrad branch of the Institute of Oriental Studies of the Academy of Sciences of the USSR, was born on 1st June 1930 in Leningrad. During World War II he was evacuated from Leningrad and lived in a number of different cities — in Rybinsk, Stalingrad, Baku and Astrakhan. After the war, in 1945, his parents returned to Leningrad.[1]

In 1948, Il'ia Sholeĭmovich joined the Department of Assyriology and Hebraic Studies in the Faculty of Oriental Studies of Leningrad State University. However, he was only able to study at the Oriental Faculty for two years. In 1950, in the wider political context of the period after the foundation of the State of Israel and of Soviet policy at that time, the Department of Assyriology and Hebraic Studies was closed and Il'ia Sholeĭmovich chose to transfer to the Department of the Ancient History of Greece and Rome in the Historical Faculty. He graduated with distinction from the Historical Faculty of the University in 1953, but this duality in his education, in both the oriental and classical fields, determined much of his scientific career.

In the next four years (1953–7) Il'ia Sholeĭmovich taught history at schools, first in Central Asia, then in the Kaliningrad area.

In 1957 he returned again to Leningrad. For two years (1957–8) he worked as a salesman in the *Mir* bookstore (then located at 13 Nevsky Prospect, selling books from socialist countries, though now unfortunately closed). Then for the next two years (1958–9) he worked as a translator at the Central Design Bureau of the Navy in Leningrad.

In 1959–60 Il'ia Sholeĭmovich became a research student at the Department of the Ancient History of Greece and Rome of the Historical

---

1 The facts of Shifman's life are taken from his biography located in his personal file at the Archive of Near Eastern Specialists in the Academy of Sciences, f. 152, inv. 3, box 914.

Faculty in Leningrad State University. In July 1960 he presented his candidate's dissertation on the subject of Phoenician colonization.

For about half a year (from late 1960 to the middle of 1961) Il'ia Sholeĭmovich then worked as a senior engineer in the Department of Scientific and Technical Information in the Leningrad Scientific Research Institute of the Academy of Public Utilities.

Finally, at the request of Nina Viktorovna Pigulevskaia, the renowned Soviet specialist in Near Eastern studies and corresponding member of the Academy of Science of the USSR., Il'ia Sholeĭmovich was accepted on 1st July 1961 into the Leningrad Branch of the Institute of Oriental Studies, with subsequent approval of the rank of Junior Researcher. Here, combining research with teaching at the Historical Faculty of Leningrad State University, Il'ia Sholeĭmovich worked until his death on 4th March 1990.

Documents preserved in his personal file show that he worked assiduously. On 18th May 1962 at the Institute of Archaeology in Moscow he defended his dissertation on Phoenician colonization in the Western Mediterranean, which he had submitted two years earlier.

In the annual report of the Institute of Oriental Studies for 1965–6 the following words deserve particular attention: 'He participated in all conferences of Semitologists, all conferences of historians of the ancient Near East and in the annual sessions of the Leningrad Department of the Academy of Science.'

On 10th November 1967 Il'ia Sholeĭmovich was recommended for the post of Senior Research Fellow.

In 1970 he completed his monograph on *Social and Economic Relations in Syria in the 1st–3rd Centuries*. This work was also presented as his Ph.D. research, which he successfully defended in Moscow after two years on 19th December 1972. Il'ia Sholeĭmovich's examiners were the well-known specialist in Byzantine Studies, Georgiĭ L'vovich Kurbatov, and the specialist in Near Eastern Studies and in the history of Meroe, Isidor Savich Katsnelson. According to the documents, the doctoral degree was awarded eight months later, on 21st August 1973.

There are relatively few documents in Il'ia Sholeĭmovich's personal file relating to the last period of his life. As before, he took an active part in many conferences. He regularly taught courses at the Historical Faculty. Among the papers in his file there is a letter of May 1989 written by I.Ia. Froianov and E.D. Frolov to Iu.A. Petrosian, Director of the Leningrad Branch of the

Institute of Oriental Studies of the Academy of Sciences of the USSR, expressing gratitude for the course on the analysis and criticism of the Bible which had been taught in 1988–9. In fact this was by no means the only course that Il'iā Sholeĭmovich taught within the walls of that Institute. He also often conducted courses on the history of Carthage and the Punic Wars.

Il'iā Sholeĭmovich was for about 30 years the head of the public lectures and seminar series at the Leningrad Branch of the Institute of Oriental Studies. In Soviet times, once a month, on Fridays, lecturers presented public seminars for all who were interested. Sometimes these seminars were quite crowded. Especially popular were lectures on the history of Christianity by Il'iā Sholeĭmovich and lectures on Islam and the life of Muhammad by O.G. Bol'shakov. These lectures stopped taking place after Il'iā Sholeĭmovich's death and the new management of the Institute did not renew this activity (and apparently does not intend to do so).

It is also notable that in 1989–90 Il'iā Sholeĭmovich was the head of the Jewish Cultural Society in Leningrad.

Il'iā Sholeĭmovich died on 4th March 1990, just a few months before his sixtieth birthday. His death involved a coincidence which reminds me of the dramatic twists in a Greek tragedy. He died a few days before making a first visit to his 'homeland', Israel. Although he regarded himself as a Russian and a communist, he had never forgotten his Jewish roots. He considered himself a participant in two cultures. In March 1990 several members of the Institute of Oriental Studies, including Il'iā Sholeĭmovich, were to be part of an official delegation to Israel on behalf of the Academy of Sciences of the USSR. He prepared for this visit very thoroughly, intending to deliver his presentation in Modern Hebrew, despite the fact that he did not know the modern language very well. Unfortunately the stress of the preparation for the trip to Israel triggered a fatal heart attack just a few days before his scheduled departure. In fact his general health was already not very good, and another probable factor was the death in the summer of 1989 of his wife, Galina Semenovna, who had worked in the State Public Library (now the Russian National Library). This had been a severe blow to Il'iā Sholeĭmovich. In the event his written presentation was read out at the meeting in Israel by S.M. Iakerson, an expert in medieval Hebrew manuscripts.

It will be useful to share a few personal memories of Il'iā Sholeĭmovich and give a general characterization of his work. Thanks to a chain of circumstances which also involved E.D. Frolov, on 1st November 1979 I began my postgraduate work at the Leningrad Branch of the Institute of Oriental Studies of the Academy of Sciences of the USSR, and I then communicated with Il'ia Sholeĭmovich frequently and regularly for eleven years.

For obvious reasons, everything Jewish meant a lot to him. It was different for me since I dealt with Jewish studies merely in the course of my academic work. Il'ia Sholeĭmovich knew this and we hardly talked about biblical or Jewish topics. Yet sometimes these conversations did happen and I was always amazed at how his voice and appearance changed when he talked about these subjects. From an ordinary man, he would be instantly transformed into an inspired prophet. Every September he greeted the staff members of the Institute on the occasion of the Jewish New Year.

Il'ia Sholeĭmovich was very well organized and systematic. On his desk there was a box with a beautifully written Latin inscription, *index librorum articulorumque*, where he placed cards with information on all his published and 'in press' works. I held the box in my hands many times and the number of published works by the end of his life was about 120; the total number of published and unpublished works written by him was somewhere between 130 and 140.

To some extent Il'ia Sholeĭmovich appreciated and liked public attention. He was always happy to act as chairman in conferences and meetings.

Il'ia Sholeĭmovich was a careful person. I realized this truly only recently, when I was looking through his work on the Nabataeans, completed in 1970, just at the beginning of the Arab-Israeli conflict. In this book (actually published in 1976) he presented an episode from the time of Pompey's attacks on the Middle East in a very careful way to avoid any unnecessary political associations. Pompey, as we know, was involved in the battle between two potential heirs to the Hasmonaean throne. In this battle, one of the candidates asked the Nabataeans for military support and at one point their troops were even near the walls of Jerusalem, before the Romans drove them away.

Il'ia Sholeĭmovich was my supervisor. The main thing that he taught me was to appreciate strict criteria in determining the quality of scientific work. I rewrote my master's dissertation three times. Only the third version, presented in the spring of 1986, was considered by Il'ia Sholeĭmovich as worthy of defence. Now, when I examine and evaluate somebody's research, I unconsciously use the criteria Il'ia Sholeĭmovich applied to me.

Turning to Il'iă Sholeĭmovich's scientific heritage, his written work can be divided into three categories of material: writings on ancient subjects in the classical sphere, on the interface between the Near Eastern and classical worlds and on the ancient Near East more specifically. The number of articles published by him is much larger than the number of monographs, but I will here comment only on the latter.

There are only a few monographs by Il'iă Sholeĭmovich on purely classical subjects. There are, above all, two books that fall into the category of popular scientific works — his writings on Alexander the Great and Caesar Augustus.[2]

There are more books on the Near East in its relation to the classical world. Here I would mention first of all several projects on Phoenician-Carthaginian subjects. For unknown reasons, these were of special interest to Il'iă Sholeĭmovich. I can only speak about these on the basis of the style of his work. He had great skill in expressing his ideas and this is particularly notable in two of his works: *The Rise of Carthaginian Power*[3] and his brilliantly written biography of Hannibal, which was the first monograph he wrote, published under the pseudonym of Korablev.[4] His last work about the Phoenicians, *Phoenician-Punic Mythology*, was written in German and published in Rome. The Russian edition of the book was translated from the German and does not fully reflect the individual characteristics of the style and language of the author.[5]

This group of works should include a series of books, related in one way or another to the Middle East, and mostly to Syria. They are *Syrian Society in the Time of the Principate*,[6] *The Palmyrene Tax Tariff*[7] and *The Nabataean State and Its Culture*.[8]

---

2 Shifman, I. Sh., Александр Македонский (*Alexander of Macedon*), Leningrad, 1988; Цезарь Август (*Caesar Augustus*), Leningrad, 1990.

3 Возникновение Карфагенской державы, Moscow/Leningrad, 1963.

4 Korablev, I. Sh., Ганнибал (*Hannibal*), Moscow, 1976 (2nd ed. 1981).

5 In German: Schiffmann, Ilya, *Phönizisch-Punische Mythologie und geschichtliche Überlieferung in der Widerspiegelung der antiken Geschichtsschreibung*, Rome, 1986; Russian translation by A.C. Chetverukhin: Финикийская мифология и античная историческая традиция (*Phoenician Mythology and Ancient Historical Tradition*) in Финикийская мифология (*Phoenician Mythology*) (ed. Iu.S. Dovzhenko), St Petersburg, 1999, pp. 188-324.

6 Сирийское общество эпохи принципата (I-IIIвв. н. э.), Moscow, 1977.

7 Пальмирский пошлинный тариф. Введение, перевод и комментарий, Moscow, 1980.

8 Набатейское государство и его культура, Moscow, 1976.

The work on the Nabataeans was part of Il'ia Sholeĭmovich's socialist commitment, written in 1970 in connection with the centenary of Lenin's birth. The book was eventually published in 1976 and is a sound popular-scientific essay meeting the criteria of scientific work of the time. In recent years much more material has been published about the Nabataeans, which was, for obvious reasons, not available to Il'ia Sholeĭmovich.

His book *The Palmyrene Tax Tariff* is an interesting project. It gives a brief outline of the history of Palmyra, as well as an edition of the text and a translation into Russian of both the Greek and Aramaic of the Palmyrene Tariff. The book was published in 1980 when the computerization of books in the Soviet Union was still in the distant future and the entire Greek and Aramaic texts that appear in the book were diligently written in by Il'ia Sholeĭmovich's own hand. I have been told that there are in this work some inaccurate translations from the Aramaic text, but I cannot comment on this since it is outside my own area of expertise.

Il'ia Sholeĭmovich's book *Syrian Society in the Time of the Principate* is a significant piece of research. It examines and analyses large amounts of information on the social and economic history of the region of Syria in both the Hellenistic and Roman periods. Unfortunately, careful reading of this monograph reveals numerous examples of typographical and other mistakes and indications of haste.

The most numerous group of Il'ia Sholeĭmovich's books is on general Near Eastern Studies. They form the largest part of his research and, no doubt, they will have a long scientific life — longer than his work on general ancient subjects. I do not have a clear explanation of this, but can only assume the following. The first Arab-Israeli conflict had an impact on Il'ia Sholeĭmovich's life. In the Oriental Department at the University, he could not finish his education in Near Eastern Studies. He was forced to enter the Historical Faculty in the Department of the Ancient History of Greece and Rome because the Department of Assyriology and Hebraic Studies in the Oriental Faculty was closed. Apparently, classical education was imposed on Il'ia Sholeĭmovich by external circumstances, but it was not his natural choice for life and scientific work.[9] Everything connected with the Near East was much closer to his heart

---

9 We must admit that this was reflected in the quality of his work; Shifman's research on Near Eastern subjects is more painstaking.

and more interesting for him.

This certainly influenced the nature of his work on the general history of the Middle East. Among the monographic studies, I want to mention in chronological order, first of all, his work *The Old Testament and its World*, published in 1987 by Politizdat.[10] According to Il'iā Sholeĭmovich, this book was published twenty-two years after it was written. In fact it is hard to imagine how a work like this could have troubled those responsible in the Soviet period for publication of books, because there is nothing seditious in this highly scientific monograph. It is probable that the long delay was caused by the nature of the subject matter itself.

In his later years, Il'iā Sholeĭmovich also translated the Pentateuch into Russian, focusing on the narrative aspect of the Old Testament. The book was published three years after his death.[11] The biblical text can, of course, be interpreted from different perspectives. Il'iā Sholeĭmovich's translation presented Russian readers with a monument of ancient Near Eastern literature which has universal significance. The ancient oriental flavour is created primarily by using unusual forms of names reflecting transcription (Hava for Eve, Moshe for Moses, etc.). The edition of the text is accompanied by a short commentary and a long introduction. Apparently, the author and the publishers expected a lot from this book: they printed what was for 1993 a striking number of copies — 25,000. Their expectations were not realized, however. The publication did not draw a wide public response, and from a scientific point of view, it is interesting rather than significant. The commentary provided is too brief.

Ugarit held a special place in the scientific work of Il'iā Sholeĭmovich. In the middle of the last century in northern Syria, archaeologists discovered a rather large cuneiform archive of the fifteenth–thirteenth centuries BCE. These documents revealed to us information about a settlement, the city of Ugarit; its previously unknown history and culture became known in detail through this happy accident. Il'iā Sholeĭmovich wrote altogether four monographs on Ugarit: on the history of Ugarit,[12] the culture of Ugarit,[13] as well as two

---

10 Ветхий Завет и его мир, Moscow, 1987.
11 От Бытия до Откровения. Учение. Пятикнижие Моисеево (*From Genesis to Revelation. Teaching. The Five Books of Moses*), Moscow, 1993.
12 Угаритское общество (XIV-XIIIвв. до н. э.) (*Ugaritic Society, 14th-13th cents B.C.*), Moscow, 1982.

volumes of Russian translations of the Ugaritic literature that were published after his death.[14] Ugarit presents us with examples of an ancient Near Eastern literature which is similar in type to the biblical literature.

The language of the author in these books, as well as in his studies of the history of Phoenicia and Carthage, is lively and interesting. This attests to his particular interest in these subjects.

To conclude, I would like to put it on record that Il'iă Sholeĭmovich remains in the memory not only because of his positive qualities as a man, but also because of his devotion to science and his robust ability to work, both of which are worthy of respect.

His scientific legacy is significant. Although his publications are a little uneven in value, the majority of Il'iă Sholeĭmovich's writings will have a long academic life. In this context I would mention especially all his work on Ugarit and his two works on biblical subjects, *The Old Testament and its World* and his translation of the Pentateuch as a monument of ancient Near Eastern literature. Finally, I would list here his brilliantly written biography of Hannibal and, despite some technical flaws in the way it was published, *The Palmyrene Tax Tariff*.

---

13 Культура древнего Угарита (XIV-XIIIвв. до н. э.) (*The Culture of Ugarit, 14th–13th cents B.C.*), Moscow, 1987.

14 Угаритский эпос. Введение, перевод с угаритского и комментарии (*Ugaritic Epic. Introduction, translation from Ugaritic and commentary*), Moscow, 1993; О Ба'лу. Угаритские поэтические повествования. Перевод с угаритского и комментарии (*O Ba'lu. Ugaritic Poetic Narratives*), Moscow, 1999.

Introduction

1. Preliminary Remarks

One of the tasks that has been passed on to Soviet Near Eastern Studies, especially to Soviet Semitic Studies, is the scholarly edition and publication of the Palmyrene Tax Tariff that was found in 1882 by S.S. Abamelek-Lazarev and is kept at present in the Hermitage Museum. This goal was established by P.K. Kokovtsov, who devoted several decades to the thorough study of the Tariff but who could not finish his work. His transcripts and interpretations arrived at during his research, the samples of the Palmyrene font that were moulded under his supervision, the photographing of the inscription itself and its transportation to Russia, form Kokovtsov's memorial. A.Ia. Borisov and O.O. Kriuger had a special interest in the Tariff but they too could not complete their studies. N.V. Pigulevskaia repeatedly emphasized its importance for the socio-historical and cultural history of the ancient Near East. The emergence of this work is due to her initiative.

The Palmyrene Tax Tariff has been published and commented on several times. Much has been done for its correct reading, reconstruction and understanding. However, new collections of comparative historical material, including Palmyrene material, and the discovery and publication of inscriptions from Hellenistic-Roman Syria give good reason to study this document again.

The above data determine the tasks for this work. First, to compare the existing publications with the original inscription. Unfortunately, the major part of the original inscription, known through an *estampage*, which had been foundational for the existing publications, is now erased. Thus, it becomes necessary to turn again to the *estampage*, which, however, is not accessible to the author of this work (with the exception of the Aramaic part that is kept in the French *Académie des Inscriptions et Belles-Lettres* and is available in the *Corpus Inscriptionum Semiticarum*).

Another task is to study and interpret the document in the light of the new data that has arisen from research (both general and specific) on the epoch of the Principate and the history of the Near East, especially Syria, in the Hellenistic and Roman periods.

The Palmyrene Tax Tariff

As has been stated before, the Palmyrene Tax Tariff is the most significant source for the socio-economic and cultural history of Syria in the second century AD. It allows us to examine the structures of the city government, the relationship between the city and imperial authority, the legislative system, taxation and methods of tax collection, the trading system and traded goods, the transportation of goods, and so on. Since this document is bilingual, it also provides the opportunity for us to see the relationship between Aramaic and Greek culture. Finally, the task of this work is to review the data of the Tariff in the light of new material.

The author is grateful to the staff of the Hermitage Museum, especially B.B. Piotrovskiĭ, V.G. Lukonin and E.V. Zeĭmal', for their kind permission to reproduce photographs of the stone stored in the Hermitage; to the French *Académie des Inscriptions et Belles-Lettres*, especially A. Dupont-Sommer and J. Starcky for permssion for reproduction of the photographs of the Tariff taken *in situ* by E. Lütticke. The author expresses great appreciation for the valuable comments and suggestions of K.B. Starkova, I.F. Fikhman, A.G. Lundin, V.A. Livshit͡s, E.N. Meshcherskai͡a, R.G. Rylova, S. Kodama and A.V. Paĭkova, and to Y.D. Michaĭlova for her generous help with the Japanese text of an article.

2. Sources on the History of Palmyra

The history of Palmyra, which drew the attention of many scholars after the discovery of the Palmyrene Tariff, undoubtedly presents theoretical interest. Drawing information from existing sources, one can assume that Palmyrene society existed for at least two to two and a half thousand years. Its birth dates back to the end of the third millennium BC and its fall to AD 270–80. Studying this city's history will, hopefully, help us to find new ways of addressing the whole set of problems related to the origins and historical development of Hellenism. It will help to unveil the bigger historical picture during the period of Roman domination, and, finally, it will shed some light on the crisis in the second half of the third century AD, in which Palmyra played an exceptional role.

However, the Palmyrene Tariff does not itself provide enough information for the study of these questions. In general, sources on the history of Palmyra are divided into narrative literary sources, cuneiform texts and inscriptions.

Introduction

If we are to review sources referring to Palmyra, we need to pay special attention to pre-Hellenistic Judaeo-Israelite literature, because it contains significant data on the history of this city in the second and first millennia BC. According to this tradition (1 Kgs 9:15–19; 2 Chr. 8:4) king Solomon was the founder of Palmyra; Josephus Flavius refers to the same idea (*Ant.*, 8, 6, 1).

In post-biblical Jewish literature we find indications of the Palmyrenes' participation in the destruction of Yahweh's temple in Jerusalem (Bereshit Rabba 56: 11), as well their other activities (Yevamot, 16b–17a; Jerusalem Talmud Terumot, 8:10 [46b], etc.). All these records are quite tendentious: they present us with a sinful people, seen in the worst light, who participated in the destruction of the sacred place; and they express hope in their imminent downfall. It is interesting that even the Semitic name for Palmyra, Tadmor, is intentionally distorted in order to avoid its pronunciation: instead of the expected תדמור it is written as תרמוד. However, these references give some apparently genuine facts about Palmyrene society at the time of Roman dominion and, as such, deserve special attention.

The information about Palmyra in the literature of the Graeco-Roman writers of the first–third centuries AD, as well as in the works of Byzantine authors, is quite diverse. It can be provisionally divided into two groups. The first collection of information consists of brief descriptions of Palmyra that are found in Appian's account of Mark Antony's invasion of the city (the oldest surviving description related to the history of Graeco-Roman Palmyra); and in Pliny the Elder's geographical essay about Syria (*NH*, 5, 88). Both Appian and Pliny emphasize the significant role of Palmyra in international life, especially, in the foreign trade of the first century BC. The second group are sources from the third quarter of the third century AD, i.e. from the time when power was in the hands of Odenathus and after his death in the hands of Bat-Zabbai-Zenobia.

Much of this latter information comes from the Hellenistic biographies of the *Thirty Tyrants*, attributed to Trebellius Pollio and included in the collection *Scriptores historiae Augustae*. The biographies of Odenathus, his (real or imaginary) sons, Herannianus and Timolaus, and Zenobia are particularly significant. This collection also contains the biography of Aurelian. The author of this particular biography is allegedly Flavius Vopiscus. In the biography there is a description of Aurelian and Zenobia's struggle for power in the East (Fl. Vop., *Aurel.*, 25–7), and, more importantly, the description of the national insurrection in Palmyra after Zenobia's defeat (Fl. Vop., *Aurel.*, 31). These sources suffer from some shortcomings that are intrinsic to the whole collection: superficial brevity of the material, doubtful facts (including imaginary events and people), forgery of documents and excessive propensity for unimportant details. The author or authors were not interested in giving many valuable details. At the same time, the *Scriptores historiae Augustae*, including records on Palmyra and its rulers, contains a reliable tradition that probably derives from an imperial historical source of the second–third centuries AD which did not itself survive (Shtaerman 1957; Dovatur 1957). The surviving fragments from the work of Peter Patricius (*FHG*, IV, p. 187, fr. 10) and the so-called *Anonymous Fragments* (*FHG*, IV, p. 195–7) provide valuable references on the relationship between Odenathus and Shapur I. Orosius on the other hand presents only brief remarks about the political activities of Odenathus and Zenobia (*Hist. adv. pag.*, 7.22.12–13; 7.23.4).

Zosimus (I.39–44, 50–61), Zonaras (XII.23–27) and Syncellus (*Chronogr.*, 716–7; 382 in Goar's original edition) give a more detailed history of Odenathus and Zenobia. Their accounts help us to follow the history of the Palmyrene kingdom and its struggle for hegemony in the Near East. In one form or another they probably reconstruct information from the same sources that were used in *Scriptores historiae Augustae*.

The account of John Malalas on how Palmyra was defeated by Nebuchadnezzar II (Malal., *Chronogr.*, book 18, 426) is particularly distinct. As is known, this event is not mentioned in Nebuchadnezzar's annals. Perhaps Malalas drew on Jewish traditions that made their way into Christian literature. In any case, a Jewish text (Bereshit Rabba 56) tells us about Palmyrene archers who participated with Nebuchadnezzar in the campaign against Jerusalem. This may well be a doubling of the tradition — ascribing of later facts to an earlier date.

We also find valuable information concerning Palmyrene history of the first half of the second century AD in Stephanus of Byzantium (see Πάλμυρα: Ἀδριανοπολῖται).

Cuneiform sources on the history of Palmyra are not numerous. First, the Palmyrenes are mentioned in the Cappadocian texts (E. Bilgiç 1945–51: 36)[1]

---

1   These documents are certainly not 'an Assyrian inscription of the XIXth century B.C.' (Saverkina 1971: 7).

Introduction

and Mari (Michelini Tocci 1960: 94–5). Secondly, there are reports about Palmyra as the most significant Aramaic centre in the annals of Assyrian kings in the second and first millennia BC (Dupont-Sommer 1949).[2]

In spite of their relative brevity and extremely laconic character, these sources present an outline of the major events in the history of Palmyra of the second millennium BC.

The Palmyrene inscriptions have been known to European scholarship since the twenties of the seventeeth century: Jan Gruter published the first Graeco-Palmyrene bilingual in 1616 (Gruter 1616). In fact, from that event the history not only of Palmyra but of the whole of north Semitic epigraphy counts its beginning. However, the first attempts to read and to interpret the Palmyrene texts by S. Petit and J. Rhenferd were unsuccessful (Lidzbarski 1898: I, 89–90).

A new stage in the history of Palmyrene epigraphy began after J. Dawkins and R. Wood visited Palmyra in the middle of the eighteenth century. They published a report about their visit in French and English in 1753 (Wood 1819). They published thirteen texts that were discovered in the area of the ancient city itself. Based on their material, Abbé Barthélemy attempted to date the Palmyrene script. He presented a report on this topic already on 12th February 1754 at the French *Académie des Inscriptions*. However, the report was published only in 1759. As often happens, independently of him J. Swinton came to similar conclusions. Swinton's research became available to the public in 1754. Barthélemy and Swinton not only read all the Palmyrene inscriptions published by that time, but also built a solid foundation for Palmyrene epigraphy. In subsequent years there have been needed only detailed corrections without any essential changes.

The collection of Palmyrene texts and their publication cannot be considered completed. Every new expedition to Palmyra and its surrounding area reveals new findings. In 1861 W. H. Waddington found a whole collection of Palmyrene inscriptions (140 in total); M. de Vogüé (de Vogüé 1868–77) published them. In 1870 A.D. Mordtmann found thirty inscriptions; that group of texts was published by him in 1875. The year 1882 is the year of the discovery of the present document (the Tariff). In 1885 J.R.S. Sterrett copied an extensive collection of Greek inscriptions from Palmyra. Among the

---

2 I.I. Saverkina (Saverkina 1971: 7) also mistakenly claims them here as Amorites.

publications of the Palmyrene inscriptions in the 80s and 90s of the nineteenth century the most significant are the works by E. Ledrain (1885; 1888; 1889; 1891; 1892; 1893) and D. Müller (1884; 1892; 1894; 1898).

I͡a.I. Khouri (Yaʿqūb Khūrī) made one of the most valuable discoveries after the discovery of the Palmyrene Tariff in 1900 when he went to Palmyra to organize the transportation of this document. While searching in the north-western necropolis, Maghārat Abū Suhayl, Khouri found four grave inscriptions. He made *estampages* and gave them to the director of the Russian Archaeological Institute in Constantinople, F.I. Uspenskiĭ. In 1903 these inscriptions were published by P.K. Kokovt͡sov. Although the number of texts that were copied by Khouri was not numerous, their publication played an important role in research on Palmyra. For the first time scholarship was presented with texts that contained information about transactions related to funeral chambers and niches. The importance of the texts becomes especially clear if we take into account the fact that we did not before this have any business documents from Palmyra. The inscriptions of Khouri/Kokovt͡sov and others related to them remain the only sources that shed light on property relationships in Palmyra (Shifman 1965b).

In the same year, 1900, on 4th and 5th May, an American expedition visited Palmyra. It travelled from northern Syria to the Hauran. E. Littmann participated in that expedition. He copied fourteen inscriptions and later published them as a part of the expedition report (Littmann 1905: 57–84). Among the texts there were some previously unknown inscriptions, but some which were already published by his predecessors. In his commentaries, though, Littmann suggested his own interpretations which in many cases were substantially different from the previous ones. The historical-religious problems of that era drew the particular attention of this scholar. However, the inscription that contained valuable information about the state system of Palmyra (no. 10 in his publication, see *CIS* II, 3941) exhibited no interest for him (he describes it as 'short and uninteresting'.)

O. Puchstein found forty inscriptions in 1902. In 1905 they were published by M. Soberheim. H. Spoer found three inscriptions in 1904 (Spoer 1904). Drs Lamer and Jäckel brought several inscriptions to Germany in 1907. Their publication was undertaken by Lidzbarski (Lidzbarski 1902–15: III, 32–6). A. Jaussen and R. Savignac visited Palmyra in July 1904. They made a substantial number of *estampages* there which served as a significant source for a subsequent volume of the *Corpus Inscriptionum Semiticarum*.

After World War I the discovery and publication of Palmyrene inscriptions became more systematic. Numerous publications by A. Gabriel, H. Ingholt, J. Cantineau and after World War II by D. Schlumberger, J. Starcky, K. Michałowski and by the followers of the latter, especially M. Gawlikowski,[3] made many new inscriptions known. The most significant research, in our opinion, was done by J. Cantineau (1930a and 1930b) and H. Ingholt (1935 and 1962). They introduced into scholarship previously unknown material on the socio-economic history of the city. The inscription from the mausoleum of Malkū published by H. Ingholt in 1962 is of a special importance: it contains a copy of a document concerned with the alienation of part of the tomb. Generally the publications by Cantineau and Ingholt continue the work begun by P.K. Kokovtsov. M.I. Rostovtzeff (1932c and 1935) published a series of Greek inscriptions on the subject of Palmyrene caravan trading. In 1939 a famous scholar in Palmyrene studies, R. du Mesnil du Buisson, published a collection of Palmyrene inscriptions from Dura-Europos (1939). Finally, D. Schlumberger's publication of the inscriptions from the area surrounding Palmyra deserves special attention (1951).

The period after World War I was marked by the emergence of the collected publication of Palmyrene inscriptions. J.-B. Chabot prepared a collection of texts that was published in 1926 as the third volume of the second part of the *Corpus Inscriptionum Semiticarum* (*CIS*). It contained all the texts known at that time and remains the most complete manual of Palmyrene epigraphy. In 1930 the *Inventaire des inscriptions de Palmyre* began and continued to be published until 1933 by Cantineau (*Inv.* I–IX). After a long pause and after World War II the publication was continued by J. Starcky and J. Teixidor (*Inv.* X–XI). The publications differed not only in content but also in their approach. Chabot's publication included all the texts in the Palmyrene language (for bilinguals the Greek text is also provided) that were found not only in Palmyra but also outside — from Britain and Italy and from North Africa to Mesopotamia. Cantineau and his successors limited their publication to the inscriptions of Palmyra itself. Chabot grouped the inscriptions thematically while Cantineau and his successors grouped them in terms of location, though they did not follow this very successfully in *Inv.* VIII. Finally,

---

3   The collection of inscriptions published by M. Gawlikowski in Paris was not available to us.

the *Inventaire* publishes some inscriptions simply in Greek, where a parallel Palmyrene text is absent. Sometimes the *Inventaire* adds inscriptions to the *Corpus* which the latter does not take into account. Since there was a continuous increase of other publications, as well as a continuous process of the preparation of new inscriptions, the combined publications cannot be considered exhaustive. In any case the *Inventaire* was not completed. The task of publishing the full corpus of the Palmyrene inscriptions or at least a supplement to *CIS* remains on the agenda. [Ed.: note now D.R. Hillers and E. Cussini, *Palmyrene Aramaic Texts*, 1996, for a systematic one-volume corpus.]

Based on their content the Palmyrene inscriptions can be divided into grave inscriptions, dedications, building inscriptions and honorific inscriptions associated with statues. The Palmyrene Tariff is separate from these categories. It represents a kind of business document and is the object of this research.

The most common grave inscriptions are the ones that contain a name or names of those buried and usually a list of ancestors. In front of the name of the most remote ancestor of whom the list takes account the word בר, 'son', is omitted. Sometimes there are indications of the social and family status of the person buried, the type of burial facility and when and for whom it was built. The grave inscriptions sometimes tell us about business transactions: the sale or alienation of the whole burial facility or of part of it; they show what type of transactions might be involved in relation to the tomb and whether this transaction is prescribed or prohibited. The inscriptions that have the form of business documents belong to the texts of this category. Their analysis shows that in structure they are similar to documents of alienation of land from the area around the Dead Sea and from Dura-Europos (Shifman 1965b).

The dedicatory and construction inscriptions are similar in content. The first group records the dedication of an object to a deity. The second records the building of a sacral facility, usually dedicated to a deity. In addition, these texts give data on the dedicator or initiator and on the organizer of the construction: his name, genealogy, family and social status, career, etc. All these data except for the name are optional. The honorific inscriptions related to statues indicate the name, genealogy, social status, the *cursus honorum* of the person honoured, whether it is a governmental or public body that decrees the celebration of honour involved and the motive for the celebration.

The inscriptions are dated according to the Seleucid Era; they indicate the year and month, sometimes the day.

From the above it is evident that the Palmyrene inscriptions contain significant and important historical material. They help us not only to discover historical facts that are not mentioned in the narrative sources (for example, that the emperor Hadrian visited Palmyra: see inscription 3959[4]), but also to see some essential aspects of Palmyrene social life, including types of property transaction, changes in social structure, etc., also peculiarities of tribal and political organization (Février 1931a; Shifman 1977). The Palmyrene inscriptions give valuable data about the forces that supported the regime of Odenathus and Zenobia and about the character of their reign.

Tesserae have a special place among the sources on the history of Palmyra. They are unique coupons that gave their holders the right to participate in funeral feasts, distributions that confirmed hospitality relationships, etc. Sometimes *tesserae* played the role of talismans placing a person under the protection of a particular deity and preventing misfortune. In spite of their laconic character, the *tesserae* give us important historical information: proper names, names of Palmyrene tribes, names of certain products (wine, etc.). In other words, they provide data about the socio-economic history of Palmyra of the first–third centuries AD and about the history of Palmyrene religion (Borisov 1937, 1939; *RTP*; Mesnil du Buisson, 1962).

Finally among the sources on the history of Palmyra there are coins. The bronze Palmyrene coins give information about the religious symbolism and ideology of Palmyra. The coins from Vahballat's and Zenobia's time convey titles which allow us to trace the development of Palmyrene and even Roman statehood in the second half of the third century AD.

The first European[5] to visit Palmyra after Syria became Arab was a very famous traveller and Spanish rabbi, Benjamin of Tudela (1172). He was interested, though, not in the antiquity of the city but in the local Jewish community. It was another 500 years before the first attempts to study the Palmyrene remains were undertaken. In 1616 and 1625 an Italian missionary and scholar, Pietro della Valle, visited Palmyra, and in 1630 a Frenchman, J.-B. Tavernier. In 1678 a group of English merchants from Aleppo wanted to see the ruins of Palmyra. However, when they approached the oasis, they were captured by the bedouins. The travellers were released only after paying a

---

4   Here and later the inscriptions published in *CIS*, II are referred to by a simple number.
5   For the history of archaeological studies on Palmyra see Starcky 1952; Champdor 1953; Rosenthal 1964; Bounni 1967.

ransom. Only in 1691 could they organize a new and a more successful trip; they spent four days in Palmyra. One of the travellers, the Rev. William Halifax, copied some inscriptions which he published later in the *Philosophical Transactions of the* [British] *Royal Society*. When Halifax and his companions described their adventure in Syria and Palestine, they were not silent about the overwhelming impression they received of the colonnades, mausolea and temples of Palmyra.

For years the main purpose for all researchers on Palmyra remained the collection of inscriptions. Later this was followed by archaeological explorations. In 1751 J. Dawkins and R. Wood visited Palmyra and two years later they published a description of the city which was prefaced by research (obviously now out of date) on Palmyrene history (Wood 1819). It is interesting that in the architecture of Palmyra Wood discovered a closeness to the architecture of Athens. In the more simple style of the funeral facilities he saw the traces of local pre-Hellenistic art. The presence of the Corinthian style made it possible for Wood to date the Palmyrene structures to the time of Roman rule. He identified the construction in the north-east corner of Palmyra as the temple of the Sun god. To his book he attached a plan of the city which remained the only archaeological plan of Palmyra for more than 200 years (until the 20s of this [twentieth] century). In 1787 C.-F. Volney included in his *Voyage en Syrie et en Égypte* some data on Palmyra. This author was totally dependent, however, on R. Wood. He reproduced Wood's plan and description without any alterations. In 1789 J.-J. Barthélemy mentioned Palmyra in his *Voyage du jeune Anacharsis en Grèce*. A more consecutive but still only sporadic study of the city began in the middle of the nineteenth century when a French expedition headed by M. de Vogüé visited Palmyra (in 1853). The works by M. Sobernheim, O. Puchstein, the expeditions of the Russian Archaeological Institute in Constantinople headed by F.I. Uspenskiĭ, B.V. Farmakovskiĭ and P.K. Kokovtsov (systematic work started from 1900), and of the German expedition in 1902–17 headed by T. Wiegand played a significant role in the period before World War I.

The outcome of the German expedition was the drawing up of a new plan of the city and its surrounding necropolises. J. Strzygowski and B.V. Farmakovskiĭ published special works on Palmyrene art. They based their research on the material that was found at the end of nineteenth and the beginning of the twentieth centuries.

Introduction

Since 1924 French archaeologists have directed most of the systematic research on Palmyra, at the same time conserving its antiquities. Already in 1924 Gabriel drew up a new plan of the city. Thanks to H. Seyrig and R. Amy, between 1929 and 1932 the Arab village that was located in the temple of Bēl was moved to the north-west of the Palmyrene oasis. This made the temple accessible for research. That year the exploration of the temple of Bēl began under the leadership of H. Seyrig, D. Schlumberger and R. Amy. The research continued in 1933–5. In 1933–5 there were explorations of the temple of Ba'alshamīn (the director of the research was M. Écochard). Seyrig and Amy explored the north-west necropolis; Schlumberger and H. Ingholt explored the area of Jabal Bil'ās and Jabal Abū Sha'r. Amy restored the monumental arch and numerous tombs. In 1939–40 Seyrig and R. Duru cleared up the *agora*. Duru's excavations to the east of the temple of Bēl led to the discovery of several ancient buildings with mosaics. At the same time there was a systematic exploration of the southern and western necropolises (mainly thanks to Ingholt's efforts). To the south of the 'Camp of Diocletian' J. Cantineau discovered the ruins of the 'Funerary Temple'. After World War II the results of D. Schlumberger's research in the north-eastern part of Palmyra were published (1951).

A new stage in the archaeological study of Palmyra began after Syria obtained political independence and in 1950 its government founded the Syrian Directorate-General of Antiquities and Museums. Already in 1952 new excavations under the director-general, S. Abdul-Hak, began in the north-eastern necropolis and in the location of the theatre (1952–5). The latter were led by N. Khair and O. Taha. At that same time the excavations of the temple of Ba'alshamīn continued (with a Swiss expedition under P. Collart). In 1957–8 A. Bounni, N. Saliby and O. Taha led the excavations in the area of the Grand Colonnade (Section B), the main city street; and in 1959 and later in 1962–3 in the area of the street that connects the theatre with the *agora*. In 1963 excavations were carried out in the area of the Grand Colonnade (Section A) between the temple of Bēl and the Monumental Arch. Since 1957 much work was done in the Valley of the Tombs. In 1963–4 it became possible to determine that the so-called 'Corinthian Temple' was dedicated to Nabu and to specify its layout.

The excavations of the Polish expedition under K. Michałowski (1959–64) in the Camp of Diocletian and in the Valley of the Tombs under R. du Mesnil du Buisson, who discovered not only the remains of the Hellenistic period temple of Bēl (second century BC) but also archaeological material of the Bronze Age and fragments of ceramics of 2200–2110 BC in the immediate area of Efqa, all played a significant role in research on Palmyra.

The archaeological findings from Palmyra enable us not only to date more or less accurately the origin of the city, but also to imagine the typical Syrian city of the Hellenistic era with its theatre, temples, baths, colonnades, *agora* and houses. One should note that the discoveries in Dura-Europos (where a temple of the Palmyrene gods and material of the rich and populous Palmyrene settlement were found) are also very important for Palmyrene studies.

There are only a few monographic works on Palmyrene history, especially on political and socio-economical history. Of course, we do not count here popular scientific literature that is written for the broader audience and does not contain original conclusions. Before the 30s of the nineteenth century scholars were mainly interested in the history of Odenathus and Zenobia and their fight for domination in the Near East in the second half of the third century AD. Ch. Cellarius devoted the first work in modern European literature on Palmyrene studies to this theme in 1693. In 1696 A. Seller published his book on the antiquities of Palmyra and it also contained a summary of Palmyrene history, especially of the third century AD. In the nineteenth century A.G. van Capelle (1817), A. von Sallet (1866), L. Double (1877) and, at the beginning of the 20th century, F. Müller (1902) devoted works to this theme. The works of van Capelle and von Sallet had importance because they used and analysed very significant numismatic sources. Müller used Arabic sources for the first time in his research. Recently this line was continued with M.B. Piotrovskiĭ (1977).

There is another theme that drew particular interest among scholars, Palmyrene trade and its role in the life of the Near East. The first work devoted to this theme was published in 1831 by a famous historian, A. Heeren. The scientific significance of this research is quite remarkable. Although there has been almost one and a half centuries since its publication, new epigraphic material has confirmed Heeren's conclusions. The discovery and the publication of the Palmyrene Tariff brought forward a new theme: the organization and character of Palmyrene trade and traded goods, as well as the Palmyrene political system. The work of M.I. Rostovtzeff deserves special attention in this regard. Rostovtzeff studied tax farming in the ancient world and in Palmyra especially (1899).

A very important event in the study of Palmyra was the publication of Février's monographs in 1931. These texts were devoted to the political and economic history of Palmyra (Février 1931a) and to Palmyrene religion (Février 1931b). The first monograph contains (apart from a general summary of the political history of Palmyra) a detailed description of the political system of the city, as well as some information about economic life (mainly trade). However, as in every first attempt, Février's monograph has some shortcomings. He left out the problem of the social structure of Palmyrene society and property relations. He did not shed much light on the political status of Palmyra. The second monograph contains a detailed summary of Palmyrene religion (based on material available at the end of 1920s and the early 1930s).

In the 1930s Rostovtzeff studied the Palmyrene trade system intensively (Rostovtzeff 1932a, 1932c, 1935). He continued Heeren's research. But it is because of Rostovtzeff's work that we get the popular idea that Palmyra was a 'caravan city' or mainly a centre of caravan trade. In 1957 E. Will published a detailed article on the caravan trade system. D. Schlumberger published a number of important articles on Palmyra, on its borders, on the structure of the society and on the history of Palmyrene art. H. Seyrig focused particularly on Palmyrene history and culture, especially in his series of articles entitled 'Antiquités syriennes'.

In 1952 Starcky published a new monograph on Palmyrene history. A year later, A. Champdor published the sixth edition of his own work (1953). Both sources used all the data known by that time on the political history, political system and culture of Palmyra, but they did not shed much light on social history.

In our own country works on Palmyra came from P.K. Kokovt͡sov (1903), A.I͡a. Borisov (1937, 1939) and B.V. Farmakovskiĭ (1903). A.I͡a. Borisov made some important observations on the legal status and the administrative system of Palmyra. In his lecture on Palmyra delivered in 1938 in the Hermitage (a summary of the lecture was kindly provided by K.B. Starkova), he says: 'Palmyra was part of the Asian provinces of the Roman Empire and had a considerable administrative and military independence and self-government like other Greek cities.' In the book of A.B. Ranovich of 1949 discussing the eastern provinces of the Roman Empire there is an essay (though very brief, superficial and, by the time of publication, already out-of-date with regard to both original sources and bibliography) on the socio-economic and political history of Palmyra. In the 1960s the author of this present book published his research about property and land relations in Palmyra on the basis of the tomb inscriptions (Shifman 1965b). In the same year I.I. Saverkina published her research on Palmyrene portraiture (Saverkina, 1965a, 1965b). In 1971 she published another work on Palmyra, mainly describing the funerary memorials of Palmyrene art.

In the 1960s there was a rapid growth in studies on Palmyra in Poland, undoubtedly because of the archaeological discoveries from expeditions that were led by Professor K. Michałowski. Among important publications of archaeological materials and inscriptions there were descriptions of the city (Michałowski 1966). Also there saw the light a series of monographs on different Palmyrene problems, including monographs by M. Gawlikowski on the Palmyrene tomb inscriptions (Gawlikowski 1970) and on the Palmyrene temple (Gawlikowski 1973).

3. Palmyrene History and Culture

As noted before, the archaeological material of R. du Mesnil du Buisson (1966 and 1967) made it possible to date the origin of Palmyra (Tadmor) to the last centuries of the third millennium BC. The settlers chose a convenient place in an oasis near the spring called Efqa (later the site of one of the local shrines), which was very close to the main trade routes of Northern Mesopotamia and Syria, but at the same time more or less protected by the desert from outside attack. Du Mesnil du Buisson suggests that the settlers were Amorites. Taking into consideration the general historical situation in the Near East of that time, this seems to be the most plausible conclusion. To support his view du Mesnil du Buisson points out that the word אפקא as a designation for the spring and ירח as a name for the moon god occur in the Canaanite context, especially at Ras Shamra (Mesnil du Buisson 1966: 186–7). The latter case, however, is less convincing, since in Palmyra Yariḥbōl is a sun god.

The first Palmyrene inhabitant known to us, mentioned in the Cappadocian tablets, has an Akkadian name, Puzur-Ishtar (Bilgiç 1945–51: 36; Starcky 1952: 27–8; Champdor 1953: 25; Michelini Tocci 1960: 94). It is possible that

Introduction

he is an Amorite who was assimilated in the Akkadian environment. Or, perhaps, Puzur-Ishtar was descended from Akkadians who lived in Palmyra. In any case, his participation in the business life of the Assyrian trading colony in Cappadocia is quite significant. It also proves that at that time Palmyra had trading relationships with Anatolia and, apparently, with Mesopotamia.

The other two Akkadian documents that mention Palmyra come from Mari (Michelini Tocci 1960: 94–5). One of them (*ARM* V, no. 23) is the letter of Tarim-Shakīm written to the king of Mari, Iasmaḫ-Addu. The letter tells of Sutû nomads in the Syrian desert who attacked Palmyra and the neighbouring Nashalâ. Although the enemies were defeated, they killed a Palmyrene. [Ed.: in fact it is better here to read the text as stating that the men of Palmyra killed one of the Sutaeans: see A. Finet, *ARM* XV, 135, fn. 2.] In the other document (Dossin 1951: 20) the author mentions four Palmyrenes who came from Qatna to Mari to appear before their lord, king Iasmaḫ-Addu.

In spite of their extremely laconic character these sources allow us to draw some significant conclusions. They confirm the earlier observations about extensive Palmyrene relationships with neighbouring states in the early period of its history. They show that kings of Mari were interested in Palmyrene affairs. The latter detail may possibly be connected with the fact that the king of Mari was the lord of the four Palmyrenes mentioned. It is also possible that the Palmyrenes in the document were the servants or officials of the king of Mari. Or perhaps the king of Mari was the lord of these Palmyrenes because the whole city of Palmyra was under his dominion. Finally, Palmyra was rich enough to draw the attention of nomad robbers and strong enough to defend itself against their attacks.

According to a report kindly provided by M.N. van Loon, among the cuneiform documents dated to the second half of the second millennium BC that were discovered at Emar (Arnaud 1975) there is a document that describes the relationship between Emar and Tadmor (Palmyra). D. Arnaud (1975: 90) clearly describes the content of this document: in the presence of four witnesses, two of whom are Palmyrenes, someone named Imlik-Dagan buys his freedom, paying 74 shekels of silver to the slave of Atteu. [Ed.: in Arnaud 1975 he too is described as Palmyrene but this is not confirmed by Arnaud's later publication of the text: *Recherches au pays d'Aštata. Emar VI.1–3*, 1986.] The agreement has an international legal character to it, though it is private. It is interesting to note the presence of a slave in this transaction, although from

Arnaud's brief account it is not clear whether he received the money for himself or for his owner. [Ed. clearly for his owner: Arnaud publication of 1986.] The names show that the majority of the Palmyrene population was still Amorite.

In the last centuries of the second millennium BC the situation in Palmyra changed. In the fourteenth to twelfth centuries BC Aramaean tribes settled in the territory of northern Syria and Mesopotamia (Dupont-Sommer 1949: 16–17) and made Palmyra one of their important political centres (in that period). We do not have information on how exactly these events took place (perhaps they settled there as a result of invasion), but the sources show that the Aramaeans relied on Palmyra when they tried to resist the Assyrian king Tiglath-Pileser I (end of the twelfth century BC). Thus, in the inscription fragments of the eight-sided prism (*KAH* 2, no. 63) Tiglath-Pileser I reports: 'For the twenty-eighth time, in pursuit of the Aḫlamê Aramaeans, I crossed the Euphrates, — the second time in one year. From Tadmar of Amurru, Anat and Suḫi, even as far as Rapiku of Karduniash I defeated them ... including their fortresses, I captured them, multitudes of them I slew. Their booty which was countless, I carried off' (*ARAB*, I, §287). These words are repeated in other inscriptions of this king (*ARAB*, I, §§292, 308, 330). They describe quite precisely the area where the Aramaean tribes were living, the role that Palmyra (Tadmor) played for them and their defeat. In this connection it is interesting to consider the finding (although preliminary) made by R. du Mesnil du Buisson (1966: 185) that Palmyra was populated from the last third of the third millennium BC and until the end of the Bronze Age it did not experience any serious catastrophes. This scholar suggests that in the following period (of about 1000 years) Palmyra had a less powerful status than in the Bronze Age. In any case he thinks (and it is hard to disagree with him) that the Iron Age period was very likely a time of decline in Palmyra. He persuasively explains this on the basis of the defeat of the city by Tiglath-Pileser I.

Further possible information about Palmyra comes from the Bible. In 1 Kgs 9: 17–18 we read: 'Solomon built up Gezer, lower Beth Horon, Ta<d>mor in the wilderness in the land' (וְאֶת־תַּמֹר בַּמִּדְבָּר בָּאָרֶץ); the *qere* here suggests reading תדמר instead of תמר, i.e. Palmyra. In the parallel text in 2 Chr. 8:4 we read, 'And he (Solomon) built Tadmor (תַּדְמֹר) in the wilderness.' The text also tells us about Solomon's construction of the storage cities in Hamath, i.e. in Syria.

The question of the reliability of the biblical tradition as well as the

Introduction

secondary information of Josephus (who seems to confirm the biblical tradition: *Ant.*, 8, 6, 1) is the subject of great debate. Some scholars believe that 1 Kgs 9:17–18 describes the construction of the 'city of the palms' in southern Palestine and has nothing to do with Palmyra (Février 1931a: 3). They think that the replacement of תמר by תדמר takes place in the Jewish community in Palmyra of the Hellenistic period (Starcky 1952: 29–30). Others assume that the biblical tradition (1 Kings and 2 Chronicles) is reliable (Malamat 1963; Gichon 1963). In our opinion, this second view is preferable. First, we do not have other material that calls the biblical tradition into question. Secondly, the Jewish community in Palmyra, as far as we know, was never so influential that its traditions would be considered as generally accepted by all Jews. Thirdly, 2 Chronicles repeats the information of 1 Kings and the tradition they represent goes back to pre-Hellenistic times. Solomon possibly wanted to secure his dominion in Syria and so, while building up many other storage cities, he decided to restore Palmyra, which had been destroyed by the Assyrians. His successors could not hold on to their Syrian domains and lost the city.

According to one tradition, several centuries later Palmyra was defeated by the Babylonian king Nabuchadnezzar II (Malal., *Chronogr.*, book 18, 426) and the Palmyrene archers helped in defeating Jerusalem in 586 BC (Bereshit Rabba, 56). Whether this tradition is correct is hard to say. The former information does not as yet find corroboration in any cuneiform material of Nabuchadnezzar's reign (Mesnil du Buisson 1966: 184). The latter statement (about events in 586) corresponds to the later tradition that describes the Palmyrene participation in the siege of Jerusalem in AD 66–73.

We do not have any information about Palmyra in the Persian Empire period and almost nothing about Palmyra in the Hellenistic period (before the Roman conquest). Evidently, the city did not play any significant role in the political life of that period. It probably shared the destiny of other Near Eastern societies that were ruled by Persian and Seleucid kings. If so, the administrative and legal situation in Palmyra under both Persian and Seleucid kings was not different from any other Near Eastern city. One of the Palmyrenes known in those days was probably Zabdibēl, who gave orders among the Arab troops fighting with Antiochus III in the battle at Raphia (217 BC) (see Polyb., 5. 79. 8; 5, 82. 12). In any case the name Zabdibēl (= Zabdibōl) is known only in Palmyra (Seyrig 1971). It is also noteworthy, as we will see further, that not only did the Aramaic language become prominent in

Palmyra (which can be explained by the Aramaean settlement already in the second millennium BC), but also the traditions of the Achaemenid chancelleries survived there. Evidently, the traditions of the Persian Empire could not be eradicated even after centuries of Hellenistic rule and Hellenistic culture. The other thing worth stressing is that the beginning of the Seleucid epoch coincided with the construction of the first temple of Bōl-Bēl (third century BC) on the levelled Bronze Age surface (Mesnil du Buisson 1966: 184; *Inv.* IX). Probably, as Palmyra came into the Seleucid kingdom, it began to experience an economic revival. It became an intermediary place for trading between Mesopotamia and the coastal area of the Mediterranean Near East. As a matter of fact, Appian (*BC*, 5, 9) reports accurately about it.

We find the first written reference to Palmyra in Appian's account of the civil wars, particularly in the part that deals with the events after the murder of Julius Caesar. Appian writes (App., *BC*, 5, 10) that after Caesar's death power was taken by tyrants who were supported by the Parthians (κατὰ πόλεις ὑπὸ τῶν τυρράνων εἴχετο, συλλαμβανόντων τοῖς τυρράνοις τῶν Παρθυαίων); Antony drove the enemies of Rome away into Parthia (οὓς ὁ Ἀντώνιος ἐξελαύνων ὑποφεύγοντας ἐς τὴν Παρθυηνήν), laid heavy taxes on the people (τοῖς πλήθεσιν ἐπιβάλλων ἐσφορὰς βαρυτάτας) and undertook similar acts towards Palmyra (ἐς Παλμυρηνοὺς τάδε ἁμαρτῶν). In other words, Antony's campaign against Palmyra was part of his actions directed towards the restoration of Roman rule in the whole of Syria, including Palmyra.

A bit earlier, though, Appian had explained Antony's motives differently (*BC*, 5, 9). He sent a unit of cavalry to pillage Palmyra, motivated as follows: Palmyra allegedly used its frontier position to deceive the Romans and the Parthians. At least that was the official version. In reality, Antony probably wanted to let the cavalry capture booty. The Palmyrenes, when they learnt that enemies were approaching the city, took themselves across to the eastern side of the Euphrates, taking along all their possessions, and bows and arrows in case of a fight. The cavalry entered the empty city and returned without booty, never crossing the river. The main goal, however, was achieved (App., *BC*, 5, 10): Antony demonstrated Roman power over Palmyra and made it pay heavy taxes. All these events took place in 41 BC.

Appian's account shows that in the second half of the first century BC Palmyra was under Roman control. When he says that Palmyra was the neighbour of the Parthians and Romans (Ῥωμαίων καὶ Παρθυαίων ὄντες

Introduction

ἐφόριοι), Appian refers to the geographical position of Palmyra between the two states, not its political standing.[6] Appian's story demonstrates that in the first century BC Palmyra was a significant intermediary trading centre (*BC*, 5, 9): 'Being traders they bring from Persia Indian and Arabian goods and sell them in the Roman provinces' (ἔμποροι γὰρ ὄντες κομίζουσι μὲν ἐκ Περσῶν τὰ Ἰνδικὰ ἢ Ἀράβια, διατίθενται δ' ἐν τῇ Ῥωμαίων). Finally, it shows that at that period there was oppression in Palmyra.

The subsequent history of Palmyra until the third century AD, as far as we can follow it according to the material available to us (Shifman 1977), presents a typical 'career' for the period of the Principate, that of the so-called *civitates stipendiariae*. In its everyday life and particularly in customs policy, Palmyra not only had to follow precedents and norms dictated by Roman administrators (an imperial freedman Kilix, Germanicus, Corbulo, Mucianus) but also to implement tax tariffs according to the agreement concluded in the presence of the Roman administrator (in the title of the 'old' tariff mentioned in the text dealt with in this volume his name was mentioned — Marinus). In other words, although officially Palmyra had the status of a *polis*, in fact it was totally under Roman control. It is important to note that the Roman government always tried to use Palmyrene trading skill in Mesopotamia to strengthen its influence in that region. For that reason, probably, Germanicus sent a Palmyrene as an ambassador to Mesene.[7] [Ed.: Shifman's text has 'Emesa' here; there was also an embassy to Emesa (Starcky 1952: 32).] This also explains, as Pliny the Elder noted in his description of Palmyra (*NH*, 5, 88), why during Roman conflict with Parthia the two enemies worried about the political alignment of Palmyra, since the outcome depended largely upon it. At the same time, Palmyra had to provide Rome with 'extra' troops. Thus, the Palmyrene archers participated in the Jewish defeat of 66–73 (Bereshit Rabba, 56). A Palmyrene garrison that was transformed into a Roman military division was present in Dura-Europos.

---

6 Février assumes that Mark Antony perhaps thought of subordinating Palmyra, because in 41 B.C. it was independent of Rome (Février 1931a: 5–6). Starcky (Starcky 1952 and 1967) shares Février's view. Eissfeldt writes that even Tiberius (although he exercised certain 'rights of supremacy') refused to incorporate Palmyra into the Empire. He was sure that the advantages that Palmyra received on the Roman side connected it firmly with the Empire. And Palmyra's interrelations with Parthia should not be a concern for the Empire (Eissfeldt 1941: 66).

7 We do not have any documents that prove that the economic growth of Palmyra began from the first half of the first century AD (Saverkina 1971).

The Palmyrene Tax Tariff

A new period in Palmyrene history started when in AD 129 Hadrian visited the city (*Inv.* I, 2). There was a rededication of the city when it (like other cities in the Near East) received the emperor's name (St. Byz., see under Πάλμυρα: Ἀδριανοπολῖται). We see this new name in the Aramaic title of the Tariff: הדרינא תדמר (cf. in *Inv.* X, 38, dated to April AD 131: Ἀδριανὸς Παλμηρηνός). The new customs Tariff of 137 showed a drastic change in Palmyra's administrative status. It was enacted by local magistrates based on the decision of the Council and according to the agreement between the city government and the tax farmer. Evidently, in the time of Hadrian (and as a result of his visit) the city government received more real rights than before.[8]

Finally, at the end of the second and at the beginning of the third centuries AD Palmyra was a colony of the 'Italic Law' (*Dig.*, L, 15, 1).

In the period from the first to the middle of the third centuries AD Palmyrene society experienced serious social changes that can be described generally as follows. There was a clear division between the trading upper echelon of society, the poor and the middle class (petty traders, merchants, smallholders and so on). At the same time there was social degradation of some of the élite. Different forms of patronage became widespread: from 'neighbourly help' that was expressed in different forms of benefaction, to client patronage in its direct sense. Roman citizens played more and more significant roles in Palmyrene life. They were former solders of the Roman army (Palmyrenes served in military units that were stationed in Britain, Numidia and Dacia: Starcky 1952: 43–5), former higher magistrates, etc. Eventually, these changes led to the weakening of the *polis* organization. We are aware of several social conflicts in the city. An outcome of one of those conflicts, when the tax farmers abused their power while collecting taxes, was the issuing in AD 137 of the new Tariff which is the subject of this research. Another outcome in the second century AD (we do not know the exact reasons) led to the establishment by the Roman authorities of a special magistrate whose job was maintaining the peace. Probably, at some stage of the different social conflicts the preconditions were created for the establishing of a single ruling power (Shifman 1977).

---

8   It is certainly a mistake to suppose that under Hadrian the leadership in Palmyra was reorganized according to the Greek pattern (Saverkina 1971: 18). In Syria the homogeneous Hellenistic system was already built up under the Seleucids and Palmyra was not an exception.

Introduction

The best known and perhaps the most successful period in the history of Palmyra is the second half of the third century AD. This saw the rise of the dynasty of Odenathus and Zenobia and the establishment of a single ruler who began an active struggle, first for the domination of the Near East, and then of the whole Roman Empire (Starcky 1952: 53–69; Shifman 1977). The other reason for the rise of Palmyra was the decline of central Roman power in the crisis of the end of the second and the third centuries, when the emperors were less and less capable of providing basic social stability and of protecting their territory from outside invasions. Local political figures capable of bringing and maintaining order could have received the support of influential groups of people.

Inscription 4202 [ed.: Shifman gives a date of AD 225, but in fact this inscription is not dated; 4022 has this date] contains the first description (known until now) of the earliest representatives of the dynasty.

Τὸ μνημῖον τοῦ ταφεῶνος ἔκτισεν ἐξ ἰδίων Σεπτίμιος Ὀδαίναθος, ὁ λαμπρότατος συνκλητ[ικός,] Αἱράνου Οὐαβαλλάθου τοῦ Νασώρου, αὐτῷ τε καὶ υἱοῖς αὐτοῦ καὶ υἱωνοῖς εἰς τὸ παντελές, αἰώνιον τειμήν	Septimius Odenathus, the most splendid senator, son of Hairan son of Vaballathus son of Nasōr, built this tomb from his own means for himself, for his sons and grandsons for eternal honour.
קברא דנה בנא אדינת סקלטיקא בר חירן והבלת נצור לה ולבנוה ולבנא בנוהי לעלמא	Odenat, senator, son of Ḥairan son of Wahballat son of Naṣōr, built this tomb for himself, for his sons and grandsons for eternity.

From the inscription it is evident that Septimius Odenathus derives his genealogy from a certain Naṣōr, his great grandfather, who was probably quite significant in forming the destiny of this family. Naṣōr must have lived in the second half of the second century AD. According to his *nomen*, Naṣōr's dynasty received Roman citizenship at the end of the second or the beginning of the third century, in any case before the Edict of Caracalla. The person who built the tomb apparently continued his career and secured the political influence of his family. Since no title was mentioned in relation to his earlier ancestors, it seems he was the first who received the title of senator. The phrase, ἐξ ἰδίων, 'from his own means', is usually used to describe personal funds used for public constructions or other expenses for official needs. In a grave inscription it sounds a little awkward. A plausible way to explain its appearance here is to argue that Odenathus wanted to emphasize his independence from other members of his family (other descendants of Naṣōr in other lines of descent).

Inscription 3944 (Palmyra, October AD 251) is another text that helps us to follow the history of the Odenathus and Zenobia family.

Σεπτίμιον Αἱράνην Ὀδαινάθου τόν λαμπρότατον συνκλητικόν, ἔξα[ρχον Παλμυ]ρηνῶν Αὐρήλι[ος Φιλεῖνο]ς [Μα]ρ‹ίου› Ἡλιοδώρου [τοῦ Ραα ίου] στρατιώτης λεγ[εῶνος Κυρηνα]ϊκῆς τὸν πάτρωνα, τειμῆς καὶ εὐχαριστίας χάριν, ἔτους γξφ´	Septimius Hairan son of Odenathus, the most splendid senator and exa[rch of the Palmy]renes, Aureli[us Phileino]s son of [Ma]r[ius] son of Heliodorus [son of Raaios], soldier of the Cyrenaican leg[ion], the patron, in honour and gratitude, in the year 563.
צלמא דנה די ספטמיוס חירן בר אדינת סנקלטיקא נהריא ורש תדמור די אקים לה אורליס פלינוס בר מריא פלינא רעי פלחא די בלגיונא די בצרא ליקרה בירח תשרי די שנת 563	This is the statue of Septimius Ḥairan son of Odenat, the most splendid senator and chief of Palmyra, which was made for him by Aurelius Phileinos son of Marius Phileinos [son] of Ra'ay, soldier of the legion in Boṣra, in his honour, in the month of Tishri, the year 563.

This inscription confirms the assumption that Septimius Odenathus was the first in his dynasty to receive the title of senator. He also probably intentionally limited his genealogy (although it was well known to him) to his father. Presumably, the new line in the dynasty began with Septimius Odenathus. This was the line of rapid political advancement. The first step in this line was Odenathus' inclusion in the list of senators. That is also probably why there is no title next to Odenathus' name in the inscription: his title was well known and there was no need to repeat it again. His son, Septimius Ḥairan (in whose honour the inscription was made a quarter century later) had kept the title of senator. His name, however, is also related to another title ('Chief of Palmyra') that was not mentioned before. This inscription shows not only the growing influence and power of this dynasty but also (because of its distinctness from other Palmyrene inscriptions) the rise of the new political regime. In fact, the Palmyrene expression רש תדמור, 'the chief of Palmyra', denotes only the fact that Septimius Ḥairan was the head of the local government, who overshadowed other ordinary magistrates, including higher *stratēgoi* (in that period).

It is plausible that Septimius Ḥairan son of Odenathus was the first member of his dynasty who was able to establish a single dictatorship (a local tyranny) which ten years later grew into the power of an emperor-king held by his descendants.

In relation to the previous statement it is important to note that in the Greek inscription Septimius Ḥairan has the title ἔξαρχος Παλμυρηνῶν. Literally, this means 'the chief of the Palmyrenes' which corresponds with the Palmyrene expression רש תדמור; however, if we consider that in the period of the late Roman Empire *exarchoi* were commanders of cavalry units, we may assume that Septimius Odenathus was able to gain power in the city because he was in command of local military forces. The fact that the inscription in his honour was made by a client — probably an ex-soldier of the Cyrenaican legion stationed in Boṣra — proves the previous point and shows that patronage was one of the means of political power in Palmyra.

We meet Septimius Odenathus II, the son of Ḥairan, for the first time in inscription 3945 (Palmyra, April AD 258).

Σεπ[τίμιον Ὀδαίναθον] τὸν λαμ[πρότατον ὑπατικ]ὸν συντέ[λεια τῶν χρυσοχ]όων καὶ ἀργυ[ροκόπων, τ]ὸν δεσπότην, τειμῆς χάριν, [ἔτ]ους θξφ´ μηνεὶ Ξανδικῷ	To Sep[timius Odenathus], the most spl[endid cons]ul, the gui[ld of the gold]smiths and silv[ersmiths], to the(ir) master, for the sake of honour, the year 569, in the month Xandikos.
צלם ספטמיוס אדינת נהירא הפטיקא מרן די אקים לה תגמא די קיניא עבדא דהבא וכספא ליקרה בירח ניסן די שנת 569	This is the statue of Septimius Odenat, the illustrious consul, our lord, which was set up for him by the corporation of the gold- and silversmiths, in his honour, in the month Nīsān, the year 569.

This text confirms the successful career of the family. Septimius Odenathus does not feel it necessary to have his genealogy inserted: it is probably well known. His fame does not need validation. He is a consul. In other words, he was able to achieve the highest Roman magistracy (outside the actual imperial administration) which automatically put him in the circle of the noblest senators. Finally, he is 'lord' for the local corporation of the smiths. The Greek term δεσπότης (the Palmyrene מרן, 'our lord' is less specific and less expressive) implies that Septimius Odenathus II was not only the leader of the Council (which would require a different term), but he was in fact the *chief* of Palmyra. This means that he kept and even secured the power of his father.

Septimius Odenathus conducted quite an active foreign policy. We know from Petrus Patricius (Petr. Patr., fr. 10; *FHG*, IV: 187) that he tried to make an agreement with the Persian king Shapur I ('fawning upon him'), probably after Shapur I defeated the Roman emperor Valerian at Edessa (AD 260). Odenathus sent the king rich gifts and a letter in which he emphasized a kind of neutrality with regard to Iran. Shapur, however, arrogantly rejected the gifts (by his orders the slaves threw them into the river) and the letter ('he tore it into pieces and trampled it under foot'). Laying claim to rule of Palmyra, Shapur ordered Odenathus, who had had such impudence (in writing to his lord), to come to see him if he did not want to be punished. Otherwise, Shapur threatened to destroy Odenathus, his whole family and his homeland. In our opinion, the story told by Petrus Patricius is quite plausible. Taking into consideration political changes and the military capacity of Iran, Odenathus could well have made efforts to negotiate with a new ruler. Shapur's rude response forced Odenathus to choose a different path. He formalized his control over the Near East (Treb. Poll., *Gall. duo*, 10, 1) and organized a Syrian peasant volunteer corps (Oros., *Hist. adv. pag.*, 7.22.12). He thus defended Syria by his own means, moved the war into Mesopotamia, conquered Carrhae and Nisibis, and even laid siege to Ctesiphon (Treb. Poll., *Gall. duo*, 10, 3; 10, 6; 12, 1; Eutrop., 2, 10; Oros., *Hist. adv. pag.*, 7.22.12; Zosim., 1, 39). According to Zosimus, Odenathus obeyed the orders of Gallienus: he probably wanted to create the impression that he was acting as an official and loyal deputy of the central power rather than as a usurper.

In any case, in accordance with ancient Roman tradition, after the victory over Shapur Odenathus and his son Herod were declared *imperator* (Treb. Poll., *Tyr. trig.*, 15, 5). This meant that Odenathus, at least formally, was a co-ruler with the Emperor. In fact, he became an independent ruler of the eastern (more exactly, of the Near Eastern) part of the Empire, because the central power in Rome did not have enough forces to maintain dominion in the East. In spite of the fact that Odenathus was shown resistance in some places, such as Boṣra (Seyrig 1941a), he was still able to bring under his control a large territory as far as the Red Sea (Evagrius, *Hist. eccl.*, 3, 41).

The epigraphic records that mention Septimius Odenathus II, although they were written after his death, allow us to reconstruct at least to some degree his rank after the victory over Shapur. In inscription 3946 (Palmyra, August AD 271) he is called מתקננא די מדנחא כלה, which in Cantineau's view corresponds with the Roman *restitutor totius Orientis*, a title that indicates Odenathus' power in the East and that it was recognized by the central Roman government (Cantineau 1933b: 217–33).[9] At the same time, Odenathus had a Persian title, 'king of kings', (מלך מלכא; see 3971, Palmyra, AD 268–70; 3946, Palmyra, August AD 271; Treb. Poll., *Gall. duo*, 10, 1: *Odaenathus rex Palmyrenorum*, but in *Tyr. trig.* he is *princeps Palmyrenorum*). This title undoubtedly shows Odenathus' claims of status equal to that of the kings of Iran.

In the year 267, Septimius Odenathus and his son Herod, the inheritor of his power, were killed, most likely as a result of a conspiracy that was organized by his wife Zenobia (Bat-Zabbai) (Treb. Poll., *Tyr, trig.*, 16, 1–3).[10] According to Trebellius Pollio, she took power and ruled in the name of her sons, Herennianus and Timolaus. The epigraphic and numismatic sources, however, indicate only one son of Zenobia, in whose name she ruled. This was Vahballathus Athenodorus. The title of the son was that of consul, *imperator* and Roman general (ὑπατικὸς αὐτοκράτωρ στρατηγὸς Ῥωμαίων; *vir consularis Romanorum imperator dux Romanorum*) (Sallet 1866). According to inscription 3971 (Palmyra, AD 268–70), Vahballathus had the title of 'restorer of the whole East' (אפנרתטא די מדנחא כלה), as well as 'illustrious king of kings' (נהיר[א מלך מלכא]).

Thus he fully inherited the title of his father. Zenobia called herself *Augusta* on coins (Σεβαστή) (Sallet 1866). In the inscriptions she is referred to as 'the most illustrious queen, the mother of the king of kings' (τῆς λαμπροτάτης βασιλίσσης μητρὸς βασιλέως; אמה די מלך מלכא נהירתא מלכתא) (3946, Palmyra, August AD 271) or 'the most illustrious and pious queen' (τὴν λαμπροτάτην

---

9 According to Clermont-Ganneau (1920: 382–419) this title needs to be translated *corrector totius Orientis* (the same in *CIS*).

10 There is another opinion on this: Odenathus II together with Herod and, close to him Vorod, were killed on the order of emperor Gallienus (Eissfeldt 1941: 69).

εὐσεβῆ βασίλισσαν; [א]מלכתא [נהירתא וצדקתא] (3947; see also *IGRR*, III, 1027). Perhaps Zenobia had pretensions to a position equal to the position of Julia Domna after the death of Septimius Severus. Vahballathus and Zenobia followed the policy of Odenathus II and retained in their political management both Roman and Persian features (Treb. Poll., *Tyr., trig.*, 30, 2; 13–14).

In AD 270 Zenobia and Vahballathus seized power in Egypt; the Palmyrene rulers also established their dominion in Asia Minor. In 271 the emperor Aurelian himself regained Egypt and in 272 he defeated the Palmyrenes at Tyana, forcing them to leave Asia Minor. After victory near the Orontes he entered Antioch. Then he again defeated Zenobia at Emesa and laid siege to Palmyra. Zenobia and Vahballathus tried to flee to Iran. However, they were captured and sent to Rome. Afterwards, Aurelian suppressed revolts in Palmyra twice in autumn 272, suppressing those who tried to restore the Odenathus-Zenobia dynasty. Finally, the rebellious city was pillaged and burnt. Zenobia participated as a prisoner of war in Aurelian's triumph in 274. She lived in a villa given to her by the victor until her death. This final defeat was fatal for Palmyra. Even Diocletian's and Justinian's attempts to restore the city were unsuccessful. In 634 the troops of Khālid ibn al-Walīd entered Palmyra. Palmyra (what was left of it) as well as the whole of Syria came under Arab dominion.

In medieval Arabic literature the kingdom of Odenathus and Zenobia was long remembered. The image of the queen who fought for power in the world was especially fascinating. In Arab oral tradition, however, these images were forgotten. The great remains of Palmyra were remembered in connection with the biblical king Solomon and his wife Bilqīs, the queen of Sheba. The hill where the well-known grave inscription of Yamliku is located is called Umm Bilqīs; the construction near the *agora* was considered to be Solomon's temple (Starcky 1952: 29–30).

Before we begin discussion about the spiritual life of the Palmyrenes, it is important to notice that the sources in this area of research are limited and incomplete. The main source are the inscriptions, which help us to understand the language of business transactions and the origins and development of the chancery style in Palmyra, as well as cultural life and religion. There are also remains of Palmyrene art, sculpture and architecture and there is, finally, very limited information about the writers and philosophers at Zenobia's court. Zenobia, probably imitating Julia Domna, also tried to play the role of the educated patroness of science and art. Despite their incompleteness the sources

Introduction

enable us to envisage the ambience of Palmyrene society. They all belong to the time of the Principate.

Another problem that we face in research is the problem of the ethnicity of the Palmyrenes. The analysis of the names that appear in the Palmyrene inscriptions shows that in a majority of cases they are Arabic, which causes us to think that the majority of the population in Palmyra of the first to third centuries AD was descended from Arabs.[11] It would, however, be wrong to limit ourselves to stating this fact. It is essential to note that the Palmyrene population, including Arabs, were an inseparable part of the Graeco-Aramaic environment and culture. This may mean that in the end the Palmyrenes were the same as the Hellenized Syrians of the rest of Syria. Finally, self-awareness is extremely important for ethnicity. If there are indications in Palmyra of the first half of the second century about belonging to one's tribe (Shifman 1977), this never occurs in terms of 'Arab' or 'Syrian' ethnicity. In some cases the inhabitants of Palmyra are called Palmyrenes, which points to citizenship. There is one case (*Inv.* IX, 6) where the term 'Greeks' is opposed to the term 'Palmyrenes'. From the above it is evident that the Palmyrenes of the period of the Principate considered themselves as an ethnically separate society, neither Greek nor Hellenistic. Whether they considered themselves Syrians (Aramaeans or Arabs), we do not know.

We have already noted that many of the inscriptions that survive till now are in Aramaic; in many cases they are Graeco-Aramaic bilinguals. We will return to the detailed analysis of the Graeco-Aramaic Palmyrene Tariff, but at the moment we need to discuss the following.

According to Cantineau (1935) and Rosenthal (1936, 1964), the Aramaic language in the Palmyrene inscriptions represents the 'Imperial Aramaic' of the Achaemenid period, though also influenced by the Eastern Aramaic language spoken in Palmyra. Some scholars, like J. Cantineau, with reference also to D. Schlumberger, think that the presence of this traditional Near Eastern language in Palmyrene business affairs emphasized Palmyrene independence, at least

---

11 Goldmann (1935: 3–5) is absolutely right in assuming that in many cases Palmyrene names can be interpreted as Aramaic or as Arabic. This fact makes it hard to determine the ethnicity of a person. On the other hand, he identifies characteristics of Arabic names that are shared by others: the presence of the Arabic nominative case (with ending in ו-) and the meaning of the name, for example אשד (corresponding with the Arabic أَسَدٌ), 'lion'. The book written by Stark about proper names in the Palmyrene inscriptions is not available to us.

formally, from the Hellenized countries of the Near East and from the Roman Empire itself. In our opinion, this interpretation is incorrect, because Palmyra was never independent of the Roman Empire, and its administrative and political status was not different from the status of other Syrian cities of the Hellenistic and Roman period. A more simple explanation is likely: in spite of Greek influence Palmyra kept its ancient tradition of composing written documents in Aramaic, understandable by the whole population.

The Palmyrene Aramaic script originated in the Aramaic square script of the first millennium BC and ultimately in the linear Phoenician script. Palmyra was a part of the Near East's Aramaic culture of the first millennium BC. It kept and developed this tradition further. The analysis of some Palmyrene inscriptions shows that the form and the terminology of business documents came from the Aramaic documentary tradition of the first millennium BC (Shifman 1977).

There is much more to say about Palmyrene culture. As we have noted earlier, many Palmyrene inscriptions have two almost identical parallel texts set side by side: Aramaic and Greek. Some are written only in Greek. Greek was possibly provided for the purpose of informing as many people as possible, including those who did not speak Aramaic. A more significant conclusion is that the presence of the Greek texts shows that the author, without refusing his Aramaism, has assimilated Greek culture, language and education — the question how deep this assimilation was remains, however — and thus belongs to 'civilized' Hellenistic society. It is important to note that the Greek texts were composed according to the regular Greek form and, once again, while conveying the meaning, they do not always repeat the Aramaic text word-for-word. They were written according to Hellenistic norms and traditions. Palmyra probably belonged to Hellenistic culture, while remaining Aramaic. It had all the possibilities for developing both Aramaic and Greek literature, as well as the whole tradition of Hellenistic Eastern philosophy, religion and ethical teachings. During Zenobia's reign Palmyra became an important centre of late Hellenistic philosophy.

As was said before, Palmyra was dominated by Rome probably as early as the first century BC. One could expect that Palmyra would be influenced also by Roman culture. However, Roman culture itself was developing under the strong influence of Hellenistic civilization. During the Empire these two cultures were so merged that the main influence of Rome on the East was probably the extension of the Latin language.¹² The main sources for the Latinization of Palmyra would be the Roman provincial chancery and the Roman army, where many Palmyrenes served. Inscriptions of Palmyrene soldiers who served in the Roman army were found in Britain, Numidia and Dacia. Many Palmyrenes had high military ranks (Starcky 1952: 44–5, Shifman 1977). They returned home as Romans and this was surely reflected in their lifestyle, habits, etc. The Latin language, however, was not widespread in Palmyra. It was only the official language of documents composed by Palmyrene archers accommodated in Dura-Europos when they became an official subdivision of the Roman army (all the documents are published in *DEPP*).

We have reason to assume that Palmyra was also influenced by Iranian culture. Studies of clothing styles in Palmyrene art indicate this (Seyrig 1937: 4–31). The Palmyrene pantheon that we know from the surviving inscriptions and cultic images presents an astonishing combination of gods of different origins. In Palmyra there is veneration of Aramaean (mainly local Palmyrene), Arabian, Mesopotamian and Canaanite gods. All of them are also identified with Greek deities.

According to R. du Mesnil du Buisson (1964: 169–95), who based his arguments on the study of the Palmyrene *tesserae*, the most ancient cult in Palmyra (so far as can be traced) was the cult of the gods Yariḥbōl and ʿAglibōl, alongside the image of Arṣu with horned ram's head (du Mesnil du Buisson sees here the earliest Palmyrene triad). [Ed.: in mentioning the ram's head Shifman may be confusing du Mesnil du Buisson's comments on Arṣu with his comments on Malakbēl.] They were venerated on the hill near the Efqa spring. According to du Mesnil du Buisson, these deities were gods of the well and oasis; they represent the moon-father (ירח, 'moon, month') and the moon-son (עגל, 'calf'). A more plausible hypothesis was suggested, however, by O. Eissfeldt (1941: 85–6). He believes that the root ירח needs to be understood as meaning 'to go, to walk', and עגל as 'to ride, to travel'. Accordingly, Eissfeldt explains further that ירחבול means 'the herald of Bōl', and עגלבול means 'charioteer of Bōl'. There are several arguments against du Mesnil du Buisson's hypothesis. The first is the symbolic meaning of the

---

12 In any case, we cannot assume the immediate influence of the architectural skills of the Romans on Palmyra (Saverkina 1971: 9). Rather we should assume the influence of Hellenistic architecture.

names. The second is that the names need to be divided: בול needs to be separated as a later addition if we accept du Mesnil du Buisson's reading of the names. His version cannot be proved. In fact both names probably contain בול as a leading name in a compound. In the first name it is linked with ירח; in the second with עגל. In our opinion, the triad of the Bēl-Bōl, Yariḥbōl and ʿAglibōl played a very important role in the Palmyrene pantheon.

The other question that is related to the Palmyrene cults is that of the origin of Bēl. It is now commonly recognized (Hoftijzer 1968: 27) that the name Bēl represents the Neo-Babylonian variant of the name of the deity that came into Palmyra and became parallel to the local god Bōl. Following Eissfeldt (1941: 84–5; see Starcky 1952: 87) we believe that the most probable date of that event is the middle of the first millennium BC.[13] The name Bōl remained, first of all, in the names of the above-mentioned gods — Yariḥbōl and ʿAglibōl; secondly, in proper names (like Zabdibōl, Gaddibōl, etc.). The Bēl element, בל, also appears in Palmyrene proper names (like Nūrbēl, Elahbēl) (Goldmann 1935: 19). This means that both variations (local and Neo-Babylonian) had existed for some time. According to the plausible explanation of Eissfeldt (1941: 84), the word 'Bōl' came from Canaanite-Amorite *Baʿal*, which turned into *bāl* and then to *bōl* (with loss of the ʿ between vowels). If so, we have a case (common among western Semitic peoples) of the substitution of other words, like 'master,' 'lord', instead of the taboo name of the deity. Substitutions later developed into proper names themselves and in this case survived in the Aramaic of Palmyra. Thus, 'Bōl' was quite possibly identified with the Akkadian word 'Bēl', having a similar origin, pronunciation and meaning; and those who knew the Palmyrene spoken language would not be aware of the difference.

Seyrig rightly reckons that the origin of this cult goes back to a time when Palmyra was not yet Aramaic-speaking (Seyrig 1971: 86–7).

Now we will focus on the functions of Bōl-Bēl. We have an inscription (3970) dated to April AD 203 that contains the title ἀρχιερεὺς καὶ συ[μποσία]ρχος ἱερέων μεγίστου θεοῦ Διὸς Βή[λου]. From this it is evident that by the third century the image of Bēl in the minds of believers, including priests, was associated with Zeus. The name was also accompanied by the

---

13 R. du Mesnil du Buisson (1962: 177) thinks that this took place in the second half of the fourth or beginning of the third century. There is an opinion that *bōl* is a Palmyrene dialect variation of Akkadian *bēl* (Goldmann 1935: 19, n. 1).

epithet 'the greatest god'. The identification with Zeus was possible only if, even before Hellenization in Palmyra, Bōl-Bēl played the role of the highest deity in the pantheon. This particular representation of Bōl-Bēl as the heavenly lord is found on a fresco in a Palmyrene temple (Cumont 1926) and in the relief from the temple of Bōl-Bēl, where he represents the overlord of everything (Eissfeldt 1941: 83).[14] Perhaps, in connection with the latter, the name of Bōl-Bēl on the *tesserae* is sometimes accompanied by the picture of the mask of Pan (*RTP*, 56–7) which corresponds well with the Pan cult itself in the period of the Principate. Based on a variety of *tesserae* (*RTP*, 41–144), we can assume that Bōl-Bēl was a protector of wine-making and olive cultivation (Hoftijzer 1968: 29–30). In some *tesserae* the epithet 'Gad (Gr. τύχη and Lat. *Fortuna*) of olives' (גד משחא) is attributed to Bōl-Bēl (*RTP*, 131–2). He is often pictured with palm leaves.

The ancient image of Bōl-Bēl was probably expressed as בול תורא, 'Bōl- (or Bēl-) bull' (*RTP*, 59). On one of the images of the head of the bull there is the inscription [ל]אגן ב, 'Protect, O Bō[l]' (*RTP*, 89). On another image of the bull there is the inscription בל שמש, 'Bōl, assist' (*RTP*, 139). On *tessera* 75 there is an image of a human-like figure with the head of a bull and the inscription בל, 'Bōl'. Here there is a similarity with the Ugaritic images of the Bull El. Most common, however, is an anthropomorphic image of Bōl-Bēl with a horned crown, often with a spear in his right hand and in Roman armour (Cumont 1926).

The material that survives does not contain any information on the mythology of Bōl-Bēl. However, based on the *tesserae* we can reconstruct the scene of the fight between Bōl-Bēl and Typhon (Mesnil du Buisson 1962: 192).

The cult of Yariḥbōl — the god of the sun — is very much connected with the veneration of Bōl-Bēl. Yariḥbōl is part of the triad headed by the latter. As we have mentioned before, the most plausible hypothetical interpretation of the name of this deity was suggested by O. Eissfeldt: Yariḥbōl as 'the herald of Bōl'. J. Hoftijzer (1968: 32) describes the role of Yariḥbōl as that of the one who gives oracles. He refers to the inscription that accompanies the honorific statue of Zubayda son of Shaʿadu son of Taymishamsh (3919; April AD 117):

---

14 According to Seyrig (1933: 238–46) the god Bōl-Bēl was probably the lord of heaven. His opinion is more likely than that of Février (1931b: 55), who considered Bōl-Bēl as the god of the sun. In the triad Bōl-Yariḥbōl-ʿAglibōl the second plays the role which Février ascribes to Bōl. See also Seyrig 1971: 85–114.

The Palmyrene Tax Tariff

וסהד לה ירחבול אלהא, 'and Yariḥbōl the god testified for him'. In the commentary on the inscription in *CIS* it is suggested that Zubayda received the testimony of the god most likely through oracles. An analogous formula is present in the inscription of Julius Aurelius Zabdila (3932, October, AD 242): ὡς διὰ ταυτὰ μαρτυρηθῆναι ὑπὸ θεοῦ Ἰαριβώλου; מטלכות סהד לה ירחבול אלהא, as well as in another inscription dated AD 162 (al-Hassani, Starcky 1957: 102–11 [ed.: see Greek part]). As is known (Mesnil du Buisson 1964), Yariḥbōl is often depicted as a *baetyl* with a head surrounded by solar rays. He is connected to the well of Efqa. Yariḥbōl appears as a *maṣṣēbā* (pillar) — the protector and the personification of the well (מצבא די עינא: cf. Dura-Europos no. 33 in Mesnil du Buisson 1939: 18). J. Hoftijzer (1968: 32, n. 37) notes that in inscriptions 4064 and 4065 there is reference to the priest of the *maṣṣēbā* of the well (אפכלא די מצב עינא). Usually Yariḥbōl appears in the form of a warrior; his head rests on a disc that emits (sun) rays.

ʿAglibōl was the god of the moon and also a member of the Bōl-Bēl triad. According to Eissfeldt, as we have already mentioned, ʿAglibōl means 'driver, charioteer' of Bōl. Like Yariḥbōl, ʿAglibōl, who was venerated in connection with the well of Efqa, was depicted in the form of a *baetyl* crowned with a crescent moon (Mesnil du Buisson 1964: 170). There are also images of him in the form of a bull (Mesnil du Buisson 1962: 222–4). The most common and probably later images of ʿAglibōl represent him as a Roman warrior with a spear in his right hand and his head resting on a lunar disc.[15]

There is another triad[16] parallel to the one mentioned above and connected with the veneration of the heavenly lord Baʿalshamīn, the sun (Malakbēl) and the moon (ʿAglibōl). The presence of ʿAglibōl both in the first and the second triad presses home the idea that Baʿalshamīn and Malakbēl (the variant Malakbōl is also possible) were originally the hypostasis of Bōl-Bēl and Yariḥbōl respectively and only later isolated in the Palmyrene pantheon. Having said that, though, we do not exclude the suggestion that at some point Malakbēl was a god of fertility (Hoftijzer 1968: 36).

Baʿalshamīn is one the ancient gods of the Asian Near East. His cult was certainly spread among pre-Aramaic populations of Syria and among the Aramaeans. In Palmyra Baʿalshamīn was the god of lightning and thunder

---

15 Seyrig thinks that the understanding of the triad of Bōl-Bēl was formed in the period 33 BC–AD 32 (Seyrig 1971: 89–94).

16 According to Seyrig (1971: 97) this triad was formed in the first half of the first century AD.

(depicted with lightning in his hand, reminding us of the Ugaritic images of mighty Ba'al) and the god of fertility (Hoftijzer 1968: 34; Drijvers 1971; Teixidor 1972: 424). Ba'alshamīn is described sometimes as 'the kind and rewarding god' (3983: אלהא טבא ושכרא), 'great and compassionate' (3988: רבא ורחמנא).

As far as Malakbēl is concerned, his name (מלכבל), according to Eissfeldt (1941: 86–8), comes from מלאך בל, 'the herald of Bōl-Bēl'. The famous altar found in Trastevere (third century AD) helps us to see some scenes that are related to the mythology of this deity. One side of the altar depicts the birth of the god from a cypress: he is holding a goat in his hands. The other side shows the beginning of his heavenly flight in a chariot harnessed to four griffins. The third side depicts Malakbēl in zenith (an eagle carrying the bust of Helios on its wings). The fourth side shows Malakbēl in the night in the form of Saturn, 'the sun of the night' (Cumont 1928: 101–9; Eissfeldt 1941: 88; Mesnil du Buisson 1962: 269). Thus, the myth identifies Malakbēl with Helios; it presents the motion of the sun from sunrise to sunset (i.e. from the birth of the god until his old age, and, probably, death), and the annual cycle of changing nature.

In addition the veneration of τύχη, the goddess Atargatis (Tar'atē), was widespread in Palmyra. The image of Atargatis was very likely an imitation of a similar statue from Antioch that was found in the temple of the Palmyrene gods in Dura-Europos, as well as in the two temples of the Gaddē in Palmyra and in Dura-Europos. Rabasīrē, the god of the underworld, was also venerated: the temple of Rabasīrē is mentioned in the Tax Tariff. There were also some West Semitic deities (for example, the sun-god Shamsh, Elqōnēra-Poseidon, Ba'alḥammōn, Shadrafa-Apollo), Mesopotamian deities (Nabu, Nergal, Tammuz, Ishtar, Nanai; the cult of Anahita also came into Palmyra from Mesopotamia) and Arab deities (Arṣu, Shay' al-Qawm, Du'anat, Ma'nu, Manāf, Sha'ru, Abgal, Manawat [the goddess of fate], Allat-Pallas Athene) (Hoftijzer 1968: 40–9).[17]

The so-called 'anonymous god', 'the one whose name is blessed forever' (a cult probably widespread from the second century AD), also played a very important role in the life of Palmyra (Seyrig 1933: 246–52; Eissfeldt 1941: 90–92; Hoftijzer 1968: 3–40; Shifman 1974: 88–94). Since in the parallel Greek

---

17 Rostovtzeff's attempt (1933: 58-63) to show the presence of the Haddad cult in Palmyra did not succeed. See Seyrig 1933: 238, n. 1.

texts this formula corresponds to Ζεὺς ὕψιστος καὶ ὑπήκοος, one can suppose that behind the title is one of the highest Palmyrene gods, such as, for example, Baʿalshamīn. However, we do not have any decisive proofs of this hypothesis. The 'anonymous god' appears, however, in the triad of Malakbēl and ʿAglibōl (for example, 3981). It is not impossible that the 'anonymous god' expelled other gods and was associated with Zeus beginning to be part of the triad.

Usually the formula 'the one whose name is blessed forever' is also accompanied by the epithets 'kind', 'compassionate', 'giving'. In one of the inscriptions (4047) the author says that he appeals to this god 'on the sea and on the dry land' (קרלה בימא ובישׁא). In another (4100) we read that the authors appealed to him in time of misfortune, and he replied to them 'in the breadth' (קרו לה בעקא וענון ברוחא). Scholars have several times pointed out the similarity between the latter formula and Psalm 118:5 (especially in the Syriac translation). The title of the deity also finds equivalence in Psalms (72:19). However, to assume that the cult of the 'anonymous god' developed under the influence of Judaism or early Christianity is probably premature. It would be equally wrong to speak of a Palmyrene tendency towards monotheism. It is important to emphasize, however, that with the cult of the 'anonymous god' there were notions (to some extent related to Baʿalshamīn) of the 'kind', 'compassionate' and 'giving' god. This led to the appearance and spread of moral and ethical religious concepts which, in their turn, led to the transformation of the Palmyrene pantheon.

Palmyra looked like a typical Hellenistic *polis*. According to the travellers of the eighteenth century, it is one of the most beautiful cities of the world (Champdor 1953; Michalowski 1966).

The main axis of the city was the Grand Colonnade, 1100 m long, built in the second century AD. Along both sides of the street, together with warehouses and commercial factories, there were Corinthian columns 9.5 m high and 0.95 m in diameter. One of the bends in the colonnade was disguised by the *tetrapylon* that was located at the intersection of two main city streets. The other was hidden by a monumental arch that was built in the shape of a trapezium.

The most important monument in Palmyra and the centre of its spiritual life was the temple of Bōl-Bēl. The temple most likely existed already before the Roman conquest. However, in the first century AD it was radically reconstructed. Stones with dedicatory inscriptions were used as building material for that reconstruction (see publication in *Inv.* IX). We have an

Introduction

inscription (*Inv.* IX, 1) that tells us about Lishamsh son of Tayibbōl son of Shōkaybēl from the tribe of 'the sons of Komara', who dedicated the temple of the gods Bēl, Yariḥbōl and ʿAglibōl on the day of their feast, the sixth day of Nīsān, in the year 343 (= 6th April AD 32). The inscription concerns the *cella*, the holy of holies; perhaps the act of dedication in April (particularly at the appointed day) is connected with certain spring festivals and rituals, similar to the Jewish Passover. In any case, Cantineau in his commentary on this text, notes that in a Greek inscription (*Inv.* VI, 13) 6th April (= 6th Xandikos = 6th Nīsān) is described as a 'good day' (the formula is τ[ῇ] ἀγαθῇ ἡμέρᾳ; see also the Hebrew expression יום טוב, 'feast day', literally, 'good day').

In its final stage the temple of Bōl-Bēl looked like a large square courtyard on a platform (205 x 210 m.), paved with massive slabs and surrounded by a high wall. On the inside the wall was decorated with pilasters with Corinthian capitals. Seen from outside, on the southern, northern and eastern sides the wall had windows with pediments above. Access into the inner courtyard was opened through a *propylaeum* of eight columns, with towers on both sides. Along the walls in the courtyard there were covered porticos. In the western portico there was a room for slaughtering and dressing sacrificial animals. There was an altar in front of the *cella*. The walls of the *cella* rested on a high *podium* surrounded by a peristyle that was made up of forty-two gilded-bronze, fluted Corinthian pillars. Inside the *cella* on the northern wall there were niches with divine images. The temple of Bōl-Bēl was decorated with vegetal ornaments in the form of vines and bunches of grapes. The reliefs depicted gods, sacrificial ceremonies, sacred processions and mythological scenes (the battle with the monster).

Another temple, that of Baʿalshamīn, probably also existed before the Christian era. It was remodelled more than once. Several inscriptions (*Inv.* I, 4; *Inv.* I, 2) give us information about it. According to the former, Yarḥay son of Lishamsh son of Raʿay from the sons of Maʿazyan built the entrance (מ[ע]לתא) into the temple and the colonnade in September AD 67. According to the second, Male son of Yarḥay son of Lishamsh son of Raʿay, i.e. the son of the aforementioned and the same person who subsidized the meeting with Hadrian, 'built', i.e. probably rebuilt, the temple of Zeus (= Baʿalshamīn), its *pronaos* and porticos. The temple of Baʿalshamīn looks very similar to the temple of Bōl: the courtyard is surrounded by a wall and porticos, with an altar and a holy of holies or *cella* surrounded by a peristyle (pillars with Corinthian capitals). There is a special room devoted to sacred rituals. The bas-reliefs of the temple depict Baʿalshamīn in the form of an eagle, as well as Yariḥbōl and ʿAglibōl.

Archaeological excavations in the 1960s found the temple Nabu, dated to the first century AD. Its plan is not different from the previous ones. There is an entrance through the *propylaea* into a courtyard that is surrounded by porticos. In the middle of the courtyard, opposite the entrance, there was a *cella* on a high *podium*. Between the entrance and the *cella* there is a chamber (or maybe an altar) that is decorated at each corner with three half-columns.

Just like other Hellenistic Syrian cities, Palmyra had its own theatre in the Greek style (built in the first half of the second century AD) and *agora*, a trading square surrounded by a wall and on the inside by four porticos. Not far away from the theatre and *agora* there was a building for the Palmyrene council. In 1968 another building near the *agora* was discovered. It was either a huge trading store or a shelter for caravans. It was built in the first half of the second century AD (Bounni, Saliby 1968: 99–100).

The Palmyrene funeral constructions deserve special note. Two types of these kinds of construction are particularly well known: the multi-storied funeral towers with many chambers for burials, and the *hypogaea*, underground tombs in T- and cross-form, also with many chambers (this latter type of construction becoming dominant from the beginning of the second century AD). The *hypogaeum* of the Three Brothers with frescos is particularly interesting. The frescos depict the dead and allegorical scenes (Will 1949: 87–116; Gawlikowski 1970). The period between the first and third centuries was very fruitful for Palmyra in terms of the great development of the art of portraiture. Burials were accompanied by bas-relief portraits of the dead. One could also see honorific statues on the streets in those days, made by the order of the local authorities or by the initiative of different individuals. Palmyrene sculptors (undoubtedly under the influence of Roman and Hellenistic experts) were very skilled in communicating the inner lives of their models and the unique beauty of each personality (Ingholt 1928, 1954; Saverkina 1971).

The works of the Palmyrene artists also survive: the scene of priests offering sacrifice and of worshippers in the Palmyrene temple in Dura-Europos; also images of gods and burial paintings (Strzygowski 1901; Farmakovskiĭ 1903; Cumont 1926). They are very similar to the famous Fayyūm portraits in their technique, a fact which links them to Hellenistic art. In its composition the scene of sacrifice is very reminiscent of the Byzantine portraits of Justinian and Theodora in their court. The style of the Palmyrene artists was probably common to the whole Hellenistic world and a forerunner of Byzantine art.

The Palmyrene mosaics recapitulate mythological stories common in the Hellenistic period (Achilles amongst the daughters of Lycomedes, the myth of Cassiopeia).

4. The Circumstances Surrounding the Finding of the Palmyrene Tariff and the History of its Interpretation.

The Palmyrene Tariff was found accidentally not far from the *agora* on 4th (16th) March 1882 (Arch. AS, f. 779, inv. 1, no. 44). A well-known archaeologist-dilettante, S.S. Abamelek-Lazarev, found the document while visiting Palmyra as a part of his Near Eastern tour. He describes it this way:

> On the third day of my visit to Palmyra two Bedouins showed me an inscription located towards the east of the main ruins and about a mile away from the entrance into the courtyard of the temple of the sun [i.e. the temple of Bōl-Bēl] between beautiful ruins called the 'Saray' and the Muslim graveyard. The writing was made on a small stone positioned vertically in the ground and protruding above it to a height of half an *arshin* [c. 35 cm.]. I began to read large and very beautiful script:
>
> ....ου υἱοῦ θεο....
> ....ατου τὸ $\overline{\gamma}$ πατρὸς πατρίδος ὑπατ....
>
> Based on the meaning of these lines and on the position of the stone I assumed that this must be the title of the inscription. I dug a bit more in the sand and immediately under these letters I saw the beginning of a large and very well preserved Aramaic inscription. The stone was quite large and I hired six people, who in a day and a half uncovered a slab (Abamelek-Lazarev 1884: 41–2).

When Abamelek-Lazarev uncovered the slab (though not yet completely) he made an *estampage* and a copy of it. He writes:

> I was doing this work, being in a very narrow (70 cm) ditch below ground level in the broiling sun and without any possibility of bending in order to read the lowest lines. I had to adjust to the circumstances. After working from 8 a.m. till 6 p.m. I had completed an *estampage* that was equal to the area of 20 square *arshin*s. I was so exhausted that on the next day I could not even copy the inscriptions (1884: 42).

A.V. Prachov, a co-traveller of Abamelek-Lazarev, completed his work. They made many *estampages* of both the Greek and Aramaic and copied the Greek text.

They were not able to bring the material intact to St Petersburg. During the customs examination in Odessa the *estampages* were damaged. The inscription had to be copied again and in the autumn of 1882 Abamelek-Lazarev sent back to Palmyra a photographer from Beirut named Kvareli. His assignment was to take pictures of the stone. However, this mission was unsuccessful too. The local Turkish administrator Selim Effendi prohibited the clearing of the ground in front of the stone to allow the taking of a picture. Abamelek-Lazarev received only some *estampages*, although, in his own words, 'of a worse quality' (Abamelek-Lazarev 1884: 41–3).

In St Petersburg Abamelek-Lazarev began to study the Greek text. V.V. Latyshev, a master of the Greek language, probably played a very important role in that process. Together with his report about the trip to Palmyra, Abamelek-Lazarev published the Greek text with a short commentary.

However, research on the Tariff began right after its discovery and even before Abamelek-Lazarev published his report, even though he took the first steps. He wrote to the French *Académie des Inscriptions et Belles-Lettres* informing them about the details of the discovery and explaining the context of the document. At the end he wrote: 'I am intending to send to the Academy an *estampage* that I made from the Palmyrene inscription. I ask you to send me the translation of this historical document.' Based on this material, already in May 1882 W.H. Waddington reported to the Academy about the discovery and gave a brief description of the document (*CRAIBL*, 1882: 80; Arch. AS, f. 779, inv. 1, no. 40, p. 27).

On 25th May 1882 Abamelek-Lazarev presented a report to the Russian Archaeological Society about his discovery (Arch. LO IA, f. 3, no. 409, pp. 91–3). In the same year P.-F. Foucart published some samples of the Greek text that the Academy had received from Abamelek: the decree of the council, fragments with references to the rescripts of Germanicus and Corbulo and to the practice of the emperor's freedman Kilix, and, finally, a fragment dealing with complaints by tax farmers and about them (Foucart 1882: 439–42). In 1883 M. de Vogüé (1883a, b) published the complete text of the whole inscription — both Greek and Aramaic — based on Abamelek-Lazarev's material. In fact he published the Tariff twice.

His first decoding of the Aramaic text based on the *estampage* sent by Abamelek-Lazarev turned out to be just a preliminary trial. Some months after the first article was published de Vogüé received new material that allowed him to clarify some paragraphs in the text. This was a photograph taken by the German vice-consul in Damascus, E. Lütticke, who sent it to Berlin, to a well-known specialist in Aramaic, E. Sachau. Sachau, in his turn, gave it to de Vogüé. De Vogüé used it to publish the complete parallel texts in Greek and Palmyrene, a translation of the Palmyrene part and a short commentary. After de Vogüé's article, Sachau reconstructed the introductory part of the inscription that conveyed the resolution of the Palmyrene council (Sachau 1883).

In 1883 new *estampages* were made by J. Euting and C. Huber; in 1887 the same was done by J. S. Gautier. P. Schröder published the Tariff for the second time in 1884. He did so on the basis of Euting's *estampage* and the photograph of the Damascus photographer Slimān Hakīm (taken in 1883) and provided it with a German translation. He was able to read and interpret some difficult passages of the inscription that were previously unclear. However, he also gave some interpretations that were not confirmed later. In 1884 H. Dessau published the Greek text of the Tariff with a detailed analysis of the clauses and legal aspects. In the same year R. Cagnat presented some research on these (Cagnat 1884). Finally, in 1888 S. Reckendorf published again both the Greek (following Dessau) and the Palmyrene parts. He provided for the latter a German translation and detailed commentary. In some cases he followed Schröder.

Meanwhile the inscription was still where Abamelek-Lazarev had seen it and copied it for the first time. This fact, and the absence of any security for the inscription or protection from the weather conditions, both made it difficult to study the document and also endangered its survival. There was, therefore, a need to move the Tariff. P.K. Kokovtsov took the initiative to have it moved to one of the Russian museums.

On 22nd April 1899 Kokovtsov spoke at a meeting of the Oriental Section of the Russian Archaeological Society. He spoke about the need to buy the inscription and bring it to Russia. In the minutes of that meeting it is recorded: 'We have decided that it is highly important to purchase the above-named historical document and to ask P.K. Kokovtsov to give a report on this issue at the next meeting of the Archaeological Society' (Arch. LO IA, f. 3, no. 428, p. 17).

On 1st May 1899 Kokovtsov participated in the meeting of the Classical Section of the Russian Archaeological Society and suggested they join in the petition of the Oriental Section (Arch. LO IA, f. 3, no. 451, p. 68). Finally, on 4th May 1899 he spoke at the general meeting of the Russian Archaeological Society. In his note he says: 'The Palmyrene Tariff is a precious historical document of one of the ancient Aramaic dialects ... Semitologists and language experts would probably agree on the great importance of the Palmyrene Trade Tariff. This is a historical document equal in its value to the inscription of Mesha and inscriptions from Zincirli. In other words, this is a highly significant document.' And then, 'I want to draw the attention of the Russian Imperial Archaeological Society to the fact that here we have a forgotten but very precious historical document that we need to make every effort to save. Our museums, that are not very rich in Semitic archaeology and epigraphy, could be proud to have such a possession, just as the Louvre Museum is proud of the inscription of Mesha, and the Royal Museums in Berlin are proud of antiquities from Zincirli' (Kokovt͡sov 1900: 3–5). The Russian Archaeological Society informed the Academy of Science about this (Arch. LO IA, f. 3, no. 232, pp. 1–2 and no. 409, p. 29). The question of purchasing the document was discussed already at the meeting the next day, 5th May 1899. The decision was 'to inform the Russian ambassador in Constantinople and after his response to compose a petition' (Arch. AS, f. 779, inv. 1, no. 40, p. 45). The President of the Academy contacted the ambassador, I. Zinov'ev, and asked him to enquire about the possibility of buying the Tariff (Arch. AS, f. 779, inv. 2, no. 1, pp. 9–10; Arch. LO IA, f. 3, no. 232, p. 3).

The Russian government began to negotiate with the Turkish authorities. The latter were very positive about the proposal. Zinov'ev asked the director of the Russian Archaeological Institute in Constantinople, F. Uspenskiĭ, and the consul-general in Damascus, A.P. Belīaev, to find ways of transportation. As Kokovt͡sov wrote to Abamelek-Lazarev, 'we must find ways to organize transportation' (Arch. AS, f. 779, inv. 1, no. 40, pp. 9–10). At that time the Institute of the Russian-Palestinian Society was organizing a trip to Syria and Uspenskiĭ visited Palmyra together with the dragoman of the Russian consulate in Jerusalem, Īa.I. Khouri. When he had studied the stone, he decided that the best way to transport it was to divide it into four parts along the borders that separate one panel from another. He gave instructions to Khouri, who was supposed to lead the transportation project (Arch. LO IA, f. 3, no. 254 and no. 60; Arch. AS, f. 779, inv. 1, no. 40, pp. 70–78). At the same time Zinov'ev completed the negotiations with the Turkish government. On

13th October 1900 the Sultan told the Russian ambassador that he was giving the inscription as a gift and allowing it to be taken to Russia. On 9th November 1900 the Academy brought the news to the Russian Archaeological Society and the latter (on 22nd November 1900) asked the Hermitage to accept the stone. The copyright on publication belonged to the society, i.e. P.K. Kokovtsov (Arch. AS, f. 779, inv. 1, no. 40, pp. 31, 44, 70–78; Arch. LO IA, f. 3, no. 232, fol. 3–4 and no. 409, p. 68).

Appreciating the role of Kokovtsov in the fate of the Palmyrene Tariff, S.S. Abamelek-Lazarev wrote: 'The efforts and persistence of one person means a lot: Russia owes you alone a great deal for this scientific victory' (Arch. AS, f. 779, inv. 2, no. 1, p. 12; Orbeli 1956: 353). Abamelek-Lazarev did not overestimate Kokovtsov's efforts. Kokovtsov had pleaded for the inscription, informed all scholarly circles and, more importantly, stimulated interest in the document in the bureaucratic sphere, as well as participating in all the discussions concerning this enterprise.

On 4th May 1901 a Russian expedition, headed by Khouri, left Jerusalem (with consular permission of 1st December 1900) and directed its way to Palmyra. On 9th May it arrived in Damascus. Khouri spent eight days there forming a caravan, hiring workers and mostly waiting for the stabilization of the situation in the Ledja. Only on the 17th, escorted by ten soldiers, did he leave Damascus and on the 21st he arrived in Palmyra. There, to his surprise, he found that the notification from the Syrian governor-general (Palmyra was not administratively under him) was not enough for the local authorities and the governor-general of Dayr ez-Zor had not had any notification from Constantinople. Khouri began work anyway and the governor-general sent to the capital for confirmation. The expedition began excavations and sawed off the lower part of the stone that did not have any text on it. On 9th June the local authorities forbade any further work until the necessary notification from Constantinople arrived. Khouri sent a telegram to the Russian consul in Damascus.

Only two weeks later, on 24th June the work resumed. As Uspenskiĭ had suggested, the stone was sawn into four parts vertically. Then the panels were placed on a carriage, without packing and with the texts upwards. On top they placed bottomless boxes and tied everything together. On 14th–15th July 1901 Khouri left Palmyra. The carriages with their heavy loads moved very slowly on the Syrian roads. Only on the eleventh day, 26th July, at midnight, did the caravan arrive in Damascus. After five days, on 1st August, the stones were sent by train to Beirut, where they were packed in special boxes. On 28th November 1901 the precious package arrived by sea in Odessa. On 11th December it arrived in St Petersburg by train (Arch. AS, f. 779, inv. 1, no. 40, pp. 50–69 and 77–8).

The problems with the inscription were not over yet. The customs duties had to be paid. Also there were extra expenses on the way from Odessa to St Petersburg (the stones having to be repacked at the customs post in Odessa). The total sum to be paid was 1692 roubles and 48 kopeks. The customs office in St. Petersburg allowed one year for payment of the duties, until 11th December 1902. Otherwise the stones would be exhibited for public sale and any other foreign museum could buy them (Arch. AS, f. 779, inv. 2, no. 1, pp. 14–15). P.K. Kokovtsov began to solicit funds and found N.P. Kondakov, who on 17th January 1902 told him: 'From the conversation with Baron V.R. Rosen I learnt that he is quite open to making some effort to help with the issue. You ought to talk to him about it.' Kokovtsov probably asked Kondakov to talk to the secretary of the Academy, N.O. Dubrovin, 'who assured me that the Academy was inclined to ask the government to help with the money to pay for the transportation and that the Academy only needed notification from the Hermitage that the museum was willing to accept the panels' (Arch. AS, f. 779, inv. 2, no. 223, p. 112).

The debates between Kokovtsov, Kondakov, Rosen and Dubrovin were not enough to solve the problem. As far as we know, Rosen changed his mind concerning the enterprise. Unfortunately, the Academy took his side as well and decided that the Ministry of the Royal Court (which was in charge of the Hermitage) had to make decisions about the document. While the discussions and squabbles among bureaucrats continued, Kokovtsov again tried to make more efforts himself. He found F.E. Korsh, who made a presentation at the meeting of the Academy of Science on 6th April 1902. In his letter to Kokovtsov Korsh writes: 'Before the meeting I had a quick conversation with Baron Rosen about the document, but he was absolutely uninterested in helping. Then I asked Dubrovin whether it is appropriate for me to even a raise a question about the Tariff. He said that the Tariff should be a concern for the Ministry of the Royal Court, which wanted the stone for the Hermitage, but it was probably unaware of its arrival in St Petersburg. He suggested talking to Kondakov who 'hung around' there (or 'lounged around' — I do not remember what exactly our kind secretary said). Kondakov did not say anything intelligible. In the meanwhile the meeting began. I sat together with Shakhmatov, who is a sincere priest of science as you are. I explained to him briefly about the Tariff and asked whether I could even touch on a subject that is not in my area and not even of our department. Shakhmatov, who knows the academic sphere so well, suggested describing the issue in written form and submitting it to the secretary' (Arch. AS, f. 779, inv. 2, no. 224, pp. 3–5). In his note F.E. Korsh insisted on taking prompt action; in particular he stated, 'We should be concerned that, as a result of announcing an auction, it [the Tariff] will pass into the hands of foreigners and this, especially after all the publicity, would offend the honour of Russian science' (Arch. AS, f. 779, inv. 1, no. 40, p. 47).

E. Radlov supported F.E. Korsh. Based on Korsh's written request the decision was made to start a conversation with the Hermitage. Korsh further tells us: 'After the meeting Nikitin, Dubrovin and Saleman came to me. The last supported me greatly, just as Radlov did. The baron (Rosen) came to me also and reproached me lightheartedly. He said that if the Academy would take the initiative, it would end up paying for the transportation. I reminded him about the extra ministerial finances (about 14,000,000 annually). Others around supported me ... So, I think that we will win the deal' (Arch. AS, f. 779, inv. 2, no. 224, pp. 3–4). Korsh's intervention broke down the bureaucratic barriers. The money for the customs duties was finally found. However, only on 23rd February 1904 did N.N. Pridik report to Kokovtsov that the Tariff was in the Hermitage (Arch. AS, f. 779, inv. 1, no. 40, p. 51).[18]

When the material was available for study Kokovtsov began preparation for its publication. Kokovtsov's handwritten material that is in the Academy of the USSR helps us to see how he was changing his plans concerning commentary on the text. We are aware of some draft titles in French (probably, the publication was supposed to be in French). The first one is in ink and crossed out, 'La partie araméenne du tarif des douanes de Palmyre de l'an 137 [après] J. Chr. Publication définitive d'après le monument conservé à l'Ermitage Impériale de St. Petersbourg par Paul Kokowzow.' The second, and probably the final one, is written in pencil, 'Le tarif bilingue de Palmyre de l'an 137 [après J. Chr.].

---

18 On the correspondence between Kokovtsov and Abamelek-Lazarev about the Tariff see also Baziiants 1978: 171–5.

The Palmyrene Tax Tariff

Édition définitive des deux textes, araméen et grec, d'après le monument conservé à l'Ermitage Impériale par P. Kokowzow' (Arch. AS, f. 779, inv. 1, no. 40, p. 108). As we see, Kokovtsov wanted initially to publish only the Aramaic part, but then he decided to publish the whole text. Among Kokovtsov's documents there are interpretations where he referred to S. Reckendorf's suggestions on the reconstruction and reading of the text (Arch. AS, f. 779, inv. 1, no. 40, pp. 83–107), as well as many notes that contain material for the commentary. From the notes it is evident that Kokovtsov wanted to include biblical, Jewish and Syriac material. He had references to some ancient works such as Lucian's *Dialogue of the Hetaerae*. He assisted in the production of a special Palmyrene font that was stored in the printing office of the Academy. Unfortunately, Kokovtsov was not able to finish his work on the Palmyrene Tariff. Possibly he was inspired to do something else. Maybe after the text was published in the *Corpus Inscriptionum Semiticarum* by J.-B. Chabot Kokovtsov thought that further studies of the Tariff were not necessary. In 1940 he wrote: 'After the French Academy published the Palmyrene Tariff, the necessity for our Academy to publish this text disappears' (Arch. AS, f. 779, inv. 1, no. 40, pp. 276–7). On 7th September 1940 Kokovtsov passed all the documents (photographs, official papers, etc.) to the Hermitage (Arch. AS, f. 779, inv. 1, no. 40, pp. 269–71), where his successor, a person who was very interested in the Tariff, A.Ia. Borisov, worked.

From the foregoing it is evident, that if Kokovtsov had published his version of the Tariff, it would probably have been a very detailed and deep scientific publication that could have enriched the history of Semitic epigraphy. Until now we have no such publication on the Tariff. Thus, we can only join Chabot in his regret that Kokovtsov did not finish his work (see *CIS* II, commenting on 3913).

Meanwhile the study of the Tariff continued. In 1905 V. Dittenberger published the Greek text that was based on H. Dessau's publication, but with his own grammatical observations and commentary (*OGIS*, 629). In the same year R. Cagnat (*IGRR*, III, 1056) prepared and published the Greek part of the Tariff. His publication does not contain any commentary (except for some textual remarks), but he inserts the Aramaic text alongside the Greek in the form of the Latin translation of it by Chabot.

A significant landmark in the history of the Palmyrene Tariff was J.-B. Chabot's publication in 1926 in the *Corpus Inscriptionum Semiticarum* (3913) of both the Greek and Aramaic texts. Chabot used the *estampages* of J.S. Gautier (the Palmyrene text) and of Seymour de Ricci (the Greek: it was made especially for this publication). As usual in *CIS*, Chabot's publication contains a reproduction of the Greek *estampage* and the Aramaic text in a special Palmyrene font, the transcription of both texts (the Aramaic in 'square' script) and a Latin translation of the Palmyrene text. The publication also contains an extensive commentary that summarizes all the previous conclusions of Palmyrene research. Chabot's main focus is on the Palmyrene text. He invites the reader to use his textual notes, his explanation of the translation, his linguistic remarks and his observations on the context. Whether all of his conclusions are plausible or not does not change the fact that his publication laid a foundation for the further historico-philological study of the document.

Finally, a significant event in the history of the Palmyrene Tariff was the discovery near the *agora* of two other fragments of the document. J. Starcky published them in 1949 (*Inv.* X, 143). This finding confirmed the previous suggestions on the title of the document. It also gave hope that in the future there is a possibility of finding other parts of the document.

Obviously, the publication of the Palmyrene Tariff enabled scholars to widen the themes of Palmyrene research. Previously research was limited to the political history of Palmyra in the last decades of its existence. The commentaries on the document (those mentioned in relation to publications) already contained valuable information about the character of Palmyrene trade (especially about the objects of the transit trade), about political structures and on the status of Palmyra. H. Dessau and R. Cagnat laid the foundation for the study of the Tariff in this context. M.I. Rostovtzeff (1899: 94–8; 1932b: 74–87) included the Palmyrene Tariff among the sources that characterize the customs system in antiquity. J. Février (1931a) and J. Starcky (1952) used the Tariff in their monographs on the general history of Palmyra. In 1937 D. Schlumberger (1937: 271–97) published specific research on the structure of the Palmyrene Tax Tariff. H. Seyrig's article, published in his famous series 'Antiquités syriennes' in 1941 (1941b), played a very important role in study of the Tariff. He suggested reconstructing one of the phrases in the Tariff in such a way that he connected the edict mentioned in the Tariff with the activity of Gaius Licinius Mucianus. As such, he was able to identify more accurately the chronology of the Palmyrene, and as a result the Syrian provincial legislation on taxes. In 1961 S. Kodama published a translation of the Tariff into Japanese, following in his translation H. Seyrig and D. Schlumberger (Kodama 1961).

In the concluding part of this section we want to want to say a few words about I.I. Saverkina's research on the Tariff in her book on ancient Palmyra (Saverkina 1971: 18–19). She writes that before AD 137 the customs duties in Palmyra were not yet determined, which led to their abuse and a decrease of the city's income. However, her last claim does not find support in the decision of the council; there is discussion there about conflicts between tax collectors and taxpayers. Saverkina further believes that the Tariff establishes the organized legal system of taxes. Her conclusion in using such wording is, however, incorrect: the text of the inscription constantly makes references to the law and to the custom that was in action in Palmyra *before* 137; it repeats the edict of Mucianus and the 'old' law that were in effect before that date. Thus an organized legal system of taxes was in place in Palmyra before our Tariff was composed. It could not be otherwise. Otherwise, the functioning of society would have been distorted. The Tariff of AD 137 was an attempt (maybe not a successful one in every respect) to improve the system by force of writing down some fixed taxes and by affirming previous resolutions.

5. Description of the Inscription

The inscription is on a limestone slab that is now sawn into four parts. Each part constitutes one of the panels of the text. The first part is 0.95 x 1.48 m, the second is 1.38 x 1.48 m, the third is 1.38 x 1.48 m and the fourth is 1.02 x 1.33 m. Above the second and third panels there were two lines of Greek text that contained the dating formula according to the commonly accepted calendar. The height of the letters is 4 cm, the width 2.5 to 3 cm.

The text fragments (*Inv.* X, 143) consist of two pieces of the dating formula. They were found in front of the construction attached to the *agora* at its south-east corner, near a half-column in front of the *agora*'s south-eastern wall. Fragment A 1078 has the following size: the height is 16 cm and the width is 16.5 cm; the height of the letters is 4.3 cm. Fragment A 1058: the height is 18 cm and the width is 29 cm; the height of the letters is 4.3 cm.

The first panel contains the resolution of the Palmyrene council in Greek (13 lines) and in Aramaic (11 lines). Under the resolution there are three lines of identical Greek and Aramaic text that were omitted by the lawgiver during the preparation of the law. The height of the Greek letters is 2 cm and the width is 1.4 to 2 cm; the height of the Aramaic letters is 2 cm and the width is from 0.8 to 1.7–2 cm.

The second panel is divided into three columns and contains the Aramaic text of the Tariff. The first line (the title) is above all three columns. One line is at the bottom under the three columns. All three columns have forty-nine lines otherwise. The height of the letters in the title is 4 cm.; the width is from 1.5 to 3.8 cm. The height of the letters in the text itself, including the line under the columns, is 2 cm. The width of the letters in the text is from 0.8–1 to 2–2.5 cm; and in the line under the columns it is from 1 to 2 cm.

The third and the fourth panels contain the Greek text of the Tariff. The third panel is divided into three columns (47, 46 and 47 lines). The fourth is divided into two (57 and 40 lines). The height of the letters in the third panel is 1.8 cm; the width is from 1–1.5 to 2 cm. The height of the letters in the fourth panel is 1.5 cm.; the width is 0.8–1 cm.

The panels are ordered from left to right. The inscription is much damaged because of weathering and transportation. The text in the third and the fourth panels is especially badly damaged. Some parts, in particular lines of the second panel, are erased. The first panel is less damaged. The Greek dating formula above the second and third panels is almost totally destroyed.

6. The Structure of the Text

The text of the Palmyrene Tariff consists of the Greek dating formula (according to the Roman standard), the resolution of the Palmyrene council and the Tariff itself. In the latter there is a clear representation of the 'new' Tariff (composed as a fulfilment of the decree which had been passed), as well as the 'old' tax law, attached to it as a supplement (in Aramaic, together with the title). An essential part of the 'old' tariff is the attachment of the edict of Mucianus. In the old tariff there are citations of the edict and rescripts of Germanicus and Corbulo.

The dating formula

The dating formula, as we have stated earlier, is located above the second and third panels, which underlines the fact that it refers to the whole document and not to a part only. It is composed according to the Roman standard and — in contrast to other parts of the inscription — is only in Greek. Such dating formulae are not typical for other Palmyrene texts. In inscriptions composed by Syrians the Roman calendar is quite rare: it appears in the inscriptions that were composed in Italy (*OGIS*, 594–5) and in the later documents from Dayr al-Laban (*OGIS*, 619; A.D. 320).

The formula has two parts. The first part has the date indicating which emperor (in this case Hadrian) was in power and it describes his authority and prerogatives (tribunicial power, consulate and the position of *pontifex maximus*) and mentions when the emperor was invested with them. This was typical in the Principate period in inscriptions deriving from the Roman authorities, veterans and so on. The second part contains, as is traditional for Roman dating formulae, the year of the governing consuls.

The insertion of this formula demonstrates the acknowledgment of supreme Roman power over Palmyra.

The resolution of the Palmyrene council

In the decree of the Palmyrene council there are the following structural parts: 1) the dating formula, 2) the title, 3) the introductory formula, 4) the explanation, 5) the resolution. We adopt here the arrangement that is found in the Greek version. The Aramaic version starts with the title followed by the dating formula. For the rest the structural parts match in both texts.

The dating formula of the decree gives the year, the month and the day when the decree was accepted according to the Seleucid Era, common for the whole Near East. It has the following layout.

Greek text: Ἔτ]ους ημυ΄ μηνὸς Ξανδικοῦ ιη΄ — year, month, day (gen. abs.).
Aramaic text: בירח ניסן יום 18 שנת 448 — month, day, year (with the preposition ב).

Apart from the differences that can be explained in terms of the grammatical and syntactical differences between Aramaic and Greek, there is a difference in the location of the main dating formula in the two texts. A similar difference appears in other Palmyrene inscriptions. Thus 3934 has the following dating formula: ἔτους ςξφ΄ Ὑπερβερεταίῳ (Greek text), but 566 שנת תשרי בירח (Aramaic text). There are cases where the structure of the dating formulae is identical.

The order in the Greek text of the Tariff (except for indicating the day) is common for the Greek inscriptions from Palmyra (cf. 3912: ἔτους εμυ΄ μηνὸς Λώου; 3925 ἔτ[ους] ηκ[τ΄] μηνὸς Γορπιαί[ου]; 3928 ἔτους ϛξυ΄ μηνὸς Λώου). The other version: month-year (also with the name of the month in *dat. temp.* and the year in *gen. possess.*) (cf. 3933: Ξανδικῷ τοῦ ηνφ΄ ἔτους), imitates the Aramaic construction and is less common.

Formulae that are analogous to the dating formula of the Aramaic text of the Tariff are quite common in the Palmyrene inscriptions (cf. 3925: בירח אלול שנת 328 [בירח] קנין] שנת 451 :3927; [בירח] קנין] שנת 466 :3928, etc.). The title in the Greek text of the resolution follows the dating formula while in the Aramaic it opens the document. The terminology in both texts is Greek: the syntactical constructions match: δόγμα βουλῆς and in parallel: דגמא די בולא.

The absence of any other resolutions of the Palmyrene council raises the question, to what extent this formula (cf. analogous constructions δόγμα δήμου in *IGRR*, III, 74–5; δόγμα βουλῆς καὶ δήμου in *IGRR*, III, 593; δόγμα κοινοβουλίου in *IGRR*, III, 63) was typical for Palmyrene documents. In other Palmyrene documents we have terms like πρόσταγμα (*Inv.* X, 44) and תוחית (*Inv.* 1, 2 = 3959; *Inv.* X, 44).

The introductory formula of the resolution consists of following parts: a) the list of magistrates in post at the time of the making of the resolution; b) a statement of the legitimacy of the meeting. The forms of the Greek and Aramaic texts are different.

In the Greek text the magistrates are just listed and the list starts as usual with the preposition ἐπί (ἐπὶ Βωννέους Βωννέους τοῦ Αἱράνου προέδρου, Ἀλεξάνδρου Ἀλεξάνδρου τοῦ φιλοπάτορος γραμματέως βουλῆς καὶ δήμου, Μαλίχου Ὀλαιοῦς καὶ Ζεβείδου Νεσᾶ ἀρχόντων). The composer of the Aramaic text put emphasis on the magistrates, placing them at the beginning of the syntactical construction (with the preposition ב) and using a *nomen abstractum*:

בפלהדרותא די בונא בר בונא בר חירן וגרמטיא די אלכסדרס בר אלכסדרס בר פלפטר
גרמטוס די בולא ודמס וארכוניא מלכו בר עליי בר מקימו וזבידא בר נשא

Also, in the Aramaic version there is a more detailed genealogy of Maliku son of ʿOlaya.

The Greek version says that the meeting of the council was held according to the law (βουλῆ[ς] νομίμου ἀγομένης). The Aramaic text says that the meeting was assembled according to the law (כד הות בולא כנישא מן נמוסא).

The formula of the decree in both texts is the same. The reason for the decree in the Greek text is introduced by the word ἐπειδή, which corresponds with the Palmyrene בדיל די, 'because'. It consists of the following points: a) a description of the 'old' law in which the taxes of many items were not specified and there was only implied reference to custom; b) a report of the conflicts in this area between merchants and tax collectors. Both Greek and Aramaic versions literally reproduce each other.

The decision of the council is introduced in Greek by the verb δεδόχθαι (the subject of the action is missing), in Aramaic it is introduced by the formula אתחזי לבולא די, where there is a logical subject. Both sentences are main clauses (in Greek — infinitive acting as predicate; in Aramaic — impersonal construction) that are connected with a subordinate clause of cause or reason, as well as with the decision itself: in Greek as an *accusativus cum infinitivo* expression; and in Aramaic as an additional subordinate clause. The decree contains the following instructions: a) to set a fixed tax for each article of trade; b) to write the 'new' law together with the 'old' on a stone stele; c) to oblige the magistrates to maintain the law.

There are some discrepancies between the Greek and Aramaic texts. The Greek δεδόχθαι corresponds with Aramaic אתחזי לבולא. However, the literal meaning of these verbs δοκέω and חזי is different. Also, the form of the verb in Greek is infinitive, while in Aramaic a finite form is used. The Greek could have had ἔδοξε instead, which was quite common in analogous formulae. The council is not mentioned in this clause in the Greek text. The Aramaic parallel of Greek τοὺς ἐνεστῶτας ἄρχοντας καὶ δ[εκα]πρώτους is ולעשרתא ארכוניא אלן, although the Aramaic אלן is different in meaning from the Greek ἐνεστῶτας. Instead of Greek τῇ ἔγγιστα μισθώσει the Aramaic has בשטר אגריא חדתא, although again the meaning of ἔγγιστα and חדתא are not the same. Finally, where the Greek has ὑποτ[ά]ξαι, the Aramaic has ויכתב; and in this case there is no correspondence in meaning.

In general, the resolution is composed according to the Greek standard (Reinach 1885: 335) which is reproduced in the Aramaic text also. The Greek and the Aramaic are very close to each other. However, certain clauses and forms do not match.

An additional resolution is written on the first panel; perhaps there was no space on the other panels, so it was decided to include this resolution with the text of the decree. It is noticeable that the formula of this clause is quite general: there are no particular details.

Introduction

The Tax Tariff

The law itself in the Palmyrene Tariff is located on the second panel (in the Aramaic text) and on the third and fourth (Greek text).

The Aramaic text of the law begins with the title, located in the second panel above all three columns. There is no corresponding title in the Greek text. The title is written with letters which are bigger than those in the rest of the text (height 4 cm; width 1.5–3.8 cm) and it indicates the scope of the Tariff (the Palmyrene market and the water sources). The title corresponds to the form that was accepted for this kind of document, as is clear from comparison with the title of the 'old' law (II, 2, 13–15).

Title	II, 2, 13–15
נמוסא די מכסא	נמ[ו]סא די מכ[סא
די למנא	
די הדרינא תדמר	די תדמר
ועינתא די מיא	ועינתא די מיא
[די אי]לס קיסר	
	ומל[חא ד]י ב[מ]דיתא ותחומיה

The title undoubtedly applies to the whole text: its location proves that. The additions to the title either reflect changes in the system of legislation of Palmyra after Hadrian's visit (הדרינא and [די אי]לס קיסר) or clarify the first text. The new title does not mention the places where they mined the salt.

From the text that is prior to the Tariff itself it is evident that the Palmyrene council suggested composing a new tax tariff that would correct the shortcomings of the previous one, while attaching a copy of the tariff that was previously in force. Accordingly, the question arises, what part of the Tariff is 'new' and what is 'old.' Commonly (Février 1931a: 34–6) the first part of the Tariff (before the title in the Aramaic text at II, 2, 13) is considered to be the 'new' law and the following text 'old.' However, Chabot attempts to prove that the first part of the Tariff is the 'old' law and the second is 'new', followed by a specific commentary which forms the third part (*CIS* II, iii, pp. 58–64 in relation to 3913; Chabot 1922: 31–2). Rostovtzeff joins Chabot in this opinion (Rostovtzeff 1932b: 75–6). He thinks that the Palmyrene Tariff consists of two parts: the 'old' law that was composed before Tiberius' reign and additions to the law dated to the Hadrianic period or a bit earlier. These additions are based on the practice of local tax collectors and Roman officials. Among these additions there are earlier ones and later ones. Rostovtzeff assumes that in

The Palmyrene Tax Tariff

general the Tariff was a collection of legal orders issued by the council of Palmyra that regulated the amount of taxes. Eventually, other rules for taxpayers and tax farmers were attached to the Tariff.

In 1937 Schlumberger attempted to shed some light on this problem. His main conclusions can be summarized as follows. The document consists of 1) a common title, 2) the first part (61 lines) that Schlumberger names section A, 3) the separate law (section B according to Schlumberger), the beginning of which is indicated by a title, 4) additional articles (section C). The presence of the internal title (II, 2, 13–15), according to Schlumberger, is a serious argument in favour of those who do not consider section B as a 'new' law. Schlumberger also points out that the title תדמר without the description הדרינא (as in II, 2, 13) is impossible for an official document of AD 137 (and we indeed see in the general title the formula הדרינא תדמר). In the text of section A there are two references to custom. Schlumberger thinks that the codification of custom was precisely what was intended by the council. The difference in taxes in sections A, B and C he explains as follows: section A is the norm in action, sections B and C are norms that had lost their power. These arguments lead to the conclusion that section B is an 'old' law. On the other hand, according to Schlumberger, these arguments do not give reason to consider section A as a 'new' law. The latter is only an addition to the old law, which is being clarified in several articles. Seyrig (Seyrig: 1941b) shares this opinion with Schlumberger. We will consider the characteristics of the text of the Tariff that follows the internal title at II, 2, 13–15 later. At this point we only state that just as Schlumberger convincingly concludes, this part of the text could belong only to the 'old' law. It would be very strange to insert a 'new' law under a special heading that copies the general title and which does not correspond with the political status of Palmyra in AD 137. At the same time the heading is very appropriate if it is the beginning of the 'old' law that is attached to the 'new' (or to the new articles, if we follow Schlumberger and Seyrig). The concept that the 'new' and the 'old' laws chronologically precede the edict of Mucianus (Laet 1949: 356 with reference to Piganiol [ed.: cf. A. Piganiol, 'Observations sur le tarif de Palmyre', *Revue Historique* 195 (1945), 10–23]) is unacceptable.

So the Aramaic text starts from the beginning of the first column on the second panel. This text contains (just as the council requires) clarifications in accordance with 'custom,' i.e. the current situation with taxation in Palmyra. The first part of this text (II, 1, 4–II, I, 44) indicates taxes for import and export (slaves, dry goods, precious oil and aromatics, purple wool, salted fish, cattle; in one case the object of taxation cannot be identified). The second part (II, 1, 45–II, 2, 12) has resolutions that regulate taxes for market trading, handicrafts, for use of the city water-supply, import and sale of major food items, as well as for unloaded camels coming into the city. All this can be considered more or less a detailed 'new' law and not just a collection of articles or legal decisions that are added to the 'old' law. The Greek text of the 'new' law is located at III, 3, I–III, 2, 46.

We will now study the particular articles of the first part of the 'new' law in the Aramaic text. The conclusions from studying Table 1 are the following. (The symbols are listed at the beginning of the Tables, which are printed at the end of this section.) The author of the Tariff evidently tries to formalize the text, but he does not do it very successfully. The formulae within an article are very similar (and in many cases are almost identical); the clauses that deal with taxes for a load on a donkey are similar in structure. Particular components of the formulae are not always similar, however; in some cases they are substituted for by wordy descriptions. Also syntactical constructions that are used for similar situations are not always the same. Thus, together with the construct state: טעון גמל there is the analytical genitive construction with the preposition די, where both components are in the emphatic state state: טעונא די גמלא. [Ed.: the term 'emphatic' is generally preferred to 'definite' in this English translation.]

The Greek text of the first part of the 'new' law is constructed according to the chart that is given in Table 2.

The other articles in the first part of the 'new' law are almost totally erased.

The study of Table 2 shows that the Greek text, although corresponding with the Aramaic, is not the literal translation of the latter. In the Greek text there are words that are missing in the Aramaic text and *vice versa*; in the Greek text there is a more logical and systematic formula on the authority of the tax farmer; the syntactical constructions are not the same in the two versions. The Greek text, like the Aramaic, is not completely formulaic, but the formulae within one particular article of the Tariff are very similar.

As we study the structure of the Aramaic text of the second part of the 'new' law (Table 3), it is easy to see that the first three articles in the Aramaic text are constructed according to a similar scheme (as are also the particular clauses in the second article). The pattern of the first part is similar to that of the fourth and the seventh articles (and the beginning of the seventh is like the beginning of the first three); the fifth article is similar in pattern to some clauses in the second; the sixth and the eighth in general do not follow a set formula.

The Greek text in the second part of the 'new' law is constructed as is shown in Table 4.

This table shows that only the last two articles in the Greek text of the second part of the 'new' law correspond with the Aramaic text in content and form. In all other cases the Greek text either has words that are lacking in the Aramaic version, or the Greek omits some instructions that are present in the Aramaic. There are differences in the structure of the text: the Greek text tends to have formal openings for some articles (the beginnings match in the first, second, third and, possibly, seventh articles); the rest of the text has a free structure.

The question of the structure of the text of the Tariff that follows in the Aramaic version after the internal title (II, 2, 13–15) has been debated for some time. Already J. Février (1931a: 31–6) writes that the 'second' law, which was composed during the rule of the Roman prefect Marinus, probably ends with the article about the water-supply and is followed by a commentary on detailed matters. He also notes that the 'second' law and the commentary predate the 'new' law. According to D. Schlumberger (1937), his 'section B' runs from the internal title (II, 2, 13–15; in Greek III, 3, I) to the new edict that is issued, as will become clear later, by Mucianus (II, 2, 24; in Greek IV, I, 10). He divides this section into two parts: Ba (the entire Aramaic text and the parallel Greek text III, 3, 1–33) and Bb which is only found in the Greek version (III, 3, 34– IV, 1, 9). Of these two parts, Schlumberger continues to argue, only Ba maintains the characteristics of the Tariff. He thinks that they are in fact two different documents. Ba is the 'old' law in the real sense of this word (or at least what is left of it). In Bb Schlumberger sees the part of the tax-farming contract dated to the end of AD 136 or the beginning of 137. He finds the proof for this in the reference to 'water-springs of Caesar' (III, 3, 46: [πη]γῶν ὑδάτων Καίσαρος), which, as he thinks, corresponds with the expression 'the water-springs of Aelius Caesar' in the general Palmyrene title. Schlumberger considers this passage as an addition to the previous contract ('section C'), composed in 137 together with the main resolution of the council. The rest of the text, or section C according to Schlumberger, is the Palmyrene contract of tax farming. Finally, Seyrig (1941b) considers Ba as the 'old' law, Bb as a fragment of the edict of a Roman official which is not translated into Aramaic, and C as an edict of another Roman official, probably Mucianus (AD 68–9).

Before the question of whether the above viewpoint is valid can be answered, it is necessary to study the text in the form that it has come down to us. Almost all scholars agree that the Aramaic text of the 'old' law opens with the internal title (II, 2, 13–15; to remind the reader, Chabot sees here the beginning of the 'new' law). The internal title says: נמ[ו]סא די מכ[ס]א די תדמר וּעינתא די מיא ב[מ]דיתא ותחומיה היך א[גור[י]א [ד]י א[ת]אגר קדם מרינס היגמונא. As we see, in structure it is divided into two parts: 1) characterization of the context and scope of the law; 2) explanation of its function.

The context and scope of the law are clear: they are concerned with taxation in Palmyra, including taxes for using local wells and salt mines.

The explanation of the function of the 'old' law, the reference to the contract made in the presence of the Roman governor (i.e. probably confirmed by the governor), is interesting not only because it shows the dependency of Palmyra on the Roman government in Syria, but also because it witnesses to the fact that the 'old' law literally reproduces the statements of the tax-farming contract. This means that the sections which scholars tend to see as fragments of a tax-farming contract are indeed such fragments. Also as an integral part of the 'old' law they cannot be anything else. From the resolution of the Palmyrene council it is also clear that the articles of the 'new' law correspond with the 'new' contract for tax farming. Probably this is a common procedure. Even if this is not so, we still do not have reasons to assume that the parts that follow the internal title and that were seen as fragments of the tax-farming contract are not, at the same time, parts of the 'old' law. A final conclusion will be possible after analysis of the text.

There is something else very essential. As we know, the decree of the Palmyrene council refers to the tax law that was in operation in Palmyra in AD 137: [ἐν το]ῖς πάλαι χρόνοις ἐν τῷ τε[λω]νικῷ νόμῳ πλεῖστα τῶν ὑποτελῶν οὐκ ἀνελήμφθη, ἐπράσ[σετο] δ[ὲ ἐ]κ συνηθείας, ἐνγραφομέ[νου] τῇ μισθώσει τὸν τελωνοῦντα τὴν πρᾶξιν ποιεῖσθει ἀκολούθ[ω]ς τῷ νόμῳ καὶ τῇ συνηθείᾳ (I, 4–7); בזבניא קדמיא בנמוסא די מכסא עבידן שגין חיבן מכסא לא אסקו והוו מתגבין מן עידא במדען די הוא מתכתב באגוריא די מכסא {ו}הוא גבא היך בנמוסא ובעידא (I, 17–19).

This means that in the old days the majority of the goods that had to be taxed were not listed in the law of taxation. The tax farmer collected the taxes according to custom because the contract about taxation said that the tax

55

farmer had to collect taxes according to law and custom. This was the same law which, according to the council's decree, had to be written down together with the text of the 'new' Tariff. From the foregoing we can conclude that the text that follows the inner title has to conform to the previous legislation mentioned in the council's decree. Now, we need to see whether this conclusion truly reflects the reality of things. There is a problem that makes the issue complicated: whether the internal title belongs to all of the text which follows or only to a particular part of it.

If Harrer (1915: 21–2 [citation according to Seyrig 1941b: 165, n. 3]) is right and there is a link between Marinus in this text and Lucius Julius Marinus, then the 'old' law can be dated to the end of the first decade of the second century AD.

Let us study the Aramaic text II, 2, 16–23 and the parallel Greek text III, 3, 1–33 (in the latter only the ending is preserved — lines 23–33), which is section Ba according to Schlumberger (Table 5).

As we can see, the text that follows the internal title and that Schlumberger considers as a textual unity is divided into three unequal parts. The first part contains articles about dry goods and purple wool. The formula is similar to the formula of the majority of the articles in the first part of the 'new' law, although it does not match the formulae of the articles in the 'new' law which are similar in content (particularly in the article on dry goods). The list of goods stops at this point and another article starts (this article forming the second part of the text) that requires the tax farmer to collect taxes 'as it is written above' (היך די כתיב מן למעל). This article most likely refers here to the 'new' law (because that is what 'is written above') (the words מן גנסיא כלהון, 'from all kinds of goods' are especially important here) and therefore cannot be a part of the 'old' law. Maybe this article substitutes for a resolution in the 'old' law which has not survived, i.e. to collect taxes according to the law and custom? This assumption may well be possible. Then there is a third part, the article about taxes on salt. There are no parallels to this article in the 'old' law.

So, if we exclude the article about collecting taxes from all kinds of goods (as 'it is written above'), which is inserted by the later legislation of AD 137, then we see that the 'old' law (at least in this part of it) has three articles — about dry goods, purple wool and salt. Since the first two articles clearly contradict the 'new' law and are included in the inscription only because the later legislator did not want to omit them, even though they were not in operation any more, one may assume that this text reproduces entirely the text of the 'old' law after the title and that none of its articles is omitted (only one is partially changed). In the third article as well as in the Greek version there is a fourth clause that talks about the penalty for the failure to pay tax. In the Aramaic text this fourth clause is absent.

The continuation of the text before we come to the edict of Mucianus is only found in the Greek version of the Tariff (III, 3, 28–IV, I, 9). Here are preserved fragments of articles referring to the procedure for solving arguments between tax farmers and taxpayers, about redeeming pledges and also about the fact that the tax farmer is not allowed to pass his responsibilities to anyone else. There is no uniform construction in these articles. Every article has its own structure determined by the content.

III, 3, 46 is very significant, according to Schlumberger, for dating the document. It refers to: λιμένος Π[αλμύρων καὶ πη]γῶν ὑδάτων Καίσαρος. In his research on the Palmyrene Tariff Schlumberger (1937: 278–81) shows that out of four places where the inscription mentions the water-supply only two (in the general Aramaic title and in III, 3, 46) carry the name of Caesar (in both cases probably Aelius Caesar). After V. Dittenberger (*OGIS*, 629), Schlumberger believes that unlike other nameless natural wells in the city, 'the water-springs of Aelius Caesar' is probably a water-supply system that was built in the name of the latter. On this basis, he thinks that the present text was composed together with the new articles of the law and represents a fragment of the tax-farming contract that was composed at the end of AD 136 or beginning of 137.

In our opinion, Schlumberger's conclusions are not well grounded. Indeed, the first reference in the inscription to the wells in the general title of the Aramaic text reads ועינתא די מיא [די אי]לס קיסר, 'the water-springs of Aelius Caesar'. However, this title belongs to the whole Tariff, not only to part of it. It is hard to believe that one group of water sources and water-supply systems in Palmyra required taxes for usage while the other was free. More plausible is the idea that for the composer of this Tariff all water sources in and outside the city are named after Aelius Caesar. Another fact also supports this idea. Palmyra bore the name of Hadrian in those days since he was considered its founder. And so such a generous gesture, the giving of the name of his expected successor to significant water sources by the local government, is not surprising.

Another reference to the wells in the 'new' law (II, 2, 8: עינן תרתן די מ[י'] די במדיתא; III, 2, 41: πηγῶν β΄), although without mentioning the name of Aelius

Caesar, occurs in relation to taxes for using water supplies. This text presumably corresponds with the (Aramaic) title in its content: they refer to the same subject. This fact also rules out the assumption that the 'water-springs of Aelius Caesar' refers to aqueducts built during Hadrian's reign. This passage is very important in the light of Schlumberger's hypothesis: it shows that the name Aelius Caesar could be omitted in the text composed in AD 137; therefore the presence or absence of this name is not the determining factor for dating. In any case, the absence of this name does not prevent us from dating this article to AD 137, which also follows from the context.

The third reference to the water sources without mentioning the name of Aelius Caesar is in the internal title that begins the 'old' law in the Aramaic version of the Tariff (II, 2, 13–14: ועינתא די מיא ומל[חא ד[י ב[מ]דיתא). Just like the previous passage this one refers to the city water-supply systems; as in II, 2, 8 we have די ב[מ]דיתא. The absence of the name of Aelius Caesar in this passage is quite natural: it was composed long before Hadrian's reign as other dating features show. Finally, the fourth reference is the passage that we are dealing with, i.e. in the article that forbids the tax farmer from passing on his responsibilities to someone else.

As we see, the situation repeats itself even though in reverse order. Now, we have a reference to the water sources in the internal title without mentioning Aelius Caesar, but in the text that follows the title there is a reference mentioning the name. It is very plausible that the insertion was made during the composing process in order to stress Palmyra's loyalty to the emperor. As we see from the previous paragraph, an adjustment of the 'old' law to the new conditions has taken place in other situations as well. The composer of the Tariff was doing this quite inconsistently.

Thus, the formula [πη]γῶν ὑδάτων Καίσαρος does not prevent him from placing the Greek text III, 3, 28–IV, I, 9 in the time before the 'new' law was composed. Another question arises though: what relationship does it have to the 'old' law? The location of the text after the internal title and after some articles of the 'old' law could be a witness in favour of its belonging to the 'old' law too. The context of the document testifies to the same assumption. It speaks of the interests of the tax farmer, of regulations on the relationship between tax farmer and taxpayer, and finally of the power of the tax farmer (which is natural after the payment sum is set). The absence of a title that would introduce the text and separate it from the previous information is

Introduction

particularly significant: the composers of the Tariff presumably considered this section not only an essential part of the 'old' law (otherwise they would have placed it *before* the internal title), but as an actual *section* of the 'old' law that was composed during the reign of the Roman prefect Marinus.

The absence of an Aramaic parallel to the Greek III, 3–IV, 1, 9 may contradict the above assumptions. It is possible to assume that in Palmyra before 137 there were two versions of the 'old' law: a shorter one (in Aramaic) where the articles that we are dealing with were missing, and a longer one (in Greek) where they were included. However, this suggestion seems to be unlikely.

It is hard to imagine that the legislator considered it unimportant to inform the Aramaic-speaking audience in the sphere of influence of the law about such important articles as those that deal with the legal rights of the tax farmer and taxpayer. The fact remains, however, that the Aramaic version of these articles is absent. Further, the difference between the Aramaic and Greek parts in Palmyrene inscriptions is visible both in this Tariff and in other inscriptions as well. For example, for the Greek phrase in 3944, στρατιώτης λεγ[εῶνος Κυρηνα]ϊκῆς, the parallel in Aramaic is פלחא די בלגיונא די בצרא. In 3953, the Greek inscription for the statue of Herod-Ḥairan son of Shurayku that was set up by the sons of Zabdibōl omits a very important addition that the Aramaic inscription has: [י]לי[קר ש]ריכו אבוה. Thus the aspect that we are discussing in the present inscription is a part of the whole Palmyrene epigraphic tradition.

We cannot shed more light on the absence of these articles in the Aramaic part of the Tariff at this point. Only one thing is clear: the Greek text has priority in the eyes of the Palmyrene legislators. It is not impossible that the lack of space for the Aramaic part on the stone made the author of the inscription omit a part of the law that did not regulate tax collection in the strict sense of the word and could be considered as less important for calculations and payment. On the one hand, the tax farmers and their contracting parties could refer to the articles in the Greek text; on the other, they were obliged to follow a certain legal procedure in any case. It is interesting that the secretary of the council that made the decision to compose a 'new' law has a Greek name. He is presumably Greek and his election into such an important position, precisely in AD 137, could not be just a coincidence.

The edict of Mucianus in the Aramaic part of the document probably begins with the words היגמונא [ס]קינ[מ] לקניס] גיס [אקם די [ן]מ, 'from that which

Gaius Licinius Mucianus, the prefect, determined' (II, 2, 24). The Greek text (IV, 1, 10–11) has Γαῖο[ς Λικίνιος Μουκιανὸς πρεσβευτὴς καὶ] ἀντι[στρατηγὸς λέγει], 'Gaius [Licinius Mucianus, legate and] pro[praetor says]'. The reconstructions in both texts do not raise any doubts in our opinion, although there is a discrepancy in Mucianus' title in the Aramaic part. According to Seyrig, who suggests this reconstruction, the edict of Mucianus, as well as the preceding text, are later than the 'old' law (Seyrig 1941b: 165). We believe, however, that the edict of Mucianus is an inseparable part of the 'old' law, which according to the resolution of the Palmyrene council is supposed to be written together with the 'new'. Our study of the text testifies in favour of the edict of Mucianus having been written before the text of the 'old' law (just as the 'old' law is being written down after the 'new', but chronologically preceded it). If we had more solid proofs that Marinus (II, 2, 15) was in fact L. Julius Marinus Caecilius Simplex (see Commentary), then the chronology of the 'old' law would be as follows: the edict of Mucianus is dated to the time of his rule in Syria in 68–9, the 'old' law in general is dated to the end of the first decade of the second century AD.

The edict of Mucianus (or an excerpt from the edict of Mucianus if we understand the Aramaic text literally) opens with an introduction that explains the motives of the Roman governor of Syria in issuing the decree and the essential principle of the edict itself. Then the edict lists the objects and persons to be taxed: slaves, wool, perfumed oil, butchers, food items, nuts, camels, camel skins, greens and fruits, prostitutes, bronze statues, salt, clothing merchants and tailors, leather, sheep and goats. An essential characteristic of the edict is reference to the resolutions of Mucianus' predecessors, Germanicus and Corbulo, to the different decrees in operation in Palmyra, to Palmyrene laws and to the practice common in other cities of Syria.

The introduction to the edict, as we have stated above, consists of two points. First the author explains the situation in Palmyra at the time of the issue of the edict (II, 2, 25–6):

[על] חשבן מכ[ס סרבן הוא] בני תדמריא ל[בני ס[קנ[ו]ת מכס[א]

'[be]cause of the tax [there was dispute] between the Palmyrenes and the tax collec[tor].'

The Greek version has only a fragment of this text, which can be reconstructed thus: μεταξὺ Παλ[μυρηνῶν πρὸς τοὺς τελώνας]. If the reconstruction and the

Introduction

interpretation are correct, then the introduction of the edict describes Palmyra at the end of the 60s of the first century AD, which is analogous to the situation in the middle of the 30s of the second century, with the same expressions as in the decree of the council in relation to the new Tariff. Presumably the edict of Mucianus concerned Palmyra only.

The general principle for the edict of Mucianus is the following (II, 2, 27–9):

[א]קימת די ... [מ]כסא חיב למהוא [היך מכ]סא די אגר בה אלקמס וח[ברה היך] נמוסא

'[I de]c[id]ed that … the [t]ax must be the same [as the ta]x collected by Alkimos and [his] pa[rtner, according] to the law.'

The Greek text of the edict (IV, 1, 12–17) has only isolated words and letter-combinations surviving. It is important to note that the principle of Mucianus corresponds with the principle explained in the decree of the council, i.e. first there must be an agreement for tax farming, then its stipulations appear in the law. The internal title that introduces the 'old' law (II, 2, 15) agrees with this principle. Presumably this is a common procedure for Palmyra. The clause that describes the rights of Alkimos and his companion contains reference to the 'law' that most probably determines the procedure of tax farming, the amount of tax and the profit of the tax farmer.

The article that is concerned with taxes on slave import, export and purchase (II, 2, 29–37) is similar to the article in the 'new' law (II, 1, 1–5), but with some differences. Both articles have sections about a) the import and export of slaves; b) the sale of slaves in the city and/or their export; c) the sale of slave-veterans. In the 'new' law there is also a section about the export of slaves by a buyer, while in the edict of Mucianus instead the export and import of slaves is mentioned a second time (the text is very damaged; however, the taxes are almost half those in the immediately preceding section; perhaps the earlier text refers to the export and import of slaves who are not intended for sale) and also the export of slave-veterans: here there is reference to the law, probably a local law (see Table 6 for comparison between the 'new' and 'old' laws and the edict of Mucianus).

There are differences and similarities in the formulae. Thus, the first section of the article about the import and export of the slaves in both the edict of Mucianus and in the 'new' law have the formulae: לתדמר או לתחומיה and לכל (רגלי) רגל. The size of the taxes is the same as well.

The differences in the text are as follows. In the 'new' law the subject of the action is the tax collector; in the edict of Mucianus the subject is the taxpayer. Therefore the formulae are different as well. The edict uses the verb פרע. The 'new' law has גבא. The person who is subject to tax is identified in the 'new' law: the text deals with the import of slaves, while the edict with the import of people/individuals. The first section in the article of the 'new' law does not mention the export of slaves, which occurs in the edict.

The article that follows the article about slaves (II, 2, 38–42 in the Aramaic text; IV, 1, 24–6 (?) in the Greek) is damaged substantially and cannot be reconstructed or interpreted at all.

Then there is an article about wool, also fragmentary (II, 2, 43–7 in Aramaic; IV, 1, 27–36 in Greek). There is no parallel here between the 'new' law and the regulation in the 'old' law prior to the edict. According to the surviving fragments, the article concerns the exemption from taxes of Italic wool. The article consists of two sections. In the first section the legislator refers to the import of Italic wool into Palmyra; in the second to export. The latter section also alludes to an agreement, most likely with the Palmyrene government, which, according to the article, was originally against such an exemption.

The article about perfumed oil in goatskins (II, 2, 48–3, 2 in the Aramaic text, IV, 1, 37–40 in Greek) is very different from the parallel article in the 'new' law. It prescribes taxes according to the law, refers to an error in the tax-farming agreement and cancels the tax that is laid down there. The article ends with a reference to the law which requires tax in the amount of 13 *denarii*. As we can see from the earlier context, the tax charge for perfumed oil in the 'new' law varies (II, 1. 12ff.), depending on the containers used for transportation and therefore on the quality of the material itself, as well as on the means of transportation and therefore the quantity of material. The tax defined by the law to which the edict of Mucianus refers corresponds with the tax in the 'new' law on perfumed oil transported on camels in goatskins (II, 1, 16–17).

There are some differences between the Greek and Aramaic versions of this article. For the Aramaic כתב the Greek version has τῷ προτεθέντι [δ]ει. For the Aramaic phrase ובנמוסא רציך, the Greek has [ἐν τῷ συν]εσφραγισμένῳ νόμῳ τέτακται.

The article on taxes on butchers or, as in the Greek version, on butchering (II, 3, 3–8 in the Aramaic and IV, 1, 41–5 in Greek) prescribes taxes of up to one *denarius*, i.e. it sets a maximum. Then there is a reference to a rescript of

Germanicus to Statilius, which sets the procedure for the payment of taxes: over a *denarius*, to be paid in Italic *assaria* (the common imperial currency), up to a *denarius*, to be paid in local currency (ערפן, κέρμα). The precise level of payment is also stated. There is no parallel to this text in the 'new' law.

The article about foodstuffs (II, 3, 10–14 in the Aramaic text and IV, 1, 47–51 in the Greek) has two sections. The first sets the tax of one *denarius* for freight transported from outside or from inside Palmyra. It is important to note that these tax terms are presented in both articles as a resolution of the Roman governor and stated on his behalf ('I have decreed'), though with reference to the appropriate (Palmyrene?) law. The second section deals with exemption from taxes for goods exported or imported from the villages outside the city. The legislator refers in this case to an agreement that was made in Palmyra itself. There is no analogy to this article in the 'new' law. There are there only references to grain and forage.

The article about nuts (II, 3, 15–18 in the Aramaic text and IV, 1, 51–3 in Greek) is written in the third person and the subject of the action (the person who made the decision) is not specified, although from the context it is clear that this is the Roman governor. Nuts are equated with dry goods in the amount of taxes charged. In the edict of Mucianus (at least in the form of it that survives) there is no article on taxes for dry goods. It is possible that Mucianus relied on Palmyrene resolutions that did not survive. The reason for composing this article is of a special interest: the legislator refers not to the law or to his own decision but to the practice that is common in other Syrian cities. There is no corresponding article about nuts in the 'new' law.

The article on bringing camels into the city (II, 3, 19–22 in the Aramaic text and IV, 1, 54–7 in Greek) is very different from the corresponding article in the 'new' law (II, 2, 11 in Aramaic and III, 2, 45–6 in Greek), although the amount of tax is the same in both articles. The edict of Mucianus sets taxation for both laden and unladen camels, while the 'new' law does so only for unladen ones. The edict of Mucianus refers to the law and to the instruction of Corbulo in his rescript sent to Barbarus. The author of the 'new' law refers to the practice of Kilix, the freedman of Caesar. For the Aramaic באגרתא די כתב לברברס the Greek equivalent is ἐν τῇ πρὸς βάρβαρον ἐπιστολῇ. It is interesting that in the Greek text of the 'new' law the camels are defined by an adjective in the singular masculine form (κενός), while in the Greek text of the edict of Mucianus (IV, 1, 54) the adjectives are in the plural feminine form (ἐάν τε κεναὶ ἐάν τε ἔγγομοι). In Aramaic the adjective is masculine in both cases.

The article on exemption from taxes for fruit and vegetables (II, 3, 24–5 in the Aramaic text and IV, 2, 4–5 in the Greek, where a few letters or combinations of letters survive) contains a rather ambiguous resolution. As in the article about nuts, this text is not clear about who is the legislator. It says that fruits and vegetables are subject to taxation because they have a certain price, i.e. they are considered to be traded goods, but the amount of taxation is not defined. There is no corresponding article in the 'new' law.

The article about prostitutes (II, 3, 26–31 in the Aramaic text, in the Greek IV, 2, 5–9 (?), almost totally erased) is identical to the corresponding article in the 'new' law (II, 1, 46ff.). It is written from the first person singular perspective ('I have established'), i.e. with Mucianus as subject, emphasizing that his actions correspond with the requirements of the law.

The article about bronze statues (II, 3, 29–31 in the Aramaic text; in the Greek text there are a few letters surviving in the second column of the fourth panel) does not have a corresponding article in the 'new' law. It is similar to the article about nuts in its composition. In both cases the amount of tax is not defined, but goods of this kind are equivalent to other goods of, in one way or another, similar status. As in the articles about nuts and about fruits and vegetables, the legislation begins with the phrase 'it seemed good'.

The article about salt is only partially similar to the corresponding article in the 'old' law (II, 2, 19ff.) located before the edict of Mucianus (II, 3, 31–7 in the Aramaic text). It begins with an unusual formula for the edict: 'it seems right/reasonable to me' (a formula in any case which is not found elsewhere in the extant part of the Tariff). The formula shows, however, that the legislation comes from Mucianus. The article has two parts. The first part prescribes the selling of salt in a 'public' place (the *agora*?) and requires the buyer to pay tax in the amount of one *assarius* for a *modius*. (The location of this clause in the Tariff is also unique.) In the corresponding article of the 'old' law the payer is not specified, though the amount of taxation is the same. From the context, however, it seems that the taxpayer is the vendor. The prescription to sell salt in a 'public' place is absent from the 'old' law. The second part of the article about salt in the edict mostly repeats the first. It also contains reference to the law that sets the tax and to the custom that regulates methods and forms of the trade. The first part has a more concrete description on this point.

Introduction

The articles about purple (purple cloth?) (II, 3, 38–9 in the Aramaic), craftsmen and tradesmen (II, 3, 40–3 in the Aramaic) are not well preserved.

The article about skins (II, 3, 43–5 in the Aramaic text) has some similarities to the article about taxes on skins in the 'new' law (II, 2, 6). The 'new' law prescribes 2 *assarii* for a skin; the edict prescribes 2 *assarii* per *ashal*. It also has a reference to an agreement made in Palmyra.

Finally, the article about sheep and goats that are brought into the city (II, 3, 46–9 plus the one line under the three columns in the Aramaic text; IV, 2, 34–40 in the Greek) has very little similarity with the corresponding article in the 'new' law (II, 1, 38ff.). While the 'new' law prescribes specific taxes for particular kinds of cattle, the old edict considers taxes for cattle generally (cattle brought from outside Palmyra are liable to taxation); there are references to the law and to an agreement.

Now we can see some of the particularities of the edict of Mucianus: 1) it does not have a strict formula, even in cases where the legislator wanted to emphasize his own initiative; 2) the legislator often refers to the law and custom of Palmyra, to the decision of the local authorities, resolutions of his predecessors and common Syrian practice.

This research shows that the Palmyrene Tax Tariff consists of the following parts: a) the 'new' law dated AD 137; b) mechanically attached to it the 'old' law dated to the end of the first decade of the second century AD; c) the edict of Mucianus dated AD 63–9, which is an integral part of the 'old' law.

The relations between the different parts of the Tariff are represented in the following tables. (Note that the articles in the second and third columns in Table 6 are not in the order in which they appear in the text.)

Full repetitions or contradictions between the articles of the 'new' and 'old' laws (including the edict of Mucianus) are not numerous. Most of the time the laws supplement each other, for example, with articles that are absent in the other document or when they both discuss the same subject from different points of view, again supplementing each other.

The Palmyrene Tax Tariff

Symbols in Tables

A — the mentioning of import

B — the mentioning of export

C — additional information

D — the amount of tax

E — the mention of sale in the city

K — word of introduction

L — the frequency of tax collection

N — the explanation about the amount of tax

P — the rights of the tax farmer

T — the individual from whom the tax is taken

X — the name of the goods

Y — the main unit of measurement

Subscript numbers indicate repetitions (T_o, T_1)

Introduction

Table 1

The items taxed	Text	Formula	Notes [ed.: extremely laconic!]
On slaves (II, 1, 1–5)	מן מעלי עלימיא די מתאעלין לתדמר או לתחומיה [יגבא מכס]א לכל רגל ד 22	mn A X dy A l-C l-Y D	A - repeated twice in the form of participles (active and passive).
	מן עלם די י[זבן ב]מדי[ת]א או י[פק ד] 10	mn X dy E 'w B D	E and B - finite verbal forms.
	מן עלם וטר[ן] די יזבן [במדיתא] ד 10	mn XC dy E D	
	והן זבונא יפק עלי[מ]ין יתן לכל רגלי [ד] 12	Not formalized	E - finite form.
On dry goods (II, 1, 6–9)	הו מ[כסא יג[בא [מ]ן טעון גמלא די יב[ן שין] למעלנא [לכלמא] די טעון גמלא ד [3]	hw P mn Y dy X l-A C dy Y D	P = m[ks yg]b'. A - noun m'ln'.
	מן [טעון] גמלא למ[ן]פקנא[ד 3	mn Y l-B D	
	מן ט[עון] חמרא למעלנא ו[למפקנא ד 2]	mn Y l-A wl-B D	
On purple wool (II, I, 10–11)	מן א[ר]גונא מלטא לכל מ[ש]ך למעלנא ולמ[פ]קנא אסרין 8	mn X l-Y l-A wl-B D	
On Perfumed oil (II, I, 12–21)	מן טעו[ן ג]מל[א] די משחא בשימא [די] מתאעל [ב]ש[טיפ]א 25	mn Y dy X dy C D	C = A + the type of container; A is a participle.
	ולמא ד]י יפק משה[א דנה למפקנ]א מן טעון] גמל לטעונא ד 13	wlm' d[y] ypq mšh' dnh l-B mn Y l-Y D	
	מן טעון גמלא די [מ]שחא בשימא [די ית]אעל[בזקי[ן] די ע[ן ל[מ]על[נ]א ד 13 ולמפקנ[א ד 7]	mn Y dy X dy C l-A D wl-B D	C = A + the type of container; A is a finite form (?).
	מן ט[עון] חמר די[משחא בשימא ד]י ית]אעל ב[ש]טיפ[י]א [ד] 13 ולמפקנא ד 7	mn Y dy X dy C D wl-B D	C = A+ the type of container; A is a finite form. Formula l-A, where the A noun m'ln' is omitted in order to avoid pleonasm.
	מן טעון חמר [ד]י משחא ב[ש]י[מא די ית]אעל[בזקי[ן] די ע[ן ד 7 ו[למ]פקנא ד 4	mn Y dy X dy C D wl-B D	All the particularities of the previous text are repeated.

The Palmyrene Tax Tariff

On (olive) oil (II, 1, 22–7)	מן טעון די מש[חא די בזק]ין ארבע די עז למעלן טעון ג[מ]לא 13 ד ולמפקנא ד [3]1	mn X dy C l-A Y D wl-B D	X - the word *ṭ'wn* + the name of the goods.
	מן טעון די מש[חא] די בזקין תרתן די עז למעל[ן ט]עו[נ]א די גמלא ד [7] ולמפקנא ד [7]	mn X dy C l-A Y D wl-B D	The same.
	מן טעו[ן] חמר די משח למע[לנא] ד 7 ול<מ>פקנא [ד 7]	mn Y dy X l-A D wl-B D	
On (fuel) oil (II, 1, 28–32)	מן טעון דהנא די בזקין א[רבע] די עז די טעון גמל <ל>מעלנא ד 13 ול[מפק]נא ד 13	mn X dy C dy Y l-A D wl-B D	The same.
	מן טעון דהנא די בזקין תרת[ן די] עז לטעון גמל למעלנא ד 7 ולמ[פ]קנא ד 7	mn X dy C l-Y l-A D wl-B D	The same.
	מן טעון [דה]נא די חמר למעלנא [ד 7 ולמפקנא ד 7	mn X dy Y l-A D wl-B D	Y - the restored word *ṭ'wn* is a component of X.
On salt fish (II, 1, 33–4)	מן טעון נ[וני]א מליחיא לטעונא די [גמלא למע[לנ]א ד 10 ומן מפק מנהון [יגבא מכסא ד]	mn X l-Y l-A D wmn mpq mnhwn P D	X - the word *ṭ'wn* + the name of the goods.

Introduction

Table 2

The items taxed	Text	Formula	Correlation with Aramaic	Notes
On slaves (III, 1, 1–8)	παρὰ τ[ῶν παῖδας εἰς Παλμύρους] ἢ εἰς τὰ ὅ[ρια Παλμυρηνῶν εἰσ]αγόντω[ν πράξει ἑκάστου σώματος X κβ´]	παρὰ τ[ῶν X A πράξει Y D	For the Aramaic מן the Greek has παρά.	A - participle In general the reconstruction follows the Aramaic text.
	παρ᾽ οὗ δ[ὲ παῖδας ἐν τῇ πόλει πωλεῖ ἢ ἐξάγει ἑκάστ]ου σ[ώματος X ιβ´]	παρ᾽ οὗ δ[ὲ... Y	Unlike in the Aramaic the objects of taxation are not the slaves but the sellers.	The text is reconstructed according to the Aramaic.
	παρ᾽ οὗ [δὲ σώματ]α οὐετραν[ὰ πωλεῖ X ιβ´]	παρ᾽ οὗ A...	The same.	The same.
	κἂν τὰ σώμα[τα ὑπ]ο το[ῦ πριαμένου ἐξ]άγηται ἑκάστου σώμα[τος διδότω X ιβ´]	Not formalized.	Unlike the Aramaic the Greek text has a passive construction.	
On dry goods (III, 1, 9–15)	ὁ αὐτὸς δημοσιώνη[ς ξηροφόρτου] πράξει ἑκάστου γόμο[υ καμηλικοῦ] εἰσκομισ[θέ]ντος [X γ´] κκομισθ[έντ]ος [γόμου καμηλικοῦ] 13 ἑκάστου [X γ´]	P X πράξει Y A D B Y D	Unlike the Aramaic this text first refers to the object of taxation, then the measure of taxation, described by the word ἑκάστου. For the Aramaic מן the Greek has *gen. separat.*	P = ὁ αυτὸς δημοσιώνη[ς]
	γόμου ὀνικ[οῦ ἑκάστο]υ εἰ[σκομισθέντος X β´] ἐκκομισθέν[τος X β´]	Y A D B D		This corresponds with the Aramaic; it differs by having component D after A.

69

The Palmyrene Tax Tariff

On purple wool (III, 1,16–18)	πορφύρας μηλωτῆ[ς], ἑκά[στου δέρμα]τος εἰσκομισθέν[τ]ος [πράξει ἀσσάρια η΄] ἐκκομισθ[έντο]ς [ἀσσάρια η΄]	X Y A [πράξει ?] D B D	This differs from the Aramaic by the introduction after A of the word πράξει and the component D.
On perfumed oil (III, 1, 19–31)	γόμου κ[αμηλικοῦ] μύρου [τοῦ ἐν ἀλαβάσ]τροις ε[ἰσκομισθέντος πράξει Χ κε΄]	Y X C A [πράξει?] D	This differs from the Aramaic in omitting the adjective equivalent to בשמא.
	καὶ το[ῦ γόμου καμηλικοῦ μυρον τοῦ ἐν ἀλαβάστροις] ἐκ[κομισθέντος πράξει Χ ιγ΄]		Completely reconstructed. Probably fully corresponds with the previous clause. If the econstruction is correct, then the structure does not match the Aramaic.
	γ[όμου καμηλικοῦ μύρου τοῦ ἐν ἀσκοις] αἰγείοις [εἰσκομισθέντος πράξει Χ ιγ΄ ἐκ[κομισθέντος Χ ζ΄]	Y X C A [πράξει?] D B D	Almost completely reconstructed. In favour of the reconstruction there is the word αἰγείοις.
	[γόμου ὀνικοῦ μύ]ρου τοῦ ἐ[ν ἀλαβάστροις] εἰσ[κομισ]θέν[τος] πράξει Χ ΄ ιγ΄ ἐκκομισ[θέν]τος Χ ζ΄]	Y X C A πράξει D B D	This corresponds with the Aramaic; additional insertion of the word πράξει after A
	γόμου ὀνικοῦ μ[ύρου τοῦ ἐν ἀσκοῖς] αἰγείοις εἰσκομ[ισθέντο]ς πρ[άξει Χ ζ΄] ἐκκομισθέντος π[ρ]άξ[ει Χ δ΄]	YXCA πράξει D B πράξει D	

Introduction

On (olive) oil (III, 1, 32–42)	γόμου ἐλεηροῦ το[ῦ ἐν ἀσκο]ῖς [τέσσαρ]σι αἰγείοις ἐπὶ καμήλ[ου εἰσκομισθέν]τος [Χ ιγ´] ἐκκομισθέντο[ς Χ ιγ´]	Χ C Y A D B D	This corresponds with the Aramaic.
	γόμου ἐλαιηροῦ τοῦ ἐ[ν ἀσκοῖς δυσὶ αἰ]γείοις ἐπὶ καμήλ[ου εἰσκομισθέντος] πράξει [Χ ζ´] ἐκκομισθέντο[ς Χ ζ´]	Χ C Y A πράξει D B D	The same.
	γόμου ἐλε[ηροῦ τοῦ ἐπ᾽ ὄνο]υ ε[ἰσκομισθέν]τος π[ράξει Χ ζ´] ἐκ[κομισθέντος Χ ζ´]	Χ C Y A πράξει D B D	The same.
On (fuel) oil (III, 1, 43– II, 4)	γόμ[ου καύσεως τοῦ ἐν ἀσκοῖς τ]έσσ[αρσι] αἰγείοις [εἰσκομισθέντος πρά]ξει Χ ιγ´ ἐκκομι[σ]θέ[ντος] Χ ιγ´	Χ C A πράξει D B D	There is no mention of the import of camel-loads.
	γόμου κ[αύσεως τοῦ ἐν] α[σ]κοῖς δυσὶ αἰγείοις ἐπὶ κ[αμήλου εἰσ]κομισθέντος πράξει Χ ζ´ [ἐκκομισ]θέντος [Χ ζ´]	Χ C Y A πράξει D B D	
	[γόμου ὀ]ν[ικοῦ καύσεως εἰσκομισθέντος πράξει Χ ζ´ ἐκκομισθ]έν[τος Χ ζ´]		The text is completely reconstructed.

The Palmyrene Tax Tariff

Table 3

The name of the trade	Text	Formula	Notes
On the sellers of perfumed oil (II, 1, 45–6)	אף [י]ג[ב]א מכ[ס]א לכל יר[ח] מן די יהוא מזבן משחא בשימא אסרין 2	K P L T D	
On prostitutes (II, 1, 46–2, 2)	אף יגבא מכסא מן זניתא	K P T	
	מן מן די שקלא דינר [או] יתיר דנרא חד מן אתתא	T_o P D T_1	T_o and T_1 specify the T of the introductory part of the article. The structure of T_o in all three clauses is of the same type.
	ומן מן די שקלא אסרין תמניא יגבא אסרין תמניא	T_o P D	
	ומן מן די שקל[א] אסר[ין ש]תא יגבא אסרין [ש]ת[א]	T_o P D	
On handicraft shops (II, 2, 3–5)	אף יגבא מכ[ס]א מן ארגסטר[ין] ופטפלי [ואשכ]יפא [ומן] ח[ז]ט[א] היך עדתא [לכל] יר[ח] מן חנותא ד 1	K P T N L Y D	
On the import and selling of skins (II, 2, 6)	[מן כ]ל משך די [י]תאעל או יזבן למשכא אסרין 2	mn X dy A 'w E l-Y D	
On taxes from pedlars of clothes (II, 2, 7)	[מזבנ]י נחתיא די הפכין במדיתא יהן מוט מכסא	Not formalized	
On the use of the water sources (II, 2, 8)	[לתש]מיש עינן תרתן די מ[י] די במדיתא ד 800	T D	T is probably introduced by the preposition ל.
On the import and selling of wheat, wine and straw (II, 2, 9–10)	[י]גבא מכסא לטעונא די חטא וחמרא ותבנא ו[כ]ל מדי דמא [להון לכ]ל גמל לארח חדא ד 1	P l-X l-Y l-Y_1 O	Y and Y_1 - two measurement units. The structure of the article is similar to the articles of the first part.
On unladen camels (II, 2, 11–12)	לגמלא כדי יתאיעל סריק יגבא ד 1 היך [די] גב[א] קלקיס בר חרי קיסר	l-X C P D N	C and N - subordinate clauses.

Introduction

Table 4

The name of the article	Text	Formula	Correlation with the Aramaic	Notes
On the sale of perfumed oil (III, 2, 25–7)	Ὁ αὐτὸς δ[η]μοσιώνης ἑκάσ[του] μη[νὸς] παρ᾽ ἑκ[άστο]υ τῶ[ν τὸ] ἔλαιον κατα... [πωλού]ντων [ἀσσάρια β´]	P L T D	There are no equivalents for אף or יגבא.	The beginning is the same as in the article on dry goods in the first part.
On prostitutes (III, 2, 28–32)	Ὁ αὐτ[ὸς ημοσιώνης] πρά[ξει ἐν τῃ πόλει [ἐκ τῶν ἑταιρ]ῶν ὅσαι [δηνάριον ἢ πλέον λαμβά]νουσιν π[ράξει δηνάριον, ὅσαι δὲ ἔλαβον ἀ]σσάρια ὀκτώ [πράξει ἀσσαρι]α η´, [ὅσαι δὲ ἀσ]σάρια ἓξ ἔ[λαβον ἑ]καστ[ης πράξει] ασσ<άρια> ς´	P [ἐν τῃ πό]λει T T₀ P D T₀ P D T₀ T₁ P D	At the beginning of the article we find [ἐν τῃ πό]λει. There is no equivalent in the Aramaic. In the first clause there is no equivalent for Aramaic מן אתתא, which, however, appears in the Greek text in the third clause (ἑκάστης), although in the corresponding Aramaic this expression is absent. In the first clause of the Greek text there is an extra word πρ[άξει].	The beginning of the article is parallel to the beginning of the previous one.
On taxes from craftsmen's shops (III, 2, 33–6)	[Ὁ αὐτὸς δημ]οσιώνης πρ[άξ]ει ἐργαστηρίων [ῥαφιδικῶν] παντοπωλ[ικ]ῶν σκυτικῶν [τὸ τέλο]ς ἐκ συνηθείας ἑκάστου μηνὸς καὶ ἐργαστηρίου ἑκάστου, X α´	P T [τὸ τέλο]ς N L Y₁ Y₂...D	In the Greek text the following is inserted: [τὸ τέλο]ς. The location of particular objects for taxation in both cases is different.	The beginning is the same as the two previous entries.

73

The Palmyrene Tax Tariff

On the import and sale of skins (III, 2, 37–8)	Παρὰ τῶν δέρματα ἰσκομιζόντ[ων ἢ πω]λούντων, ἑκάστου δέρματος ἀσσά[ρια β΄]	X A E Y D	Unlike in the Aramaic, the objects of taxation are the people exporting or importing the goods.
On taxes from pedlars of clothes (III, 2, 39–40)	Ὁμοίως ἱματιοπῶλαι μετάβολοι πωλ[οῦν]τες ἐν τῇ πόλει τῷ δημοσιώνῃ τὸ ἱκανὸν ποιεῖ[ν]	Not formalized	The Greek text has an extra word at the beginning, ὁμοίως, and after μετάβολοι there is a clarification πωλ[οῦν]τες.
On the use of the water sources (III, 2, 41)	Χρήσεος πηγῶν β΄ ἑκάστου ἔτους Χ ω΄	T L D	The Greek does not have an equivalent for Aramaic די במדיתא, but does have an additional ἑκάστου ἔτους.
On the import and sale of wheat, wine and straw (II, 2, 42–4)	Ὁ αὐτὸς <δημοσιώνης> πρά[ξ]ει γόμου πυρικοῦ οἰνικοῦ ἀχύρων καὶ τοιούτου γένους ἑκάστου γόμου καμηλικοῦ καθ' ὁδὸν ἑκάστην Χ α΄	P X Y D	The Greek text fully matches the Aramaic.
On unladen camels (III, 2, 45, 46)	Καμήλου ὃς κενὸς εἰσαχθῇ πράξει Χ α΄ καθὼς Κίλιξ Καίσαρος ἀπελεύθερος ἔπραξεν.	X C P D N	The same.

Table 5

The name of the article	Aramaic Text	Formula	Correlation with the Aramaic	Greek Text
On dry goods (II, 2, 16)	מִן יְבֵישִׁין [לכ]ל טעון די גמל מעלן 4 ד ולמפקן ד 4	*mn X l-Y A D wl-*B D	In the 'new' law the tax is 3 *denarii*. In the 'old' law the tax for a donkey-load is missing.	
On purple wool (II, 2, 17)	מִן א[ר]גונא מלטא לכל משך למעלנא ד 4 ולמפקא ד 4	*mn X l-Y l-*A D *wl-* B D	In the 'new' law the amount of taxation is 8 *assarii*.	
On taxation on all kinds of goods (II, 2, 18)	אף יגבא [מכס]א מן גנסיא כלהון היך די כתיב מן למעל	Not formalized.	There is no correspondence with the 'new' law.	
On good-quality salt (II, 2, 19–21)	ח טב [יתג]בא[מ]ל אסרא חד למדיא די קסטון עשר ו[ש]ת [ו]מא די יתבעא יתן [לה]ן לתשמישא ו[די] לא י[כ]ל י[פרע לכל מדא מן נמ[וס]א דנה סטרטין [תר]ן	The same.	The same.	
On taxes for salt in private ownership (II, 2, 22–3; III, 3, 23–7)	מן די יהוא לה מלח בתד[מ]ר או בתחו[מא ד]י ת[ד]מרי[א יכילנה ל[מסכ]א[פ]י מדיא באסרא חד	The same.	The same.	Ὃς δ᾽ ἂν ἅλα[ς ἔχ]ῃ ἐν Παλμύροις ἢ [ἐν ὅροις] Παλμυρη[ν]ῶν παραμετ-ρησάτω [τῷ δημο]σιώνῃ ε[ἰς ἕκ]αστον μόδιον, ἀσσά[ριον] ὃς δ᾽ ἂν οὐ ....ν κ.τ.λ.

The Palmyrene Tax Tariff

Table 6

'New' law	'Old' law (articles before the edict of Mucianus)	The edict of Mucianus
On slaves		On slaves
On dry goods	On dry goods	
On purple wool	On purple wool	On purple
On perfumed oil	On perfumed oil in goatskins	
On olive oil	-	
On (fuel) oil	-	
On salted fish	-	
On livestock	-	On sheep and goats that are brought into the city
On trading of the fragrant oil	-	
On prostitutes	-	On prostitutes
On taxes from craftsmen's shops	-	On tradesmen and craftsmen
On export and import of skins	-	On export and import of leather
On salesmen peddling clothes	-	-
On the use of the water sources	-	-
On the import and selling of wheat, wine and straw	-	-
On unloaded camels	-	On camels
-	On taxes from all kinds of goods	-
-	On good salt	On salt
-	On salt that anyone has in their possession	-
-	On pledges from a taxpayer (Greek only)	-
-	On solving a dispute between the tax farmer and a taxpayer (Greek only)	-
-	On the rights of the tax farmer to take and to sell a deposit (Greek only)	-
-	On the tax farmer not being allowed to pass his authority to anyone else (Greek only)	-
-	-	On wool
-	-	On taxes from butchers
-	-	On foodstuffs
-	-	On nuts
-	-	On camel-skins
-	-	On vegetables and fruits
		On statues

7. The Particularities of the Palaeography and the Language of the Document

The Greek text of the Palmyrene Tax Tariff is written in an angular-rounded script typical of the second century AD (Guarducci 1967 I: 377; Reinach 1885: 203–12).

In the table below are indicated unique features of the palaeography of the Greek part of the inscription.

A	A	N	N N
B	B	Ξ	ᴦ ≡
Γ	Γ	O	ο °ο
Δ	Δ Δ Δ	Π	π
E	ε ε ᵉ	P	ρ
Z	Z	Σ	C ᶜc
H	H ʜ ᴹ	T	T
Θ	θ θ θ	Y	Y
I	ı ' ı	Φ	φ φ
K	K k ʀ	X	X
Λ	Λ Λ	Ψ	✝
M	M M	Ω	ω ω ω

Ligatures: ντ = **NT**; νκ = **NK**; νγ = **NΓ**; ην = **HN**; νην = **NHN**. We find ligatures only in panel IV of the Tariff and not systematically.

The composer of the text marks the beginning of what is from his point of view a complete section by an outdent (a non-indented line). Within sections word-divisions are absent.

The Greek of the Palmyrene Tariff is the common Greek koine of the Hellenistic period (Thumb 1901). A distinctive (though not exclusive) aspect of koine Greek orthography is found in the use of νγ instead of γγ. This is visible throughout the text: ἐνγραφομέ[νου] < ἐγγραφομέ[νου], ἐνγράψαι < ἐγγράψαι, ἐνγραφῆναι < ἐγγραφῆναι, ἔνγιστα < ἔγγιστα, ἔνγομοι < ἔγγομοι. The writing of γχ is also found: τυγχάνοντας.

The Palmyrene Tax Tariff

The similarity in speech between the diphthong αι and the vowel ε led to variant spellings ἐλαιεροῦ and ἐλεηροῦ; the similarity in sound of the diphthong ει to the vowel ι made it possible to write γείνεσθαι < γίνεσθαι, γείνεται < γίνεται, διακρείνοντας < διακρίνοντας, Στατείλι[ον] < Στατίλιον, ῥειπτουμένων < ῥιπτουμένων, εἴστημι < ἵστημι, ἐμπορείαν < ἐμπορίαν.

The spelling of ἀνελήμφθη shows that Palmyrene Greek is the same as koine, with nasal consonants appearing before aspirants. An example of writing ου instead of ω is found in Κουρβούλων (Latin Corbulo). The writing of ῥειπτουμένων shows the convergence of ο and ω, as well as ω and ου. The iota adscript/subscript is systematically absent after a long vowel (e.g. ΤΩΝΟΜΩΚΑΙΤΗ ... = τῷ νόμῳ καὶ τῇ ... I, 6). There are cases of dissimilation: μπ > νπ: ἔνπορος < ἔμπορος, ἐνπόρων < ἐμπόρων (cf. however, ἐμπορείαν). For an Attic ττ there is an Ionic σσ: πράσσειν, τέσσαρες. The declension of nouns and the conjugation of verbs follows the regular scheme.

Some words can be omitted in sentences, for example, a subject that can be guessed from the context (ὁ δημοσιώνης, τὸ τέλος). More rarely a verb (πράξει), infinitive (λογεύεσθαι) and nouns in *genitivus absolutus* can be omitted.

Prepositions εἰς and πρός in the expressions εἰς δηνάριον ὀφείλει λο[γευεσθαι], πρὸς ἀσσάριον ἰταλ[ικὸν] τὰ τέλη λογεύεσθαι and πρὸς κέρμα πράξει introduce indirect objects and the noun which follows in the accusative case gives the sense of *dativus instrumenti*.

The infinitive is used instead of the other verbal forms: δεδόχθαι (= δέδοκται); τὸ ἱκανὸν ποιεῖ[ν] (= ποιούντων). The aorist infinitive in δεδόχθαι ... ἐνγράψαι ... καὶ ὑποτ[ά]ξαι ... ἐνγραφῆναι refers to future time.

The Aramaic text of the Palmyrene Tariff is a very significant source for the knowledge of the formal Aramaic used in Syria in the first–second centuries AD, at what is a relatively early stage (at least in terms of what has survived to us) in the history of the Syriac language. However, the absence of vowels and the need to guess at some forms from the context (where the understanding of the text depends on the correct reconstruction of the grammatical forms) make some of our assumptions only hypothetical. The palaeographical peculiarities of the Aramaic text and the place of the Tariff in the history of the Aramaic scripts are visible in Table 7.[19]

---

19 The classic description by Cantineau presents the development of Palmyrene script (1935: 17–

The inscription has a consistent writing of final ן. The final forms of ך, ם, ף ,ץ are not found. Word divisions and diacritical signs are absent. Sometimes (not clearly, though) the passages of the text important for the author seem to be emphasized by an outdent. Sometimes the endings of these passages are marked by a fleuron/rose leaf.

As Table 7 shows, the Palmyrene Tax Tariff was written in a monumental script which was typical of Palmyra in the second century. As is well known, the Palmyrene script is close to that of the Aramaic in Asia Minor, especially to the script used in Cappadocia; it derives from the Aramaic writing of the first half of the first millennium BC and, as such, from the Phoenician linear writing that had been formed by the second half of the second millennium BC. Research on these scripts shows that the common tendency of their development is towards the cursive type; the straight lines are replaced by curved ones; and the cursive itself acquires monumental characteristics (Lidzbarski 1898: I, 192–3; Cantineau 1933a: 169–209; Cantineau 1935: 17-30; Rosenthal 1936: 7–9). At the end of the second–third centuries AD (after the Tariff was composed), the 'broken' style (according to Cantineau's definition) becomes dominant. A comparison with similar script styles, although from a different area of the Near East, the area surrounding the Dead Sea, shows that Palmyrene epigraphy, as well as its contemporaries Nabataean and Greek, is characterized by a tendency to reproduce handwriting on stone. This tendency is also the reason for the existence of Palmyrene cursive (which is similar to, if not identical with, *estrangela*) carved on stone.[20]

---

30). The script of the Cappadocian [Aramaic] inscriptions is found in Rosenthal (1936: 8); the Judaean script is presented by F.M. Cross (1961). On the palaeography of the Qumran inscriptions see Birnbaum (1952). When this work was ready for publication, A. Malamat kindly provided a copy of a monograph by Naveh that presents the development of Aramaic writing (Naveh 5734).

20 On the similarities see Sachau 1882: 142–67. The question of similarities between these two systems has been discussed for some time among scholars. R. Duval considers Palmyrene writing of the second to third centuries as a chain that connects Aramaic square script and Syriac *estrangela* (Duval 1881: 47). M. Lidzbarski thinks that it is incorrect to assume that *estrangela* had developed from Palmyrene cursive. He points out that the writing on the sarcophagus of Saddan from Adiabene (first half of the first century AD) is very similar to *estrangela*.

He suggests that the Palmyrene forms and *estrangela* were developing parallel to each other (Lidzbarski 1889: I, 193–4). E. Nestle has a similar view. He also emphasizes that Palmyrene and Syriac scripts derive from one source (Nestle 1883: 3). Cantineau disagrees with Lidzbarski. He suggests that already in the first half of the first century AD Palmyrene merchants spread their cursive script, an example of which could be the inscription from

The Palmyrene Tax Tariff

Table 8 shows the correlation between Palmyrene cursive and other Aramaic cursive scripts.[21]

Table 9 shows ligatured writings which derive from handwriting style.

Adiabene (Cantineau 1935: 32). Rosenthal speaks of the use of cursive in everyday life, of mutual influence of monumental and cursive writing, and about their parallel development. Following Kokovtsov and Montgomery, he emphasizes the affinity between the Palmyrene script and the letter-forms of the magical texts from Nippur and the Manichean texts from Turfan. Thus he goes beyond the question about the correlation between the cursive and *estrangela* (Rosenthal 1936: 9–11).

The absence of early Palmyrene cursive documents prevents us from speaking firmly in favour of Palmyrene cursive influence on *estrangela*. Pirenne's hypothesis seems to be the most plausible one. She suggests that the Palmyrene cursive ('Syro-Palmyrene writing' according to her terminology) was Syrian writing that was adopted by the Palmyrenes who served in the Roman army and who were influenced by the Palmyrene monumental writing (Pirenne 1963: 101–37, especially 131–7). Her concept needs further clarification in the sense that both Palmyrene cursive and *estrangela* are local variants of the cursive script common to the whole of Aramaic-speaking Syria.

21 The forms of the Palmyrene cursive script and *estrangela* are reproduced according to Cantineau (Cantineau 1935: 34). The forms of the texts from Nippur are according to Rosenthal (1936: 11) and Montgomery (1913). The Judaean cursive is according to Cross (1961). The Mandaean follows Nöldeke (1875). Other variants are follow Perikhanian (1966: 112).

Introduction

Table 7

The Palmyrene Tax Tariff

Table 8

Table 9

				More than two letters	
בא		לה			
בג		מא		בנא	
בד		מד		כבנ	
בה		מו		כפר	
בו		מת		כתב	
בז		נא		לתחת	
בר		נת		מתג	
גו		סא		מתז	
גר		סד		נתא	
גה		עא		סוא	
דח		עו		תגר	
זח		פו		תחו	
חו		קד		תחו	
כד		קו			
כי		קצ			
כת		קר			
לה		תא			

The absence of word divisions makes connected writing and joining of words possible.

The numbers are expressed as follows:

1 - | 10 - ?   100 - ?

5 - y   20 - ?3

As stated above, the classical studies of Cantineau (1935) and Rosenthal (1936), which are characterized by thorough research on the Tariff, show that the Aramaic language of the Palmyrene inscriptions is essentially Imperial Aramaic. The vocabulary has adopted words from Greek, Latin (administrative, financial and household terminology) and Arabic (רגל, טעמתא; cf. also רגלי — an Arabic genitive). There are also Eastern Aramaic lexical elements (חשחתא, מתחשבו, נחתיא, סריק, עידא, פשק) and Palmyrisms (עדתא, מטלכות, אגוריא). To this we need to add some more observations:

The Tariff has an internal passive of the Peʿal: גבי (perfect), יכתב and יזבן (imperfect). As is known, we have the same in Imperial Aramaic and Biblical Aramaic. However, in Syriac and in the Aramaic of the postbiblical literature, this does not occur. Perhaps this research on the Palmyrene Tariff makes it possible to determine until what time the elements of the Imperial Aramaic language were a part of the written Aramaic of north-eastern Syria.

The language of the Tariff is characterized by compound tenses (the finite form of the verb הוא, 'to be', plus participle of the main verb). Combination with the verb הוא in the perfect gives a compound past tense: הות כנישא, הוו מתגבין, הוא מתכתב. Combination of this verb in the imperfect with a participle creates a future tense: יהוא מת[א]על ... או מאפק יהון, יהון יהבין תהוא שקלא, ת[ה]ו[א] מ[תאעל, יהוא מזבן. The jussive of the verb הוא together with a participle creates a compound jussive: יהוא מזבן, פרעא תהוא, יהוא מתקבל, יהוא מתגבא, יהוא יהב, לא יהוא גבא. A participle without any auxiliary verb gives a present tense: מן די לא מסק בנמוסא. J. בנמוסא רציף, מדי דמא, מכס לא חיבין, מן מפק מנהון, [מזבנ]י די הפכין במדיתא, שקלא דינר. Cantineau notes this peculiarity and sees a durative in all the above cases. The expressions הות כנישא (i.e. the בולא) and הוא מתכתב show that compound verbal forms could be used to indicate a single, 'instantaneous' and completed action.

The corresponding phenomenon occurs in both Biblical Aramaic (Kautzsch 1884: 139–42)[22] and in Syriac (Duval 1881: 320–2; Costaz 1955: 81–3).

Just as in the Greek text, in the Aramaic of the Tariff some parts in sentences (ones that can be easily reconstructed in the context) can be omitted, for example a subject (מכסא, בולא) or a main verb (גבא, יגבא).

The Palmyrene Tariff testifies to a lively interaction between Aramaic and Greek. We can refer to Roman titles: כשירא = ὁ κράτιστος = *vir egregius*. Words that came from Greek, acquired Aramaic endings: προεδρία > פלהדרותא, λιμήν > למנא, παντοπώλιον > פטפלי, ἀσσάριον > אסרא, σύνδικος > סדקיא, γένος > גנסיא. Also the Greek suffix -εία (א-) came into Aramaic: ארכוניא. There is visible influence of the Greek on the Aramaic syntax of the Tariff. The Greek

---

22 E. Kautzsch considers these forms as participles that function as predicates in nominal sentences or as complements to הוה in verbal sentences.

preposition ἐκ in the phrases ἐκ τοῦ νόμου, ἐκ συνηθείας produces a corresponding preposition in the Aramaic, מן — מן נמוסא, מן עידא. In expressions like מדיא די קסטון עשר ו[ש]ת there is a reproduction of the Greek genitive case: μόδιόν τῶν ξεστῶν ἐκκαίδεκα. In the Aramaic sentence לא עמרא איטליק[א ת]הוא פרעא the unusual place of the negative particle לא before a noun reflects (though not literally) a Greek construction: μ[ὴ ἀπὸ τ]ούτων ἐξαγο[μένων τὸ τέλος δί]δοσθαι. In the Greek one can sometimes notice Aramaisms, such as the use of prepositions εἰς and πρός, which corresponds with the Aramaic אפי. The expression μεταξὺ τῶν ἐνπόρων πρὸς τελώνας reflects literally the Aramaic ביני תגרא לביני מכסא.

In the light of the above data the question arises: which of the two texts of the Tariff was the primary one? As we have noted, there is some evidence showing that the Greek text had priority among the Palmyrene legislators. Besides, there are abbreviations on the stone specifically in the Aramaic text. Greek elements could penetrate into the Aramaic text only through calquing of the Greek, while Aramaisms in the Greek reflect the influence of the living Aramaic language. The edict of Mucianus was certainly composed in the chancery of the Roman governor in the Greek language. All of this makes it possible to conclude that the Greek text of the Tariff is the original and the Aramaic is a translation. It is also not accidental that in the year when the Tariff was composed the *grammateus* of the Palmyrene council was a man with a Greek patronymic – presumably of Greek origin.

8. The Palmyrene Tariff as an Historical Source

The Palmyrene Tariff contains valuable information about the socio-economic, political and cultural history of Palmyrene society, thus representing all of Syrian society of the first century and the first half of the second century AD. It provides information about the occupations of people, the legal and property status of different population groups and city government structures; also, about the political status of Palmyra within the Roman Province of Syria and the development of local regulations. The present document preserves unique materials on Palmyrene religion.

As has been mentioned earlier, the Palmyrene Tariff prescribes the following taxes: in the 'new' law one *denarius* for a camel-load of wheat, wine, straw or similar items (II, 2, 9–10; III, 2, 42–4) and in the edict of Mucianus one *denarius* for foodstuffs imported from and exported to areas outside of Palmyra (II, 3, 10–12; IV, 1, 47–9), and also for vegetables and fruits, since 'they have a price', in other words because people buy and sell them. Import and export of foodstuffs between different settlements located in the Palmyrene territory were exempt from taxation (II, 3, 10–12; IV, 1, 47–9).

Thus, by the time of compilation of the edict of Mucianus, i.e. at the end of the 60s AD, foodstuffs in Palmyra could be imported and exported. This fact alone does not provide any information about the quantities of production of such items; nor does it give any indication of their production in Palmyra at all. The document speaks only about import and export. Moreover, the edict allows for the possibility of transit traffic. Of particular interest is the clause about transportation of foodstuffs from settlements located in Palmyrene territory to the city of Palmyra and *vice versa*. The tendency here is obvious. The Roman government in Syria tries to encourage trade in local foods and the development of local agriculture in newly settled territories.

Tchalenko's research (1953–8) showed that such a policy corresponded with the goals that Roman government pursued everywhere in Syria. The clarification of the clause in question is noteworthy. It states that vegetable and fruit trade is taxed. Apparently such types of trade were so well developed by then that they did not require any sort of government encouragement. Restatement of these laws in the Tariff of AD 137 without any revocation shows that in the first half of the second century AD the Palmyrene government continued the policy of the Roman administration. Nevertheless, the article from the 'new' law mentioned earlier shows that wheat, wine, straw, etc. were still imported from outside Palmyra (obviously, local production did not satisfy demand), in spite of the fact that taxation puts these imported items at a disadvantage by comparison with local produce.

Another group of taxes, related to agriculture are livestock taxes. The edict of Mucianus (II, 3, 46 to the line under the columns of the second panel; IV, 2, 36–40) makes provision for taxation related to grazing livestock brought from outside for pasturing or shearing. The tax farmer is allowed to stamp the sheep. Animals pastured on Palmyrene territory (i.e. not brought from outside) and brought into the city for shearing are not to be taxed. In the 'new' law (if our interpretation of the Aramaic text in II, 1, 38–44 is correct) there are additional articles related to taxes for bringing in horses, mules, rams; bringing in and taking out of lambs, colts, she-goats and kids intended for trade.[23] Special attention in the Tariff is given to the taxation of camels — in the 'new' law the taxing of unloaded camels, and in the 'old' law the taxing of loaded and unloaded camels.[24]

Thus, the Tariff covers the following situations: livestock is pastured on Palmyrene territory, but is not brought from outside; livestock is brought into the Palmyrene territory for pasturing and shearing; livestock is brought into Palmyrene territory from outside and is taken away for sale. Taking all of that into consideration the question of the legal status of the pastures arises. Since taxes for using the pastures are collected only from the non-Palmyrene population[25] and paid into the city treasury, one can conclude that the law here concerns government lands, rather than private pastures.

Nevertheless, the Tariff depicts Palmyra as a society where animal husbandry, particularly for trade, played an important role. The Palmyrene oasis was the centre of gravity attracting farmers not just from the Palmyrene territory itself, but also from neighbouring lands. They brought their livestock in for pasturing and shearing.

The results acquired from research on the Palmyrene Tariff are backed up by archaeological excavations in the north-western part of the Palmyrene territory. Numerous settlements of farmers and stock-breeders were discovered there (Schlumberger 1951). In all likelihood, in Palmyra these areas were referred to as קריא and χωρίον. As we have attempted to show on the basis of the study of some grave inscriptions from Palmyra (the legal status of tombs and other landed property were the same), there was private property in the form of land, with practically no distinction between inherited and non-ancestral property (Shifman 1965b: 100–13; Gawlikowski 1970: 174). References to businesses making regular profit are few in the Tariff.

The edict of Mucianus mentions taxes collected from butchers (II, 3, 3–8

---

23 In Roman Egypt the φόρος προβάτων was a fee to hire sheep and goats that belonged to the state (Wallace 1938: 79). The Palmyrene Tariff refers to a different issue: taxes from buying and selling young livestock (lambs, kids) brought in from outside and exported outside.

24 In Egypt the τέλεσμα καμήλων was collected regularly for camels owned by private people (Wallace 1938: 89–90). It was different from the taxation described in the Palmyrene Tariff, which was collected only when a camel was crossing the Palmyrene borders.

25 A tax for using pasture (ἐννόμιον) is also attested in Egypt (Wallace 1938: 86).

and IV, 1, 41–5), prostitutes (II, 3, 26–9), apparently from tailors (II, 3, 3–8), and also from other craftsmen; the 'old' law regulates the taxation of people who exploit sources of salt (II, 3, 22–3 and III, 3, 23–5); the 'new' law establishes taxes from prostitutes (II, 1, 46–2.2 and III, 2, 28–32) and from the shops of craftsmen (II, 2, 3–5 and III, 2, 33–6).

The edict of Mucianus does not set the exact amount of tax collected for butchering. According to the rescript of Germanicus to Statilius, the tax is to be collected in *denarii*, i.e. in Roman coin, apparently, because the tax was higher than the amount (1 *denarius*) which was allowed to be paid in local coins.

As far as we can tell the edict of Mucianus did not set a strict fixed tax for craftsmen's shops; however, there were some kinds of regulation for these taxes. The edict mentions only tailors. The 'new' law sets the amount of tax collected from craftsmen's shops (specifically mentioned are shoemakers and tailors) at one *denarius* a month. Apparently, the necessity of making such a clarification indicates that in the conflicts with tax farmers, the resolution of which the Palmyrene council mentions, craftsmen played a central role. No doubt the Tariff (both the edict of Mucianus and the 'new' law) mentions shoemakers and tailors explicitly because they were the most common occupations in Palmyra. Nevertheless, they were not the only craft occupations in the land. Inscription 3945 (= *IGRR*, III, 1031 = *Inv.* III, 17; April AD 258) mentions goldsmiths and silversmiths. Construction and ceramic work were also quite common in Palmyra (Collart 1961: 427–35). Inscription 3945 testifies to the existence of craftsmen's guilds, which is important for the understanding of the social status of craftsmen in Palmyrene society.

Special attention in the edict of Mucianus is given to taxation of bronze statues, set at half of the tax amount for a unit of weight of raw bronze (II, 3, 29–31). One may note that the text does not mention any form of taxation on the import of *raw* bronze as such.[26] It is possible that this tax was collected not only from the import of statues, but also from the local sculptors.

It is probable that taxes on import of bronze were regulated by the imperial legal system, which could explain why they were excluded from the Tariff.

According to the 'old' law, 'those who have salt' in Palmyra or its territory, i.e. people engaged in salt mining, had to pay a tax of 2 *assarii* for a *modius*.

---

26 This tax in the Tariff is different from the Egyptian μερισμὸς ἀδριάντος, which was collected in order to cover expenses to build imperial statues (Wallace 1938: 159–62).

As we can judge from II, 2, 20 the oversight of exploration of salt was given to the tax farmer, who could (according to the text he was obliged to) allow exploration of new territories.[27]

Finally, according to the imperial law, established during Caligula's reign (Suet., *Calig.*, 40), τέλος πορνικόν was collected monthly — *quantum quaeque uno concubito mereret*.[28]

Thus, there were two systems of taxation of craftsmen or other people whose occupations brought in a steady income (which at that time was equated to craftsmanship). One system (dealing with butchers, craftsmen's shops) prescribed a fixed monthly tax not tied to one's profit. The other system (dealing with makers of bronze statues, salt mining) takes the profit into account and the tax is collected from the final product. In case of τέλος πορνικόν both principles are combined: tax is collected monthly but is calculated according to the profit of the taxpayer.

The main scope of the material covered in the Palmyrene Tariff deals with trade: it talks both about import and export of goods, and trade in the city (market, shops). The edict of Mucianus talks about slaves, purple, perfumed oil in goatskins, sheep and goats, skins, salt, wool, foodstuffs, nuts, vegetables and fruit. The 'old' law covers dry goods and purple wool. The 'new' law deals with slaves, dry goods, purple wool, perfumed oil, olive oil, fuel oil, salted fish, livestock, trade in perfumed oil in the city, peddling of clothes, import of and trade in skins, import of and trade in wheat, wine and straw. The fact that some regulations concerning import and export of goods and the list of goods themselves in the 'new' law is somewhat more detailed than in the 'old' law, or in the edict of Mucianus, hardly testifies to any sort of change in trade practice. More likely, it is to be accounted for as a development of the law itself, reflecting specific practices of Palmyrene society.

Nevertheless, the Tariff preserves a list of common goods shipped through Palmyra and traded in the Palmyrene territory. Most regulations deal with

---

27 In Egypt ἁλική was collected regularly from every person. It was an outcome of the state monopoly on salt (Wallace 1938: 183–4). In Palmyra, we must assume, the government owned the salt mines/beds and rented them out. Those who mined salt or sold it paid taxes.

28 A similar tax (ἑταιρικόν) existed in Egypt also (Wallace 1938: 209–11). It is interesting that in the Chersonese (*IOSPE* 2, I, 404) at least part of the τέλος πορνικόν was paid to Roman soldiers as a contribution to maintaining the Roman garrison in the city. Rostovtzeff (1916: 63–9) assumes that this was on the order of one of the emperors, possibly Hadrian or Antoninus Pius. Whether the same order was in effect in Palmyra is unknown.

The Palmyrene Tax Tariff

taxes collected from the import and export of specific goods. Judging by what kind of units of measure are established in the Tariff, one can say that the goods were transported on camels and donkeys and in carts. Numerous caravan inscriptions from Palmyra help us identify families that systematically, from generation to generation, equipped and led caravans. These inscriptions also help us understand Palmyrene trade routes: to the south of Mesopotamia as far as Spasinou Charax and to the west as far as Egypt. Palmyrenes possibly traded with South Arabia and engaged in maritime trade (Shifman 1977).

In most cases taxes were not collected for selling goods in the Palmyrene territory. The exceptions in the 'new' law were the selling of slaves (II, 1, 3–4 and III, 1, 4–6), and perfumed oil (fixed monthly tax, probably from a professional trader; II, 1, 45–6 and III, 2, 25–7), corner shops (II, 2, 3 and III, 2, 34), and clothes pedlars (II, 2, 7 and III, 2, 39). The 'old' law does not mention any taxes collected from selling goods. The edict of Mucianus regulates taxes from the selling of slaves (II, 2, 32–3), of some unknown item (perhaps perfumed oil), the name of which has not been preserved (II, 2, 38), of salt (II, 3, 31–7) and from peddling (II, 3, 40). It is evident that the legislator was aiming at professional traders who sold slaves, perfumed oil and salt. All other goods, except clothes, were probably sold through small shops. Another document, from the archive of Nebuzabad from Dura-Europos, which has been studied by us earlier (Shifman, 1977), gives an idea about the trading practices of such shops. Nebuzabad sold food, clothes etc. So, we can assume that goods that were imported into Palmyra or transported through its territory were not allowed to be sold except through such shops. Of course, such small shops could be owned by traders who also equipped caravans.

Principles of taxation in Palmyra were quite different from tax systems in other areas of the Near East, for example, in Leukē Kōmē (*Per. mar. Er.*, 19) and Soada (Suwayda) (Wadd., 2311 = *IGRR*, III, 1283), where a specified part of the goods or their value was paid as a tax. In Leukē Kōmē that part was one fourth of the cargo, and in Soada for every 100 *denarii* of the value of the cargo a golden *obol* was paid as a tax. In Palmyra taxes were fixed without reference to the value of the goods (which is why on the basis of the text of the Palmyrene Tariff itself we cannot estimate the real cost of goods). As a result, in spite of the fact that the tax amount was fixed, in practice the difference between the tax and the profit on sales varied according to prices in the

Palmyrene *agora*.[29]

As far as the social structure of Palmyrene society is concerned, we should mention the situation of slaves. The Tariff refers to them only in relation to export/import or selling/buying, accordingly only as items to be taxed, i.e. in situations where the property rights of their owners are exercised over them (see the edict of Mucianus II, 2, 30–7, in the 'new law' II, 1, 1-5 and III, 1, 1–8).

Palmyrene terms for slaves deserve special attention. In the edict of Mucianus they are called 'individuals, people' (רגלין, cf. Greek σώμα) and 'boys' ע[ל]ם; in the 'new law' 'boys' (עלם, plural על[מ]ין and עלמיא). The latter term (the corresponding term for it in *Inv.* XI, 13 is טליא, like Greek παῖς, Hebrew נער) is undoubtedly an old word which comes from the time when it was the responsibility of the younger members of a family (boys) or of other male or military associations to serve the rest of the members of these groups (Lipets 1969: 107–13). In Palmyra as well as in other Mediterranean countries this term was used only as a relic of the earlier tradition.

The Tariff shows that so-called 'slave-veterans' had a special position among other slaves. Taxes on them were half of those on other slaves. The difference in taxes must to some extent reflect a difference in their price. Based on Shtaermann (see *Dig.*, XXI, 1, 65, 2 and XXI, 1, 37; Staermann, Trofimova 1971: 243–4) we can assume that in Palmyra slave-veterans were slaves who had some sort of administrative job in the household of their owners or had been educated in the liberal arts. These slaves were cheaper because it was much harder for them to adjust to a new position in the household of a different owner.

The Tariff does not have comprehensive data on the conditions of slaves. Additional information is found in one of the other inscriptions (*Inv.* XI, 13), a dedication on behalf of a slave (טליא) 'for the health' of himself and the sons of his lord (Shifman 1974). This inscription shows that slaves in Palmyra could use money and make dedications on their own behalf.

Data on free persons in the Palmyrene Tariff is quite ambiguous. However, on the basis of it we can still imagine rich trade people sending caravans for precious foreign goods and owning large enterprises in Palmyra (numerous caravan inscriptions also support this), craftsmen in smaller local

---

[29] M.I. Rostovtzeff (1932b: 76) is probably right when he writes that the Palmyrenes accepted the tax system that existed among the Seleucids.

craft shops, shopkeepers and pedlars, rich stockmen and landowners organizing their households in Palmyra, as well as the urban poor. It is interesting that Shabbat 21b imagines Palmyrenes as collecting kindling on the streets in order to survive. Probably, the social structure of Palmyrene society was not too much different from the structure of other Mediterranean societies of that time.

The Palmyrene Tariff has brought to our attention the effects of social conflicts in Palmyra. Significant attention is given to conflicts between merchants and tax farmers. Both the introduction to the edict of Mucianus (II, 2, 25–8) and the decree of the council (I, 7–8 and 19–20) talk about them. Thus, tax adjustments in AD 68–9 and in 137 were supposed to meet the requirements of merchants and to eliminate the causes for their complaints.

Numerous references in the edict of Mucianus to the agreement made in Palmyra concerning tax show that various strata of society (who were interested in changes to the tax system) had made their demands. These demands were discussed and considered for further resolution. The Palmyrene Tax Tariff, as we have examined it, regulates tax-collecting in Palmyra: taxes for import and export of goods, for selling them and for different occupations that bring in a steady income. Based on the fact that taxes were regulated by local laws (or by the decisions of Roman administrators with regard to Palmyra), it is clear that taxes brought income to the city. We have to leave one question unanswered, whether any percentage of this income went to the Roman government; the Tariff itself does not contain any explicit or implicit references to this issue.[30]

Just as in the Near East in general, Palmyra had a system of tax farming. Numerous sources show that tax farmers (tax collectors) evoked the hatred of the population. In the New Testament tax collectors are treated as inveterate sinners and even fellowship with them is inadmissible for a righteous person or one who pursues righteousness and holiness. When the gospel writers want to emphasize that Jesus Christ does not disdain and is willing to convert even the

---

30 M.I. Rostovtzeff (1899: 94–6) supposes that a portion from the taxation in Palmyra went into the imperial treasury. He explains that in the Tariff there are references to the orders of Germanicus and Corbulo, to the precedent set by Kilix and to the jurisdiction over tax farming of the emperor's official (whom he considers, after Dessau, as *praepositus stationis*). We believe that all these facts just show the legal status of Palmyra.

worst sinners, they use tax collectors as examples. When they want to emphasize the hypocrisy of Pharisaic 'holiness', they contrast them with the tax collector who is a repentant sinner. When Jesus wants to teach his disciples that it is not enough just to follow general moral norms, he says that even tax collectors do that much. A person who strives for truth and perfection must demand much more from himself. Such a reputation of tax collectors is not surprising: people paying taxes had to deal with the tax collectors and they experienced all sorts of oppression from them, supported by authority, to say nothing of the fact that taxes were too high.

The Palmyrene Tariff enables us to imagine a tax farmer at his work. His rights and duties were regulated by a contract which, as the decree of the council (from the 130s AD) shows, was made with the local magistrates. Prior to this the procedure was probably the same. The edict of Mucianus (II, 2, 26–30) mentions tax which was farmed 'in it', namely in Palmyra, by a person named Alkimos. This shows that Alkimos made a contract of farming with the authorities in Palmyra. The title of the 'old law' (II, 2, 15) tells us about another contract which was probably made in the late decades of the first century AD 'before, in the presence of' Marinus, a governor of Syria. It is interesting that nothing is said about the contract being made *with* the governor; the latter probably functioned as an enforcing authority; however, in both cases the size of a tax and the procedure of its collecting are regulated by the Roman administration. In the law of 137 there is no reference to the Roman administration's involvement in the life of the city. Contracts between the city and tax farmers served as the basic taxation law. Contracts between tax farmers and the city set, more or less, the items to be taxed and the size of the tax, as well as the procedure for resolving disputes between tax farmers and taxpayers. Among these resolutions that are a part of the 'old law', republished in 137, there are fines for failure to pay salt tax (II, 2, 21 and III, 3, 32–3) and the rights of a tax-farmer to take pledges from non-payers and to sell them after three days (III, 3, 38–45). All the disputes concerning payments had to be resolved by a *dikaiodotēs* (δικαιοδότης), a Roman official in Palmyra (III, 3, 34–7). A striking illustration of this is this formula: δικαιοδο[τείσ]θω παρὰ τῷ ἐν Παλμύροις τεταγμένῳ.

The Tariff does not say what percentage of tax goes to the tax farmer.

The decree of the Palmyrene council was the basis for the Palmyrene Tariff composed in 137. It describes a typical Hellenistic city which is controlled by the council. The council makes all the important decisions that concern the life of the city (without the calling of a popular assembly). At the same time we cannot deny that the Palmyrene popular assembly was functioning at that period (though there is no information about it). One thing is clear, that questions of taxation were outside its competence. The council was governed by a *proedros* (chairman) and by a *grammateus* (secretary).

Two archons headed the system of magistrates in Palmyra. They and the council of *dekaprōtoi* were responsible for all practical steps in composing and publishing the text of the law. Archons, *dekaprotōi* and the council of syndics were responsible for maintaining the law. This data helps us to see the system of rights and responsibilities of particular magistrates.

The Palmyrene Tax Tariff also gives us an opportunity to see the changes in the political status of Palmyra within the Province of Syria.

In 68–9 taxes were collected according to the edict of Mucianus, although local laws and resolutions would be taken into consideration, as well as the contract of tax farming made by Alkimos, presumably with the local authority. The direct involvement of the Roman administrator in the city's finances shows that the city council in Palmyra at that time had, if not rights, then at least the possibility of enacting legal decrees in the financial sphere. It is no coincidence that the edict of Mucianus contains references to the rescripts of Germanicus and Corbulo. Perhaps, by the first half of the first century AD the Roman government in Syria set uniform principles, eliminating, or trying to eliminate, local legal initiative. The above information does not contradict the fact that Mucianus functions as an arbiter between tax farmers and taxpayers: according to the 'decree', three-quarters of a century later this function was fulfilled by the Palmyrene council.

At the beginning of the second century, according to the 'old law', this situation has not changed. The contract of tax farming was made 'before' a governor, which means that he regulated the main points and set the context. It is significant that the *dikaiodotēs* had to resolve disputes between tax-farmers and taxpayers. Whatever the reason behind this measure (we think that this action was undertaken because tax-farmers were people who were not subordinate to the Palmyrene local government), it limited Palmyrene sovereignty.

Only after Hadrian's visitation of Palmyra in the 130s AD were the rights of local government broadened and the direct involvement of the Roman

Introduction

administration in the city's affairs was eliminated. The Palmyrene Tariff is a monument to Hadrian's beneficial policy towards Syrian cities.

The Palmyrene Tax Tariff gives us an idea of Palmyrene law and its development. Analysing the term רחק, 'alienate', used in some Palmyrene inscriptions and the formulae of tomb inscriptions that mirror business documents, we can assume that the local Palmyrene legal tradition derives from the same tradition as that of Elephantine, i.e. the law that was dominant in the Achaemenid Empire (Shifman 1965b: 100–13). The Palmyrene Tariff adds to this point another. According to its structure it presents a chain: the 'old law' is attached mechanically to the 'new' resolutions. It contains even earlier resolutions, the edict of Mucianus. The structure recalls (apart from the narrative elements) the biblical Pentateuch. In other words, the methods of legal procedure of the Palmyrene council correspond with the methods and forms typical of countries in the Near East and the Mediterranean (at least of the first half of the first millennium BC).

Another significant aspect of the legal system in Palmyra is that the legal initiative before the 130s AD comes in fact from the Romans.

Finally, the third significant fact is the penetration of Greek formulae into Palmyrene administrative practice.

All of these facts show the provincial character of Syria in the time of the Principate, which created the basis for the appearance of the legal school of Berytus and the Syrian code of law in the fifth century (a fusion of local, Near Eastern, Greek [Hellenistic] and Roman legal traditions).

Finally, it is precisely from the Palmyrene Tariff that we learn about the existence in the local divine pantheon of the god of the world beyond, Rabasīrē (I, 11, and Aramaic 23). The other world, as is clear from the name of this deity, is a place where the dead abide as in captivity and Rabasīrē reigns over them.

It stands to reason that the Palmyrene Tariff does not shed full light on life in Palmyrene society at the time of the Principate. A more thorough view can be presented by studying all the narrative, epigraphic and other materials related to the city. Nevertheless, the study of the Tariff is very significant for everyone who wants to imagine a provincial city of the Antonine period or everyday life in Roman Syria in the first half of the second century AD or the operation of Roman and local government. Thus, the Palmyrene Tariff is very significant as a historical document.

Text of the Palmyrene Tariff[1]

Dating Formula

[Greek Heading (above Panels II–III)]

1 ['Επὶ Αὐτοκράτορος Καίσαρος θεοῦ Τραιανοῦ Παρθι]κοῦ υἱο[ῦ, θε]ο[ῦ Νέρουα υἰωνοῦ Τραιανοῦ Ἀδριανοῦ Σεβαστοῦ, ἀρχιερέως μεγίστου, δημαρχικῆς ἐξουσίας]

2 [τὸ κα΄, αὐτοκράτορος τὸ β΄, ὑπ]άτου τὸ γ΄, π[ατ]ρὸς πατρίδος, ὑπάτ[ων Λουκίου Αἰλίου Καίσαρος τὸ β΄, Πουβλίου Κοιλίου Βαλβίνου].

Panel I

[Decree of the Council]

1 [Ἔτ]ους ημυ΄ μηνὸς Ξανδικοῦ ιη΄. Δόγμα βουλῆς.

2 Ἐπὶ Βωννέους Βωννέους τοῦ Αἰράνου προέδρου, Ἀλεξάνδρου Ἀλεξάνδρου τοῦ

3 Φιλοπάτορος γραμματέως βουλῆς καὶ δήμου, Μαλίχου Ὀλαιοῦς καὶ Ζεβείδου Νεσᾶ ἀρχόν-

4 των, βουλῆ[ς] νομίμου ἀγομένης, ἐψηφίσθη τὰ ὑποτεταγμένα. Ἐπειδὴ [ἐν το]ῖς πάλαι χρόνοις

5 ἐν τῷ τε[λω]νικῷ νόμῳ πλεῖστα τῶν ὑποτελῶν οὐκ ἀνελήμφθη, ἐπράσ[σετο] δ[ὲ ἐ]κ συνηθείας, ἐν-

6 γραφομέ[νου] τῇ μισθώσει τὸν τελωνοῦντα τὴν πρᾶξιν ποιεῖσθει ἀκολούθ[ω]ς τῷ νόμῳ καὶ τῇ

7 συνηθείᾳ, συνέβαινεν δὲ πλειστάκις περὶ τούτου ζητήσεις γείνεσθ[αι με]ταξὺ τῶν ἐνπόρων

8 πρὸς τοὺς τελώνας· δεδόχθαι τοὺς ἐνεστῶτας ἄρχοντας καὶ δ[εκα]πρώτους διακρείνοντας

9 τὰ μὴ ἀνειλημμένα τῷ νόμῳ ἐνγράψαι τῇ ἔνγιστα μισθώσει καὶ ὑποτ[ά]ξαι

---

1 The text here is as in Shifman, though with corrections of evident minor errors. Supplementary subheadings have been added in square brackets, in part referring to Healey 2009 (see Foreword). In Panels III and IV the indentations in the layout of the Greek, indicated in *CIS* but represented by Shifman only in the form of capital letters for new sentences, have been inserted as appropriate.

The Palmyrene Tax Tariff

ἑκάστῳ εἴδει τὸ
10 ἐκ συνηθείας τέλος, καὶ ἐπειδὰν κυρωθῇ τῷ μισθουμένῳ, ἐνγραφῆναι μετὰ τοῦ πρώτου νό-
11 μου στήλῃ λιθίνῃ τῇ οὔσῃ ἀντικρὺς ἱερ[οῦ] λεγομένου Ῥαβασείρῃ, ἐπιμελεῖσθαι δὲ τοὺς τυγχά-
12 νοντας κατὰ καιρὸν ἄρχοντας καὶ δεκαπρώτους καὶ συνδίκο[υς τοῦ] μηδὲν παραπράσσειν
13 τὸν μισθούμενον.

[Healey 2009: Aramaic i: 1–13 with Greek inserted]

14 דגמא די בולא בירח ניסן יום 18 שנת 448 בפלהדרותא די בונא בר
15 בונא בר חירן וגרמטיא די אלכסדרס בר אלכסדרס בר פלפטר גרמטוס די בולא ודמס וארכוניא
16 מלכו בר עליי בר מקימו וזבידא בר נשא כד הות בולא כנישא מן נמוסא אשרת
17 מדי כתיב מן לתחת בדיל די בזבניא קדמיא בנמוסא די מכסא עבידן שגין חיבן
18 מכסא לא אסקו והוו מתגבין מן עידא במדען די הוא מתכתב באגוריא די
19 מכסא ו{ו}הוא גבא היך בנמוסא ובעידא ומטלקות זבנין שגין על צבותא אלן
20 סרבנין הוו ביני תגרא לביני מכסיא אתחזי לבולא די ארכוניא אלן ו{ל{עשרתא
21 די{ יבנ}ו{ן מדעם די לא מסק בנמוסא ויכתב בשטר אגריא חדתא ויכתב למדעמא
22 מדעמא מכסה די מן עידא ומדי אשר לאגורא וכתב עם נמוסא קדמיא בגללא
23 די לקבל היכלא די רבאסירא ויהוא מבטל לארכוניא די הון בזבן ועשרתא
24 וסדקיא די לא יהוא גבא אגורא מן אנש מדעם יתיר
25 Γόμος καρρικὸς παντὸς γένους· τεσσάρων γόμων καμηλικῶν τέ-
26 λος ἐπράχθη
טעון קרס די כלמא גנס כלה לארבעא טעונין די גמלין
27 מכסא גבי

Panel II

[Aramaic Heading at the top of Panel ii: Healey Aramaic Heading, line 1]

נמוסא די מכסא די למנא די הדרינא תדמר ועינתא די מיא [די אי]לס קיסר

Column 1

[Healey Aramaic ii a: 2–50]

1 מן מעלי עלימיא די מתאעלין לתדמר
2 או לתחומיה [יגבא מכס]א לכל רגל ד 22

Text of the Inscription

3 מן עלם די י[ז]ב[ן] ב[מדי]ת[א]‏ או י[פ]ק [ד] 12
4 מן עלם וטר[ן] די יזבן [במדיתא] ד 10
5 והן זבונא יפק עלי[מ]ין יתן לכל רגלי [ד] 12
6 הו מ[ן]כסא יג[ב]א [מ]ן טעון גמלא די יבי[ן]שי[ן]
7 למעלנא [לכלמא] די טעון גמלא ד [3]
8 מן [טעון גמלא] [למ]פקנא] ד 3
9 מן ט[עון] חמרא למעלנא ו[למפקנא ד 2]
10 מן א[ר]ג[ו]נא מלטא לכל מ[שך למעלנא]
11 ולמ[פ]קנא אסרין 8
12 מן טע[ון] ג[מ]ל[א] די משחא בשימא [די]
13 מתאעל [ב]ש[טיפ]י ד 25
14 ולמא ד[י] יפק משח[א] דנה
15 למפקנ[א] מן טעון] גמל לטעונא ד 13
16 מן טעון גמלא די [מ]שחא בשימא [די יתאעל]
17 בזקי[ן] די ע[ז] ל[מ]על[נ]א ד 13 ולמפק[נ]א ד 7
18 מן ט[עון חמר די] משחא [בשימא ד]י יתאעל
19 ב[שטיפ]י [ד] 13 ולמפקנא ד 7
20 מן טעון חמר [ד]י משחא ב[שי]מא די
21 יתאעל בזקי[ן] די ע[ז] ד 7 [ולמ]פקנא ד 4
22 מן טעון די מש[חא] די בזקי[ן] ארבע
23 די עז למעל[ן] טעון ג[מ]לא ד 13
24 ולמפקנא ד [3]1
25 מן טעון די מש[חא] די בזקין תרתן די עז
26 למעל[ן] ט[עו]נ[א] די גמלא ד [7] ולמפקנא ד [7]
27 מן טעו[ן] חמר די משח למע[ל]נא] ד ול<מ>פקנא [ד 7]
28 מן טעון דהנא די בזקין א[ר]ב[ע] די עז די
29 טעון גמל <ל>מעלנא ד 13 ול[מ]פק[נ]א ד 13
30 מן טעון דהנא די בזקין תרת[ן] די] עז
31 לטעון גמל למעלנא ד 7 ולמ[פ]קנא ד 7
32 מן טעון [דה]נא די חמר למעלנא ד 7 ולמפקנא ד 7
33 מן טעון נ[וני]א מליחיא לטעונא די [גמלא]
34 [למע]לנ[א] ד 10 ומן מפק מנהון [יגבא מכסא ד]...
35 [מן טעון]..א לטעונא די גמלא למ[עלנא ולמפקנא]...
36 [מן טעון]..א די טעון חמרא למעלנא] ד...
37 [ולמפק]נא יגבא מכסא ד 3
38 מן [מעלי סוס]י[א] ד 10 ולכוד]נ[א] ד 10

39 .... ל מן ..... אמ[רי]א..
40 .... יא ..... [אס]רין 2
41 מ[ן גדיא די] אמריא למע[לן ולמפקן] לרשא חד אסרא חד
42 מן [חור]א גמלא א[סרי]ן 3
43 מן .. [עז]א רבא [יגבא מכסא א]סרין 2
44 מן [עת]ו[ד]א מ[כ]סא אסר]א חד
45 אף [י]ג[ב]א מכ[סא לכל יר]ח מן די יהוא מזבן משחא
46 בשימא אסרין 2 ✳ אף יגבא מכסא מן זניתא מן
47 מן די שקלא דינר [או] יתיר דנרא חד מן אתתא
48 ומן מן די שקלא אסרין תמניא
49 יגבא אסרין תמניא

Column 2

[Healey Aramaic ii b: 51–99]

1 ומן מן די שקל[א] [אסרי]ן ש[תא]
2 יגבא אסרין [ש]ת[א]
3 אף יגבא מכ[סא מן ארגסטר]יו[ן] ופטפלי
4 [ואשכ]יפא [ומן] ח[ט]א היך עדתא
5 [לכל] יר[ח] מן חנותא ד 1
6 [מן כ]ל משך די [י]תאעל או יזבן למשכא אסרין 2
7 [מזבנ]י נחתיא די הפכין במדיתא יהן מוט מכסא
8 [לתש]מ[יש עינן תרתן די מ]י] די במדיתא ד 800
9 [י]גבא מכסא לטעונא די חטא וחמרא ותבנא
10 ו[כ]ל מדי דמא [להון לכ]ל גמל לארח חדא ד 1
11 לגמלא כדי יתאיעל סריק יגבא ד 1
12 היך [די] גב[א] קלקיס בר חרי קיסר
13 נמ[ו]סא די מכ[ס]א די תדמר ועינתא די מיא
14 ומל[חא ד]י ב[מ]דיתא ותחומיה היך
15 א[גור]יא [ד]י א[ת]אגר קדם מרינס היגמונא
16 מ[ן יבישין] לכ[ל] טעון די גמל מעלן ד 4 ולמפקן ד 4
17 מ[ן א]ר[גונא] מלטא לכל משך למעלנא ד 4 ולמפקנא ד 4
18 אף יגבא [מכס]א מן גנסיא כלהון היך די כתיב מן לעל
19 [מל]ח טב [יתג]בא אסרא חד למדיא די קסטון
20 עשר ו[ש]ת [ו]מא די יתבעא יתן [לה]ן לתשמישא
21 ו[די] לא י[כל י]פרע לכל מדא מן נמ[וס]א דנה סטטרטין [תר]ן

100

Text of the Inscription

22 מן די יהוא לה מלח בתד[מר או בתחו]מא ד[י]
23 ת[ד]מרי[א] יכילנה ל[מסכ]א [א]פ[י] מדיא באסרא חד
24 מ[ן] די אקם [לקניס מ]קינ[ס] גיס [ל]היגמונא
25 [על] חשבן מכ[ס סרבן הוא] ביני תדמריא ל[ביני]
26 [ס]ק[ו]ת מכסי[א א]ק[י]מ[ת די ... מ]כסא
27 חיב למהוא [הי]ך מכ[ס די] אגר בה
28 אלקמס וח[ברה היך] נמוסא מדעם להן
29 משתתף ומ....א די ... יהוא
30 פרע למכסא מן די מעל רגלין לתדמר
31 [א]ו[ן לתח]ומ[י]ה ומפק לכל רגלי ד 22
32 ו[מ]ן [די מ]זבן רגלין ומ[פ]ק יפרע למכ[סא] ד 12
33 ו[מ]ן [די י]זבן על[ם] וטרן יפרע ד [10]
34 ... [רגל ע]מ[י]א דנה ......
35 ו[ד]י מעל.. [י]פרע[] הו ד 10 ומפק [ד] 12
36 .... מן די מפק עלם וטרן
37 ..חשב..... [היך די] כתיב בנמוסא
38 [מ]ן] די יז[בן] ..... יפרע ד 9
39 ו[די מ]פק ..... לא כתיב בדיל [די]
40 מדעם לא א...א וכ..........
41 לא דמיא .... י....
42 ומעלן מכ......ב......י מ...
43 ודי עמרא ....סא די אף מ....
44 תדמ[ר] ל[מ]כ[ס .... פרעא תהוא עמרא
45 די איט[לי]א ..... מכסא למפפקנא בתר
46 כות הוו ספו[ן] ..... לא עמרא איטליק[א]
47 [ת]הוא פרעא [מכ]ס[א] למפק<נ>א
48 משחא ב[שימא די] בזקין די עז יהוא מכסא
49 מת[ג]בא היך נמוס[א] בדיל די בטעון די

Column 3

[Healey Aramaic ii c: 100–148]

1 כתב די טעא מכס[א] ... בל.........
2 כ..ש ובנמוסא רציף ד 13
3 מכסא די קצבא אפי דנר חיב
4 למתחשבו היך די אף גרמנקוס קיסר

5 באגרתא די כתב לסטטילס פשק די

6 הא כשר די[יה]ן מכסיא אפי אסר איטלק[ון]

7 גבן ומדי גו מן דנר חיב מכסא היך

8 עדתא ע[ר]פן יהוא גבא

9 פגרין די משתדן מכס לא חיבין

10 לטעמתא הי‹ך› בנמ[ו]סא לטעונא אקימת

11 די יהוא מתג[ב]א דנר

12 מדי יהוא מת[אע]ל בר מן תחומא או מאפק

13 מן די מפק ל[קרי]א [או מ]אעל מן קריא

14 מכס לא חיב היך די אף הוו ספון

15 אסטרביליא ומדי דמא להון אתחזי די

16 לכל די עלל לחשבן תגרא יהוא מכסא

17 היך ליביש היך די הוא אף במדינתא

18 אחרניתא

19 גמליא הן טענין והן סריקין יהן

20 מתאעלין בר מן תחומא חיב כל

21 גמל דנר היך בנמוסא והיך די אשר

22 קרבלון כשירא באגרתא די כתב לברברס

23 על גלדיא די גמלי[א] אף אלן כפרו די מכס

24 לא גבן עשב[י]א ו[נת]ירתא אתחזי די יהון

25 יהבין מכ[סא] בדיל די אית בהון תגרתא

26 מכסא די עלימתא היך די נמוסא מוחא פשקת

27 [ה]ן מכסא יג[ב]א מכ[סא] מן עלימתא די שקלן דנר

28 או יתיר לאת[נ]א דנ[ר] והן חסיר תהוה שקלא

29 מדי הי שקלא [יגבא על] צלמי נחשא אדרטיא

30 אתחזי די יתגב[ון] היך [נח]שא ויהוא פרע צלם

31 בפלגות [טעו]ן וצלמין תרן טעון על מלחא

32 קשט[א א]תחזי לי באתר די דמס תהוא

33 מתזבנא באתר די מתכנשין ומן מן תדמריא

34 יזבן לחש[חת]ה יהוא יהב למדיא אסר איטלק[ון]

35 היך בנמוסא ואף מכסא [מ]לחא די הויא

36 בתדמר היך בה[ו]ן נמוס[א] אפי אסר יהוא

37 מתקבל ול[תדמרי]א יהוא מזבן היך עידא

38 .... [מכ]סא די ארגונא בדיל די

39 .... ארבעא ופלג...ב..

40 ..[מזבני נחתיא די] מ[ה]מ[ה]לכין ב[מד]ית‹א› וחיטא

Text of the Inscription

41 ד די יהוא........................
42 א..................... יהוא מתגבא
43 מכסא היך די כ[תיב מן ל[על ⸗ למעלן שלחא
44 אסרין 2 אשל[א יהוא] מתגבא ול{מ}מפקנא
45 לטעונ[א יגב]א [היך די א]ף הוו ספון
46 ענא ת[ה]ו[]א מ[תאעלא מ]ן בר] מן תחומא אף הן
47 [למגז תהוא מת]אעלא מכסא חיבא והן לגו מן
48 [תחומא תהוא] מתאעלא למדיתא למגז מכס לא חיב[א]
49 מ............נותא ומן די < > היך <ד>י הון הון

Line under the three Aramaic columns

[Healey Aramaic line 149]

[ס]פון מכסא .. [יתגב]א היך בנמוסא דנר מתגבא [אף] מן .... מ[די] פרע מכסא לא יהוא
מתגבא אלא לענ<א> די תהוא מאעלא ל]גו מן תחום] תדמר אן יצבא מכסא <למחתם> יהוא
[שביק]א לה

Panel III

Column 1

1	Παρὰ τ[ῶν παῖδας εἰς Παλμύρους]	
2	ἢ εἰς τὰ ὅ[ρια Παλμυρηνῶν εἰσ-]	
3	αγόντω[ν πράξει ἑκάστου σώματος	X κβ´.]
4	Παρ' οὗ δ[ὲ παῖδας ἐν τῇ πόλει πωλεῖ ἢ]	
5	μι[... ἐξάγει ἕκαστ]ου σ[ώματος	X ιβ´.]
6	Παρ' οὗ [δὲ σώματ]α οὐετραν[ὰ πωλεῖ	X ι´.]
7	Κἂν τὰ σώμα[τα ὑπ]ὸ το[ῦ πριαμένου ἐξ-]	
8	άγηται ἑκάστου σώμα[τος διδότω	X ιβ´.]
9	Ὁ αὐτὸς δημοσιώνη[ς ξηροφόρτου]	
10	πράξει ἑκάστου γόμο[υ καμηλικοῦ]	
11	εἰσκομισ[θέ]ντος	[X γ´.]
12	Ἐκκομισθ[έντ]ος [γόμου καμηλικοῦ]	
13	ἑκάστου	[X γ´.]
14	Γόμου ὀνικ[οῦ ἑκάστο]υ εἰ[σκομισθέντος	X β´.]

The Palmyrene Tax Tariff

15 ἐκκομισθέν[τος] ✗ β΄.]
16 Πορφύρας μηλωτῆ[ς], ἑκά[στου δέρμα-]
17 τος εἰσκομισθέν[τ]ος [πράξει ἀσσάρια η΄.]
18 Ἐκκομισθ[έντο]ς [ἀσσάρια η΄.]
19 Γόμου κ[αμηλικοῦ] μύρου [τοῦ ἐν ἀλαβάσ-]
20 τροις ε[ἰσκομισθέντος πράξει ✗ κε΄.]
21 Καὶ το[ῦ γόμου καμηλικοῦ μύρου τοῦ ἐν ἀλαβάστροις]
22 ἐκ[κομισθέντος πράξει ✗ ιγ΄.]
23 Γ[όμου καμηλικοῦ μύρου τοῦ ἐν ἀσκοις]
24 αἰγείοις [εἰσκομισθέντος πράξει ✗ ιγ΄.]
25 [Ἐκ]κ[ομισθέντος ✗ ζ΄.]
26 [Γόμου ὀνικοῦ μύ]ρου τοῦ ἐ[ν ἀλαβάστροις]
27 εἰσ[κομισ]θέν[τος] πράξει ✗ ιγ΄.]
28 [Ἐκκομισ]θέν[τος ✗ ζ΄.]
29 Γόμου ὀνικοῦ μ[ύρου τοῦ ἐν ἀσκοῖς]
30 αἰγείοις εἰσκομ[ισθέντο]ς πρ[άξει ✗ ζ΄.]
31 Ἐκκομισθέντος π[ρ]άξ[ει ✗ δ΄.]
32 Γόμου ἐλεηροῦ το[ῦ ἐν ἀσκο]ῖς [τέσσαρ-]
33 σι αἰγείοις ἐπὶ καμήλ[ου εἰσκομισθέν-]
34 τος [✗ ιγ΄.]
35 Ἐκκομισθέντο[ς ✗ ιγ΄.]
36 Γόμου ἐλαιηροῦ τοῦ ἐ[ν ἀσκοῖς δυσὶ αἰ-]
37 γείοις ἐπὶ καμήλ[ου εἰσκομισθέντος]
38 πράξει [✗ ζ΄.]
39 Ἐκκομισθέντο[ς ✗ ζ΄.]
40 Γόμου ἐλε[ηροῦ τοῦ ἐπ' ὄνο]υ ε[ἰσκομισθέν-]
41 τος π[ράξει ✗ ζ΄.]
42 Ἐκ[κομισθέντος ✗ ζ΄.]
43 Γόμ[ου καύσεως τοῦ ἐν ἀσκοῖς τ]έσσ[αρσι]
44 αἰγείοις [εἰσκομισθέντος πρά]ξει [✗ ιγ΄.]
45 Ἐκκομι[σ]θέ[ντος] ✗ ιγ΄.
46 Γόμου κ[αύσεως τοῦ ἐν] ἀ[σ]κοῖς δυσὶ αἰγείοις
47 ἐπὶ κ[αμήλου εἰσ]κομισθέντος πράξει ✗ ζ΄.

Text of the Inscription

Column 2

1 ['Εκκομισ]θέντος [✳ ζ´.]
2 [Γόμου ὀ]ν[ικοῦ καύσεως εἰσκο-
3   μισθέντος πράξει ✳ ζ´.]
4 ['Εκκομισθ]έν[τος ✳ ζ´.]
5 ......ο.κου...........
6 ['Εκκ]ο[μισθέντ]ο[ς πράξ]ει [✳ ι´.]
7–16 *not preserved*
17 ....φο.............
18
19 ....σ........
20 ....λλησ....
21 [κα]μήλου το......κης ......
22 [θ]ρέμματος .εσ...ενου
23 ....δ.........θ....
24 ..νκαδ..[τ]εθυμένη........
25 Ὁ αὐτὸς δ[η]μοσιώνης ἑκάσ[του] μη[νὸς]
26   παρ᾿ ἑκ[άστο]υ τῶ[ν τὸ] ἔλαιον κατα...
27   π.ον......ις [πωλού]ντων [ἀσσάρια β´.]
28 Ὁ αὐτ[ὸς δημοσιώνης] πρά[ξει ἐν τῇ πό]λει
29   [ἐκ τῶν ἑταιρ]ῶν ὅσαι [δηνάριον ἢ πλέ-]
30   [ον λαμβά]νουσιν π[ράξει δηνάριον, ὅσαι
31   δὲ ἔλαβον ἀ]σσάρια ὀκτὼ [πράξει   ἀσσαρι]α η´,
32   [ὅσαι δὲ ἀσ]σάρια ἓξ ἔ[λαβον ἑ]καστ[ης πράξει] ασσ<άρια> ς´.
33 [Ὁ αὐτὸς δημ]οσιώνης πρ[άξ]ει ἐργαστηρίων
34   [ῥαφιδικῶν] παντοπωλ[ικ]ῶν σκυτικῶν
35   [τὸ τέλο]ς ἐκ συνηθείας ἑκάστου μηνὸς
36   καὶ ἐργαστηρίου ἑκάστου ✳ α´.
37 Παρὰ τῶν δέρματα εἰσκομιζόντ[ων ἢ πω-]
38   λούντων ἑκάστου δέρματος ἀσσά[ρια β´.]
39 Ὁμοίως ἱματιοπῶλαι μεταβόλοι πωλ[οῦν-]
40   τες ἐν τῇ πόλει τῷ δημοσιώνῃ τὸ ἱκανὸν ποιεῖ[ν.]
41 Χρήσεος πηγῶν β´ ἑκάστου ἔτους ✳ ω´.
42 Ὁ αὐτὸς <δημοσιώνης> πρά[ξ]ει γόμου πυρικοῦ οἰνικοῦ ἀχύ-
43   ρων καὶ τοιούτου γένους ἑκάστου γόμου

The Palmyrene Tax Tariff

44   καμηλικοῦ καθ᾽ ὁδὸν ἑκάστην   ☧ α´.

45 Καμήλου ὃς κενὸς εἰσαχθῇ πράξει   ☧ α´.

46   καθὼς Κίλιξ Καίσαρος ἀπελεύθερος ἔπραξεν.

Column 3

1   ....

2   πο......................

3   τῆς γ......................

4   κο......................

5

6

7   σ..........................

8   πορφ......................

9   .....εκ........................

10–20 *not preserved*

21 ....μ..η.γο............

22 ....[γ]εινέτω

23 Ὃς δ᾽ ἂν ἅλα[ς ἔχ]ῃ ἐν Παλμύροις ἢ [ἐν ὅροις]

24   Παλμυρη[ν]ῶν παραμετρησάτω [τῷ δημο-]

25   σιώνῃ ε[ἰς ἕκ]αστον μόδιον, ἀσσά[ριον·]

26   ὃς δ᾽ ἂν οὐ ....ν παραμετρήσ[ῃ] ......

27   ση ἔχων το ..... δημο[σιών]....

28 Παρ᾽ οὗ ἂν ὁ δ[ημοσι]ώνης .... [ἐνέ-]

29   χυρα λά[βῃ]....................

30   ἀποδο[θῶ]σιν ο.............αβρει

31   δημο[σιώνῃ] τοῦ διπ[λοῦ] τὸ ἱκανὸν λαμβα-

32   νέτω· περὶ τ[ο]ύτου πρὸς τὸν δημοσιώνην

33   τοῦ διπλοῦ ε[ἰσα]γέσθω

34 Περὶ οὗ ἂν ὁ δημ[ο]σιώνης τινὰ ἀπαιτῇ, περί τε

35   οὗ ἂν ὁ δημοσιώ[νης ἀ]πό τινος ἀπαιτῆται, περὶ

36   τούτου δικαιοδο[τείσ]θω παρὰ τῷ ἐν Παλμύ-

37   ροις τεταγμένῳ.

38 Τῷ δημοσιώνῃ κύρι[ον] ἔ[σ]τω παρὰ τῶν μὴ ἀπο-

39   λ[υόντων ἐν]έχυρα [λ]α[μβάνει]ν δι᾽ ἑαυτοῦ ἢ δι[ὰ

40   τῶν ὑπη]ρ[ετῶν· κἂν τα]ῦτα τὰ [ἐνέ]χυρα ἡμέραις

Text of the Inscription

41 [τρισίν μὴ λυθῇ, ἐξέστω τῷ δημ]οσιώνῃ πωλεῖν
42 [τοιαῦτα τὰ ἐνέχυρα ἐν τόπῳ δημ]οσίῳ χωρὶς
43 δόλου πο[νηροῦ] ....ωλ..... ἐπράθη
44 ἢ δοθῆναι ἔδει π[ράσσ]ειν τῷ δη[μοσιώνῃ] καθὼς
45 καὶ .....στιν...... τοῦ νόμου [ἐξέσ]τω
46 Λιμένος Π[αλμύρων καὶ πη]γῶν ὑδάτων Καίσαρος
47 τῷ μισθωτῇ ......εντος .... παρασχέσ[θαι]

Panel IV

Column 1

1 ἄλλῳ μηδενὶ πράσσειν διδόναι λαμ[βάνειν]
2 ἐξέστω μήτε τι..ε....νωφο. ἀνθρ[ωπ.. μή-]
3 τε τινὶ [ὀν]όματι τὸ στ....οε..υπ......ν
4 τούτων εἰ ποιήσῃ ἢ ε.......... [πραχ-
5 θήτω τὸ] διπλοῦν..................
6 ....ητε..................οι..
7
8 κ...............................
9 κα.........................
10 Γαῖο[ς Λικίνιος Μουκιανὸς πρεσβευτὴς καὶ]
11 ἀντι[στρατηγὸς λέγει]..............
12 μεταξὺ Παλ[μυρηνῶν πρὸς τοὺς τελώνας]
13 γνούς ἐστι ....
14 γείνεσθαι καθ᾽ οἱ...................
15 εὐ....σατο μ.....................
16 ......οσα δὲ ἐξ....................
17 ....ως.
18 Αὐτο[ῖ]ς...τα....λεισπ.............
19 τω[ν τ]α......ωνυ................
20 τῷ τελών[ῃ διδός]θω.
21 Οἳ δ᾽ ἂν ε..α...ασω.... ἐξα[γ]........
22 ....ει........................
23 .εο..............δο...
24 καθ᾽ ἣν ἀναλο...................

The Palmyrene Tax Tariff

25   τοῦ δὲ ἐξαγω......................
26   αδωσε...νο..............
27   ἐρίων................................
28   θαρ................................
29   π...................ειμ..........
30   .ρ..................διαγ..............
31   .....φορον.........ματουμεν......φορι..
32   ....αγωγη........ι Ҳ ϛ´ τοῦ δὲ........ [Ҳ] θ´
33   ἀξιοῦντος το.....νου εἰ καὶ μὴ ... [ἐρίων]
34   [ἰτ]αλικῶν ἐξαγ[ομένω]ν πράσσειν ὕστ[ερον ὡς συν-]
35   εφωνήθη μ[ὴ ἀπὸ τ]ούτων ἐξαγο[μένων τὸ τέλος δί-]
36   δοσθαι.
37 Μύρου τοῦ ἐν ἀσκο[ῖς αἰγεί]οις πρά[ξει ὁ τελώνης]
38   κατὰ τὸν νόμο[ν] .... οὔτε .... ἀμ[άρ-]
39   τημα γέγονεν τῷ προτεθέντι [δ]εῖ κ[αθὼς ἐν τῷ συν-]
40   εσφραγισμένῳ νόμῳ τέτακται.
41   Τὸ τοῦ σφάκτρου τέλος εἰς δηνάριον ὀφείλει λο[γεύεσθαι]
42   καὶ Γερμανικοῦ Καίσαρος διὰ τῆς πρὸς Στατείλι[ον ἐπισ-]
43   τολῆς διασαφήσαντος ὅτι δεῖ πρὸς ἀσσάριον ἰτα[λικὸν]
44   τὰ τέλη λογεύεσθαι· τὸ δὲ ἐντὸς δηναρίου τέλο[ς]
45   συνηθείᾳ ὁ τελώνης πρὸς κέρμα πράξει· τῶ[ν δὲ]
46   διὰ τὸ νεκριμαῖα εἶναι ρειπτουμένων τὸ τέλο[ς οὐκ ὀφείλεται.]
47 Τῶν βρωτῶν τὸ κα<τὰ> τὸν νόμον τοῦ γόμου δην[άριον]
48   εἴστημι πράσσεσθαι ὅταν ἔξωθεν τῶν ὅρων εἰσά[γηται]
49   ἢ ἐξάγηται. Τοὺς δὲ εἰς χωρία ἢ ἀπὸ τῶν [χω-]
50   ρίων κατακομίζοντας ἀτελεῖς εἶναι, ὡς καὶ συνεφώ-
51   νησεν αὐτοῖς. Κώνου καὶ τῶν ὁμοίων ἔδ[ο-]
52   ξεν ὅσα εἰς ἐμπορείαν φέρεται τὸ τέλος εἰς τὸ ξη-
53   ρόφορτον ἀνάγεσθαι, ὡς καὶ ἐν ταῖς λοιπαῖς γείνεται πόλεσι.
54 Καμήλων ἐάν τε κεναὶ ἐάν τε ἔνγομοι εἰσάγωνται ἔξωθεν
55   τῶν ὅρων ὀφείλεται δηνάριον ἑκάστης κατὰ τὸν
56   νόμον ὡς καὶ Κουρβούλων ὁ κράτιστος ἐσημι-
57   ώσατο ἐν τῇ πρὸς Βάρβαρον ἐπιστολῇ.

Text of the Inscription

Column 2

1 ....ρλ.....................
2 ...οι.......νο..........οξη........
3 ἄγεσ[θαι]......τ<α>.......οποστ......
4 .... π[ρ]ος ....
5 ....υσ...π.............
6 [Παρὰ τῶν] ἑταιρῶ[ν αἴ δηνάριον ἢ πλέον λαμβά-
7 νουσιν .. ἑ]κάστης..................α.αν
8 ....εου...................ναλα
9 ....οσ............ [πρ]άσσειν
10 ....τον θ...αν
11 ....ντος ο......
12 ....του....
13 ....ι.......
14
15 ....νιτ...ον....
16 ....μενοιτ.........
17 .ειποι.........................
18 νόμον .τ.......................
19–30 *not preserved*
31 .....πατ.......................
32 ....ω......................
33 ...πας συνφων....................
34 τελώ[ν]ην γείνεσθαι· ἐπει......[τὸ ἐκ τοῦ]
35 νόμο[υ] τέλος πρὸς δηνά[ρ]ιον φ[έρειν.]
36 Ἐννόμιον συνεφωνήθη μὴ δεῖν πράσσε[ιν ἐκτὸς τῶν]
37 τελῶν· [τ]ῶν δὲ ἐπὶ νομὴν μεταγομένων [εἰς Παλ-]
38 μυρηνὴν θρεμμάτων ὀφείλεσθαι· χαρα[κτη-]
39 ρίσασθαι τὰ θρέμματα ἐὰν θέλῃ ὁ δημο[σιώνης]
40 ἐξέστω.

The Palmyrene Tax Tariff

Fragments, *Inv.* X, 143

[Two fragments from the right side of the Greek Heading]

[... Τρ]αιανο[ῦ].........................
[..Καί]σαρος [τὸ β´ Πουβ]λίου Κοιλίο[υ Βαλβίνου]

Translation[1]

Dating Formula

1. [IN THE REIGN OF THE EMPEROR CAESAR TRAIANUS HADRIANUS AUGUSTUS, SON OF THE DIVINE TRAIANUS PARTH]ICUS, [GRANDSON OF THE D]I[VINE NERVA, SUPREME PONTIFF, INVESTED WITH

2. TRIBUNICIAN POWER] FOR THE [21ST TIME, TWICE *IMPERATOR*], THREE TIMES [CON]SUL, *PAT*[*ER*] *PATRIAE,* IN THE CONSU[LSHIPS OF L. AELIUS CAESAR FOR THE SECOND TIME AND PUBLIUS COELIUS BALBINUS].

Panel I

Column 1

1. [IN THE YE]AR 448, ON THE 18TH OF THE MONTH OF XANDIKOS. DECREE OF THE COUNCIL.

2. IN THE TIME OF BŌNNĒS SON OF BŌNNĒS SON OF HAIRANĒS THE *PROEDROS*, ALEXANDROS SON OF ALEXANDROS SON OF

3. PHILOPATŌR, THE *GRAMMATEUS* OF THE COUNCIL AND PEOPLE, MALICHOS SON OF OLAIĒS AND ZEBEIDAS SON OF NESA BEING THE ARCH-

4. ONS, AT A LEGALLY CONSTITUTED MEETING OF THE COUNCI[L], THE FOLLOWING WAS DECREED: SINCE [IN] FORMER TIMES

5. MOST OF THE DUES WERE NOT SET DOWN IN THE TAX LAW BUT WERE EXAC[TED] B[Y C]USTOM, FOR IT WAS WRIT[TEN]

6. INTO THE CONTRACT THAT THE TAX COLLECTOR SHOULD MAKE HIS EXACTION IN ACCORDA[N]CE WITH THE LAW AND

---

[1] Ed.: Small capitals are used for translation of Greek, normal font for Aramaic. Square brackets marking [restorations] are impressionistic rather than precise, having been adapted from the original, into Russian and then into English.

The Palmyrene Tax Tariff

7. WITH CUSTOM, AND BECAUSE OF THAT DISPUTES OFTEN ARO[SE] ON THIS MATTER [BE]TWEEN THE MERCHANTS

8. AND THE TAX COLLECTORS, IT WAS DECIDED THAT THE ARCHONS IN OFFICE AT THE PRESENT TIME AND THE D[EKA]PRŌTOI SHOULD DETERMINE THE THINGS

9. NOT SET DOWN IN THE LAW AND WRITE THEM INTO THE NEXT (TAX) CONTRACT, AND SET F[O]RTH FOR EACH CLASS OF GOODS

10. THE TAX ACCORDING TO CUSTOM; AND THAT, WHEN THEY HAVE BEEN CONFIRMED BY THE ONE WITH WHOM THE CONTRACT IS MADE, THEY SHOULD BE WRITTEN DOWN TOGETHER WITH THE FIRST

11. LAW ON A STONE STELE OPPOSITE THE TEMP[LE] CALLED RABASEIRE; AND THAT

12. THE ARCHONS IN OFFICE AND THE DEKAPRŌTOI AND THE SYNDIC[S] SHOULD TAKE CARE TO SEE [THAT]

13. THE ONE WITH WHOM THE CONTRACT IS MADE DOES NOT EXACT ANYTHING EXTRA.

14. Decree of the Council. In the month of Nisan on the 18th day, in the year 448, during the *proedria* of Bōnā son of

15. Bōnā son of Ḥairan, and the *grammateia* of Alexandros son of Alexandros son of Philopatōr, *grammateus* of the Council and People, the archons being

16. Maliku son of ʿOlayā son of Moqimu and Zebeida son of Nesa, when the Council was assembled in accordance with law, it established

17. what is written below: Since in former times many items subject to

18. tax were not listed in the tax law and were taxed according to custom as was written in the contract, so that the tax collector

19. was collecting according to the law and according to custom, and therefore

20. there were often disputes concerning these things between the merchants and tax collectors, it has been determined by the Council that the said archons and the *dekaprōtoi*

Translation

21. should consider whatever was not listed in the law and it should be written in the new tax contract and there should be written for each

22. item its tax which is according to custom. And after it has been confirmed by the tax farmer it will be written down with the former law on the stele

23. opposite the temple of Rabasīrē. And it is for the archons in office at the time and the *dekaprōtoi*

24. and the syndics to forbid the tax collector to collect anything more from anyone.

25. FOR A WAGON-LOAD OF MERCHANDISE OF ANY KIND, THE TAX IS TO BE EXACTED

26. AT THE RATE OF FOUR CAMEL-LOADS. For a wagon-load of any merchandise,

27. the tax is collected at the rate of four camel-loads.

Panel II

Above the columns

The Tax Law <established> at the market of Hadriana-Palmyra and <at> the water-springs of [Ae]lius Caesar.

Column 1

1. From the importers of slaves imported into Palmyra

2. or into its territories the t[ax collector will collect] 22 *d<enarii>* for each individual.

3. For a slave who will be [so]ld in the [ci]t[y or ex]ported – 12 [*d*].

4. For a vetera[n] slave who will be sold [in the city] – 10 *d*.

5. And if the buyer exports the sla[v]es, he will give [12 *d*] for each individual.

6. The same t[ax collector must col]lect [for] a camel-load of d[ry goods] –

7. For import for [a] camel-load [3 *d*].

8. For a [camel-load] for exp[ort] 3 *d*.

The Palmyrene Tax Tariff

9. For a donkey-lo[ad] for import and [for export 2 *d*].

10. For purple wool, for every fle[ece for import]

11. and ex[po]rt 8 *assarii*.

12. For a cam[el]-lo[ad] of perfumed oil [which]

13. is imported [in] al[abaste]r jars – 25 *d*.

14. And with regard to the fact that this oi[l is exported],

15. for expor[t] for a camel-lo[ad], for a load 13 *d*.

16. For a camel-load of perfumed [o]il [which is imported]

17. in go[at]ski[ns], [for] impor[t] 13 *d* and for expor[t 7 *d*].

18. For a [donkey]-lo[ad] of [perfumed] oil [whi]ch is imported

19. in alaba[ste]r jars 13 [*d*] and for export 7 *d*.

20. For a donkey-load of p[er]fumed oil which

21. is imported in [goa]tskin[s] 7 *d*, [and for ex]port 4 *d*.

22. For a load of olive oi[l] in four

23. goat[sk]ins, for import for a ca[me]l-load 13 *d*,

24. and for export 1[3] *d*.

25. For a load of olive o[il] in two goatskins,

26. for impor[t] for a camel-l[oa]d 7 *d*, and for export [7] *d*.

27. For a donkey-loa[d] of olive oil for impo[rt] 7 *d*, and for [ex]port [7 *d*].

28. For a load of (fuel) oil in fo[ur] goatskins, which

29. is a camel-load, [for] import 13 *d*, and for [exp]ort 13 *d*.

30. For a load of (fuel) oil in tw[o] goatskins,

31. for a camel-load, for import 7 *d*, and for ex[port] 7 *d*.

32. For a donkey-load of (fuel) oil, for import 7 [*d*] and for export [7] *d*.

33. For a load of salted f[i]sh, for a [camel]-load,

Translation

34. [for imp]or[t] 10 [*d*], and if somebody exports, the [tax collector must collect] from them [...] *d*.

35. [For a load] ... for a camel-[load] for i[mport and for export *d*. ...].

36. For a [load] ... which is a donkey-load, for impor[t] ... *d*,

37. [and for expo]rt the tax collector must collect 3 *d*.

38. For [import of a hor]se 10 *d*, and for a mul[e] 10 *d*.

39. ... for ... sh[ee]p ...

40. ... 2 [*assa*]*rii*.

41. For [lam]bs, for impor[t and export], one *assarius* per head.

42. For a young camel 3 *a*[*ssari*]*i*.

43. For a large [goa]t the [tax collector must collect] 2 [*a*]*ssarii*.

44. For a [k]i[d, the t]a[x] is – one [*assar*]*ius*.

45. Also the tax colle[ctor must co]l[le]ct every mo[n]th from those who are selling perfumed

46. oil 2 *assarii*. ✥ Also the tax collector must collect from prostitutes,

47. from the one who takes a *denarius* [or] more, one *denarius* from each woman,

48. and from the one who takes eight *assarii*

49. he must collect eight *assarii*,

Column 2

1. and from the one who takes [s]ix *assar*[*ii*]

2. he must collect [s]i[x] *assarii*.

3. Also the tax collec[tor] must collect from a [craf]tsma[n]'s shop, and a general shop,

4. [and shoemak]ers [and] ta[ilo]rs according to custom

5. [for every] mont[h] from each shop, 1 *d*.

6. [For ea]ch hide which is imported or sold, for a hide – 2 *assarii*.

The Palmyrene Tax Tariff

7. [Vendor]s of garments who circulate in the city must satisfy the tax collector.

8. [For usa]ge of two springs of wat[er] which are in the city – 800 *d*.

9. The tax collector [must co]llect for a load of wheat, and wine, and straw,

10. and [suc]hlike, [for ev]ery camel, for one journey 1 *d*.

11. For a camel when it is imported unladen he must collect 1 *d*,

12. just [as] Kilix, freedman of Caesar, di[d].

13. The Ta[x La]w <applicable in> Palmyra and <at> the sources of water

14. and sa[lt wh]ich are in the [c]ity and its territories according

15. to the co[ntracts whi]ch were dra[w]n up before the prefect Marinus.

16. For [dry good]s, for eve[ry] camel-load, for import 4 *d*, and for export 4 *d*.

17. For purple [w]o[ol], for every fleece, for import 4 *d*, and for export 4 *d*.

18. Also the [tax collecto]r must collect for all kinds <of goods> as is written above.

19. Fine [sal]t – one *assarius* [must be collec]ted per *modius* of si[xt]een *sextarii*

20. [and] whatever is (sought and) found, he must give [th]em for use.

21. And [who]ever does not measure it out, he [must] pay for every *modius* according to this l[aw] t[wo] *sestertii*.

22. Whoever has salt in Palmy[ra or in the terri]tory

23. of the P[almyre]nes must measure it out for the t[ax collect]or at the rate of one *assarius* [pe]r *modius*.

24. Fr[om what] Gaius [Licinius Mu]cianus, the prefect, [established]:

25. [Be]cause of the t[ax there was dispute] between the Palmyrenes

26. and the ta[x coll]ector. [I de]c[id]ed that ... the [t]ax

27. must be the same [as the ta]x collected by

28. Alkimos and [his] pa[rtner, according] to the law. Anything they have

29. in common, and ..., which ... will be

30. paid to the tax collector by whoever imports individuals into Palmyra

Translation

31. [o]r into its territ[or]ies and exports, for each person 22 *d*.

32. And [wh]oever [sells individuals and ex]ports them must pay the tax collect[or] 12 *d*.

33. And [wh]oever s[ells] a veteran [sla]ve must pay [10] *d*.

34. ... for each [individual and sl]aves of this ...

35. And [wh]oever imports ... he [must pay] 10 *d*, and exports – 12 *d*.

36. ... whoever exports a veteran slave,

37. ... calculation ... [as] is written in the law.

38. [Who]ever se[lls] ... will pay 9 *d*,

39. and [whoever ex]ports ... not written, because

40. nothing ... and ...

41. is not like ...

42. and import........

43. And whoever ....wool...., who also ...

44. Palmy[ra]. Wool from Ita[ly] will n[ot] be [t]axed ...

45. tax for export later,

46. as agre[ed] ... Italic wool

47. will not [b]e [t]a[xed] for ex<p>ort.

48. P[erfumed] oil in goatskins – there must be tax

49. colle[cted according to the la]w, because by an error

Column 3

1. in the written record, where the ta[x] was determined erroneously for ....

2. ....but in the law it is established as 13 *d*.

3. The tax from butchers is due in *denarii*,

4. as also Germanicus Caesar, in the letter he

5. wrote to Statilius, made clear,

The Palmyrene Tax Tariff

6. indeed it is right that that taxes must [b]e collected in Ital[ic] *assarii*.

7. And whatever is due less than a *denarius*, according

8. to custom, will be collected in *arpan*s.

9. Carrion which is thrown away is not liable to tax.

10. Regarding foodstuffs, as in the l[a]w, I have decreed for a load

11. that a *denarius* will be collected

12. whenever it is being im[port]ed from outside the territory or exported.

13. Whoever exports to the [villa]ges [or i]mports from the villages

14. is not liable to tax as they also agreed.

15. (Pine) nuts and suchlike – it seems good that

16. for everything which comes in to be sold, tax should be

17. as for dry goods, as it is also in

18. other cities.

19. Camels, whether they are imported laden or unladen

20. from outside the territory, each camel is liable for

21. a *denarius*, as in the law and as the noble Corbulo established

22. in the rescript he wrote to Barbarus.

23. Concerning camel-hides: they too are free from tax, because the tax

24. is not collected. ҂ Vegeta[b]les and [fr]uit: it seemed good that they should

25. pay ta[x], because they have a price.

26. The tax on prostitutes, as the law shows, I have decided:

27. if the tax collector coll[ects ta]x from prostitutes who take a *denarius*

28. or more, then from each wo[man] (he will collect) a [*dena*]*rius*. And if she takes less,

29. whatever she takes he will [collect. ҂ Concerning] bronze images, statues:

30. it seemed good that they should be tax[ed] as [bron]ze and an image should be paid

31. for as for half a [lo]ad, and two images, as for one load. ↩ Concerning salt:

32. it [s]eemed rig[ht] to me that it should be put on sale in a public place,

33. in the place where (people) gather, and whoever from the Palmyrenes

34. buys it for his own ne[e]ds should pay for a *modius* an Italic *assarius*,

35. as in the law. And also the tax on salt which exists

36. in Palmyra, according to this law, must be collected in *assarii*,

37. and it must be sold to the [Palmyren]es according to custom.

38. ....[t]ax on purple because

39. ....four and a half....

40. ..[vendors of garments who] circ[u]late in the [ci]ty, and tailors

41. ....which will be

42. ....tax will be collected

43. according to what is written above. ↩ For import of hides,

44. 2 *assarii* <per> *asha[l* must] be collected, and for export,

45. for a loa[d], he [must colle]ct [according to wh]at they agreed.

46. Sheep imported f[ro]m outside the territory, if

47. brought in even [for shearing], are liable to tax, but if they are brought into the city from

48. within the [borders] for shearing, they are not liable to tax.

49. ....and from whoever < > [a]s they

Line under the columns

agreed, tax ... [must be collect]ed, as in the law. A *denarius* is collected also from ... After [he] paid, the tax will not be collected except for the small livestock which are brought into the [territory] of Palmyra. If the tax collector wishes to <stamp> [the sheep], he will be allowed to do so.

The Palmyrene Tax Tariff

Panel III

Column 1

1. FOR S[LAVES IMPORTED INTO PALMYRA]
2.   OR [PALMYRENE] TERRI[TORY]
3.   TAX [WILL BE EXACTED FOR EACH ONE] X 22.
4. FROM WHOEV[ER SELLS SLAVES IN THE CITY OR
5.   EXPORTS, FOR E]A[CH ONE X 12].
6. [FROM WHOEVER SELLS] VETERAN [SLAVES X 10].
7. AND IF THE SLAV[ES] ARE
8.   [EX]PORTED [BY THE BUYER], FOR EACH SLA[VE HE MUST PAY X 12].
9. THE SAME TAX COLLECTO[R] WILL EXACT [FOR DRY GOODS]
10.   FOR EVERY [CAMEL-]LOAD,
11.   WHEN IMPO[R]TED [X 3],
12. WHEN EXP[OR]TED, FOR EACH [CAMEL-LOAD],
13.   FOR EACH [X 3].
14. FOR [EVER]Y DONK[EY]-LOAD, WHEN IM[PORTED X 2],
15.   WHEN EXPO[RTED, X 2].
16. FOR PURPLE WOO[L], FOR EV[ERY FLE]ECE,
17.   WHEN IMPO[R]TED, HE [WILL EXACT 8 *ASSARII*],
18. WHEN EXPO[R]TED, [8 *ASSARII*].
19. FOR A C[AMEL]-LOAD OF PERFUMED OIL [WHICH IS IN ALABAS]TER JARS,
20.   WHEN IM[PORTED, HE WILL EXACT X 25].
21. AND.......
22.   WHEN EX[PORTED, HE WILL EXACT X 13].
23. FOR A C[AMEL-LOAD OF PERFUMED OIL WHICH IS]
24.   IN GOAT[SKINS, WHEN IMPORTED, HE WILL EXACT X 13,

Translation

25. WHEN E]X[PORTED, ✕ 7].

26. [FOR A DONKEY-LOAD OF PERFUMED O]IL WHICH IS IN [ALABASTER JARS],

27. WHEN I[MP]OR[TED], HE WILL EX[ACT ✕ 13],

28. [WHEN EXPO]R[TED, ✕ 7].

29. FOR A DONKEY-LOAD OF PERFUMED O[IL WHICH IS IN]

30. GOAT[SKINS], WHEN IMPO[R]TED, HE WILL EX[ACT ✕ 7],

31. WHEN EXPORTED, HE WILL E[X]A[CT ✕ 4].

32. FOR A LOAD OF (OLIVE) OIL WHI[CH IS IN FOU]R GOAT[SKINS],

33. WHEN [IMPORT]ED ON

34. A CAM[EL, ✕ 13],

35. WHEN EXPORT[ED, ✕ 13].

36. FOR A LOAD OF OLIVE OIL WHICH IS IN [TWO GOA]TSKINS,

37. WHEN [IMPORTED] ON A CAM[EL],

38. HE WILL EXACT [✕ 7],

39. WHEN EXPORT[ED, ✕ 7].

40. FOR A LOAD OF OLIVE O[IL WHICH IS] IM[PORT]ED ON A [DON]KEY,

41. HE WILL E[XACT ✕ 7].

42. WHEN EX[PORTED, ✕ 7].

43. FOR A LO[AD OF FUEL OIL WHICH IS IN F]O[UR] GOAT[SKINS],

44. [WHEN IMPORTED, HE WILL EX]ACT ✕ 13,

45. WHEN EX[P]ORT[ED], ✕ 13.

46. FOR A LOAD OF [FUEL OIL WHICH IS IN] TWO GOATS[K]INS,

47. WHEN [IM]PORTED ON A CA[MEL], HE WILL EXACT ✕ 7,

Column 2

1. [WHEN EXPO]RTED, ✕ 7.

2. [FOR A D]O[NKEY-LOAD OF FUEL OIL LOAD, WHEN IMPORTED,

The Palmyrene Tax Tariff

3. HE WILL EXACT ✗ 7,

4. WHEN EX]PO[RTED, ✗ 7].

5. ....

6. [WHEN EX]P[OR]TED, HE [WILL EX]ACT [*10].

(lines 7–20 are not preserved)

21. [CA]MEL.....

22. [SH]EEP

23. ....

24. .....[WHICH HAS BEEN SACRIFI]CED.....

25. THE SAME TAX CO[LL]ECTOR FOR EVE[RY MO]NTH

26. FROM E[AC]H ON[E, WHO] OLIVE OIL .....

27. .... [SEL]LS [2 *ASSARII*].

28. THE [SAME TAX COLLECTOR] WILL EX[ACT IN THE CI]TY

29. [FROM PROSTITU]TES, FROM THOSE WHO [TA]KE [A *DENARIUS* OR MORE,

30. HE WILL EXACT A *DENARIUS*; FROM THOSE

31. WHO TAKE] EIGHT [*A*]*SSARII*, [HE WILL EXACT] 8 [*ASSARII*,

32. AND FROM THOSE WHO] T[AKE] SIX [*AS*]*SARII*, [FROM EACH ONE HE WILL EXACT] 6 *ASS<ARII>*.

33. [THE SAME TAX CO]LLECTOR WILL EX[A]CT [TAX] FROM WORKSHOPS,

34. [OF TAILORS], OF GENERAL DEALERS, OF SHOEMAKERS,

35. ACCORDING TO CUSTOM, EVERY MONTH

36. AND FROM EACH SHOP, ✗ 1.

37. FROM THOSE WHO IMPO[RT] HIDES [OR

38. SE]LL THEM, FOR EVERY HIDE, *ASSA*[*RII* 2].

39. ALSO VAGRANT VENDORS OF GARMENTS

40. TRA[DI]NG IN THE CITY [MUST] SATISFY THE TAX COLLECTOR.

Translation

41. FOR USAGE OF 2 SPRINGS (OF WATER), FOR EVERY YEAR, ✕ 800.

42. THE SAME <TAX COLLECTOR> WILL EX[A]CT FOR A LOAD OF WHEAT, WINE,

43.   STRAW AND SUCHLIKE, FOR EVERY

44.   CAMEL-LOAD FOR EACH JOURNEY ✕ 1.

45. FOR A CAMEL THAT IS BROUGHT IN UNLADEN, HE WILL EXACT ✕ 1,

46.   JUST AS KILIX, FREEDMAN OF CAESAR, EXACTED.

Column 3

(lines 1–22 are not preserved)

23. WHOEVER [H]AS SA[LT] IN PALMYRA OR [IN THE TERRITORY]

24.   OF PALMY[R]A, MUST MEASURE OUT TO THE [TAX

25.   COLLECT]OR FO[R E]ACH *MODIUS* AN *ASSARIUS*.

26.   WHOEVER DOES NOT.....WILL COUN[T OUT]....

27.   .... HAVING......TAX COLLE[CTOR]....

28. FROM WHOMSOEVER THE TA[X COL]LECTOR.....

29.   WILL TA[KE SUR]ETIES.....

30.   LET THEM BE SO[L]D.....

31.   TO THE TAX COLLE[CTOR] DOUBLE, LET HIM TAKE WHAT IS APPROPRIATE;

32.   FOR T[H]IS LET HIM P[A]Y TO THE THE TAX COLLECTOR

33.   DOUBLE.

34. CONCERNING ANYTHING THAT THE TAX CO[LL]ECTOR DEMANDS FROM ANYBODY,

35.   AND CONCERNING ANYTHING THAT ANYBODY DEMANDS FROM THE TAX COLLECTOR,

36.   CONCERNING THIS THERE MUST BE AN ENQUIRY BY THE *DIKAIODOTĒS*

37.   STATIONED IN PALMYRA.

38. THE TAX COLLECTOR WILL HA[VE] THE RI[G]HT

The Palmyrene Tax Tariff

39. TO [T]A[KE SUR]ETIES FROM THOSE WHO DO NOT P[AY], PERSONALLY OR THRO[UGH

40. OF]F[ICIALS]; [AND IF TH]ESE [SU]RETIES ARE NOT REDEEMED WITHIN

41. [THREE DAYS, THE TAX C]OLLECTOR WILL HAVE THE RIGHT TO SELL

42. [THESE SURETIES IN A PU]BLIC PLACE, BARRING

43. EV[IL] INTENTION..... IS TO BE SOLD,

44. OR IT DOES NOT PRODUCE ENOUGH, IT IS PERMITTED TO THE TAX C[OLLECTOR] TO EXACT

45. IN THE SAME WAY AND..... LAW.

46. THE MARKET OF P[ALMYRA AND WA]TER SPRINGS OF CAESAR

47. TO THE TAX COLLECTOR....... HE WILL NOT HAVE THE RIGHT TO PERMIT

Panel IV

Column 1

1. ANYONE ELSE TO EXACT, GIVE, T[AKE].

2. AND NO....MA[N.... AND]

3. IN THE [NA]ME OF ANYONE.....

4. IF HE DOES THIS, OR.....[WILL WILL BE EXACTED]

5. DOUBLE....

(lines 6–9 are not preserved)

10. GAIUS [LICINIUS MUCIANUS, LEGATE AND]

11. PRO[PRAETOR, SAYS].....

12. AMONG THE PAL[MYRENES AGAINST THE TAX COLLECTORS]

13. IT HAS BEEN DECREED....

14. WILL BE ACCORDING.....

15. ....

Translation

16. .... FROM ....

17. ....

18. TH[EM]............

19. ....

20. [MUST GIV]E TO THE TAX COLLEC[TOR].

21. WHOEVER.......

22. ....

23. ....

24. ACCORDING TO..........................

(lines 25–31 are not preserved)

32. .... X 6 .... X 9

33. DEMANDING................ IF NOT..................[WOOL]

34. FROM ITALY, WHEN IT IS EX[POR]TED, TO EXACT TAX, AFT[ER THEY

35. AG]REED, WHEN BEING EX[PORTED], IT MUST N[OT

36. PA]Y [TAX].

37. FOR PERFUMED OIL WHICH IS IN [GOA]TSK[INS], THE [TAX COLLECTOR] MUST EX[ACT]

38. ACCORDING TO THE LA[W]......AND NOT.....

39. MI[STA]KE HAS BEEN MADE IN WHAT WAS ESTABLISHED EARLIER; IT [MU]ST BE <EXACTED> [JUST AS

40. HAS BEEN] DECREED IN THE LAW WHICH HAS BEEN RATIFIED.

41. THE TAX FOR CATTLE SLAUGHTER MUST BE RECK[ONED] IN *DENARII*,

42. JUST AS GERMANICUS CAESAR EXPLAINED IN THE [RES]CRIPT TO STATILIUS

43. THAT THE TAX MUST BE PAID OUT IN ITA[LIC] *ASSARII*;

44. THE T[A]X LESS THAN A *DENARIUS*

45. HE WILL EXACT IN SMALL COINS ACCORDING TO CUSTOM. [AND] FO[R]

The Palmyrene Tax Tariff

46. WHAT IS THROWN AWAY AS CARRION, T[AX IS NOT REQUIRED <TO BE EXACTED>].

47. FOR FOODSTUFFS, I DECREE, ACC<ORDING> TO THE LAW, FOR A LOAD A *DEN[ARIUS]* WILL BE EXACTED,

48. IF IT IS IMPO[RTED] FROM OUTSIDE THE BORDERS

49. OR IF EXPORTED. WHATEVER IS BROUGHT IN FROM OR TAKEN

50. TO THE RURAL [ARE]AS, IS NOT LIABLE TO TAX, AS THEY HAVE

51. AGREED. (PINE) NUTS AND SUCHLIKE: IT HAS BEEN D[E]CIDED:

52. THOSE THAT ARE BROUGHT IN FOR SALE, THE TAX SHOULD BE AS

53. FOR DRY GOODS, AS IT IS ALSO IN OTHER CITIES.

54. CAMELS, WHETHER THEY ARE IMPORTED UNLADEN OR LADEN FROM OUTSIDE

55. THE TERRITORY, EACH CAMEL IS <LIABLE> FOR A *DENARIUS*, ACCORDING

56. TO THE LAW, AS THE NOBLE CORBULO

57. ESTABLISHED IN THE RESCRIPT TO BARBARUS.

Column 2

(lines 1–2 are not preserved)

3. CAR[RY].......

4. ....

5. ....

6. [FROM] PROSTITU[TES WHO TAKE A *DENARIUS* OR MORE,

7. FROM EA]CH.....

8. ....

9. ....[MUST EX]ACT

(lines 10–17 are not preserved)

18. LAW..........

(lines 19–33 are not preserved)

34. THE TAX COLLE[C]TOR.........THE TAX [ESTABLISHED] BY

35. LAW IS TO BE BE PAID IN *DENA[R]II*.

36. GRAZING – IT HAS BEEN DECIDED, TO EXAC[T] NO [FU]RTHER TAX.

37. BUT [F]OR GRAZING SHEEP BROUGHT [INTO PAL]MYRA

38. TAX IS TO BE CHARGED.

39. IF THE TAX COLLEC[TOR] DECIDES TO BR[AND] THE SHEEP,

40. HE IS ALLOWED TO DO SO.

Fragments (*Inv.* X, 143)

1. ......[TR]AJA[N]......

2. ......[CAE]SAR FOR THE [SECOND TIME, PUB]LIUS COELI[US BALBINUS].

Commentary

Dating formula

Lines 1–2

For the restoration of the rank of Hadrian see Lazarev-Abamelek 1884: 44, though he suggested δημαρχικῆς ἐξουσίας τὸ κ′. H. Dessau arrived independently at the same restoration; see also *OGIS*, 629. It is clear from the extant sources that the inscription gives the precise rank of Hadrian. See *OGIS*, 624 (from Jerash): Αὐτοκράτορα Καίσαρα, θεοῦ Τραιανοῦ Παρθικοῦ υἱόν, θεοῦ Νέρουα υἱωνόν, Τραι[αν]ὸν Ἀδριανὸν [Σεβαστό]ν, ἀρχιερέα μέγιστ[ο]ν, δημαρχικῆς ἐ[ξουσίας] τὸ δι′, ὕπατον τὸ γ′, πατέρα πατρίδος τὸν ἀγ[αθὸ]ν κύριον. The latter detail is absent from the Tariff.

Nerva - was the first emperor from the Antonine dynasty and declared emperor by the Senate (Marcus Cocceius Nerva; as emperor: Emperor Caesar Nerva Augustus, AD 96–8).

Trajan - the adopted son and successor of Nerva (Marcus Ulpius Traianus; as emperor: Emperor Caesar Nerva Traianus Augustus, AD 98–117). He led an active military campaign in the Near East. In 106 he prompted the annexation of the Nabataean kingdom and turned it into the Province of Arabia. Thus, the Romans gained access to the important trading routes into the Arabian peninsula. In successful military attacks against Parthia (AD 114–17) he annexed Armenia and Northern Mesopotamian (hence the title Παρθικός). During that war he brutally put down the revolts of the Jews in the eastern provinces.

Hadrian - the adopted son and successor of Trajan (Publius Aelius Hadrianus; as emperor: Emperor Caesar Traianus Hadrianus Augustus; AD 117–38). Hadrian stopped the war with Parthia, handed back northern Mesopotamia and turned Armenia into a dependant kingdom. In the thirties of the second century he travelled to the East and visited Palmyra. He intended to carry out administrative reforms in the Province of Syria and to separate Phoenicia from it (see Ael. Spart., *Vita Hadr.* 14, 1). However, he apparently did not implement his intentions. He suppressed the Jewish revolt led by Bar Kokhba.

ἀρχιερέως μεγίστου - *pontifex maximus*. Hadrian held this position from 117. (See Ael. Spart., *Vita Hadr*. 22, 10–11: *Sacra Romana diligentissime curavit, peregrina contempsit. Pontificis maximi officium peregit*).

δημαρχικῆς ἐξουσίας το κα΄ - *tribunicia potestas*; beginning from AD 117 the *tribunicia potestas* of Hadrian was renewed annually on 10th December. Accordingly, his *tribunicia potestas* XXI began on 10th December 136 and continued until 9th December 137. For the meaning of *tribunicia potestas* see Mashkin 1949: 397–8.

αὐτοκράτορος τὸ β΄ - Hadrian was pronounced emperor for the second time in 135 (see *CIL*, II, 478; VI, 974; XIV, 4235).

ὑπάτου τὸ γ΄ - Hadrian was a consul three times: in 108 *consul suffectus* — together with M. Trebatius Priscus (see *CIL*, VI, 2016), in 118 (Cass. Dio, 2, 6) together with Gn. Pedanius Fuscus Salinator and in 119, first with Rusticus, then with A. Platorius Nepos (see *CIL*, V, 877).

πατρὸς πατρίδος - Hadrian first declined the title of *pater patriae* (Ael. Spart., *Vita Hadr*. 6, 4: *patris patriae nomen delatum sibi statim et iterum postea distulit*), although this title was used on coins (cf. *CIL*, III, 1445, 2828, 3968a; VII, 1169 etc.). From 128 it became an official title.

Lucius Aelius Caesar - Hadrian's adopted son (?-138), adopted in 136 (before adoption L. Ceionius Commodus; see Ael. Spart., *Vita Hadr*. 23, 10–16; Cass. Dio, 69, 17, I). He was designated Hadrian's successor. He was a consul for the first time together with G. Vettulenus Civica Pompeianus (*CIL*, III, 720; VI, 975a, 10242; XIV, 2112, 2852; XV, 1056, 1058), for the second time in 137 together with P. Coelius Balbinus.

P. Coelius Balbinus Vibullius Pius - consul in 137 (*CIL*, III, 1933; VI, 1854; IX, 5839; XIV, 2390; XV, 900, 1057, 1059, 1218; *ILS*, 2102). His *cursus honorum* is known because of inscription *CIL*, VI, 1383 = *ILS*, 1063: *P. Coelius P. F. Ser[gia] Balbinus Vibullius Pius X vir stlitib[us] iudic[andis] VI vir equit[um] Roman[orum] turm[ae] quint[ae] tr[ibunus] mil[itum] leg[ionis] XXII Primig[eniae] p[iae] f[idelis] adlectus inter patric[ios] ab imp[eratore] Caes[are] Traiano Hadriano Aug[usto] salius Collinus quaest[or] Aug[usti] flamen Ulpialis pr[aetor] de fidei commiss[is] co[n]s[ul] designatus*.

Commentary

Panel I

Line 1

Ἔτους ημυ΄, μηνὸς Ξανδικοῦ ιη΄ - the 18th day of the month of Xandikos in the Seleucid calendar is equated with 18th April AD 137. S. Reckendorf (1888: 390) joined H. Dessau (1884: 492) in the opinion that in the month of Xandikos the renewal of contracts concerning tax laid down by custom might have taken place. We do not have the material to confirm this assumption.

δόγμα - decree (cf. *SIG*, 630, 690, 761, 858, 878 etc.) below (I, 8) δεδόχθαι is from the same root. The usage of the verb ἐψηφίσθη (I, 4) presupposes the term ψήφισμα. See the term πρόσταγμα in the same sense (*Inv.* X, 44).

βουλή - the Palmyrene city council; its structure and the way it was constituted are unknown. There are numerous inscriptions that have survived which refer to the 'council' or 'council and people' who decreed the establishment of statues in honour of those who did good service to the city.

Line 2

Ἐπὶ Βωννέους Βωννέους τοῦ Αἱράνου προέδρου - Bōnnēs, son of Bōnnēs son of Hairanēs is not as yet mentioned in other Palmyrene inscriptions. According to his name and genealogy, he belonged to an Aramaean-Syrian or Aramaean-Arab ethnic group and was probably born after his father's death. The nominative form of Βωννέους is probably Βωννῆς (*SDGY*, 51).

Proedros - president of the council; cf. *Inv.* X, 55.

Lines 2–3

Ἀλεξάνδρου Ἀλεξάνδρου τοῦ Φιλοπάτορος γραμματέως βουλῆς καὶ δήμου - Alexandros son of Alexandros son of Philopatōr is not mentioned in other Palmyrene documents as yet. According to his name and genealogy, he is a Greek or Hellenized Syrian.

Grammateus of the council and people - secretary of the council meetings and people's gatherings. See also *Inv.* X, 39 (AD 75/6): [κ]αὶ ἀγνῶς γραμματ[εῦσα]ντα and *Inv.* I, 2 (which corresponds with *IGRR*, III, 1054; *CIS*, II, 3959, AD 130/1): γραμμ[α]τέα γενόμενον τὸ δεύτερον, though without the addition of βουλῆς καὶ δήμου. Apparently, the magistracy had a fixed term;

this post could be occupied by the same person serving repeatedly (at least in the second quarter of the second century AD).

Lines 3–4

Μαλίχου Ὀλαιοῦς καὶ Ζεβείδου Νεσᾶ ἀρχόντων - Malichos son of Olaiēs, and Zebeidas son of Nesa are not mentioned in other Palmyrene inscriptions as yet. According to their names and patronymics (cf. I. 16: Maliku son of 'Olaya son of Moqimu) they both belonged to the Aramaean-Syrian or Aramaean-Arab ethnic group.

ἀρχόντων - archons, probably the highest group of magistrates in Palmyra (there were two archons) but not mentioned in other Palmyrene inscriptions as yet. Cf. *CIS*, II, 3934, which corresponds to *IGRR*, III, 1047 (AD 254): δυα[νδρικὸν φιλοτεί]μως στρατ[ηγήσαντα]. This refers to the duumvirate of the third century AD which was established on the basis of archons in connection with the fact that Palmyra received the status of a colony and *ius Italicum*. *OGIS*, 629 and *IGRR*, III, 1056 erroneously state that in other Palmyrene documents the archons were called *stratēgoi*. See in this regard *CIS*, II, 3913; Dessau 1884: 491; Reckendorf 1888: 393. [Ed.: *CIS*, II, 3913 is the *CIS* publication of the Tariff, frequently referred to as 3913 below.]

Line 4

βουλῆ[ς] νομίμου ἀγομένης - This clause points probably to the fact that the meeting of the council took place when the quorum was reached (cf. *Dig.*, L, 9, 2). According to *OGIS*, 629 the reference is to the institution meeting regularly, like Athenian ἐκκλησίαι νόμιμοι, in contrast to σύγκλητοι that would take place occasionally: see also *CIS*, II, 3913; *IGRR*, III, 1056. This parallel, though, is inaccurate for the simple reason that the Palmyrene Tariff talks about the council and not about the people's gatherings. According to Reckendorf 1888: 394, this clause means that the council either took place at the appointed time, or was authorized to make decisions.

Line 5

ἐν τῷ τε[λω]νικῷ νόμῳ - in the tax law. The law that is meant here is the law on the procedure for tax collection and on the size of the tax. It had been in operation in Palmyra before this decree was issued and it was attached to the new Tariff.

The whole Greek inscription is characterized by the omission of *iota subscriptum* that is typical for Syro-Greek epigraphy under Roman rule.

ἀνελήμφθη instead of typical ἀνελήφθη. V. Dittenberger (*OGIS*, 629, *ad locum*) points to παραλήμπτης (*OGIS*, 202). In his comment on this he writes, 'the writing of μ in verbals (λήμψομαι, ἐλήμφθην, λημφθήσομαι) is so common in inscriptions and papyri that it is unnecessary to give further examples'.

ἐνγραφομέ[νου] - a very common writing of νγ instead of typical ἐγγραφομέ[νου].

Line 6

τῇ μισθώσει - agreement on the farming out of taxes; literally ἡ μισθώσις - tax agreement. Apparently, tax farming was considered as an employment of a person who would fulfil a certain job for the *polis* for a reward. The reward in this case would be all the extras above the tax that the tax farmer collected. Cf. *IGRR*, III, 1056.

τὸν τελωνοῦντα - one of the terms describing the specific role of the tax farmer in the Greek text (literally, 'the one who collects the tax').

Line 7

γείνεσθ[αι] - instead of γίνεσθαι. With the advance of itacism the representing of *i* by ει became common in the Greek inscriptions of the first–third centuries AD, as well as in later centuries, including the inscriptions from Palmyra.

Lines 7–8

[με]ταξὺ τῶν ἐνπόρων πρὸς τοὺς τελώνας. According to *OGIS*, 629 we would expect either τοῖς ἐμπόροις πρὸς τοὺς τελώνας or μεταξὺ τῶν ἐμπόρων καὶ τῶν τελωνῶν. In Greek the preposition μεταξύ is usually used to indicate space or time relations ('between' particular points of space and time [*SDGY*, 287]). In the construction in the present text (μεταξύ - πρός) it is not used in this way. In the text we probably have a literal translation from the Aramaic (I, 20): סרבנין הוו ביני תגרא לביני מכסיא.

τῶν ἐνπόρων - instead of the common form in literary koine Greek, τῶν ἐμπόρων (μπ > νπ). Cf. *KBN*, 1252.

τοὺς τελώνας - tax collectors, therefore tax farmers; the term is common in the administrative practice of the Hellenistic and Roman periods.

Line 8

δεδόχθαι (sc. τῇ βουλῇ) - a common formula (from the fourth century BC) introducing a decree or resolution (cf. *SIG*, 159, 227 etc.), cf. I, 1: δόγμα. Cf. Reinach, 1885: 344–55. Pleonasm: cf. earlier ἐψηφίσθη τὰ ὑποτεταγμένα.

δ[εκα]πρώτους - the board of Palmyrene magistrates, unknown from other inscriptions. According to some other sources, the *dekaprotia* was one of the lowest magistracies (cf. *IGLS* IV, 1303; Balanea, second cent. AD), which could be filled by individuals even younger than twenty-five years of age (*Dig.*, L, 4, 3, 10–11). Some of their responsibilities included enforcing tax payment and other duties (*Dig.*, L, 4, 18, 26). It seems that in Palmyra of the second quarter of the second century AD *dekaprōtoi* had to enforce tax collection and ensure it was done correctly. See Rostovtzeff 1899: 229–31; Turner 1936.

διακρείνοντας - instead of common διακρίνοντας (ει < ι).

Line 9

ἐνγράψαι - instead of common ἐγγράψαι (γγ > νγ).

ἔνγιστα - instead of common ἔγγιστα (γγ > νγ).

Line 10

τέλος - taxation.

τῷ μισθουμένῳ - one of the terms used in the inscriptions to denote a tax farmer ('the one with whom a tax agreement is made'). Compare with μίσθωσις (I, 6) - agreement for the farming out of taxes.

κυρωθῇ τῷ μισθουμένῳ - According to R. Cagnat (1884), *dativus commodi* is used here and correspondingly the authorities of Palmyra act as logical subject (compare with in *IGRR*, III, 1056: τῷ μισθουμένῳ = ὑπὸ τοῦ μισθουμένου). *OGIS*, 629 indicates that H. Dessau is more correct in seeing this as *dativus auctoris* and in τῷ μισθουμένῳ an indication of a logical subject. See I, 22.

ἐνγραφῆναι - instead of common ἐγγραφῆναι (γγ > νγ).

Line 10–11

ἐνγραφῆναι μετὰ τοῦ πρώτου νόμου - H. Dessau thinks that the earlier law was not mentioned again even though it had been sanctioned by the committee. Indeed, in the Greek part of the Tariff there is no indication of transition from

Commentary

the new to the old law. However, it is present in the Aramaic part, where there is even mention of the title of the old law. Thus Dessau's point of view does not fit the facts.

Line 11

ἀντικρὺς ἱερ[οῦ] λεγομένου Ῥαβασείρη - a temple, apparently situated not far from the place where the inscription stood. According to R. du Mesnil du Buisson, the temple was situated at the southern corner of the *agora* (1966: 176–7). According to the evidence discovered by H. Pognon from the Mandaean holy book, the *Ginza* (Pognon 1907: 84, note 2; compare *CIS*, II, 3913, *ad lin.* 23), Rabasīrē is a god of the underworld. The relevant passage from the *Ginza* in Pognon's translation says: 'Lorsque vous sortirez de vos corps pour aller vers la Grande Vie, quel certificat donnerez-vous? Que direz-vous au messager qui vous aura délivrés du monde? Que direz-vous aux génies infernales et à Rab-Essiré qui réside là-bas? Que direz-vous au génie Anouche?' The expression רב אסירא on its own means 'the lord of the bound, captives' (i.e. in the underworld) and, according to Pognon, it is the name of an ancient god of the underworld. Schröder 1884: 419 saw here the expression 'Rab Osiri' and noted the existence of a temple of Osiris in Palmyra. F. Rosenthal (Rosenthal 1935: 77–8, note 2) refers to the other texts of the *Ginza*, which contain the same expression in this form: רביהון דעסיריא. He also suggests that, since there is no information about ideas of the underworld in Palmyra (unlike among the Mandaeans), then there were no such ideas. Therefore, we cannot (according to him) talk about a common prototype. The comparison between the Palmyrene and Mandaean is, then, only a comparison of language. For R. du Mesnil du Buisson (1962: 275–8; cf. 1966: 177), Rabasīrē is 'the lord of (two) bound (lions)'. We ourselves believe that the Palmyrene-Mandaean comparison shows that there was a cult of the underworld lord in Palmyra. (For the religious situation of the second century AD such views are completely normal.) Moreover, this helps us to see the origins of the Mandaean view. In any case רב אסירא is an epithet of a deity whose real name is a taboo.

Ῥαβασείρη - ει for the ι which might be expected according to the later norms of the literary Greek koine (for similar non-standard spellings see Introduction, section 7).

Line 12

συνδίκους - syndics, the collective Palmyrene magistrates; this group is not mentioned in other Palmyrene texts. According to *Dig.*, L, 4, 1 and L, 4, 18, 13, the responsibility of the syndics was the legal protection of the society. Perhaps to fulfil these responsibilities the Palmyrene syndics would have overseen the actions of the tax farmers. According to Dittenberger (*OGIS*, 629) this corresponds with other aspects of the magistracy of the ἔκδικος. However, this point of view is hardly plausible.

παραπράσσειν παρὰ τοῦ νόμου πράσσειν - cf. *OGIS*, 629.

Line 14

דגמא - Greek δόγμα. In inscriptions *Inv.*, I, 2 (which corresponds with *CIS*, II, 3959; AD 130) and *Inv.* X, 44 the Palmyrene term is preserved which describes the resolution: תוחית (in formulae בתוחית בולא ודמוס, מן תוחית בולא ודמס). The chronological closeness of the inscriptions does not allow us to determine whether one term was at some stage substituted for the other. The form דגם is known in the Palmyrene inscriptions (JH, 55). Therefore, the word דגמא in the Palmyrene language is treated as a purely Aramaic one: *st. abs.* דגם; *st. emph.* דגמא. In Syriac the word ܕܘܓܡܐ gained the meaning 'creed', 'sect' and 'law' (*BLS*, 141–2); in the Jewish parabiblical literature דוגמא (variant דיגמא) comes from Greek δεῖγμα and has the meaning 'example', 'pattern' and 'image' (*KGLL*, II, 187–8).

א - *mater lectionis*, conveying the Greek α.

בולא - Greek βουλή. The proper Aramaic equivalent of this term is unknown. Cf. Syr. ܒܘܠܐ - council (*BLS*, 62); in Jewish parabiblical literature בולי (*KGLL*, II, 140; itacism: η = י), often in the formula בולי ודמוס = ἡ βουλὴ καὶ ὁ δῆμος. In the Palmyrene variant ו conveys the Greek ου and א the Greek η.

ירח - noun, singular, masculine, absolute state. In the Aramaic documents from Egypt ירח (JH, 111, V., 7, 235); in Biblical Aramaic ירח (Gesenius-Buhl, 902); in the Jewish parabiblical literature (*DAN*, 187), Syr. ܝܪܚܐ.

ניסן - a month in the Aramaic calendar, corresponding with the Greco-Macedonian Xandikos and the month of April of our calendar (*BLS*, 427); cf. the documents from Elephantine (V., 11, 210). The name comes from the Mesopotamian (Nippurian) calendar (D'iakonov, Dandamaev, Livshits 1975: 301).

Commentary

פלהדרותא - *nomen abstr.* with the suffix -ות, from the Greek πρόεδρος: it corresponds with the Greek ἐν τῇ προεδρίᾳ (JH, 228). In contrast to the Greek part of the decree, here we have abstract descriptions, common in the Palmyrene formulae (cf. Shifman 1965a: 177–86). Reckendorf (1888: 392) notes the shift of the letters [l] and [r], probably as a result of dissimilation. Cf. פרהדרין, variant פלהדרין (*KGLL*, II, 480) according to Krauss emerging from Greek πάρεδροι. The Palmyrene material shows the weakness of this view.

Lines 14–15

בונא בר בונא בר חירן - in the Greek text: ἐπὶ Βωννέους Βωννέους τοῦ Αἱράνου. There is some graphic correspondence: ו = ω; א = η (nominative - βωννής; genitive - βωννέους); חי = Αἱ (in other words י reflects *ay*).

Line 15

גרמטיא - Greek γραμματεία (JH, 54) - magistracy of the *grammateus*. It is not clear, however, whether the י reflects *ei* or, because of itacism, *ī*.

אלכסדרס בר אלכסדרס בר פלפטר - in the Greek text: Ἀλεξάνδρου τοῦ Ἀλεξάνδρου τοῦ Φιλοπάτορος. כס (ס after a vowel but before the consonant ס) = ξ; ν is assimilated in Aramaic to the following δ; פ = φ (at the beginning of the word); פ = π (between vowels); ט = τ.

גרמטוס - Greek γραμματεύς (JH, 53); ט = τ; ו = ευ. Cf. Syr. ܓܪܡܛܐܣ = γραμματεῖς (*BLS*, 133).

דמס - Greek δῆμος (JH, 59); cf. Syr. ܕܡܘܣ (variant ܕܝܡܘܣ) (*BLS*, 158); Hebr. דימוס (*KGLL*, II, 204–5). In inscriptions *CIS*, II, 392 (which corresponds with *Inv.* IX, 8; March A.D. 51) and *Inv.* IX, 12, the Greek ἡ πόλις and ὁ δῆμος correspond with the Semitic גבל which is certainly derived from Arabic tribal terminology; cf. inscriptions from Lihyan: גבל דדן (Caskel 1954: nos 52, 71, 77, 91; Shifman 1966: 38–44) and the Classical Arabic جبل. According to Février (1931a: 12–13), the corporate body called גבל תדמריא is not identical with the *boulē*, the *dēmos* or the *polis*. Starcky (1952: 36–7) believes that the term גבל refers to the popular assembly as the union of all the Palmyrene tribes. We believe that the parallel גבל = δῆμος proves that both terms mean the same: the civil population of Palmyra. The intrusion of the term דמס in the first century AD relects the process of Hellenization of administrative and legal terminology (and possibly their offices).

ארכוניא - *nomen abstr.* There is an analogy with גרמטיא, the word being adopted from the Greek ἄρχων (JH, 25). Cf. Syr. ܐܪܟܘܢ, ܐܪܟܘܢܐ and ܐܪܟܘܢܘܬܐ (*BLS*, 49); Hebrew ארכון (also in inscription A5 from the synagogue at Dura-Europos; variant ארכן) and ארכונטוס (variant ארכונטס) (*KGLL*, II, 129). כ between vowels = χ, ו = ω.

Line 16

מלכו בר עלײ בר מקימו - Greek Μαλίχου Ὀλαιοῦς. כ (between vowels) = χ; ו = o (the name Μαλίχος); יי = αι.

זבידא בר נשא - Greek Ζεβείδου Νεσᾶ. י = ει (possibly reflecting itacism); א = α (the name is presumably Ζεβείδας) and ᾶ; ש = σ.

כד הות בולא כנישא מן נמוסא - temporal subordinate clause, corresponding with the Greek *gen. abs.* (βουλῆ[ς] νομίμου ἀγομένης); introduced by a temporal subordinating conjunction כד. The predicate consists of the auxiliary verb הות and feminine passive participle.

כנישא (√כנש) - forming a compound past tense, passive. S. Reckendorf (1888: 393) construed it with the word כד with perfective aspect to convey completed action; he also noted the possibility of using כד simply with a participle. This is the general pattern of the compound past tense: the auxiliary verb is in the perfective form, Peʻal + participle.

הות - third singular feminine perfective, Peʻal. Cf. Aramaic documents from Egypt הוה (JH, 63); Biblical Aramaic הוא (Gesenius-Buhl, 683); parabiblical Jewish literature הוא (*LW*, I, 458); Syriac ܗܘܐ (*BLS*, 175).

כנישא - feminine passive participle, Peʻal (agreeing with feminine בולא), with the ending א-. The verb כנש occurs in the Ethpaʻʻal in the Aramaic documents from Egypt (V., 9, 146; see also JH, 123).

נמוסא - Greek νόμος in Aramaic form: *st. emph.* (ending א-) (JH, 179); cf. Syriac ܢܡܘܣܐ (*BLS*, 431) and Hebrew נימוס (rarely נומוס) and in *st. emph.* נימוסא (*KGLL*, II, 359–61); analogous to the latter is the Palestinian-Syriac form ܢܡܘܣܐ; so ו = o.

אשרת - third feminine singular perfective, Afʻel (root שרר); it agrees with the earlier בולא (= βουλή, feminine). In the Greek text it corresponds with ἐψηφίσθη. It is possible that the Palmyrene derivative of the root שרר could be parallel to the Greek ψήφισμα; cf. JH, 320–1.

Line 17

מדי כתיב מן לתחת - in the Greek it is τὰ ὑποτεταγμένα.

מדי - defective writing instead of מא די (cf. *CIS*, II, 3913, *ad locum*).

כתיב - the root כתב; masculine singular passive participle, Pe'al. י is a *mater lectionis* for *ī*.

בדיל די - in the Greek ἐπειδή (cf. parabiblical Jewish literature and translations of the Bible into Aramaic . . . בדיל די (*LW*, I, 193; *DAN*, 48]).

זבניא - cf. Syriac ܙܒܢܐ (*BLS*, 187); masculine plural, *st. emph.* (ending -יא).

מכסא - in the Aramaic documents from Egypt מכס (V., 11, 194), Syr. ܡܟܣܐ (*BLS*, 385); in parabiblical Jewish literature: Hebrew מכס (*DAN*, 236; *LW*, III, 113) and Aramaic מכסא (*DAN*, 236; *LW*, III, 113–14). For the Palmyrene בנמוסא די מכסא the Greek has ἐν τῷ τε[λω]νικῷ νόμῳ. There is also a correspondence between מכסא and τέλος. The word was adopted from Akkadian (Akk. *miksu(m)*: von Soden 1966: 652). Cf. JH, 150. P.K. Kokovtsov (Arch. AS, f. 779, inv. 1, no. 40, p. 163) points to the Hebrew מכס and refers to parallels from the Septuagint, Vulgate and Targum, as well as from Syriac and Arabic.

עבידן - the root עבד; cf. Aramaic עבידה (JH, 202); Syr. ܥܒܕܐ (*BLS*, 505); in parabiblical Jewish literature עבידתא (*DAN*, 304). The form is probably feminine plural here (cf. agreement with שגין חיבין [*CIS*, II, 3913, *ad locum*]). In this case, however, we have to note the violation of agreement with the following verbs, אסקו and הוו מתגבין. If agreement is *not* violated, we could assume that (1) the words עבידן שגין חיבן are masculine plural, with the archaic ending *-ān* and (2) in Palmyrene there was a masculine word עביד.

חיבן - root חוב; cf. in Aramaic documents from Egypt חוב (V., 7, 216); Syr. ܚܒ and its derivative ܚܘܒܐ (*BLS*, 218); also in the parabiblical Jewish literature חיב and חיבא (*DAN*, 144). The Pe'al passive participle agrees with עבידן. Cf. JH, 83.

Line 17–18

עבידן שגין חיבן מכסא - the Greek parallel is πλεῖστα τῶν ὑποτελῶν.

Line 18

אסקו - root סלק; Af'el third masculine plural perfective; it agrees with עבידן (I, 17). F. Rosenthal (1936: 64) cautiously assumes here third feminine plural passive. The Greek parallel οὐκ ἀνελήμφθη presupposes a passive form of the verb.

הוו מתגבין - root גבא; cf. Syr. ܓܒܐ (*BLS*, 100); in parabiblical Jewish literature גבה and גבא (*DAN*, 69; *LW*, I, 292–3); third masculine plural, compound past tense, Ethpaʻʻal or Ethpeʻel, agreeing with עבידן and corresponding with the Greek third person singular middle imperfect ἐπράσ[σετο]. Cf. JH, 46–7.

עידא - Syr. ܥܝܕܐ, root ܥܘܕ (*BLS*, 515). The expression מן עידא is a loan translation from Greek [ἐ]κ συνηθείας (cf. on this expression *SDGY*, 274); cf. also I, 16: מן נמוסא and the Greek parallel νομίμου. In the pre-Hellenistic Aramaic texts there is no similar recorded use of the preposition מן (in the sense of 'according to' or 'in accordance with').

במדען די - conjunction introducing the subordinate clause of cause. The parallel in Greek is *gen.abs.*

מדען - cf. in the Aramaic documents from Egypt מנדעם (V., 11, 198) and מדעם (V., 11, 190); Syr. ܡܕܥܡ (*BLS*, 375); in parabiblical Jewish literature מנדעם, מידם, מדעם (*LW*, III, 31). The Palmyrene writing of the letter ע is probably a left-over from the earlier orthography; the comparison with the Syriac spelling raises a question: was the letter ע a *mater lectionis* for the designation of *ē*? In the Palmyrene there is assimilation נ > ד.

הוו מתכתב - root כתב; third masculine singular compound past tense, Ethpeʻel. In the Greek text ἐνγραφομέ[νου].

אגוריא - The Palmyrene term designates contracts of hire; in the Greek text τῇ μισθώσει. Root אגר (V., 3, 188); Syr. ܐܓܪ (*BLS*, 4–5); in the parabiblical Jewish literature אגר (*LW*, I, 23–4; *DAN*, 6); feminine singular noun in *st. abs.*: אגרי + א (cf. I, 20: בשטר אגריא חדתא).

Line 19

מכסא – 'tax collector'; in the Greek text τὸν τελωνοῦντα (cf. Reckendorf 1888: 384; *CIS*, II, 3913, *ad locum*). Syr. ܡܟܣܐ (*BLS*, 385); in the parabiblical Jewish literature מכסא (*DAN*, 236; *LW*, III, 114).

הוא{ו} - the initial ו evidently breaks the construction of the sentence, which corresponds exactly with the Greek text. Cf.:

Greek text	Palmyrene text
ἐνγραφομέν[ου] τῇ μισθώσει τὸν	הוא מתכתב באגוריא
τελωνοῦντα τὴν πρᾶξιν ποιεῖσθαι	די מכסא {ו}הוא גבא

Accordingly, the writing of ו is most likely a mistake of the engraver. Cf.,

however, Reckendorf 1888: 384 and *CIS*, II, 3913, *ad locum*, where די באגוריא
מכסא is translated: *in stipulatione cum publicano*.

הוא גבא - third masculine singular compound past tense, Pe'al, agreeing with
מכסא. In the Greek text τὴν πρᾶξιν ποιεῖσθαι (as a compound part of the
accusativus cum infinitivo).

היך - أَمِ (*BLS*, 14); in the parabiblical Jewish literature היך, היכי (*LW*, I, 464;
DAN, 112). In the Greek text there is the parallel ἀκολούθ[ω]ς.

מטלכות - compound preposition: מטל + כות; the Greek parallel is possibly διὰ
ταῦτα (*CIS*, II, 3913). מטל - Syr. ܡܛܠ, ܡܛܠ (*BLS*, 382). כות - see V., 9, 144;
JH, 117.

זבנין שגין - in the Greek text πλειστάκις.

על צבותא אלן - in the Greek text περὶ τούτου.

צבותא - Syr. ܨܒܘܬܐ (*BLS*, 619).

אלן - plural demonstrative pronoun. In the Aramaic inscriptions of Sefire and
Zakar, king of Hamath and Lu'ash, אל; in the Aramaic documents from Egypt
אלן, אלה (JH, 78; V., 3, 199, 201); in Biblical Aramaic אֵל, אִלֵּן, אֵלֶּה, אִלֵּין
(Gesenius-Buhl, 887–8); in parabiblical Jewish literature אלין (*DAN*, 19); in the
Syriac ܗܠܝܢ (Nestle 1883: 23).

Line 20

סרבנין Syr. ܣܪܒܢܘܬܐ (*BLS*, 496); in parabiblical Jewish literature *nomen abstr.*
סרבנותא (*DAN*, 300); absolute plural. The Greek parallel is ζητήσεις.

תגרא - plural, *st. emph.*; Syr. ܬܓܪܐ (*BLS*, 816); in parabiblical Jewish literature
תגר and תגרא (*DAN*, 438; *LW*, IV, 627). In the Greek text τῶν ἐνπόρωιν.

מכסיא - in the Greek text τοὺς τελώνας; plural. *st. emph.* (ending -יא).

אתחזי לבולא - loan translation from Greek δεδόχθαι (sc. τῇ βουλῇ).

אתחזי - root חזי; third masculine singular perfective, Ethpe'el. In the Aramaic
documents from Egypt חזה (V., 7, 217); Syr. ܚܙܐ (*BLS*, 224); in parabiblical
Jewish literature חזא (*LW*, II, 28–9; *DAN.* 141).

עשרתא - in the Greek text δ[εκα]πρώτους. As P.K. Kokovtsov (Arch. AS, f.
779, inv. 1, no. 40, p. 149) notes, in ולעשרתא the ל is pleonastic; to prove his
point he refers to Isa. 32:1: וּלְשָׂרִים.

Line 21

די - reduplication of the conjunction די (I, 20). Since the word breaks the construction of the phrase, it is possible that the carver inserted this word by mistake.

יבנ[ו]ן - root בין; third masculine plural imperfective, Af'el; Syr. كَّ (*BLS*, 68–9); in parabiblical Jewish literature בין (*DAN*, 53). In the Greek text the parallel participle form is διακρείνοντας.

מדעם - cf. I, 18: מדען.

מסק - root סלק; Af'el passive participle, masculine, absolute.

מדעם די לא מסק בנמוסא - in the Greek text the exact parallel is τὰ μὴ ἀνειλημμένα τῷ νόμῳ.

ויכתב - root כתב; the Greek parallel is ἐνγράψαι. According to Sachau (1883: 565), this form is imperfective passive Pe'al. In this case, the subject of the sentence must be מדעם. Schröder (1884: 422–3) agrees with that. The Pe'al form occurs in the Aramaic documents from Egypt (Leander 1966: 55); also in Biblical Aramaic (Bauer, Leander; Rosenthal 1963). R. Duval (1884: 61) thought that the basic form was יתכתב with the assimilation of the ת to the following כ. According to Reckendorf (1888: 398), יכתב is an active form; the implicit subject is the council of Palmyra. Chabot (*CIS*, II, 3913) assumes that the form יכתב is active imperfective Pe'al. It would mean the same as the French 'qu'on écrire'; however, he translated it: 'et ea in nova stipulatione scriberentur'. We agree with E. Sachau; the verb agrees with the preceding מדעם.

בשטר אגריא חדתא - in the Greek text τῇ ἔνγιστα μισθώσει.

אגריא - *scriptio defectiva*; cf. I, 18: אגוריא.

חדתא - cf. Syr. ܚܕܬܐ (*BLS*, 217); in parabiblical Jewish literature חֲדָתָא (*DAN*, 138). However, J. Levy (*LW*, II, 19) prefers the alternative vocalization חַדְתָּא. It is not clear whether the Palmyrene Tariff has a historical spelling or reflects a stage when the assimilation ת > ד was not yet complete.

ויכתב - in the Greek text ὑποτάξαι.

מדעמא - cf. I, 18: מדען; I, 21: מדעם.

Lines 21–2

למדעמא מדעמא - in the Greek text ἑκάστῳ εἴδει.

Line 22

מכסה די מן עידא - loan translation from Greek τό ἐκ συνηθείας τέλος. מכסה - enclitic pronoun ה-, third masculine singular.

מדי - Syr. ܡܢ (*BLS*, 372; cf. *CIS*, II, 3913); in the Greek text ἐπειδάν.

אשר לאגורא - loan translation from Greek κυρωθῇ τῷ μισθουμένῳ (passive form with *dativus auctoris*).

אשר - according to Sachau, third person singular masculine perfective aspect, passive, Peʻal (Sachau, p. 564). Reckendorf (1888: 399) has a more plausible suggestion: Afʻel from the root שרר. Sachau translates: 'nachdem dann der Steuerpächter den Vertrag genehmigt'. Reckendorf's translation is 'und sobald er (der neue Gesetz) dem Pächter recht gemacht habe'. Chabot takes Sachau's view. He translates it this way: 'postquam fuerit a publicano comprobata (stipulatio)'.

כתב - third person singular masculine perfective aspect, passive, Peʻal; in the Greek text ἐγγραφῆναι. Sachau (1866: 565) and, following him, Rosenthal (1936: 13) read יכתב...וכתב .

גללא - in the Greek text στήλη λιθίνη. Cf. in parabiblical Jewish literature גללא (*LW*, I, 335); in Biblical Aramaic גלל.

Line 23

היכלא - Syr. ܗܝܟܠܐ (*BLS*, 174); in parabiblical Jewish literature היכלא (*DAN*, 112; *LW*, I, 464). Derived from Akk. *ekallu* (*CAD* 4/E, 1958: 52–61) and through this from Sumerian é-gal. In the Greek text ιερ[οῦ].

ויהוה מבטל - root בטל; in the Greek text ἐπιμελεῖσθαι. Cf. Syr. ܚܒܛܝܠܐ 'care, fervour', *BLS*, 66. However, in Paʻʻel Syr. ܚܒܛܠ 'to cause to cease, forbid'; in parabiblical Jewish literature בטל 'to destroy, make invalid' (*LW*, I, 212; *DAN*, 52). Cf. Sachau (1866: 563): 'sollen darüber wachen, dass ...'; Reckendorf (1888: 385): 'sollen dafür sorgen, dass ...'; *CIS*, II, 3913: 'et curandum erit'; JH, 33: 'il est du devoir des archontes que ...' The latter comes from בטל in Peʻal: 's'occuper de'. Third masculine singular compound future tense, passive, Paʻʻel. The compound future is built as follows: the conjugated form of the imperfective aspect of the verb הוא in Peʻal + the necessary participle.

הון - active Peʻal plural participle of הוא.

די הון בזבן - loan translation from Greek τοὺς τυγχάνοντας κατὰ καιρόν.

Line 24

סדקיא - This comes from Greek; cf. Greek συνδίκο[υς]. Cf. similar Syriac forms: *BLS*, 484. There is progressive assimilation נ > ד. Plural, *st. emph.*, with the ending -יא.

143

יהוא גבא - third masculine singular compound future tense, active voice, Pe'al; it agrees with אגורא.

לא יהוא ... יתיר - in the Greek text παραπράσσειν.

אגורא - in the Greek text τὸν μισθούμενον. The stem is אגר (cf. I, 18 and 21); singular, emphatic.

אנש - singular, absolute. Cf. *scriptio plena* (singular, absolute): אנוש (*Inv.* IX, 12a).

Lines 25–7

This additional paragraph of the Tariff is written after the decree of the council and before the Tariff itself. The engraver was probably using the gap left after the first part of the inscription was made. It is interesting that the tax for all kinds of goods depends on whether the load is carried on a cart or a camel. The ratio 4:1 accepted in the Palmyrene Tariff does not agree with the average numbers in the *Edict of Diocletian*. There the load of 1200 (Italic) *litra*s (c. 392.4 kg) carried on a cart would cost 20 *denarii* per mile; the load of 600 *litra*s (c. 196.2 kg) carried by a camel 8 *denarii*; the load carried by a donkey costs 4 *denarii*. Therefore, the accepted camel:cart load ratio in the *Edict of Diocletian* is 2:1. (It is known that the standard load for a camel is 50% of the weight of the animal; as the average weight of a camel is between 400 and 800 kg, so the weight of the load could be 200–400 kg.) If we accept the weight given in the *Edict of Diocletian* for a camel-load (about 200 kg), so we can conclude that it was the norm in Palmyra to transport about 800 kg on a cart, i.e. four times the camel-load and twice what was normal elsewhere in the Empire (cf. also Reckendorf 1888: 401, where the load for a camel is given as 300 kg and for a cart 1200 kg). [Ed.: figures have been adjusted here.]

Line 25

Γόμος καρρικός - a normal load of the Gaulish cart, *carrus* (Caes., *B. Gall.*, I, 3, I; I, 26, I; I, 26, 3; Liv., 10, 28, 9), that was common in the Near East, probably after the Roman invasion. The *carrus* was used for the transportation of goods as well as as a military chariot. According to the *Edict of Diocletian* (15, 38–40), a *carrus* could be two-wheeled or four-wheeled; according to the Mishnah, Bava Bathra 5: 2, a *carrus* was drawn by a mule in the Near East (Mau 1899; *TA*, II, p. 336).

καμηλικῶν - the word κάμηλος comes from Semitic (LS, 872)

Line 26

טעון קרס - in the Greek text γόμος καρρικός.

טעון - masculine singular construct state. In the *Words of Aḥiqar* from Elephantine we find טעון גמלא (V., 7, 227); cf. Syr. ܛܥܢܐ (*BLS*, 283–4); in parabiblical Jewish literature טעונא (*LW*, II, 174; *DAN*, 172).

קרס - Lat. *carrus*. The word came into parabiblical Jewish literature in the form קרון (*KGLL*, II, 565), the Greek equivalent τὸ κάρρον.

כלמא גנס כלה - in the Greek text παντὸς γένους.

כלמא - in the Bar-Rekub inscriptions (*KAI*, 222A and 224): כל מה; in the texts from Sefire כלמה (JH, 119–20). Reckendorf 1888: 401 points to Syr. ܟܠܡܕܡ.

גנס - Greek γένος. Cf. Syr. ܓܢܣܐ (*BLS*, 125) and in parabiblical Jewish literature גנוס, גניס and גניסא (*KGLL*, II, 180).

גבי - Pe'al passive participle; cf. in the Greek text the conjugated passive form ἐπράχθη.

Panel II

Title

למנא - Greek λιμήν with marker of the Aramaic emphatic state (cf. *CIS*, II, 3913). Reckendorf 1888: 402 thinks that the accusative-case form λιμένα was borrowed here, though this is unlikely. Cf. Syr. ܠܡܐܢܐ (*BLS*, 367) and in parabiblical Jewish literature לימין and לימן (*KGLL*, II, 314–15). In Greek the word λιμήν usually means 'pier, harbour, haven', hence in the Palmyrene Tariff — 'trading centre, market'. Cf. in *Dig.*, L, 16, 59 the definition of the Latin word *portus*, which corresponds with Greek λιμήν: *portus appellatus est conclusus locus, quo importantur merces et inde exportantur*, '*portus* means an enclosed place into which goods are brought and from which they are taken out'. J.-B. Chabot in his translation uses the exact Latin equivalent *portus* (*CIS*, II, 3913); Reckendorf 1888: 402 thinks that the translation 'customs' (Zollstation) is possible here. Similar usage of the word has been observed for the Akkadian *kārum* — not only 'harbour, pier', but also 'haven' — a settlement of traders, not associated with sea trade (Īankovskaīa 1968: 65–6). P. Schröder (1884: 422) suggested a fanciful interpretation: מנא plural emphatic from מאן, מן, 'Waare, Handelsartikel', with preposition ל: this does not offer a satisfactory meaning. Starcky (1952: 82) thinks that what is meant here is a warehouse (entrepôt). Finally, Rostovtzeff (1932b: 79–80) believed that λιμήν in the Tariff meant 'taxation district'. It is interesting that in a neo-Punic inscription from Tripolitene, *KAI* 124 (which corresponds to Trip., 31), the word המחז (literally 'pier') corresponds with Latin *forum*. Concerning Phoenician *mḥwz* see also Borger 1969: 1–3.

הדרינא - cf. Ael. Spart., *Vita Hadr.* 20, 4: 'Although he (i.e. Hadrian) was not fond of inscriptions on buildings, he named many cities Hadrianopolis, as, for example, Carthage and a part of Athens.' In AD 129 Hadrian visited Palmyra: see *CIS*, II, 3959: ἐπιδημ[ία] θεοῦ Ἀδριανοῦ; אלהא הדרינ[וס] תנ[א] את[י] וכדי. According to Stephanus of Byzantium (St. Byz., s.v. Πάλμυρα: Ἁδριανόπολις), the city was rededicated and received the name Hadrianopolis. However, this name of the city is not completely correct; in a Greek text (*CIG*, 6015; AD 236) there is preserved the formula, Ἁδριανὴ Πάλμυρα, that fully agrees with the Aramaic הדרינא תדמר. It undoubtedly conveys the name that Palmyra received at the rededication. The analogous name for Petra is also known: Ἁδριανὴ Πέτρα (Starcky, Bennett 1968: 41–66, no. 8). Cf. *CIS*, II, 3913, *ad locum*; Reckendorf 1888: 402; Dobiáš 1928: 190–9. Reckendorf is mistaken in thinking that הדרינא is the Greek name for the city, which, in contrast to the original Semitic, is Πάλμυρα, which does not occur in the Aramaic texts from Palmyra. Perhaps it derives from πάλμυς = βασιλεύς, which came into Greek from Lydian and has the meaning 'kingly' (LS, s.v.).

תדמר - This ancient Semitic name for Palmyra occurs already in the Assyrian documents from Cappadocia and in the documents from Mari of the first half of the second millennium BC (Bilgiç 1945–51: 36; Michelini Tocci 1960: 94–5; Starcky 1952: 27–8), in the annals of the Assyrian kings of the last quarter of the second millennium BC (Dhorme 1924: 106–8), and in the Bible (2 Chron. 8:4 and the *qere* in 1 Kgs 9:18). The Assyrian texts retain the vocalization Tadmar; the biblical text has תַּדְמֹר, while Josephus (*Ant.*, 8, 6, 1) has the form Θαδάμορα. Eusebius (*Onom. sacr.*, s.v.) has Θερμώθ which corresponds with the name תרמד in parabiblical Jewish tradition (cf. for example Yevamot, 16; *LW*, IV, s.v.).

תדמר probably derives from the root *dmr* (nominal *taqtal* form with transition under stress a > ā > ō), which in Aramaic has the meaning 'to be amazing, wonderful'. In Syr. ܬܕܡܘܪܬܐ corresponds with the feminine form in

Josephus, Θαδάμορα, 'wonder, marvel' (*BLS*, 159). Cf. in the south Arabian texts the form *tḏmry* which probably comes from *tḏmr*, with the fricative pronunciation of /t/; cf. Ryckmans 1964: 277–88; Jamme 1965: 16–17; Ja(mme) 931 [Jamme, *The Al-'Uqlah Texts*, 1963: 44–5]). R. du Mesnil du Buisson (1966: 187) suggested that the word תדמר derives from *Tl-'mr* (with transition l > d and omission of '); the first part would correspond with the word 'tell', the second would go back to the Amorite ethnonym ('*mr*, '*mwr*). Although this suggestion is interesting, it is unlikely to be correct for philological reasons: the transition l > d is not known in the Canaanite languages.

עינתא - √עין; cf. Syr. ܥܝܢܐ (*BLS*, 522) and ܥܝܢܬܐ (Payne Smith 1903: 411); the latter form is linked with ܡܝܐ. In parabiblical Jewish literature עין and עינא. One of the wells in this context is Efqa, the other is either Bi'r al-ʿAmyā which is 7 km to the north of Palmyra or Abū-l-Fawāris (Starcky 1952: 82).

[אי]לס קיסר - reconstruction accepted by Chabot (*CIS*, II, 3913). קיצר, from Latin *Caesar*, possibly through Greek Καῖσαρ.

Column 1

Line 1

מעלי - √עלל, construct plural, Afʿel active participle. Found in the documents from Elephantine and in the Aramaic inscriptions (V., 11, 228).

עלימיא - √עלם; noun in plural, emphatic state; the Greek parallel is παῖδες. An analogous usage (in the sense of 'slave') is known in Ugaritic (the word *ǵlm*; see Aistleitner 1963: 248, no. 2150) as well as in the Bible (1 Sam. 20:22) and in the documents from Elephantine (V., 11, 227–8): עלים and עלימא. Plural עלימין and עלימיא. Cf. Syr. ܥܠܝܡܐ (*BLS*, 528), as well as Classical Arabic غلام.

מתאעלין - Ettafʿal participle.

Line 2

תחומיה - masculine plural noun with enclitic feminine singular pronoun ה. In Imperial Aramaic תחם (JH, 325); in parabiblical Jewish literature תחום (*LW*, IV, 637); in Syr. ܬܚܘܡܐ (*BLS*, 820). The Palmyrene borders are established according to the frontier posts that were published by Schlumberger in 1939 (Schlumberger 1939: 43–7). Presumably, these posts were along the river Euphrates in the north and northeast; in the steppes from Reṣāfa to the south of

Khirbet al-Bilʻās, from there to Khirbet al-Fayé and through Qaṣr al-Ḥayr to the valley of ad-Daw. (See also Schlumberger 1951).

יגבא מכסא - reconstruction by de Vogüé (1883b: 153), accepted by Reckendorf 1888: 380, and *CIS*, II, 3913. יגבא - third masculine singular jussive Peʻal.

כל - indefinite pronoun 'every' (Rosenthal 1936: 52–3). In the Old Aramaic inscriptions and the documents from Egypt כל (JH, 119; V., 9, 144); in Biblical Aramaic כֹּל (Gesenius-Buhl, 903); in parabiblical Jewish literature כל (*DAN*, 197); in Syr. ܟܠ (V., 1, 5, 326).

רגל - the Greek parallel is σῶμα. Dessau 1884: 504 translates the whole phrase as: 'pro singulis hominibus(?)' – and says (504, note 2): 'The word in the Aramaic text here actually means something completely different, "foot", but in IIa line 5 it corresponds with the Greek ἑκάστου σώμ[ατος] (IIIa 8); however, even without this evidence, there can be no doubt [on the interpretation].' Cf. Arabic رَجُل. Reckendorf (1888: 403) rightly believes that this is a case of borrowing from Arabic. Cf. also: *CIS*, II, 3913, *ad locum*.

Line 3

י[זב]ן - √זבן; cf. in documents from Elephantine (V., 7, 205); Syr. ܙܒܢ (*BLS*, 187); in Jewish parabiblical literature זבן (*DAN*, 123). M. de Vogüé (1883b: 153) read ... די ל; Reckendorf (1888: 381): די ..ן. We accept Chabot's reconstruction: י[זב]ן - third singular imperfective passive Peʻal (the word agrees with the עלם implied in the subordinate clause, the logical object).

מדינתא [מדי[ת]א] < - reconstruction from *CIS*, II, 3913. In the Palmyrene inscriptions the word had a meaning analogous to the Greek word πόλις (cf. *CIS*, II, 3994: Διὶ ὑψίστῳ καὶ ἐπηκόῳ ἡ πόλις εὐχήν; in the parallel Palmyrene text: עבדת מדינתא לבריך שמה לעלמא). In the documents from Elephantine מדינא, מדינה, as well as מדינתא and מדנתא (V., 11, 190). Cf. Syr ܡܕܝܢܬܐ, ܡܕܝܢܐ (Payne Smith 1903: 252); in parabiblical Jewish literature מדינה and מדינתא (*DAN*, 225).

[או י]פק - our reconstruction, third person singular, imperfect passive Peʻal of the verb נפק by analogy with the previous, undoubtedly personal, י[זב]ן. This reconstruction also corresponds with the logical sequence of lines 1–3 on business transactions involving slaves: import into Palmyra, sales on its Paʻʻel territory and export abroad. M. de Vogüé (1883b: 153) suggested [מת]פק[א]; Reckendorf (1888: 380) read [ל]מפק[נא]. However, neither of these readings corresponds with the syntactical construction of the phrase. They also do not fit the *lacuna*. J.-B. Chabot (*CIS*, II, 3913, *ad locum*) considered the following reconstruction possible although he did not insert it into the published text: קפ[מ אל]. In that case, though, the construction of the phrase and the logic of the narrative are violated. The verb נפק appears in the documents from Elephantine (V., 11, 211–12); cf. Syr ܢܦܩ (*BLS*, 438–9) and the parabiblical Jewish literature נפק (*DAN*, 274–5; *LW*, III, 424).

Line 4

וטר[ן] - from Latin *veteranus* through the Greek οὐετρανός; cf. in the parallel Greek text (III, 1, 6): οὐετραν[ά]. Already Dessau (Dessau 1884: 505) pointed to the passage from the *Digest* (*Dig.*, XXXIX, 4, 16, 3) which contains the description of the *mancipia veterana*: 'sunt autem veterana, quae anno continuo in urbe servierint; novicia autem mancipia intelleguntur, quae annum nondum servierint' (cf. similar points by Dittenberg and Chabot). However, more light can be shed by the *Digest*, which refers to slave-veterans. (The similarity between the terms 'veteran' and 'veterator' is clear; cf. *Dig.*, XXI, I, 37, where they are interchangeable.) According to the fragment from Venuleius (*Venuleius libro quinto actionum* [*Dig.*, XXI, 1, 65, 2]), 'either a *veterator* or a *novicius* can be called a slave. But a *veterator* is to be defined not according to the time of his servitude, but because of its type and cause. Caelius says: if anyone who was purchased from the slave-trader as a *novicius* becomes a head of any service, he is immediately considered as a *veterator*. A *novicius* is not a new slave, but determined as such by the condition of his servitude. It does not matter whether a *veterator* knows Latin or not. He is a *veterator* if he has been educated in liberal arts' (*Servus tam veterator quam novicius dici potest. Sed veteratorem non spatio serviendi, sed genere et causa aestimandum. Caelius ait: nam quicumque ex venalicio noviciorum emptus alicui ministerio praepositus sit, statim eum veteratorum numero esse: novicium autem non tirocinio animi, sed condicione servitutis intellegi. Nec ad rem pertinere, Latine sciat necne: nam ob id veteratorem esse, si liberalibus studiis eruditus sit*). From the foregoing it is evident that the slave-veterans in Palmyra were first of all slaves that had some sort of leading position and/or had studied the liberal arts, i.e. had a Hellenistic education. Ulpianus' directive clarifies further (*Ulpianus libro primo ad edictum aedilium curulium* [*Dig.*, XXI, 1, 37]): 'The *aediles* prescribe that a *veterator* should not be sold as a *novicius*. This edict prevents the fraudulent tricks of traders because generally the *aediles* take care to prevent buyers being taken in by traders. For example, many vendors are accustomed to sell slaves as *novicii* who are not such, in order that they may sell them for more, since it is presumed that slaves who did not receive an education are easier to deal with, better adapted to service, more tractable and skilful in every kind of work, while it is difficult to change or adapt to one's customs those slaves who are experienced and veteran. Hence, because slave-traders know that persons are rather inclined to the purchase of slaves who are *novicii*, they, for this reason, mingle *veteratores* with them and sell them as *novicii*. It is in order to avoid this that the *aediles* prohibit it by this edict; and therefore, if this kind of purchase takes place without a buyer's knowledge, the slave shall be returned.' (*Praecipiunt aediles, ne veterator pro novicio veneat. Et hoc edictum fallaciis venditorum occurrit: ubique enim curant aediles, ne emptores a venditoribus circumveniantur. Ut ecce plerique solent mancipia quae novicia non sunt, quasi novicia distrahere ad hoc, ut pluris vendant: praesumptum est enim ea mancipia quae rudia sunt, simpliciora esse et ad ministeria aptiora et dociliora et ad omne ministerium habilia: trita vero mancipia et veterana difficile est reformare et ad suos mores formare. Quia igitur venaliciarii sciunt facile decurri ad noviciorum emptionem, idcirco interpolant veteratores et pro noviciis vendunt. Quod ne fiat, hoc edicto aediles denuntiant: et ideo si quid ignorante emptore ita venierit, redhibebitur.*)

Thus, to judge from the size of the tax, slave-*veterator*s were cheaper in Palmyra. The reason for that is given by Ulpianus. See on slave-*veterator*s Shtaerman, Trofimova 1971: 233–4. It is noticeable that there is no ending -*us*/-*os* on וטרן. De Vogüé (1883b: 153) has פט[יר], but the original text does not support this.

[במדיתא] - reconstructed by analogy with the previous line. Against Chabot (*CIS*, II, 3963, *ad locum*), the text lacks six, not four symbols.

Line 5

הן - in the inscriptions from Sefire הן; in the Aramaic texts from Egypt הן (JH: 66; V., 7, 199); in Biblical Aramaic הֵן (Gesenius-Buhl, 896–7]; in parabiblical Jewish literature הן (*DAN*, 115); in Syr. ܐܢ (*BLS*, 27). See below אן (II, 3).

זבונא - see Syr. ܙܒܘܢܐ (*BLS*, 187); in parabiblical Jewish literature זבונא (*DAN*, 123).

יפק - √ נפק - third singular imperfective, active Pe'al.

עלי[מ]ין - cf. line 1 עלימיא.

יתן - third masculine singular jussive, active voice, Pe'al. Root נתן.

לכל רגלי - Arabism, with singular genitive ending.

Line 6

הו - in the Greek text this corresponds with ὁ αὐτός.

מ|ן |מ|כסא יג|בא| - reconstruction by de Vogüé (1883b: 153). Cf. Greek text ὁ αὐτός δημοσιώνης ... πράξει.

יבי|שין| - reconstruction by Reckendorf (1888: 404). The form יבי[שיא] is also possible. M. de Vogüé (1883b: 153) read יבל and translated (p. 166): 'Le fermier lui-même percevra un droit sur toute charge de chameau qui sera apportée.' Cf. Syr. ܟܡܫܐ (*BLS*, 295); in parabiblical Jewish literature יבש (*DAN*, 179).

Line 7

מעלנא - √עלל - verbal noun derived from the Af'el participle, plus suffix -ān. On this type of derivation in Syriac see Duval 1881: 234. In the Greek text εἰσκομισ[θέ]ντος.

|לכלמא| - our reconstruction in correspondence with the parallel Greek ἑκάστου γόμο[υ]. M. de Vogüé suggested לתדמר. This does not find support in the Greek text of the Tariff.

Line 8

מן |טעון גמלא| למ|פקנא| - reconstruction by de Vogüé (1883b: 153).

מפקנא - this form is analogous to מעלנא (see comments on line 7). In the parallel Greek text ἐκκομισθ[έντ]ος.

Line 9

ט|עון| חמרא - reconstruction by de Vogüé (1883b: 153). In the documents from Egypt חמר and חמרא (V., 7, 220; cf. also JH, 91); cf. Syr. ܚܡܪܐ (*BLS*, 241); in parabiblical Jewish literature חמרא (*DAN*, 152). Since the difference from the size of the tax on a camel-load in lines 7–8 must correspond with the difference in weight of the imported and exported goods, it is plausible to suggest that the average load for a donkey was 200 kg.

Line 10

א|רג|ונא מלטא - the parallel from the Greek is πορφύρας μηλωτῆ[ς]. de Vogüé (1883b: 153) read פרפ]רא[; Reckendorf (1888: 380): א[רג]ונא. The latter refers to the Biblical Aramaic אַרְגְּוָן, Syr. ܐܪܓܘܢܐ and Arabic أَرْجَوَان. See also in parabiblical Jewish literature ארגונא (*DAN*, 39). מלטא comes from Greek (μηλωτή - fine, fibrous, white sheep's wool). To get this kind of wool the sheep would be covered with a special wrapping, which enabled the wool to stay clean and not to get rough (*TA*, I, p. 137: the sources are given there also; cf. especially Shabbat 52a). Purple wool was made in Phoenicia (cf. Strabo XVI. 2. 23; Luc., *Phars.*, 3., 217; *Tot. orb. descr.* 31) and from there was probably imported to Palmyra.

מ|שך| - reconstruction by de Vogüé (1883b: 153); cf. in the parallel Greek [δέρμα]τος. Cf. Syr. ܡܫܟܐ (*BLS*, 407); in parabiblical Jewish literature משכא (*DAN*, 257); in the Aramaic documents from Egypt משך (V., 11, 204; JH, 170); literally 'skin' as a unit of measure for wool – the fleece shorn from one sheep.

[למעלנא] - reconstruction of de Vogüé (1883b: 153), confirmed by the following word: ולמ[פ]קנא.

Line 11

אסרין - adopted from Greek ἀσσάριον; cf. Syr. ܐܣܪܐ (*BLS*, 38) and in parabiblical Jewish literature איסר, plural אסירין (*KGLL*, II, 37).

Line 12

טע|ון ג|מלא - de Vogüé (1883b: 153) read ט[עון גמלא]. We adopt Reckendorf's suggestion (1888: 380).

משחא בשימא - in the Greek variant μύρου. Cf. in the Aramaic texts from Egypt משח and משח בשם (V., 9, 203; JH, 170); in Syr. ܡܫܚܐ (*BLS*, 407) and ܚܡܫܚܐ (*BLS*, 80). Reckendorf (1888: 405) and after him I.N. Vinnikov (V., 4, 222) pointed to Luke 7:46 where the Greek ἐλαίῳ τὴν κεφαλήν μου οὐκ ἤλειψας· αὕτη δὲ ἤλειψεν τοὺς πόδας μου (cf. also Vulgate: *oleo caput meum non unxisti: haec autem unguento unxit pedes meos*) has in the Syriac Peshitta: ܐܢܬ ܡܫܚܐ ܠܪܫܝ ܠܐ ܡܫܚܬ. ܗܕܐ ܕܝܢ ܒܡܫܚܐ ܘܒܣܡܐ ܡܫܚܬ ܪܓܠܝ. Cf. also in parabiblical Jewish Literature משחה and משח, משחא (*LW*, III, 273) (cf. the writing מישחא), also בוסם (in the Bible בֹּשֶׂם; [*LW*, I, 244]). In Hebrew בסם and בשם are interchangeable in words that derive from this root (cf. בסם/בשם 'being pleasant, agreeable'; בשם/בסם 'pharmacist, trader of spices'; בשומא/בסומא – 'delicious food'; *LW*, I, 244). A similar interchange probably took place in Syriac-Aramaic writing in the time of the Principate. In parabiblical Jewish literature בשמים are precious oils (*unguenta*) mixed with dry fragrant spices (*TA*, I, 237).

Commentary

|די| - reconstruction: Reckendorf 1888: 380.

Line 13

מתאעל - masculine singular Ettafʿal participle, agreeing with משחא (except in state: משחא emphatic, מתאעל absolute). This is a deviation from the common form: למעלנא.

|ב|ש|טיפ|א - our reconstruction. Reckendorf's variant is [ב]ש|טיפית]א (Reckendorf 1888: 380). He justifies his translation by referring to the Syriac translation of several passages from the Gospels. Matthew 26:7: Greek προσῆλθεν αὐτῷ γυνὴ ἔχουσα ἀλάβαστρον μύρου βαρυτίμου (cf. Vulgate: *accessit ad eum mulier habens alabastrum unguenti praetiosi*), in the Peshitta ܘܚܡܣܐ ܘܚܡܐ ܥܠܝܩܐ ܕܐܝܬ ܒܐܢܐ ܐܬܐ ܠܘܬܗ; Mark 14:3: Greek ἦλθεν γυνὴ ἔχουσα ἀλάβαστρον μύρου νάρδου πιστικῆς πολυτελοῦς (Vulgate: *venit mulier habens alabastrum unguenti nardi spicati praetiosi*), in the Peshitta ܐܬܬ ܐܢܬܐ ܕܐܝܬ ܥܠܝܗ ܥܠܝܩܐ ܘܚܡܣܐ ܕܢܪܕܝܢ ܪܝܫܝܐ ܣܓܝܐ. Luke 7:46: see comments on line 12. Reckendorf also points to the expression μύρου ἀλάβαστρον in Herodotus 3. 20. We think that ש[טיפ]א is more plausible by analogy with II, 1, 19 ש[טיפ]א. Cf. also III, I, 13–20: γόμου κ[αμηλικοῦ] μύρου [τοῦ ἐν ἀλαβάσ]τροις.

Line 14

M. de Vogüé (1883b: 153) reconstructed ולמא די [מן משח]א. However, Reckendorf (1888: 405) was very sceptical about any reconstruction of the text ('Mit dieser Zeile ist nichts anzufangen'). Chabot (*CIS*, II, 3913, *ad locum*) referred to 'scriptura deleta,' although he accepted de Vogüé's reading of the penultimate word [משח]א. Reckendorf (1888: 380) reads this line as ולמא ד......ל. וסר דנה, stating on p. 405, 'Ob am Schlusse כנה oder דנה steht, ist nicht zu entscheiden'.

The context of lines 14 and 15 is clear: it is about taxes for camel-loaded export of perfumed/sweet oil (משחא בשימא) in alabaster jars. This explains the presence of the pronoun דנה which together with [משח]א must refer clearly to משחא בשימא in line 12. However, the opening words ולמא show that the authors of the Tariff avoided here the common formula. This makes any reconstruction of the text (where there is no parallel Greek text — see on the reconstruction of III, 1, 21 below) extremely hypothetical and presumptuous.

The expression למא has the following meanings in Syriac (ܠܡܐ), as R. Duval (1881: 373–4) shows: a) in a question it expresses doubt or negation

The Palmyrene Tax Tariff

(this meaning is not possible in the present case because of the nature of the document); b) it can indicate the *possibility* of something coming to pass. This latter meaning is also inappropriate because after it we have the particle ד[י] which is either *nota genitivi* or an introduction to a subordinate clause. Reckendorf (1888: 385) translated the expression ולמא ד[י] – 'und wofür', Chabot (*CIS*, II, 3913) – 'et quod'. We think that the meaning of the whole expression ולמא ד[י] is clear in the light of the parallel from a Biblical Aramaic context (Ezra 6:8): וּמִנִּי שִׂים טְעֵם לְמָא־דִי תַעַבְדוּן עִם שָׂבֵי יְהוּדָיֵא אִלֵּךְ 'I also hereby issue orders as to what you are to do with those elders of the Jews.' Cf. Septuagint: καὶ ἀπ' ἐμοῦ γνώμη ἐτέθη, μήποτε τὶ ποιήσητε μετὰ τῶν πρεσβυτέρων τῶν Ἰουδαίων; Vulgate: *sed et a me praeceptum est, quid oporteat fieri a presbyteris Iudaeorum illis*; and especially in the Peshitta ܘܡܢܝ ܣܝܡ ܛܥܡ ܢܥܒܕܘܢ ܗܟܢܐ ܥܡ ܐܚܘܗܝ ܗܢܘ ܣܒܐ ܝܗܘܕܝܐ. Therefore the above expression can be translated as 'as to what, regarding what'. By analogy, after it there must be a conjugated verb in a subordinate clause that links either with מש[ח]א דנה or has it as an indirect object. The verb, according to the context, could refer to either the export of oil or the collecting of taxes. The first meaning is possible on the basis of the previous discussion of the export of this product. The presence of למפקנ[א] in line 15 makes this hypothesis even more plausible. Taking into consideration all of this we argue for the following reading of line 14: ולמא ד[י] יפק משח[א] דנה, taking יפק as a passive form, perfective Pe'al of נפק (on passive forms of this stem, see above). Translation: 'With regard to the fact that this perfumed oil is exported, …'.

Line 15

The context of the previous lines shows that it is common for this part of the Tariff to have גמל (or גמלא) after the expression מן טעון. Therefore, we suggest the following reconstruction of the line: למפקנ[א] מן טעון [גמל לטעונא.

Line 16

[די יתאעל] - Reckendorf's reconstruction (1888: 380) by analogy with the last part of line 18 (cf. line 13 where there is a participle); יתאעל - third masculine singular imperfective, Ettaf'al.

Line 17

[זקין] - plural absolute; singular: זק. Cf. Syr.: ܙܩܐ, 'stomach, belly' (*BLS*, 203);

154

in parabiblical Jewish literature זקא, plural זקין - 'pot' (*DAN*, 131). In the parallel Greek text [ἐν ἀσκοῖς] αἰγείοις.

ע|ז| - in the Aramaic documents from Egypt ענז (V., 14, 230); Syr. ܥܙ, construct ܥܙ (*BLS*, 535); in parabiblical Jewish literature עז (*DAN*, 309).

Line 18

מן ט|עון חמר די| משחש |בשימא ד|י - Reckendorf's reconstruction (1888: 380) by analogy with line 16. Cf. also line 20. The Greek text (III, 1, 26) has: [Γόμου ὀνικοῦ μύ]ρου, reconstructed by analogy with line 29: Γόμου ὀνικοῦ κ.τ.λ.

Line 19

בש|טיפ|יא - reconstruction of Reckendorf (1888: 380), who reads בש|טיפ|תא by analogy with line 13. *CIS*, II, 3913 reads ש|טיפ|יא. P.K. Kokovtsov (Arch. AS, f. 779, inv. 1, no. 40, p. 83) suggested בשפשיא but this does not correspond with the Greek parallel: ἐν ἀλαβάστροις. Reckendorf (1888: 380) suggests the words [למעלנא ד] after this. However, as Chabot correctly notes, there is no space for למעלנא in the text. It is also unnecessary, because the previous line has די יתאעל. Cf. lines 20–1: [ז|] משחא ב|שי|מא די יתאעל בזקין without the word מעלנא.

Lines 20–1

The formula is identical to the formula in lines 18–19.

Line 22

מש|חא די בזק|ין ארבע - reconstructed by de Vogüé (1883b: 154), who reads, however, ארב|עא; Reckendorf (1888: 380): ארב|ע|; Chabot (*CIS*, II, 3913): ארבע.

Line 23

מעלן - de Vogüé (1883b: 155): מעלי. This is a construct state instead of the emphatic מעלנא, which is common in this text. The parallel word to this, מפקנא (line 24), is emphatic.

Line 24

ד |3|1 - de Vogüé (1883b: 153) takes the number to be 10. Reckendorf (1888: 406) briefly notes that 'the number is 13 not 10'. It is reconstructed according to line 29.

The Palmyrene Tax Tariff

Line 25

תרתן - 'two' (feminine). Cf. documents from Elephantine תרתין (V., 13, 262); Jewish Aramaic תרתין (JH, 334); in parabiblical Jewish literature תרתין (Dessau 1884: 449); Syr. ﺗَﺮْﺗَﯿﻦ (BLS, 834–5). Cf. the agreement: בזקין תרתן (feminine) but in line 22 [בזק]ין ארבע (feminine + masculine).

Line 26

למעל[ן] ט[ע]ונ[א] די גמלא... ולמפקנא - cf. lines 23–4.

[7] ד - Reckendorf (1888: 406) notes, 'Numbers are provided by analogy with lines 23–4 [lines 22–3 of the present edition] in comparison with lines 29 [28] and 31 [30].'

In lines 22–6 there is a possibility that the perfumed oil will be transported on camels in either four or two skins.

Line 27

ל<מ>פקנא - the reconstruction is clear in accordance with the formula. Cf. CIS, II, 3913.

In the light of the size of the export and import tax, it seems a donkey-load for transporting perfumed oil in goatskins consisted of *two* goatskins.

Line 28

דהנא - masculine singular emphatic from the root דהן. Cf. in parabiblical Jewish literature דהן - 'to be fat, corpulent' and דהנא 'fat' (DAN, 92); Syr. ܕܗܢܐ 'fat' (BLS, 143). Reckendorf 1888: 406 points to Arabic دُهْن. He states that in Arabic this word is used in relation to the expensive sorts of oil. P.K. Kokovtsov (Arch. AS, f. 779, inv. 1, no. 40, p. 227) also asked whether the word came from Arabic. Chabot (CIS, II, 3913) follows Reckendorf in his commentary. Cf. our comment on III, 1, 43.

א[רבע] - de Vogüé (1883b: 155) reconstructs [א]רבעא; Reckendorf 1888: 381 - א[רבע]. Cf. line 22: מן טעון א[רבע] די בזקין די דהנא די עז and an analogous form in lines 22–3, though there there is a genitive (with די): טעון די מש[חא] instead of a construct state.

די - At the end of the line the די belongs with the expression טעון גמל. Compare, however, lines 28–9: מן טעון דהנא .... די טעון גמל with lines 30–1: .... מן טעון דהנא לטעון גמל. Structurally די is equivalent to ל.

Line 29

למעלנ<ל> - the restoration of the preposition ל fits the formulary of this part of the Tariff. According to Reckendorf (1888: 406) the preposition is omitted because the previous word ends with ל (גמל). The same restoration is found in *CIS*, II, 3913. de Vogüé (1883b: 155) clearly read ל.

ול[מפק]נא - restored by de Vogüé (1883b: 155) on the basis of the formulary in this part of the Tariff.

Line 30

מן טעון דהנא די בזקין תרת[ן די] עז - the whole line is almost identical to lines 25 and 28. The differences are: in 25 there is משחא instead of דהנא and there is an analytical genitive construction (טעון די מש[חא]) instead of construct (טעון דהנא); in line 28 בזקין א[רבע]. Accordingly, the reconstruction is clear (Reckendorf 1888: 381); in fact de Vogüé (1883b: 155) read all the reconstructed symbols clearly on the *estampage* that he had.

Line 31

לתעון גמלא - cf. lines 28–9: די טעון גמלא.

ול [מפקנא ד] 7 - reconstructed according to the formulary; cf. (de Vogüé 1883b: 155).

The regulation in lines 28–31 is analogous to that in lines 22–6.

Line 32

[דה]נא - see de Vogüé 1883b: 155.

[ד 7 ולמפקנא] 7 - see again de Vogüé, though he mistakenly thought that the tax was three *denarii*. Reckendorf (1888: 381 and 407) suggested a clear reading.

The regulation of line 32 is identical to that of line 27.

Line 33

נ]וני[א - masculine plural emphatic; de Vogüé reads טעו[נא די] מליחיא (1883b: 155); more precisely, however, see in Schröder (1884) טעו[ן נ]וניא. Reckendorf also refers to Schröder when he explains his reading טעון [נונ]א (Reckendorf 1888: 381, 407). He reads this on the basis of the size of the *lacunae*. *CIS*, II, 3913 reads the first נ clearly. In the Aramaic documents from Egypt plural נונן, emphatic נוניא (V., 11, 209; JH, 176); in parabiblical Jewish literature נונא (*DAN*, 266); Syr. ܢܘܢܐ.

מליחיא - masculine plural emphatic, agreeing with the preceding נ[וני]א. In parabiblical Jewish literature מליח (*DAN*, 238); in Syr. ﻣﻠﻴﺤﺎ (*BLS*, 390). [גמלא] - see de Vogüé 1883b: 155.

Line 34

ד [למע]ל[נ]א 10 - reconstructed in accordance with the previous forms. However, the words ומן מפק begin a phrase which does not correspond with the formula that was found in the earlier clauses. Cf. de Vogüé 1883b: 157: [למעלנא], also Reckendorf 1888: 381; in *CIS*, II, 3913 we have [למ]ל[א].

מן - in ancient Aramaic texts as well as in the documents from Elephantine מן (V., 11, 197; JH, 157); in Biblical Aramaic מִן; in parabiblical Jewish literature מאן, מן (*DAN*, 240); Syr. ﻣﻦ (*BLS*, 393).

מפק - √נפק - Af'el participle (masculine singular) used to convey the present tense.

מנהון - הון - enclitic pronoun, third masculine plural, together with the preposition מן. In Biblical Aramaic, הוֹן-, הוֹם-, (Rosenthal 1963: 20); in Aramaic documents from Egypt הם-, הום- (Leander 1966: 27–32); in parabiblical Jewish literature -הם; in Syr. ﻫﻮܢ and ܐܢܘܢ (*BSG*, 48–9).

After the word מנהון there must be a reference to tax collection from those who export salted fish. By analogy with line 37 there would be an additional phrase, [יגבא מכסא ד ...]. Here the section that refers to tax collected on salted fish probably ends.

Line 35

The middle part of the line clearly reads לטעונא די גמלא and shows that the preceding words refer to which particular item must be taxed. By analogy with the previous lines the line could start with [מן טעון], where טעון is in the construct state before the item, which, as the א before לטעונא shows, is in the emphatic state. Thus, the beginning of the phrase can be hypothetically reconstructed as: [מן טעון] א.. לטעונא די גמלא.

Following this there are the letters ... למ which, based on the typology of the structure of the text, must begin the word [למ]עלנא or absolute [למ]עלן. Since line 36 begins with a clause that refers to transportation of what is possibly the same material by donkey, it is plausible that the phrase ends with the words ... [למ]עלנא ולמפקנא ד] (cf. analogous forms in lines 9 and 32).

Commentary

Line 36

The symbols that are readable, די טעון חמרא, show clearly that the discussion in the text is about collecting tax from a load transported on a donkey; on the basis of the previous discussion the goods being transported are probably the same as in line 35 (since, as a rule, there is first a reference to the tax for a camel-load and then for a donkey-load). Accordingly, the beginning of the line can be reconstructed as follows: [מן טעון] .. א די טעון חמרא; cf. analogous forms in lines 28–9: מן טעון דהבא ... די טעון גמל and our comment on that. Cf. de Vogüé 1883b: 157: [מן מליחיא] די טעון חמרא למעלנא.

Assuming that the import tax, as the Tariff indicates, is in most cases twice the export tax, it must have been 5–6 *denarii*; if it is the same as the export tax (cf. the analogous situation in line 32), then it would have been 3 *denarii*.

Line 37

Following the preceding formulary, this clause continues line 36; if previously the discussion was about import ([א]למעלנ) then here it is about export; accordingly the reconstruction is clear: [ולמפק]נא. Thus in de Vogüé 1883b: 157.

Line 38

ולכודנ[א] - Chabot's reading (*CIS*, II, 3913); masculine singular emphatic. In Imperial Aramaic כדן; plural, absolute state כדונן (JH, 116); in parabiblical Jewish literature כדונא, variant כדוניא (*DAN*, 193–4; *LW*, II, 297); Syr. ܟܘܕܢܐ (*BLS*, 318, where the Akkadian is also given: *kidānu*, *kidannu*, *kudīnu*, *kudūnu*).

From the beginning of this line until line 44, the text discusses taxes for import and export of livestock; in the readable fragments the discussion is about mules, sheep and camels.

Therefore, by analogy with line 1 of this column, we can assume that after the word מן in this line was the word מעלי (construct state), after which there should be a description of imported livestock, of which we have left only the -יא ending of the masculine emphatic plural [ed.: or singular if the noun is סוסיא: below]. Since the line ends with a clause that is about mules, it is very plausible that the previous discussion is about horses (*CIS*, II, 3913 *ad locum*). If this is the case then the line could be read as follows: מן [מעלי סוס]יא ד 10 ולכודנ[א] ד 10.

סוס[יא] - masculine emphatic singular: cf. Syr. and the following כודנ[א]. In the inscriptions of Sefire סס; in the documents from Elephantine and other documents of Imperial Aramaic סוס (variant סוסו and סוסא [V., 11, 217; JH, 195]); in Nabataean סוס (*CIS*, II, 890); in parabiblical Jewish literature סוס, סוסא (*DAN*, 286); in Syr. ܣܘܣܝܐ (*BLS*, 464). Cf. also in a Palmyrene inscription (Cantineau 1936: 280) סוסי - masculine singular absolute.

Line 39

The context of this line is almost impossible to reconstruct. Only מן, 'from', which most likely starts a new phrase, is readable in the middle of the line. It is possible that the combination of signs at the end of the phrase can be reconstructed as אמ[רי]א; in this case we have the beginning of a clause about sheep (cf. also line 41) (*CIS*, II, 3913, *ad locum*).

אמ[רי]א - masculine plural emphatic. In the inscriptions from Sefire אמר; in Imperial Aram. אמרא (JH, 18); in Biblical Aramaic אִמַּר (there is a plural form אִמְּרִין [Gesenius-Buhl, 888]); in parabiblical Jewish literature אמר, אמרא (*DAN*, 24); Syr. ܐܡܪܐ (*BLS*, 26).

Line 40

The context of this line too is almost impossible to reconstruct. The readable symbols are -יא which is probably the ending of an emphatic masculine plural noun. We can also clearly reconstruct 4 [אס]רין. Cf. de Vogüé 1883b: 157, who reads 4 [אס]רין; cf., however, Reckendorf 1888: 381: 2 [אס]רין (see also CIS, II, 3913).

Line 41

The line starts with מ, most likely part of the word מ[ן] (cf. lines 42–4); after this there should be something related to 'sheep', which is liable to tax. Since the formula [למע]לן ולמפקן follows the word אמריא, it is plausible to assume that before it there was no reference to export or import. The parallel Greek text uses the word [θ]ρέμμα (III, 2, 22: [θ]ρέμματος; cf. the detailed commentary on this line below). Also it is interesting that just a line above, the tax for sheep is 2 *assarii*, while here it is 1 *assarius* per head. Therefore, it is possible to assume that this line deals with lambs; then the beginning of the line could be reconstructed as follows: מ[ן גדיא די]. Cf. in the inscriptions from Sefire גדה (JH, 47); in parabiblical Jewish literature גדיא (*LW*, I, 301); Syr ܓܕܝܐ (BLS, 104).

למע]לן ולמפקן - de Vogüé (1883b: 157) read ......א מדיא למע]לנ[א ; Schröder

(1884) has the better reading אמריא; Reckendorf 1888: 381: .... שאמריא למע[לנא]. We accept the reconstruction of *CIS*, II, 3913; it fits the context of this part of the Tariff the best.

רשא - masculine singular emphatic. In the inscriptions from Sefire ראש; in the Aramaic documents from Egypt ראש, emphatic רשא (JH, 269; V. 13, 236); in the Nabataean inscriptions ראש; in the Palmyrene ones רש and רשא (JH, 269); in Biblical Aramaic רֵאשׁ (Gesenius-Buhl, 917); in Jewish parabiblical literature ראשא (*DAN*, 395); Syr. ܪܫܐ, ܪܝܫܐ, (*BLS*, 728).

חד - agrees with רשא. It is interesting that this is absolute חד. In the Bar-Rekub and Sefire inscriptions חד; in the Aramaic documents from Egypt חד (V., 7, 215; JH, 9); in Biblical Aramaic חַד (Gesenius-Buhl, 898); in the Nabataean inscriptions חד; in the Palmyrene ones (outside the Tariff) אחדא, אחד, חד (JH, 9). According to F. Rosenthal, in the Palmyrene inscriptions the pronunciation of the two consonants at the beginning in the feminine was eased by the prosthetic א → אחדא, whence a new masculine form appeared, אחד, together with the common one חד (Rosenthal 1936: 31). In the parabiblical Jewish literature חד (*DAN*, 137); Syr. ܚܕ.

Line 42

At the beginning of the line Schröder (1884) and Reckendorf (1888: 381) read מן [טעו]נא גמלא. However, Chabot's response to this reading is well-founded: their reading would require the particle די before the word גמלא. Besides, he continues, the word טעונא, 'load, burden', does not fit the context because the discussion is about animals or other items that can be counted item by item and not transported in bulk. In this connection, we note that the Tariff sets a tax for a camel without load as 1 *denarius* (II, 2, 11). Therefore, it is reasonable to suppose that the present clause refers to a tax for a camel calf. The ending א- before the word גמלא is possible in the following cases: 1) either on a verb ending with third א in the stem or on a similar noun, 2) or as an emphatic noun ending, in which case גמלא would have to be considered as an explanatory addition. If the discussion in the text in II, 1, 42 is about a camel calf, then it is very plausible to suppose that the *lacuna* must have had a reference to this fact.

Among many Arabic terms for a camel calf one is particularly interesting بَكْر (Hommel 1879: 160). The term occurs in the Bible twice.

The first text is Isa. 60:6 – שִׁפְעַת גְּמַלִּים תְּכַסֵּךְ בִּכְרֵי מִדְיָן וְעֵיפָה. Its translation is represented as follows: Septuagint (as a continuation of ἥξουσί σοι at the end of the previous verse): ἀγέλαι καμήλων, καὶ καλυψουσί σε κάμηλοι Μαδιὰμ καὶ Γαιφά; Vulgate: *Inundatio camelorum operiet te, dromedarii Madian et Epha*; Targum Jonathan: שִׁיָרַת עַרְבָאֵי תַּחְפֵּי סַחְרָנִיךְ הוּגְנֵי מִדְיָן וְהוֹלָד (as we see, this version does not agree with the Masoretic text); Peshitta: ܐܰܚܕ̈ܳܐ ܕܓܰܡ̈ܠܶܐ ܐܶܬܟܰܣܝܰܬ ܚܕܡܣ ܘܓܶܒܳܝ ܘܥܰܠܰܝܟܽܘܢ. ('A multitude of camels will cover you, young camels from Midian and Ephah'). The passage which follows this shows that camels, בֶּכֶר, could be used for transportation.

The second text is Jer. 2:23: בִּכְרָה קַלָּה מְשָׂרֶכֶת דְּרָכֶיהָ. In the Septuagint, Vulgate, and Peshitta there is no parallel text. In Targum Jonathan (a different variant of the text): הֲוֵית דַּמְיָא לְיַנְקָא קַלִּילָא דִמְקַלְקְלָא אָרְחָתָהָא ('You were like a restive young she-camel that criss-crosses its path.')

From the foregoing we can organize the following table of correspondences:

Hebr.	Lat.	Greek.	Aram.	Syr.
בֶּכֶר	*dromedarius*	κάμηλος	הוגן	ܚܽܘܓܢܳܐ
בִּכְרָא			ינקא	

Among these the Aramaic הוגן refers to a noble, white, single-humped camel (in a metaphorical sense of the adjective 'noble, worthy' applicable to people; see analysis of *LW*, I, 451 [ed.: see also Hommel 1879: 193–4]); as a noun הוגן (variant הגונא) means 'camel' or 'young camel' (*LW*, I, 451). *LW*, I, 451 illustrates the latter meaning vividly with a proverb (Sanhedrin 52a): גמלי סבי דטעיני משכי דהוגני, 'old camels which carry the skins of young ones'. In Syr. ܚܽܘܓܢܳܐ, 'strong and vigorous camel' (the meaning 'donkey' is also possible, cf. *TS*, I, 988–9; *BLS*, 171).

Another Aramaic term is ינקא, literally 'suckling, baby' (*LW*, II, 247–8), Syr. ܝܰܢܩܳܐ - 'suckling' (*TS*, I, 1608; *BLS*, 304).

It is interesting that the word בכר is absent in the Targum but appears in the Syriac translation of the Bible (ܒܟܪܐ). In Hebrew and in Hebrew-Aramaic intertestamental texts the derivatives from the stem בכר mean 'firstling, firstborn', as well as everything which comes for the first time or early (*LW*, I, 230). In Syriac the meanings are the same, though the word ܒܟܪ̈ܐ, 'young camels', also occurs (*BLS*, 74); *TS*, I, 525 gives the word ܒܟܪܐ the following meaning: 'a camel calf weaned from the mother' (*pullus camelinus a matre ablactatus*).

In sum, the terms that derive from the Semitic stem *bkr* and that were common in this region of the Near East where the Canaanite and Aramaic languages were current, mean the following: a) camel calves weaned from their mothers; b) young camels already suitable for carrying loads. From the foregoing it is evident that the phrase from the Tariff could be reconstructed as follows: 3 א[סרי]ן [בכר]א גמלא מן. The Aramaic words used in the Targum are not technical terms. The term בכרא would be attractive because it occurs both in Aramaic and in Arabic (in accordance with the situation in Palmyra).

There is one other Arabic term meaning a young camel, خُوَارٌ (Hommel 1879: 151–2). In Syriac (*TS*, I, 1228) the word ܚܘܪܐ means 'a year old animal'. Taking this into consideration it is also possible to reconstruct the phrase as: מן [חור]א גמלא א[סרי]ן 3.

In either case, בכרא or חורא, the word plays the grammatical role of an adjective before גמלא. This order (attribute followed by defined word) is possible in Syriac (Duval 1881: 342–4, where there are appropriate examples; cf. especially ܟܠܒܐ ܕܩܦܠܐ). It is very plausible that this occurs in the language of the Palmyrene inscriptions, i.e. the combination of two nouns, where the first is in apposition to and specifies the first like an adjective.

א[סרי]ן - see *CIS*, II, 3913.

Line 43

Reckendorf 1888: 381 reads ..מן ארב.........[א]סרין... . Our suggested reading is recorded also in *CIS*, II, 3913.

The adjective רבא suggests that the preceding word was a masculine singular emphatic noun (only the ending left: -א). As in the earlier context this line is presumably about a type of animal that is imported into Palmyra. It is also clear that there is a contrast between grown and young animals here. According to the size of the tax given in the next line (one *denarius*) it is possible to assume that the discussion here and there is about animals of the same breed (line 43 –'big', line 44 – 'smaller'). If the reconstruction in line 44 is [עת]ו{.}ד[א] then it is also possible to assume that the word עז[א] 'he-goat' follows the word מן here.

By analogy with II, 1, 37 it is possible to think that after the word רבא there was a formula like יגבא מכסא.

Line 44

After the word מן there should be the definition of the item liable to tax; *CIS*, II, 3913, however, reads only the symbols ד.נ.... We think that an interpretation of these remnants can be based on the Arabic عَنُود - 'one-year-old, young adult he-goat' (Hommel 1979: 247). The analogous word is known in Biblical Hebrew, where it occurs twenty-eight times in the masculine plural (in the forms עַתּוּדִים and עֲתֻדִים: Gesenius-Buhl, s.v. עַתּוּד), though in Aramaic and Syriac, as far as we know, the word does not occur. It is possible that this word was in the emphatic, in which case the reconstruction of the beginning of the line could be מן [עת]ו{.}ד[א].

מ]כ]סא אסר]א - see *CIS*, II, 3913.

Line 45

This line starts the second part of the newly enacted law (II, I, 45–II, 2–12), which refers to traders, craftsmen and people with other occupations who made their living on the Palmyrene market. There are many other sections among the resolutions that define taxes collected from them.

אף - conjunction. In the Aramaic documents from Egypt אף (V., 3, 208); in Biblical Aramaic אף (Gesenius-Buhl, 888); in parabiblical Jewish literature אף (*DAN*, 32); in Syr. ܐܦ (*BLS*, 38). Cf. also: Rosenthal 1935: 86.

י]ג]ב]א מכ]סא לכל יר]ח - see *CIS*, II, 3913, reconstructed according to the Greek ἑκάσ[του] μη[νός] (III, 2, 25).

יהוא מזבן - third masculine singular compound future, Pe‛al, consisting of a conjugated form of the auxiliary verb הוא 'to be' in the Pe‛al and participle in the Pa‛‛el. It is dependant on the expression מן די - 'that which, the one who' etc.

Line 46

זניתא - feminine plural emphatic. In parabiblical Jewish literature זניתא (*DAN*, 130), in Syr. ܙܢܝܬܐ (*BLS*, 200).

Line 47

שקלא - feminine singular active Pe‛al participle, absolute state, giving the present tense. It is dependent on the expression מן די. In parabiblical literature שקל (*DAN*, 434); in Syr. ܫܩܠ (*BLS*, 788–9).

דינר - *denarius*, a Roman monetary coin (1 *denarius* = 4 *sestertii* = 16 *assarii*). A masculine singular absolute state noun (the *plene* writing דינר = *denarius* has י conveying the Latin *e*). Cf. in this same line דנרא: emphatic singular with defective spelling. In parabiblical Jewish literature דינר (*KGLL*, II, 207); in Syr. ܕܝܢܪ (*BLS*, 160). Schröder (1884: 427) puts forward a fanciful understanding of

Commentary

the phrase ... מן די שקלא מן - 'von einem Geräth (?), dessen Gewicht einer Dinar oder mehr beträgt ... .' It would then be left unclear, however, why זניתא, 'prostitute', is mentioned in the text earlier.

|אן] - cf. Reckendorf 1888: 381.

אתתא - Reckendorf (1888: 381) reads איתא. Schröder (1884: 427) finds here a measurement of weight. However J.-B. Chabot, after his analysis of the *estampage*, suggests a more accurate reading: אתתא (*CIS*, II, 3913). In the inscriptions from Sefire נשי; in the Aramaic documents from Egypt אנתה, אנתתא (JH, 26; V., 3, 207); in parabiblical Jewish literature אתתא (*DAN*, 46); in Syr. ܐܢܬܬܐ (*BLS*, 31); in other Palmyrene inscriptions אתת (JH, 26). In this text it is feminine singular emphatic.

Line 48

תמניא - cardinal number, feminine, agreeing with אסרין (Reckendorf 1888: 408). In the Aramaic documents from Egypt תמניה (JH: 309, V., 13, 260); in Jewish parabiblical literature תמני (*DAN*, 444); in Syriac ܬܡܢܐ, ܬܡܢܝܐ, ܬܡܢܝܢ, ܬܡܢܝܬܐ (*BLS*, 827).

Column 2

Line 1

|ש]תא - cardinal number, feminine, agreeing with אסרין. Cf. in the Greek text (III, 2, 32) ἕξ (Reckendorf 1888: 408). In Aramaic documents from Egypt שתה (JH, 321; V., 13, 257); in Biblical Aramaic שֵׁת (Gesenius-Buhl, 922); in Syr. ܐܫܬܐ, ܫܬ (*BLS*, 811)

Line 2

|ש]ת[א] - Reckendorf (1888: 381) reads אסרין [ו ע] He explains 'This restoration follows the Greek ἀσσάρια ϛ' (1888: 408).

As far as the section about taxes on prostitutes is concerned (II, 1, 46–II, 2, 2), Dessau (1884: 517), Cagnat (1884: 137) and, following them, J.-B. Chabot (*CIS*, II, 3913) argue that this tax was imposed by Caligula and they refer to Suetonius in terms of its size: *Ex capturis prostitutarum (exigebatur) quantum quaeque uno concubito mereret* (Suet., *Calig.*, 40). Our text shows that Caligula's resolution was in force in the Empire even in the first half of the second century AD and the size of this tax was also the one established by

Caligula for the benefit of the city administration. According to the previous section (line 45), collecting takes place once a month.

P.K. Kokovtsov (Arch. AS, f. 779, inv. 1, no. 40, p. 196), referring to Luc., *Het. dial.*, XI, 1, argues that in the time of Lucian prostitutes paid 5 *drachma*s. See also Rostovtzeff 1916: 63–9, where there is discussion of how the Chersonese government tried to lessen the size of this tax which had been taken to pay wages to the Roman garrison already during the reigns of Hadrian and Antoninus.

Lines 3–5

Based on the parallel Greek text (III, 2, 33–5), the passage talks about craftsmen's shops and small stores. Therefore, in the Aramaic there must be words equivalent to the Greek ones, ἐργαστηρίων and σκυτικῶν.

Line 3

Reckendorf (1888: 381) reads this line אף יגבא ... ודי ח[נו]תא ופטפלי and emphasizes that the reading ח[נו]תא is unreliable, in spite of the fact that the word can have the same meaning as the Greek ἐργαστήριον. We accept the reading of *CIS*, II, 3913 because the editor, who studied the *estampage*, points to the combination of יו, where Reckendorf saw ח. Taking into consideration the presence of the Syriac loanword from Greek, ܐܪܓܣܛܪܝܢ, which is mentioned by Reckendorf, it is possible to reconstruct ופטפלי after [ארגסטר[יו]]. In general, the line can be reconstructed as follows: יגבא מ[כסא מן ארגסטר[יו]ן] אף ופטפלי.

פטפלי - adopted from Greek παντοπώλιον; cf. III, 2, 34: παντοπωλ[ικ]ῶν. It is interesting to note that in the Palmyrene variant of the word there is no ending -ον; there is also assimilation of /n/ to the following /t/(ντ > ט)

Line 4

Reckendorf (1888: 381) reads in this line only the last two words and the letter פ in the fifth place from the beginning; *CIS*, II, 3913 accepted the reading יפא..... ח ...א... עדתא היך עדתא. According to the Greek variant of this passage we can assume that the discussion here is about a shoe workshop. Since there is a conjunction ו before פטפלי in line 3, this line 4 (because it continues the list) must begin with the same conjunction. Also there is a clear ending ....יפא here, which means that after the conjunction ו there must be a word similar to the Syriac ܐܘܫܟܦܐ (Payne Smith 1903: 31) (for pointing out this word the author is grateful to A.V. Paĭkovaia) and אשכפא, common in Jewish parabiblical literature (*DAN*, 44), 'shoemaker', although with an interesting alternate vowel: אָשְׁכִּיפָא (plural אָשְׁכִּיפֵא).

The combination of symbols ה...א can also be read as ח[נות]א, but it is analogous with II, 3, 40, where חיטא, 'tailors', are mentioned in the context of the old law. The word חנותא also appears in the following line (II, 2, 5) where it functions as a unit for measurement of certain taxes. It is probable that before the words היך עדתא the enumeration of these objects ends (cf. III, 2, 35).

א[שכ]יפא - masculine plural emphatic from the root שכף; in parabiblical Jewish literature אשכפא; in Syr. ܐܘܫܟܦܐ (see references earlier).

ח[יט]א - masculine plural emphatic; in parabiblical Jewish literature חיטא (*DAN*, 144).

עדתא - feminine singular emphatic. Cf. I, 18–19: עידא [which is masculine].

Line 5

חנותא - feminine singular emphatic; in parabiblical Jewish literature חנותא (*DAN*, 153); in Syr. ܚܢܘܬܐ (*TS*, II, 1318).

Line 6

מן כ[ל] - see Reckendorf (1888: 381), though reading [מן כל].

Line 7

[מז]בני - see *CIS*, II, 3913; masculine plural construct, active participle, stem זבן.

נחתיא - masculine plural emphatic; in Syr. ܢܚܬܐ (*BLS*, 425).

This is the reading by de Vogüé (1883b: 157) and also J.-B. Chabot (*CIS*, II, 3913). Reckendorf (1888: 381) reads ימנתיא and, referring to the Greek ἱματιοπῶλαι (III, 2, 39), he thinks that it is possible to restore [ה]ימנתיא, though he does not exclude the possibility of נחתיא. Schröder (1884: 430) was the first to suggest the reading ימנתיא. Chabot argues against it because when Aramaic adopts words from the Greek, the Greek τ is usually transmitted as ט.

הפכין - masculine plural active participle, Peʿal, absolute. In ancient Aramaic inscriptions from Sefire אהפך and יהפך (JH, 68); in Jewish parabiblical literature הפך (*DAN*, 117); in Syr. ܗܦܟ (*BLS*, 175). In the Greek text in parallel with the Aramaic די הפכין there is the word μεταβόλοι. On pedlars (רוכלין)

The Palmyrene Tax Tariff

selling ornaments see Bava Bathra 22a.

מוט - see in Jewish parabiblical literature the verb מוט, 'totter' (*DAN*, 227) and in Syr. the verb ܡܛ in the same meaning. Reckendorf (1888: 409) argues for מוט מכסא as 'variation of tax' and interprets it as 'the tax remains undefined', as also in *CIS*, II, 3913. According to Schröder (1884: 430) the word מוט must correspond with the word ἱκανόν from the parallel Greek text. It would derive from the stem מוט (= מטא), meaning 'satisfactory' or 'sufficient'. For our part, we think that the word מוט is probably a masculine singular active Pe'al participle, absolute, to be construed with the verb יהן to form one undivided unit (jussive, using the compound future form). Since the Palmyrene and the Greek texts of the Tariff cannot contradict each other, and since the Palmyrene מוט corresponds with the Greek τὸ ἱκανόν, we accept Schröder's proposal that the Palmyrene מוט means 'to be satisfactory, satisfy'.

It is worthy of note that the auxiliary verb יהן is third plural jussive, Pe'al. It agrees with מכסא which could be plural masculine emphatic, meaning 'taxes': the translation would be then 'may the taxes be sufficient'. However, in this case the meaning of the beginning of the clause would be unclear: [מזבנ]י נחתיא די הפכין במדיתא. Therefore, it is better to suggest that יהן has [מזבנ]י as its subject and the word מכסא, plausibly understood as 'tax collector, farmer', is the object of the verb יהן מוט.

The ambiguity of this clause shows that small-scale pedlars were totally in the power of the tax farmer, who could set any size of tax. Even the reference to 'custom' that appears frequently in the text is missing here.

Line 8

לתש[מיש] - Schröder's restoration (1884: 428, 430), accepted by Reckendorf (1888: 381) and *CIS*, II, 3913; in parabiblical Jewish literature תשמישא and תשמישתא (*DAN*, 450); in Syr. ܬܫܡܫܬܐ (*BLS*, 788).

מ[ין] - Reckendorf (1888: 409), with reference to the Mandaic form, regards it as singular (masculine, absolute).

In the parallel Greek text (III, 2, 41) there is an additional detail, ἑκάστου ἔτους, which indicates the collecting of tax once a year for using the city water-supply system. Schröder (1884: 430) points out that the amount of tax shows the costliness of water in Palmyra. Reckendorf (1888: 409) emphasizes the annual usage of the water sources. According to Cagnat (1884: 138) the text is dealing with those who use a great amount of water for baths, gardens, etc. (cf. also *CIS*, II, 3919). However, there is no evidence in the text for such assumptions (cf. Dessau 1884: 522). The specific water sources are not mentioned by name in the text but one of them must be the Efqa spring.

Line 9

חטא - feminine singular absolute; in the ancient Aramaic inscriptions חטה (JH, 85); in the Aramaic documents from Egypt חנטתא, חנטא (JH, 85; V., 7, 221); in parabiblical Jewish literature חטתא (*DAN*, 144); in Syr. ܚܛܐ (*BLS*, 227).

חמרא - masculine singular emphatic; in the Aramaic documents from Egypt חמר (JH, 91; V., 7, 220); in Biblical Aramaic חַמְרָא, חֲמַר (Gesenius-Buhl, 899); in parabiblical Jewish literature חמרא (*DAN*, 152); in Syr ܚܡܪܐ (*BLS*, 241).

תבנא - masculine singular emphatic; in Aramaic documents from Egypt תבן (JH, 323; V., 13, 258); in parabiblical Jewish literature תבנא (*DAN*, 438); in Syr. ܬܒܢܐ (*BLS*, 814).

Line 10

דמא - masculine singular active participle Peʻal; in Biblical Aramaic דָּמֵה (feminine דָּמְיָה) (Gesenius-Buhl, 895); in parabiblical Jewish literature דמא (*DAN*, 100), in Syr. ܕܡܐ (*BLS*, 156).

ארחא - feminine singular absolute; in ancient Aramaic inscriptions ארח (JH, 24); in Aramaic documents from Egypt ארח (JH, 24, V., 2, 210); in Biblical Aramaic ארחא (in plural with enclitic pronouns: אָרְחָתֵהּ, אָרְחָתָךְ) (Gesenius-Buhl, 899); in parabiblical Jewish literature ארח - 'to travel' (*DAN*, 40); in Syr. ܐܘܪܚܐ (*BLS*, 48).

Line 11

יתאיעל - the second ʼ is redundant (Rosenthal 1936: 13).

סריק - masculine singular passive participle, Peʻal, absolute; in parabiblical Jewish literature סריקתא and סריקותא (*DAN*, 301); in Syr. ܣܪܝܩܐ (*BLS*, 501).

Line 12

קלקיס - proper name (Cilicius?) – 'Cilicius' in the parallel Greek text (III, 2, 46) appears as Κίλιξ. Rosenthal saw here a mistake in the Aramaic version of the correct word קליקס* (Rosenthal 1936: 13). This assumption makes sense if we also assume that in the Aramaic is derived from the Greek, but it is also possible that we have here a rendering of the Latin 'Cilicius'. According to Cantineau

(1935: 38), the Aramaic spelling corresponds with the Greek Κίλκις. The person in question is unknown in other sources. In the context of this section he would seem to have been a tax farmer in Palmyra in the first century AD.

בר חרי - freedman (בר - masculine singular construct; חרי - abstract noun, masculine plural construct). In the Aramaic documents from Egypt בר חרן (V., 4, 219); in parabiblical Jewish literature בר הרין, בר חריא (*DAN*, 63; *LW*, I, 258); Syr. ܒܰܪ ܚܺܐܪܶܐ, ܒܰܪ ܚܺܐܪܳܐ (*TS*, I, 587–8).

The formula בר חרי קיסר = Καίσαρος ἀπελεύθερος = *Caesaris libertus* shows that Cilicius lived in the first half or middle of the first century AD (cf. in detail Chantraine 1967: 143–5, as well as Shifman 1977). This reference also shows that in this period Palmyra was under Roman dominion.

Line 13

נמ[וסא די מכ]סא - restoration of *CIS*, II, 3913.

Line 14

מל[חא] - masculine singular emphatic, restored as in *CIS*, II, 3913. In the ancient Aramaic inscriptions from Sefire מלח (JH, 152); in the Aramaic documents from Egypt מלח, מלחא (JH, 152; V., 11, 194); in Biblical Aramaic מְלַח (Gesenius-Buhl, 906); in parabiblical Jewish literature מלח (*DAN*, 237); Syr. ܡܶܠܚܳܐ (*BLS*, 390).

Line 15

א[גור]יא - Schröder (1884: 430) translated the remaining text of the line as follows: 'die ... welche pachtete vor dem Marinus dem Hegemon', suggesting that this must be preceded by the word [מכס]יא. Reckendorf (1888: 410) shares his opinion. However, *CIS*, II, 3913 shows at the beginning of the line an א of which Schröder took no account. It thus gives the text as א[גור]יא ד[י] י[ת]אגר. *CIS*, II, 3913, discussing Schröder's translation, rightly notes that it is very unlikely that the person who had the post of the imperial governor of Syria could function as a tax farmer.

א[ת]אגר - third singular perfect Ethpeʿel, √אגר; in Aramaic documents from Egypt אגר (V., 3, 188); in parabiblical Jewish literature אגר (*DAN*, 6); Syr. ܐܓܰܪ (*BLS*, 4).

קדם - preposition; in ancient Aramaic inscriptions קדם (JH, 251); in the Aramaic documents from Egypt קדם (JH, 251; V., 13, 231); in the Aramaic text from Uruk *qu-da-am* (JH, 251); in Biblical Aramaic קְדָם (Gesenius-Buhl, 915); in Syr. ܩܕܡ (*BLS*, 647).

מרינס - G.A. Harrer (1915: 21; citation from Seyrig 1941b: 165, n. 3) suggests here L. Julius Marinus Caecilius Simplex, consul of the year 101 or 102. According to Seyrig, the restoration of the name 'Mucianus' in II, 2, 24 is 'fatal' for Harrer's view. However, we think that Seyrig's restoration there does not contradict the idea that at the end of the first decade of the second century AD L. Julius Marinus was a legate in Syria and that 'before him' the agreement about taxes was made.

L. Julius Marinus Caecilius Simplex was the son of L. Julius Marinus, who was proconsul of Pontus and Bithynia in the 80s, later consul and in 97 legate in the Provinces of Moesia, and of his wife, the daughter of Caecilius Simplex, consul in AD 69. He was born in the middle of the first century AD or a little later. His military and administrative career began with his participation in the board of three which was responsible for road maintenance (*III vir viarum curandarum*), then he was a military tribune in the IV Scythian legion, posted in Syria, a deputy governor (as *propraetor*) in the Province of Macedonia, a plebeian *aedile*, a legate in the rank of *propraetor* in the Provinces of Pontus and Bithynia, where his father was a proconsul (at the latest in AD 89–90), *curator* of the *via Tiburtina*, a member of the board of the Arval Brethren (participating for the first time in their religious ceremonies in May of AD 91), commander of the XI Claudian legion based in Upper Germany, deputy governor in the Imperial Provinces of Lycia and Pamphylia (98), proconsul in Achaia and consul in Rome (most likely in 102). We do not have any further information about his activities. He was married to Julia Tertulla, probably a daughter of G. Julius Cornutus Tertullus, consul in AD 100 (Groag 1917: cols 670–2).

היגמונא - Greek ἡγεμών (title of the Roman deputy governor: *praefectus*), with the Aramaic emphatic ending א-. In parabiblical Jewish literature הגמון (*KGLL*, II, 219); in Syr. ܗܓܡܘܢܐ, ܗܓܡܘܢܐ (*BLS*, 171).

Line 16

[יבישון] - the restoration is well based, though it is cautious, suggested by *CIS*, II, 3913, on the basis of comparison with the text of the 'new' law. The difference in taxes in the new law (II, I, 7–8), 3 *denarii* against 4 in this text, seems not to support this restoration. However, we have an analogous situation in line 17, where all the readings are clear, compared with the new law (II, 1, 10–11). The tax for purple wool is set there as 8 *assarii*, here as 4 *denarii*. So the difference in the amount of taxes does not present a problem for the hypothetical restoration (*CIS*, II, 3913). Perhaps, the composer of the new law intended to lessen taxes for particular goods. Besides, as we shall see, in II, 2, 18 there is a resolution to use the 'new' Tariff. This also removes the apparent contradiction.

We show both clauses for comparison:

The 'new' Tariff	The 'old' Tariff
הו מ[כסא יג[בא [מ[ן טעון	מ[ן יבישין[לכ[ל] טעון
גמלא די יבי[שין] למעלנא	די גמל
[לכלמא] די טעון גמלא ד [3]	מעלן ד 4
מן [טעון גמלא למ[פקנא] ד 3	ולמפקן ד 4

As we can see, the clause in the 'old' tariff is more formalized while in the 'new' the author adds details, though at the expense of clarity in formulation.

Line 17

מ[ן א[ר]גונבא] - see *CIS*, II, 3913, restored by analogy with II, 1, 10–11.

Line 18

This is the formula which probably replaces the article about collecting tax 'according to custom'.

מכס[א] - cf. Reckendorf (1888: 382): [מכסא].

גנסיא - the Aramaic form is adopted from the Greek word γένος (masculine plural emphatic).

Line 19

מל[ח טב]יתג[בא - restored in *CIS*, II, 3913. Reckendorf (1888: 411) mentions the terrain of the Palmyrene area as being rich in salt. He refers to medieval Arabic tradition and contemporary guide-books.

מל[ח טב - the title of the clause.

טב - masculine singular adjective, absolute, agreeing with מל[ח]. In the ancient Aramaic inscriptions טב (JH, 98); in the Aramaic documents from Egypt טב (JH, 98, V., 7, 226); in Biblical Aramaic טָב; (Gesenius-Buhl, 900); in parabiblical Jewish literature טבא (*DAN*, 165); Syr. ܛܒ (*BLS*, 269).

מדיא - adopted from Latin *modius* through Greek μόδιος; in Aramaic form and masculine singular emphatic. In parabiblical Jewish literature it is not attested;

in Syr. ܩܣܛܐ (*BLS*, 375). The *modius* (= 8.7 litres) is a Roman measure of volume used for measurement of dry substances; 1 *modius* was the equivalent of 16 *sextarii* (as explained here).

קסטון - As shown in *CIS*, II, 3913, adopted from Greek ξέστης which translated into Latin as *sextarius*. In parabiblical Jewish literature קיסטא (*KGLL*, II, 535); in Syr. ܩܣܛܐ (*BLS*, 679). *CIS*, II, 3913 explains the ending -ון this way: the carver had in mind the Greek form ξεστῶν, transferring it to Aramaic. Schröder (1884: 436) understood this word as a toponym, while Reckendorf (1888: 410–11) traced it to the Greek κόστος.

Line 20

עשר - cardinal number. In the ancient Aramaic inscriptions עשר (JH, 223); in the Aramaic documents from Egypt עשר (JH, 223; V., 11, 232); in Biblical Aramaic עֲשַׂר (Gesenius-Buhl, 913); in parabiblical Jewish literature עשר (*DAN*, 325); in Syr. ܥܣܪ (*BLS*, 537). ת[ש]ו עשר - 'sixteen'.

יתבעא - third masculine singular imperfect, Ethpe'el, √בעא = בעה = בעי. In the ancient Aramaic inscriptions תבעה, יבעה (JH, 39); in the Aramaic documents from Egypt בעי, בעה (JH, 39; V., 4, 213); in Biblical Aramaic בְּעָא (Gesenius-Buhl, 891); in parabiblical Jewish literature בעא (*DAN*, 60); in Syr. ܒܥܐ (*BLS*, 82); Reckendorf (1888: 385) translates: 'was verlangt wird'; *CIS*, II, 3513: 'requiretur', also notes in the commentary that the meaning of the word is unclear and ambiguous; finally JH, 40: 'être demandé, requis'. We think that the understanding of the Palmyrene יתבעא and the phrase that is connected with it can be clearly established on the basis of the fundamental and main meaning of the verb בעא, 'to search'. This is as in the Biblical Aramaic וּבְעוֹ דָנִיֵּאל וְחַבְרוֹהִי לְהִתְקְטָלָה, 'and they sought Daniel and his fellows to slay them' (Dan. 2:13). Also אֱדַיִן סָרְכַיָּא וַאֲחַשְׁדַּרְפְּנַיָּא הֲווֹ בָעַיִן עִלָּה לְהַשְׁכָּחָה לְדָנִיֵּאל מִצַּד מַלְכוּתָא, 'At this, the administrators and the satraps sought to find a complaint against Daniel in his conduct of government affairs' (Dan. 6:5). V., 4, 213 gives further examples from the Aramaic documents from Egypt: בעה עליך גבריא, '... he incited against you the men ...'; בעי א[ר]בא זי הודו [ש] זי יזבן ביתא, 'look for a person who will buy the big house of Hodo', etc. An analogous reading is recorded in the later period. For instance *LW*, I, 247 refers to Jerusalem Talmud Ta'anit 1 (3), 64a: אימת דאתון בעיי הוא בעיי, 'when you search (for God – I. Sh.) he searches (for you – I. Sh.)'. *TS*, I, 556 also refers to a similar meaning. For instance: Eph. i, 361: ܒܥܐ ܥܠܬܐ - 'he sought a pretext'; Matt. 7:8: Greek ζητῶν is translated in Syr ܒܥܐ; Luke 2:44: Greek ἀνεζήτουν is translated in Syriac ܟ̈ܒܥܘܗܝ.

Perhaps, in our case the word יתבעא, which clearly agrees with מא, has the meaning of 'will be found' and in general this clause must support the rights of possession of those who found sources of salt.

יתן [להו]ן - The ending [הו]ן-, the suffixed 3rd masculine plural pronoun, here with the preposition ל, probably refers to 'those who will find salt mines'. It is unclear who is the subject of the verb יתן. Reckendorf (1888: 387) translates, 'gebe er ihnen'; *CIS*, II, 3913: 'dabit eis'. This suggests a tax farmer, if we assume that the latter has the right to tax the production and the selling of salt, as well as the right to control the exploitation of salt-producing land and distribution in the name of the Palmyrene government.

This clause is in style very close to the legal norms and moral maxims of the Mishnah and Gemara: the absence of a clear subject ('he') and of objects ('that which will happen, them', etc.) is characteristic of that legal tradition. Cf., for example:

Tariff	Mishnah Ma'aserot 2: 2
[ו]מא די יתבעא יתן	היו יושבין בשער או בחנות
[להו]ן לתשמישא	ואמר טלו לכם תאנים אוכלין
	ופטורין

Line 21

This line clearly refers to the fine (two *sestertii* per *modius* i.e. eight *assarii*; in other words the fine is eight times bigger than the actual tax for salt) for not doing something; what exactly is involved is missing from the text. Probably, the fine is for not paying the tax on salt, because the previous line talks about collecting this tax. Therefore, the most plausible restoration is that of *CIS*, II, 3913: י[כל] or י[כיל] by analogy with the following text. Cf. also III, 3, 26: ὃς δ' ἂν οὐ....ν παραμετρήσ[ῃ].

י[כל] - third person masculine singular imperfect, Af'el (cf. II, 2, 23, the *plene* writing יכילנה). In parabiblical Jewish literature כול: in the form that is analogous to this one: יכילון (*DAN*, 194); in Syr. Af'el ܐܟܝܠ (*BLS*, 325).

י[פרע] - third masculine singular jussive, Pe'al. In the Aramaic documents from Egypt פרע (JH, 236); in parabiblical Jewish literature פרע (*DAN*, 352); Syr. ܦܪܥ (*BLS*, 603).

מדא - cf. II, 2, 19: מדיא. Schröder (1884: 431) compares it with the Arabic مدّ.

ססטרטין - adopted from Latin (*sestertius*), in the Aramaic masculine plural form (Reckendorf 1888: 411). The *sestertius* (or *nummus*), the main monetary unit in Rome, was equal to a quarter of a *denarius*, i.e. four *assarii*.

Line 22

בתד|מר או בתחו|מא - Reckendorf (1888: 382) reads [בתד[מר. Cf. III, 3, 23: ἐν Παλμύροις. The text is restored fully in *CIS*, II, 3913, matching the analogous formula in II, 1, 1–2: לתדמר או לתחומיה, taking into consideration the final letters מא.

Line 23

ת|דמרי|א - Reckendorf (1888: 382) reads it so by analogy with the Greek text; cf. III, 3, 24: Παλμυρη[ν]ῶν; adjective of origin, masculine plural emphatic.

יכילנה - Schröder (1884: 431) read *yĕkîlūnēh* ('Sie messen es'). Reckendorf (1888: 411) thinks that the verb is Af'el (third singular, with the so-called *energicum*); *CIS*, II, 3913 also shares this opinion. JH, 11 interprets it this way: Af'el imperfect (though we think that this is jussive): 3rd masculine singular, together with 3rd singular feminine enclitic pronoun.

ל|מכס|א - *CIS*, II, 3913 reads it so by analogy with the parallel Greek text (III, 3, 24: [τῷ δημο]σιώνη). Reckendorf (1888: 411) thinks that it is possible to read ל[כל מד]יא by analogy with III, 3, 25: ε[ἰς ἕκ]αστον μόδιον; see, however, later in this line: [א]פי מדיא.

א|פי - *CIS*, II, 3913. Cf. II, 3, 1: אפי דנר and II, 3, 6: אפי אסר.

Line 24

גיס |לקניס מ|קינ|ס| - cf. in Greek IV, I, 10: Γαῖο[ς]. Schröder (1884: 431) notes with regard to this line: 'There was a proper name before היגמונא, of which only two letters left: קי: traces on the photograph show that there was a name Kilix קלקיס'. Reckendorf (1888: 411) also shares this view: 'Kilix could be the *hegemon*'. *CIS*, II, 3913: גיס - '*praenomen praefecti*, whose family name is not preserved, and of the damaged *cognomen* there remains only the ending קינס'.

Following Seyrig (1941b: 165–7) we believe that in this line the reference is to G. Licinius Mucianus (C. Licinius Mucianus) who was legate in Syria with the rank of *propraetor* in AD 68–9. Therefore, we accept the reading גיס [לקניס מ|קינ|ס]. (Seyrig has מו|קינס; cf. also Starcky 1952: 82.) Mucianus came from the noble Roman family of Licinius, another member of which was also a famous colleague of Caesar in the triumvirate, M. Licinius Crassus (his full name was G. Licinius Crassus Mucianus). The former (G. L. Mucianus) played an important role in the revolution that led to the rule of T. Flavius Vespasian. He is also known as a writer (see details in Kappelmacher 1926: col. 437; cf. *CIL*, XIV, 2173: C. Licini Muciani). Tacitus (Tac., *Hist.*, I, 10) gives a detailed characterization of G. Licinius Mucianus: *Syriam et quattuor legiones obtinebat Licinius Mucianus, vir secundis adversisque iuxta famosus. Insignis amicitias iuvenis ambitiose coluerat; mox attritis opibus, lubrico statu, suspecta etiam Claudii iracundia, in secretum Asiae sepositus tam prope ab exule fuit quam postea a principe. Luxuria industria, comitate adrogantia, malis bonisque artibus mixtus; nimiae voluptates cum vacaret; quotiens expedierat, magnae virtutes; palam laudares, secreta male audiebant: sed apud subiectos apud proximos, apud collegas variis inlecebris potens, et cui expeditius fuerit tradere imperium quam obtinere.*

'Syria and its four legions were controlled by Licinius Mucianus, a man whose good and bad fortune were equally famous. In his youth he had cultivated because of his ambition the friendship of the great; his resources soon failed, and his situation became precarious, and it was suspected that Claudius had taken offence, so he was sent into a remote part of Asia, and was as much like an exile, as he was afterwards like a *princeps*. He was a mixture of dissipation and energy, of arrogance and courtesy, of good and bad. When he was at leisure, his self-indulgence was extreme, yet whenever he had been on expeditions, he had shown great virtues. In his public behaviour he deserved praise; about his private life there were bad rumours. With his subordinates, friends and colleagues, he could be charming, but preferred to hand the imperial power to another, rather than to hold it for himself.'

If this restoration of the text is correct, then we would have here a significant witness to Mucianus' administrative work in his capacity as Roman governor in Syria. It appears that there were people in Palmyra who received Roman citizenship from Mucianus, accepted his *nomen* and became his clients. The descendant of one of those people, Gaius Licinius Flavianus, son of Borrofa (Greek variant Birra), of the *gens Sergia*, Maliku (Γαίον Λικίνιον Φλαβιανὸν Βύρρου υ[ἰὸν] Σεργίᾳ Μαλίχου; [מלכו] סרגיא בר בורפא פלוינוס ס'[לקנ] גאיס), was honoured by receiving a statue from his clients, Zebeida, 'Abdai and 'Abd'astor, sons of Nesa son of 'Ate'aqab (*Inv.* X, 130; the date is not preserved). Probably, the same figure is mentioned in *tesserae*: *RTP*, 700, 776 and 835: לקניס ברס.

Commentary

Taking into consideration the fact that line 23 ends the section about collection of tax from salt production and from its sale and line 24 begins a new section, the understanding of the whole phrase in line 24 depends on the context of the following section. Chabot reconstructs a 1st singular formula: [א]קי[מ]ת in line 26 (see details in the commentary to this line) – '[I es]tab[lish]ed'. We may assume then that line 25 contains direct speech, possibly a citation from Licinius Mucianus' resolution, and that in line 24 there was an indication of that fact. Therefore, we suggest to reconstruct this text as follows: [מ]ן די אקם - 'from what he established'. F. Rosenthal (1936: 66, note 4) notes that there is a standard full form אקים (third singular masculine perfect, Af'el) and a 'defective' form (*CIS*, II, 3927: [ל]מלכב[ל] מ]ן חר[מ] ואקם 'and he established [s]anctua[r]ies for Malakb[el]').

Line 25

חשבן - M. de Vogüé (1883b: 159) reads מ...בן; Schröder (1884: 428) reads לבן...; Reckendorf (1888: 308): חשבן ...; the latter is also accepted in *CIS*, II, 3913. In his commentary Reckendorf (1888: 411) compares this word with the Syriac ܚܘܫܒܢܐ, in Jewish parabiblical literature חושבנא and Arabic حِسْبَانٌ. He also refers to other instances when the noun and the verb from the same stem occur in the Tariff. *CIS*, II, 3913 restores [על] חשבן - 'quo ad computationem' or (and Chabot seems to prefer this) ח]שב[מת] - a plural participle meaning 'supputandi sunt'. F. Rosenthal (1936: 74) sees in חשבן a noun with suffix -ān; also JH, 97: a noun with the meaning 'account'.

As is known, the word חשבן occurs outside the Tariff in Palmyrene inscription *Inv.* X, 127 in the following context: לחשבן חפיותא וחשא טב[א]. The parallel Greek text has εὐνοίας καὶ σπουδῆς ἕνεκεν. The word σπουδή corresponds with the Aramaic חפיותא, 'defence' (?), and εὔνοια to חשא טבא, 'benevolence'. לחשבן perhaps forms a compound preposition, identical to the Greek ἕνεκεν. (Starcky translates in the text 'pour' and in the commentary 'en estimation de'.) This matches the meaning of ܠܟܠ ܚܘܫܒܢ in Syriac (*TS*, I, 1396): 'because, because of, as a consequence of'. Therefore, we suggest the following reconstruction of the beginning of the line: [על] חשבן, 'because of, as a consequence of'. This restoration is the most plausible since line 26 begins the resolution of the Roman governor that is introduced by the verb [א]קי[מ]ת; it can be preceded only by the reason for that resolution.

ביני תדמריא - 'the Palmyrenes' according to Schröder (1884: 431 - בני תדמריא),

but in the Greek we have μεταξὺ Παλ[μυρηνῶν] (IV, 1, 12). The formula that contains these words ...ל ביני תדמריא... recalls a construction in the resolution of the Palmyrene council: ביני תגרא לביני מכסיא (I, 20); cf. Greek (I, 7–8): [με]ταξὺ τῶν ἐνπόρων πρὸς τοὺς τελώνας. From this we may draw two conclusions: 1) After the preposition ביני there must follow the word לביני (Ingholt's view: Schlumberger 1937: 289; cf. *CIS*, II, 3913, which suggests, however, ל[מכסא] or ל[מכסיא] after it at the beginning of line 26). So there must be reference to people who have some sort of relationship with the Palmyrenes; 2) Before the word ביני there must be a reference to the nature of that relationship. To continue the analogy with the resolution of the Palmyrene council (and the analogy is supported if we bear in mind the similar situation: the reason for the issue and composition of the Tariff), we can assume that the discussion is about conflicts and lawsuits (סרבנין) between the Palmyrenes and some other group. Besides, prior to this we have a description of the conflicts themselves ...מכ חשבן [על], i.e. based on the surviving letters in the text, מכ, a reference to taxation. Therefore, we suggest this reading: [על] חשבן מכ[ס סרבן הוא] etc.

Line 26

At the beginning of the line, where the phrase that started in the previous line ends, we have the surviving letters ק.ת. Schröder (1884: 428), however, reads [סר]קי[ן] [מס]מכסן כס... = ...cus Maximus Caesar (so also Reckendorf 1888: 382). J.-B. Chabot notes in *CIS*, II, 3913 that this does not correspond with his reading of the *estampage*. Based on the context and the presence of the ק, the closest equivalent to the word which follows in this line, מכסי[א], is the Syriac ܣܩܘܛܐ, 'tax collector' (*BLS*, 494), which is derived from Greek σκῦτος, 'tanned leather, leather whip, lash'. This word in the Palmyrene text would end with ת (clearly in the construct state), while the Syriac word has ܐ, but this fact does not make the suggestion impossible. As is known, in parabiblical Jewish literature, Greek τ is usually transmitted by ט, but there are cases when ט and ת are interchangeable in one and the same word: טרגימא and תרגימא (Greek τράγημα), טכסיס and תכסיס (Greek τάξις) etc. (*KGLL*, I, 10–11). It is possible that the Palmyrene scribe wrote the word with the letter ת and placed ו, which represents the Greek ῠ, between this letter and the ק. Therefore, the reconstruction of the line is [ס]ק[ו]ת מכסי[א]. D. Schlumberger and H. Ingholt (Schlumberger 1937: 290) read ק[מ]ס ..., the ending of the name [א]לק[מ]ס.

However, at the end of the word we clearly see a ת, which makes this reconstruction impossible. מכסי[א]ק[מ]ת is the reading in *CIS*, II, 3913.

The word [מ]כסא at the end of the line was probably preceded by an attribute which is completely erased and cannot be reconstructed.

Line 27

חיב למהוא - This is the reading by de Vogüé (1883b :161); *CIS*, II, 3913 shares his opinion. Schröder (1884: 428) reads חיב לא הוא, as does Reckendorf (1888: 382).

The resolution of the Roman administrator begins with the word [א]ק[מ]ת (II, 2, 26). It mentions, firstly, the obligation of the tax farmer — or, depending on the meaning of [מ]כסא (at the end of II, 2, 26), the taxes — [מ]כסא חיב למהוא, and, secondly, the conditions of the contract, signed by a certain Alkimos — [די] אגר בה אלקמס (II, 2, 27–8). The ending סא- before this last phrase shows that it was preceded by the word [מכ]סא. Therefore, we suggest the reconstruction of the whole phrase as: [מ]כסא חיב למהוא היך מכ]סא [די] אגר בה אלקמס etc. See the formulae in Aramaic: היך עדתא, היך בנמוסא etc.

בה - 'in it' i.e. in Palmyra.

Line 28

אלקמס - proper name (Greek Ἀλκίμος). J.-B. Chabot (*CIS*, II, 3913) notes that that Alkimos was either a freedman of Augustus who managed taxes or he was a tax farmer. The text gives more support for the latter interpretation. Although no other sources refer to a tax farmer called Alkimos, it is clear that in the history of tax farming in Palmyra Alkimos played a significant role. The reference to him in the rescript of Mucianus leads us to date his activity to AD 68–9 or a bit earlier.

וח[ברה] - Schröder (1884: 428) reads וחת ...; also Reckendorf (1888: 382). Based on the text which follow, containing a reference to the law (נמוסא) and concluding the tax farming activity of Alkimos, ... ח can only be a companion of the main tax farmer (Alkimos?) and therefore, the word is reconstructed as ח[בר] in combination with the third masculine singular enclitic pronoun: ח[ברה] or ח[ברו] (Rosenthal 1936: 43); cf. the parallel form elsewhere in Palmyrene, חברה. In this regard, it is important to note that among the Palmyrene grave inscriptions there were records of contracts that use the verb אחבר (Greek parallel: κοινωνὸν λαβεῖν), for acceptance of someone into joint ownership and exploitation of property (Shifman 1965b: 100–13).

ח[בר] - in the cuneiform Aramaic text from Uruk: *ḫa-ba-ra-an* (JH, 82); in Biblical Aramaic חֲבַר (Gesenius-Buhl, 898); in parabiblical Jewish literature חברא (cf. especially Targumic הַבְרֵיה, Gen. 11:3); in Syriac ܚܒܪܐ (*BLS*, 212).

[היך] נמוסא - The reference to precedent is often expressed in the Tariff by the preposition היך; cf. above, commentary on line 27: היך עדתא.

מדעם להן - Schröder (1884: 428) was mistaken in reading [סא]פרע מכ; Reckendorf (1888: 382), reading יפרע מ[סא], notes that 'the end of the line is highly dubious' (1888: 412).

Line 29

מִשְׁתַּתָּף - masculine singular absolute participle, Ethpa''al, from the verb שתף. Cf. the Palmyrene שותפות (Cantineau 1930b: 520–51, no. 14 bis) – 'participation, community, association'. Schröder (1884: 429) mistakenly reads משנית followed by the numeral 22; Reckendorf (1888: 382) - משתתף ד; in parabiblical Jewish literature שתף (in the manuscripts there is a form משתתפין, *DAN*, 437); in Syr. ܐܫܬܘܬܦ (*BLS*, 812).

Lines 29–30

יהוא פרע - compound future (3rd masculine singular), active Pe'al. The use of the verb פרע is common in the 'old' law (instead of גבא common in the 'new' law).

Line 32

[מזבן רגלין ומ]פק - restored by analogy with the 'new' law (II, 1, 3); רגלין – by analogy with II, 23–31.

Line 33

[על]ם - ו[מן] די י[זבן על]ם – על[ם] was read by Schröder (1884: 429) by analogy with the 'new' law (II, 1, 4) and with the following clause (cf. Schröder 1884: 131). Reckendorf (1888: 382) read it in the same way. We accept the text restored by *CIS*, II, 3913. By analogy with II, 1, 4 it is possible that at the end of the line there was [10] ד (cf. *CIS*, II, 3913).

Line 34

CIS, II, 3913 notes, 'מיא ... - is an incomplete word in the masculine singular form, as the demonstrative pronoun דנה (masculine) shows'. However, *CIS* did not take into account the fact that there might be a construct state noun

Commentary

followed by a genitive, so that the agreement would be with the definite noun that precedes מיא ... and this would be referred to by the pronoun דנה.

Since the preceding clauses in the edict of Mucianus about taxes on slaves (II, 2, 29–33) are almost identical with those of the 'new' law (II, 1, 1–4), we can assume that II, 2, 34–5 also matches II, 1, 5, if not in form then at least in content. Thus both clearly have the combination לכל (cf. also II, 2, 31). Since the theme is slaves, it is possible to read על[מיא]. Then the whole can be read as לכל [על]מיא דנה..., and therefore by analogy with the earlier text, לכל [רגל על]מיא.

Line 35

Schröder was the first to read the numeral 10 (1884: 429). Reckendorf (1888: 382) reads the phrase as: מעלנ.. ..... ה ד? וד [א]ומפקנ ע ו ו and decodes the numerals like Schröder. We accept Chabot's opinion on this (*CIS*, II, 3913). He reads the second numeral as 12, which is different from his predecessors. The comparison with the previous text and the new law (II, I, 4–5) shows that the discussion is about taxes collected from the import of slave-veterans (10 *denarii*) and their export (12 *denarii*).

The combination הו could be a third masculine singular personal pronoun (Rosenthal 1936: 42). We might also suppose that it is part of a verb in the third masculine plural with the final stem consonant -ה. However, according to the rules of the conjugation of verbs with a weak third letter in the stem (*tertiae infirmae*), this form would not show the final weak consonant of the root (cf. בנו from the stem בנה, הוו from the stem הוא etc. [Rosenthal 1936: 69]). By analogy with the preceding text (the context is about payments) it is also possible to read יפרע[הו]. After the word מעל there should be a reference to the thing being imported – slaves, through an enclitic pronoun הי- (singular masculine third person) or הן- (plural).

הו - in the Aramaic documents from Egypt הו; in Biblical Aramaic הוא; in parabiblical Jewish literature הו, הוא; in Syr. ܗܘ.

Line 36

The initial clause must have been about slave-veterans; there is also later a reference to the 'law' (in line 37). By analogy with the previous line we can assume that the discussion here is not only about the export but also about the import of slaves.

The Palmyrene Tax Tariff

Line 37

|היך די] - cf. *CIS*, II, 3913.

... חשב ... - *CIS*, II, 3913 notes that there are two possible restorations here: either a noun חשבן or a verbal form. Line 37 probably completes the clause that prescribes the law to be used in payment of taxes.

Line 38–42

These lines are damaged to the point that it is impossible to determine their content (such as the things to be taxed) without additional sources.

Line 43

עמרא - in the Aramaic documents from Egypt עמר (var. קמר, JH, 217; V., 11, 229]); in Biblical Aramaic עֲמַר (Gesenius-Buhl, 912); in parabiblical Jewish literature עמרא (*DAN*, 316); in Syr. ܥܡܪܐ (*BLS*, 533).

Line 43 starts the section on the collecting of taxes on wool. It probably corresponds with the fragmentary Greek text of IV, 1, 27–36.

Line 44

פרעא תהוא עמרא - in the language of the Palmyrene inscriptions the word עמרא is feminine in contrast with other Aramaic languages and dialects.

Line 45

איט[ליא] - cf. *CIS*, II, 3913.

בתר - in Biblical Aramaic בָּאתַר; with the suffixed pronoun בָּתְרָךְ (Gesenius-Buhl, 890); in parabiblical Jewish literature בתר (*DAN*, 68); in Syr ܒܬܪ (*BLS*, 56). Cf. in the parallel Greek text ὕστ[ερον] (IV, 1, 34).

Line 46

כות - in the Aramaic documents from Egypt כות (JH, 117; V., 9, 144); in parabiblical Jewish literature כות (*DAN*, 195); in Syr. ܐܟܘܬ (*BLS*, 17), ܟܘܬ (*BLS*, 324).

ספון[ן] - Greek σύμφωνος (Rosenthal 1936: 92). In parabiblical Jewish literature סימפון and סמפון (*KGLL*, II, 389); cf. in Syr. ܙܘܡܦܘܢ (*BLS*, 635). In the Talmud סימפון - 'written contract'; cf. Mishnah Bava Meṣī'a 1: 8: אם יש עמהם סימפון יעשה מה שבסימפון, 'if they have a contract, let be done what is in the contract'; Sanhedrin 31b: סימפון שיש עליו עדים - 'a contract for which there are witnesses'.

Commentary

In the parallel Greek text [συν]εφωνήθη (IV, 1, 34–5). The reference is probably to a written contract.

איטליק|א| - Greek ἰταλικός.

Line 47

|מכ|ס|א| - see *CIS*, II, 3913.

למפק<נ>א - see *CIS*, II, 3913.

Line 48

ב|שימא די| - see de Vogüé (1883b: 163) and Schröder (1884: 429).

Line 49

מת|גבא היך נמוס|א - the final version of the reading given in *CIS*, II, 3913.

טעון - in parabiblical Jewish literature טעות (*DAN*, 172); in Syr. ܛܥܢܐ, ܛܥܘܢܐ (*BLS*, 282).

Column 3

Line 1

כתב - in Biblical Aramaic כְּתָב (Gesenius-Buhl, 904); in parabiblical Jewish literature כתב (*DAN*, 211); in Syr. ܟܬܒܐ (*BLS*, 351).

טעא - √טעי; in parabiblical Jewish literature טעא (*DAN*, 172); in Syr. ܛܥܐ (*BLS*, 282).

Line 2

רציף - masculine singular Pe'al passive participle, absolute. The reading רציפא is suggested by Schröder (1884: 432–3). Reckendorf (1888: 383) reads ח/ציפ|בא and explains in his commentary (1888: 412): 'The argument against רצי[פא] is that this root does not occur in the meaning that is necessary here. One could think of [ג]ליפא, but the first letter is unlikely to be anything except ח or צ.' Based on the *estampage* Chabot (*CIS*, II, 3913) reads רציף clearly. In parabiblical Jewish literature the verb רצף occurs in the following meanings: 'squeeze, closely connect (things) to each other, pave a street' (*DAN*, 407); in Syr. the verb ܪܨܦ has the following meanings: 'pave a street, connect tightly, squeeze' (*BLS*, 742). *CIS*, II, 3913 refers to the Arabic word رصيف, 'firm, solid, strong', and accordingly suggests in this context the meaning 'established'.

The Palmyrene Tax Tariff

The amount of tax established by the 'law' matches the tax which the 'new' Tariff sets for the export of perfumed oil on a camel (II, 1, 14–15). We have here an interesting reference to the 'law' which was probably in place before the 'old' law was established.

Line 3

קצבא - masculine plural emphatic; in parabiblical Jewish literature קצב (*DAN*, 387); in Syr ܩܨܒܐ (*BLS*, 687).

אפי דנר - in the parallel Greek text we have εἰς δηνάριον (IV, 1, 41). According to Schröder (1884: 434), the word אפי is 'an adverbial expression' which expresses the direction and mode of an action; in combination with דנר or אסר (see below) it must mean that the payment is calculated at a *denarius* ('à einen Denar'). The whole discussion is evidently, in fact, about payment that must be collected in the common imperial coinage (Dessau 1884: 520; Reckendorf 1888: 413; *CIS*, II, 3913, referring to Cass. Dio 52.30.9). The Greek gives a loan translation of this phrase.

Line 4

מתחשבו - Ethpe'el infinitive from the verb חשב (Rosenthal 1936: 62). This form [ed.: with -*ū* at the end of the infinitive] links the language of the Palmyrene inscriptions with Syriac and Christian-Palestinian Aramaic (Reckendorf 1888: 413).

גרמנקוס - Greek Γερμανικός, Lat. Germanicus. Germanicus was the son of Nero Claudius Drusus Germanicus and Antonia, the youngest daughter of Mark Antony, member of the second triumvirate; his full name is Nero Claudius Germanicus. The date of his birth is unknown. In AD 4, by Augustus' order, he was adopted by Tiberius and was given the name Germanicus Julius Caesar (which is why this is in the Tariff: גרמנקוס קיסר). In AD 7–9 he participated in the suppression of the anti-Roman revolt in Pannonia, in 11–12 and 14–16 in the Rhine campaign; he defeated the revolts of the Germanic tribes under Arminius. In 18–19 he had a special assignment (*imperium maius*) in the East; in October 19 he died unexpectedly in Antioch (for more details see *Prosopographia Imperii Romani*, II: 178, 146; Petrov 1857). The rescript cited in the Tariff is undoubtedly dated to 18–19; it shows that Germanicus' responsibilities included tax regulation and tax collection in the whole Province of Syria, possibly even in all the eastern provinces.

Commentary

Line 5

אגרתא - feminine singular emphatic; in the Aramaic documents from Egypt אגרה and אגרתא (JH, 4; V., 3, 188–9); in Biblical Aramaic אִגְּרָא (emphatic אִגַּרְתָּא; Gesenius-Buhl, 886); in parabiblical Jewish literature איגרא (emphatic אגרתא; *DAN*, 67); Syr. ܐܶܓܰܪܬܳܐ, ܐܶܓܰܪܬܳܐ (*BLS*, 5).

סטטילס - Latin Statilius; probably one of the officials in the Roman administration in Syria at the beginning of the first century ad, possibly responsible for tax regulation and tax collection. He is unknown in other sources. In some literature (Stein, A. 1929; *Prosopographia Imperii Romani*, III: 258, 588; *CIS*, II, 3913) it was suggested that Statilius was the imperial procurator in Syria while Germanicus was in the East (18–19). However, according to the present data, the governor in Syria at that time was Calpurnius Piso (Honigmann 1932: col. 1629). Dessau (1884: 521) comments on this appointment, referring to Cass. Dio 52.30.9, where we find one of the principles of Roman policy, i.e. the requirement to use the Roman coinage, as well the Roman system of measurements and weight, throughout the whole Empire.

פשק - this is third masculine singular perfect, Pa''el. In Syr ܦܫܰܩ (*BLS*, 613).

Line 6

הא - affirmative particle. In the Bar-Rekub inscriptions הא; in the Aramaic documents from Egypt הא (JH, 62; V., 7, 192–3); in Biblical Aramaic הָא (Gesenius-Buhl, 895); in parabiblical Jewish literature הא (*DAN*, 107); in Syr. ܗܳܐ (*BLS*, 169).

כשר - verb, third masculine singular perfect, Pe'al; in parabiblical Jewish literature כשר (*DAN*, 211), in Syr. ܟܫܰܪ (*BLS*, 350).

|יה]ן - see CIS, II, 3913.

אפי אסר - see above, commentary on line 3.

איטלק]ן| - Schröder (1884: 432). Cf., however, Reckendorf (1888: 383): איטלקא and *CIS*, II, 3913: איטלק[א]. *CIS*, II, 3913 notes that the last syllable in the word is unclear. Schröder's reading makes this word agree with the preceding אסר (cf. Greek ἀσσάριον ἰταλικόν), and this seems to be more plausible.

Line 7

גו - in the expression גו מן, 'less than' (cf. Greek IV, 1, 44: τὸ δὲ ἐντὸς δεναρίου τέλος); גו, 'body'; בגו, 'inside'. In the Zakar inscription גוה; in the Aramaic documents from Egypt גו (JH, 48; V., 4, 225); in Biblical Aramaic גוא (Gesenius-Buhl, 892); in parabiblical Jewish literature גו, גוא (*DAN*, 73); in Syr. ܓܰܘ, ܓܰܘܳܐ (*BLS*, 107).

Line 8

ער|פ|ן - in Syr. ܥܘܪܦܳܢܐ. In the parallel Greek text (IV, 1, 45): πρὸς κέρμα; cf. John 2:15, where Greek κέρμα is ܥܘܪܦܳܢܐ in the Syriac version (cf. Vulgate: *aes*).

Taxes that are less than a *denarius* can probably be collected in local small coins (cf. Dessau 1884: 520). Since the taxes from butchers had to be collected in *denarii* (line 3), the least possible payment must have been one *denarius*.

Line 9

פגרין - masculine plural absolute; in the Aramaic inscriptions from Sefire פגר; in the Aramaic documents from Egypt פגר (JH, 225; V., 13, 218); in the parabiblical Jewish literature פגרא (*DAN*, 328); in Syr. ܦܰܓܪܐ (*BLS*, 556).

משתדן - masculine plural Ethpe'el participle from שדא, absolute (Rosenthal 1936: 69–70); in parabiblical Jewish literature שדא (*DAN*, 415); in Syr. ܫܕܐ (*BLS*, 757).

Line 10

טעמתא - in the parallel Greek text (IV, 1, 47) τῶν βρωτῶν; feminine singular emphatic. There are no precise parallels with a similar meaning from the other Aramaic languages and dialects; cf., however, the verb טעם - 'eat, feed'.

הי<ד> - so *CIS*, II, 3913, based on the parallel Greek text (IV, 1, 47) κα<τὰ> τὸν νόμον.

אקימת - cf. in the parallel Greek text εἴστημι (IV, 1, 48). Already de Vogüé (1883b: 173) suggested that the editor of the Greek text is here copying a passage from Germanicus' rescript, and the Aramaic translator reproduced the same error (of using the first person form). Schröder (1884: 435) and Reckendorf (1888: 413) share the same opinion, as also *CIS*, II, 3913. There are, however, other opinions also. Dessau (1884: 511, n. 2) thinks that this is a citation from the speech of the author of this decree, perhaps of the chairman of the board of the archons and *dekaprōtoi*. This hypothesis, as *CIS*, II, 3913 correctly notes, lacks plausibility. If we were to accept Dessau's view, the chairman of the board would make the decision on his own, which contradicts the concept of the board. V. Dittenberger (*OGIS*, 692) thinks that these are the words of Gaius, i.e., as H. Seyrig shows, of Gaius Mucianus. The most plausible suggestion in our view is that the editor of the text in both the Aramaic and Greek versions of the law continues to cite Germanicus' rescript; the first person singular in both texts is in favour of that.

Line 11

מתג|ב|א - cf. *CIS*, II, 3913.

Line 12

מדי - in the parallel Greek text (IV, 1, 48) ὅταν.

מת|אע|ל - cf. Reckendorf 1888: 383: [תאעלא]מ.

בר מן - in the parallel Greek text (IV, 1, 48) ἔξωθεν.

Line 13

ל|קרי|א |או מ|אעל - so Schröder (1884: 432).

קריא - in the parallel Greek text (IV, 1, 49) χωρία (plural). This allows us to see here a feminine noun in the plural emphatic (cf. Syr. ܩܘܪܝܐ, *BLS*, 695) derived from קריא or קריתא. (See on similar nouns in Syr.: Duval 1881: 258–60). This form קריא can, however, also be understood as absolute singular (cf. also Syr. ܩܘܪܝܐ, *BLS*, 695). In the Aramaic inscriptions from Sefire קריה; in the Aramaic documents from Egypt קריה (JH, 266; V., 13, 235); in Biblical Aramaic קִרְיָא (Gesenius-Buhl, 916); in parabiblical Jewish literature קריא (*DAN*, 390; *LW*, IV, 379); in Syr. ܩܪܝܬܐ and ܩܘܪܝܐ (*BLS*, 695).

Lines 13–14

This clause sets the regime for the tax-free export of food produce from Palmyra to the settlements nearby, and import from the settlements to Palmyra. Schlumberger's research (1951) shows that around Palmyra there were many settlements of livestock-farmers who had semi-nomadic households, as well as gardening settlements (there are surviving dedications to a god who is protector of gardens, cited by Schlumberger). The present resolution has two goals: first, to supply the inhabitants of these settlements with food products on favourable terms, as necessary; and, second, to provide them with favourable conditions on the Palmyrene market in comparison with those who import food products to Palmyra from abroad or who export from Palmyra to places abroad. The reasons for such a policy in the first part or middle of the first century AD in Palmyra are

The Palmyrene Tax Tariff

not clear; however, the reference to the agreement made, probably between different Palmyrene groups (היך די הוו ספון) and perhaps even in written form, suggests that this resolution was made to eliminate any conflict within Palmyrene society by means of a compromise.

Line 15

אסטרביליא - already de Vogüé (1883b: 172) indicates that this word comes from Greek στρόβιλος; he also points to the parallel in Greek (IV, 1, 51): κώνου (cf. in this regard Schröder 1884: 435), literally 'cedar or pine cones/nuts'; in this case pine nuts ('Avoda Zara, 14a explains איסטרובילין as פירי דארזא, 'fruits of the cedar, pine': Löw 1881: 60). H. Dessau (1884: 512–13) notes that in Greek στρόβιλος and κῶνος are interchangeable. Cf. also *CIS*, II, 3913. The Aramaicization of the Greek word with -א *prostheticum* and the Aramaic masculine plural emphatic ending deserve special attention; in parabiblical Jewish literature אסטרוביל, אצטרוביל (*LW*, I, 121; *KGLL*, II, 121); in Syr. ܐܣܛܪܒܝܠܐ (*BLS*, 33).

אתחזי - here impersonal (cf. Greek IV, 1, 51–2: ἔδ[ο]ξεν), although it indicates the continuation of the citation from Germanicus' rescript.

Line 16

לחשבן תגרא - in the parallel Greek text (IV, 1, 52) εἰς ἐμπορείαν. Therefore: לחשבן means 'for' and תגרא 'trading'.

תגרא - feminine singular absolute; in parabiblical Jewish literature תגרא (*DAN*, 438; *LW*, IV, 627).

Line 18

אחרניתא - indefinite pronoun (אחרן), feminine plural emphatic, agreeing with מדינתא (line 17). In the inscriptions from Sefire אחרן; in the Aramaic documents from Egypt אחרן (JH, 11; V., 3, 196); in Biblical Aramaic אָחֳרָן (Gesenius-Buhl, 887); in parabiblical Jewish literature אחרן (*DAN*, 14); in Syr. ܐܚܪܢܐ (*BLS*, 13).

Line 19

טעינין - masculine plural Peʻal participle, absolute; root טען. In the Aramaic documents from Egypt טען (JH, 102; V., 7, 227); in parabiblical Jewish literature טען (*DAN*, 173); in Syr. (*BLS*, 283) ܛܥܢ. [Ed.: see further on Greek parallel text below.]

Line 20

בר מן - cf. above line 12; in the parallel Greek text (IV, 1, 54) ἔξωθεν.

Line 21

אשר - in the parallel Greek text (IV, I, 56–7) ἐσημιώσατω.

Line 22

קרבלון - in the parallel Greek text (IV, 1, 56) Κουρβούλων. Gn. Domitius Corbulo, a Roman military commander, was probably born during Caligula's reign. In AD 46 he went to Lower Germany; during Claudius' reign he was proconsul in Asia. In 54–8 he led Roman troops in the war with Parthia, which, because of his efforts, resulted in an honourable and profitable peace for Rome. In 60–3 he was legate in Syria (Honigmann 1932: col. 1629). In 67, when he learnt that Nero wanted to kill him — the emperor saw in Corbulo's popularity a threat to his own power and decided to eliminate him — he committed suicide. He wrote memoirs about his campaigns which were widely used by Tacitus, Pliny the Elder and Dio Cassius (*Prosopographia Imperii Romani*, II: 20, 123; Stein, E. 1918: cols. 394–410; *CIS*, II, 3913).

כשירא - masculine singular emphatic adjective (JH, 127). In the parallel Greek text ὁ κράτιστος expresses the Latin title *vir egregius*, 'excellent man', which was used of men of the equestrian order. In parabiblical Jewish literature כשירא (*DAN*, 210 – one of the meanings is 'virtuous'); in Syr. ܚܣܡ (*BLS*, 351, with the same meaning).

ברברס - in the parallel Greek text πρὸς Βάρβαρον. He is unknown in other sources. *CIS*, II, 3913 notes that Barbarus was an official in the Roman administrative apparatus; in the light of his name, he was probably a freedman.

There is a difference between II, 3, 19–22 and II, 2, 11. In the latter version (the 'new' Tariff) tax is collected from unloaded camels which are imported; in II, 3, 19–22 it is specified where the camels are brought from (from outside Palmyra) and both loaded and unloaded camels are liable to tax; also, III, 3, 19–22 refers to the law (probably, the decree that was in force in Palmyra before the 'old' law) and to the resolution of the Roman governor. The two texts mutually supplement each other.

Line 23

על גלדיא - a title that indicates the content of the clause.

The Palmyrene Tax Tariff

גלדיא - masculine plural emphatic. In the Aramaic documents from Egypt גלד (JH, 50; V., 4, 227); in parabiblical Jewish literature גלדא (*DAN*, 79); in Syr. ܓܠܕܐ (*BLS*, 117).

כפרו - third masculine plural perfect, Peʿal. In the Aramaic documents from Egypt כפר (JH, 126; V., 7, 148); in parabiblical Jewish literature כפר (*DAN*, 206); in Syr. ܟܦܪ (*BLS*, 340).

די - Reckendorf (1888: 414) assumes that the particle די introduces direct speech; however, the presence of the participle in the phrase גבן (line 24) contradicts this according to Chabot.

Line 24

גבן - masculine plural Peʿal passive participle, absolute, agreeing with אלן, root גבא.

עשב[י]א ו[נת]ירדתא - the title of the new clause that expresses its content.

עשב[י]א - masculine plural emphatic; in Biblical Aramaic עֲשַׂבָּא (Gesenius-Buhl, 913); in parabiblical Jewish literature עשבא (*DAN*, 325), variant עסבא (*DAN*, 318); in Syr. ܥܣܒܐ (*BLS*, 536).

[נת]ירדתא - *CIS*, II, 3913. Feminine plural emphatic. Reckendorf (1888: 414) suggested עשב[י]א [די אס]ותא, 'herbs for doctors', which is not, however, supported by study of the *estampage* (*CIS*, II, 3913). In Biblical Aramaic we find the verb נתר only in the Hafʿel, אַתַּרוּ, 'pluck (leaves)' (Gesenius-Buhl, 909); in parabiblical Jewish literature נתר, 'fall away, fall off, cast away', and the noun נתרא, 'potash, waste' (*DAN*, 280); in Syr. the verb ܢܬܪ has the same meanings (*BLS*, 452-453); therefore *CIS*, II, 3913 translates: *decidua*, '(things) broken off, fallen off' (in connection with fruits, leaves etc.).

Line 25

יהבין - masculine plural active Peʿal participle, absolute. In the inscriptions from Sefire יהב; in the Aramaic documents from Egypt יהב (JH, 105; V., 7, 230–1); in Biblical Aramaic יְהַב (Gesenius-Buhl, 901–2); in parabiblical Jewish literature יהב (*DAN*, 180); in Syr. ܝܗܒ (*BLS*, 298–9).

אית - existential particle used in the sense 'to have, there is' (Rosenthal 1936: 83–4); in the Aramaic documents from Egypt אית, איתי (JH, 12; V., 3, 197–8); in Biblical Aramaic אִיתַי (before the enclitic pronoun: אִית; Gesenius-Buhl, 890); in parabiblical Jewish literature אית (*DAN*, 16); in Syr. ܐܝܬ (*BLS*, 16).

Commentary

תגרתא - cf. in Syr. ܐܓܪܬܐ, one of the meanings of which is 'payment, price' (*BLS*, 816); it is found in the Syriac translations of Luke 12:58; Rom. 6:23, etc. Feminine singular emphatic.

Line 26

עלימתא - feminine plural emphatic.

מוחא - masculine singular Af'el active participle, absolute; root וחא. T. Nöldeke suggested reading מחוא (Reckendorf 1888: 415); *CIS*, II, 3913 reads it the same way. Cf., however, the derivative from the same stem תוחית, 'resolution', in the Palmyrene inscriptions corresponding with the Greek πρόσταγμα (*CIS*, II, 3913 = *Inv.* I, 2; *Inv.* X, 44; JH, 324–5). On the etymology see Rosenthal 1936: 65, n. 4; Cantineau 1935: 112. In Arabic وحى (de Biberstein Kazimirski 1846: II, 1502–3).

פשקת - first singular perfect Pe'al, which shows that this is the continuation of Corbulo's rescript (Reckendorf 1888: 415). There is also a reference to the old law.

Line 27

ה|ן| - misspelled in the text as הו.

יג|בא מכ|סא - Reckendorf 1888: 383.

עלימתא די שקלן - Schröder (1884: 436) understands this as 'Sclavinnen für die Arbeit'. However, this is impossible if compared with the resolutions about taxes from prostitutes in the 'new' Tariff (II, I, 46–II, 2,2).

Line 28

לאת|תא דנ|ר - Reckendorf (1888: 383) reads דנ|רא].

חסיר - cf. in the Aramaic documents from Egypt חסירתא (V., 7, 223); in Biblical Aramaic חַסִּיר (Gesenius-Buhl, 900); in parabiblical Jewish literature חסר, 'less' (*DAN*, 156); in Syr. ܚܣܝܪ (*BLS*, 248).

Line 29

הי - feminine 3rd singular pronoun. In the Aramaic documents from Egypt הי (Leander, p. 25); in Biblical Aramaic היא (Rosenthal 1963: 19); in parabiblical Jewish literature היא (*DAN*, 112); in Syr. ܗܝ (Nestle 1883: 221).

[יגבא ⟨ על] - Reckendorf (1888: 383) reads [יגבא מן]. We accept the reading of *CIS*, II, 3913.

Compared to the 'new' Tariff (II, 1, 46–II, 2, 2) this clause sets a maximum tax to be collected from a prostitute.

צלמיא - masculine plural emphatic. In the Aramaic inscriptions from Nerab צלמא (JH, 245); in Biblical Aramaic צְלֵם (Gesenius-Buhl, 915); in parabiblical Jewish literature צלם, צילם (DAN, 364); in Syr. ܨܰܠܡܳܐ (BLS, 630).

נחשא - masculine singular emphatic. In the Aramaic documents from Egypt נחש (JH, 177; V., 11, 209); in the inscriptions from Nerab נחש; in Biblical Aramaic נְחָשׁ , נְחָשָׁא (Gesenius-Buhl, 908); in parabiblical Jewish literature נחשא (DAN, 268); in Syr. ܢܚܫܐ (TS, II, 2341–2).

אדרטיא - masculine plural emphatic, derived from Greek ἀνδριάς (-αντος). In parabiblical Jewish literature אדריינטוס (KGLL, II, 14) together with אנדרטא (KGLL, II, 65) and אנדריאנטוס (KGLL, II, 66); in Syr. ܐܘܢܕܪܝܐ (var. ܐܢܕܪܝܐ [BLS, 6]). On prices for making statues within the Roman empire see Szilágyi 1966: 214–24.

Line 30

אתחזי - reference to the resolution is made in an impersonal form. By analogy with line 15 of the same column it is possible to assume that the citation is taken from the same document as the previous clause. Cf. also II, 3, 32: [א]תחזי לי.

נח[שא] - see CIS, II, 3913.

Line 31

פלגות - feminine singular construct. In Biblical Aramaic פְּלַג (Gesenius-Buhl, 913); in the Aramaic documents from Egypt פלג (JH, 227; V., 13, 221); in parabiblical Jewish literature פלגא (DAN, 334); in Syr. ܦܠܓܐ; var. ܦܠܓܘܬܐ (BLS, 570). Cf. in other Palmyrene texts: פלג, in the construct state פלג and in emphatic פלגא (JH, 227–8).

[טעו]ן - see CIS, II, 3913.

Line 32

קשט[א] - see de Vogüé (1883b: 165): קש[טא]. According to Schröder (1884: 436) קשט is the beginning of a proper name. In fact it is an adjective, masculine singular emphatic. In the Aramaic documents from Egypt the root קשט (JH, 267–8; V., 13, 235); in Biblical Aramaic קְשֹׁט (Gesenius-Buhl, 917); in

Commentary

parabiblical Jewish literature קשטא (*DAN*, 393–4); in Syr. ܩܫܛܐ; in Palestinian Christian literature קשטא (*BLS*, 704).

|א]תחזי לי - see de Vogüé (1883b: 165). Citation of the same text continues.

אתר - masculine singular absolute. In the inscriptions from Sefire and the inscriptions of Zakar, the king of Hamath and Lu'ash, אשר; in the Aramaic documents from Egypt אתר; in the inscriptions from Nerab אשר (*JH*, 27–8; V., 3, 214–16); in Biblical Aramaic אֲתַר (Gesenius-Buhl, 890); in parabiblical Jewish literature אתרא (*DAN*, 46); in Syr. ܐܬܪܐ (*BLS*, 55).

אתר די דמס - the place where public gatherings occur (cf. line 33 אתר די מתכנשין). In Syrian cities public gatherings would usually take place in a theatre (Shifman 1977). Does this mean that shops which sold salt were not far from the local theatre? Or that public gatherings in Palmyra were exceptional and took place in the *agora*?

Line 34

לחש[חת]ה - cf. Schröder 1884, 433: לחשבנה; Reckendorf (1888: 384): לחש[בנ]ה. *CIS*, II, 3913 reads לחש[חת]ה explaining that the remains of the fourth letter visible on the *estampage* do not correspond with the letter ב and the letters בנ would not fill the *lacuna*. Therefore לחש[חת]ה is preferable. However, the meaning in either case does not change. It is a feminine singular noun, together with the preposition ל and suffixed 3rd masculine singular pronoun ה-; in Biblical Aramaic חַשְׁחוּ in the plural (hypothetically reconstructed singular form *חָשְׁחָא) and in the singular construct חַשְׁחוּת (reconstructed form in the absolute state *חַשְׁחוּ; Gesenius-Buhl, 900); in Syr. ܚܫܚܬܐ (*BLS*, 262).

איטלק[ן] - so Schröder (1884: 433). *CIS*, II, 3913 mistakenly reads איטלק[א].

Line 35

|מ]לחא - de Vogüé (1883b: 165). This is a masculine singular emphatic adjective agreeing with the preceding מכסא.

Line 36

בה]ו נמוס[א - *CIS*, II, 3913, though in the commentary Chabot prefers בה]יגמוני[א, assuming that the rescript is addressed specifically to the area of Palmyrene jurisdiction. We believe that the restoration accepted in *CIS* is more plausible, taking into account the formula היך בנמוסא in line 35.

193

Line 37

מתקבל - masculine singular Ethpaʻʻal participle, absolute. In the Aramaic documents from Egypt קבל (JH, 248–9; V., 13, 230); in Biblical Aramaic in Paʻʻel קַבֵּל (Gesenius-Buhl, 915); in parabiblical Jewish literature קבל (DAN, 369); in Syr. ܩܒܠ (BLS, 640–1).

ול[ד]תדמריא - CIS, II, 393. Reckendorf (1888: 384) reads ול[מ]די[א]; CIS, II, 3913 points out that it is more plausible to read ת after ל. However, in general the restoration remains uncertain. D. Schlumberger (1937: 284) suggests the reading ל[מכס]א.

In comparison to the earlier clause (II, 2, 19–21) this one does not have reference to the quality of the salt being sold or to the size of the *modius* or to sanctions for failing to pay taxes, but it does contain a directive on how to organize the selling of salt in the city.

Line 38

מ[כ]סא - Reckendorf (1888: 384).

ארגונא - Schröder (1884: 436) connects this word with the Greek ἐργώνης, 'entrepreneur'. This understanding is at variance with texts II, 1, 10–11 and II, 2, 17.

Line 39

It seems that this is the end of the clause that starts in the previous line. Since there are no direct parallels to this text elsewhere in the Tariff, it is impossible to reconstruct it. In comparison with II, 1, 10–11 and II, 2, 17 it appears that the discussion here is about taxes on purple dye.

Line 40

מ[ה]לכין - cf. II, 2, 7: [מזבנ]י נחתיא די הפכין במדיתא; the Greek μεταβόλοι (III, 2, 39) matches that as well. Based on the similarity of meanings between הפכין and מ[ה]לכין, as well as on the presence of במ[ד]ית<א> after the latter, it is possible to restore the beginning of the line by analogy with II, 2, 7 as: מ[ה]לכין. [מזבני נחתיא די] מ[ה]לכין ב[מד] ית<א> - masculine plural active Paʻʻel participle, absolute. In the inscriptions from Sefire the verb appears as imperfect אהך (JH, 65); in the Aramaic documents from Egypt הלך (imperfect Peʻal יהך: JH, 65; V., 7, 198); in Biblical Aramaic הלך (imperfect Peʻal יְהָךְ; Paʻʻel participle מְהַלֵּךְ (Gesenius-Buhl, 896); in parabiblical Jewish literature

Commentary

הלך (*DAN*, 114); in Syr. ܗܠܟ (*BLS*, 176–7).

ב|מד|ית<א> - the restoration in brackets comes from *CIS*, II, 3913. Since the combination ית... is possible in this word only in the emphatic, we may assume that the carver forgot to write the א after the ת.

Lines 41–2

The context of these lines is impossible to reconstruct; it is possible, though, that the discussion here is about workshops in the *agora*.

Line 43

כ|תיב מן ל|על - *CIS*, II, 3913.

שלחא - masculine singular emphatic. In parabiblical Jewish literature שלחא (*DAN*, 425); in Syr ܫܠܚܐ (*BLS*, 780). Schröder (1884: 436) suggests the meaning 'weapon', though with a question mark.

Line 44

Before the word מתגבא and by analogy with II, 3, 42, יהוא is reconstructed.

אשל[א] - the ending of the word is missing. Masculine singular emphatic. According to the context, this is either the specification of the type of אסרין or a reference to a unit of measure for the goods being traded. In the latter case the Palmyrene word matches with the word אשל that is known in the Aramaic documents from Egypt and which is a unit of measure for area or surface (JH, 27; V., 3, 214).

מ{מ}פקנא - since the word appears as מפקנא in all cases like this in the Tariff, we must have an error: the carver wrote an extra מ.

Line 45

טענ[א] - *CIS*, II, 3913.

י]גבא - our restoration is based on the context, since the discussion here is about collecting taxes.

In contrast with II, 2, 6 this clause sets a more precise unit of measurement for the collecting of taxes on the import of skins, but leaves the export tax entirely for the tax farmer to decide, though it also refers to an agreement reached with the taxpayers.

The Palmyrene Tax Tariff

Line 46

עֲנָא - feminine singular, absolute (cf. the following agreement with ת[ה]ו[א] מ[תאעלא). In the Aramaic documents from Egypt קן (JH, 218; V., 13, 233); in parabiblical Jewish literature ענא (*DAN*, 316); in Syr. ܥܢܐ (*BLS*, 533).

ת[ה]ו[א] מ[תאעלא מן בר] - *CIS*, II, 3913.

Line 47

[למגז תהוא מת]אעלא - our restoration is by analogy with the text of the following line.

מגז - Pe'al infinitive of the verb גזז. In parabiblical Jewish literature גזז (*DAN*, 75).

Line 48

[תחומא תהוא] - our reconstruction is by analogy with the preceding text, since there is a parallel in lines 46–7, where there is reference to tax collection on livestock brought in from outside of Palmyra for shearing, while livestock moved around within Palmyrene territory for shearing are not liable to taxes.

למדיתא - undoubtedly Palmyra.

Line 49

The first part of the line is impossible to reconstruct.

... בותא - the ending of a feminine singular emphatic noun.

After the words ומן די, as *CIS*, II, 3913 rightly pointed out, there is a missing word which could only be a specification of the action undertaken by 'somebody' (מן די), which is liable to taxation. It is suggested that the discussion is about pasturage.

י<ד> see *CIS*, II, 3913.

Line beneath the three Aramaic columns

After the word מכסא there could be only one word, [יתגב]א, since the discussion is about tax collecting; then there is an explanation: דנר מתגבא.

[אף] - *CIS*, II, 3913.

[מן]די - *CIS*, II, 3913.

אלא - so in the parabiblical Jewish literature (*DAN*, 18); in Syr. ܐܠܐ (*BLS*, 20), corresponds with the Greek ἀλλά, γάρ.

Commentary

<ע>א - agrees with די תהוא מאעלא.

ל|גו מן| - restored by analogy with II, 3, 47–8.

|תחום| - *CIS*, II, 3913.

אן - cf. in other clauses הן (II, 1, 5 etc.).

יצבא - Pe'al imperfect, third masculine singular. In the Aramaic documents from Egypt צבי (JH, 241; V., 13, 228); in Biblical Aramaic צְבָא (Gesenius-Buhl, 914); in parabiblical Jewish literature צבי, צבא (*DAN*, 357); in Syr. ܨܒܐ (*BLS*, 619).

After the words מכסא יצבא there should be the equivalent of the Greek χαρα[κτη]ρίσασθαι (IV, 2, 38–9), clearly missed out by the carver, i.e. probably <למחתם> - Pe'al infinitive from the verb חתם. Otherwise the text after the word אלא would not make sense. Cf. in the Aramaic documents from Egypt חתם (JH, 98; V., 7, 225); in Biblical Aramaic חֲתַם (Gesenius-Buhl, 900); in parabiblical Jewish literature חתם (*DAN*, 164); in Syr. ܚܬܡ (*BLS*, 264).

יהוא |שביק|א - restored by analogy with the Greek ἐξέστω (IV, 2, 40); Pe'al compound with jussive meaning. [שביק]א - masculine singular passive participle, emphatic. In the Aramaic documents from Egypt שבק (JH, 289; V., 13, 244); in Biblical Aramaic שְׁבַק (Gesenius-Buhl, 919); in parabiblical Jewish literature שבק (*DAN*, 414); in Syr. ܫܒܩ (*BLS*, 753).

Panel III

Column 1

Line 1–3

All the *lacunae* in the text are reconstructed by analogy with the Aramaic version; cf. II, 1, 1–2.

|Παλμύρους| - cf. III, 3, 23: Παλμύροις.

παῖδας - *OGIS*, 629 refers to the Aramaic עלימיא that has the same meaning. The same reading is adopted by *IGRR*, III, 1056; Reckendorf 1888: 374; *CIS*, II, 3913. See Amusin (1952: 46–7) on the use of the Greek παῖς as a designation for a slave in the Hellenistic Near East.

τὰ ὅ[ρια] - de Vogüé (1883b: 152) read εἰς το[ὺς ὅρους]. However, a more precise restoration is provided by Dessau (1884: 504, n. 3): τὰ ὅ[ρια], which corresponds with the Aramaic תחומיה (II, 1, 2) and is accepted in subsequent editions (*OGIS*, 629; *IGRR*, III, 1056; *CIS*, II, 3913).

The Palmyrene Tax Tariff

Lines 4–5

παρ' οὗ δ[ὲ] - so *CIS*, II, 3913. *OGIS*, 629 and *IGRR*, III, 1056 accept the reading παρ' οὗ ἄν.

In these lines there was certainly a clause that matched II, 1, 3: the discussion must have been about the selling of slaves in the *polis* itself and about their export from Palmyra. Therefore, based on the Palmyrene version, the reconstruction of the text could be as follows: παρ' οὗ δ[ὲ παῖδας ἐν τῇ πόλει πωλεῖ ἢ] μι...[ἐξάγει ἑκάστ]ου σ[ώματος Χ ιβ'].

Line 6

OGIS, 629 reads παρ' οὗ [ἄν ἀνδράποδα] ουετερα[νὰ ἢ]...., explaining that the same clause continues in the next line. *IGRR*, III, 1056: παρ' οὗ.......ουετεραν[ός?]. This line undoubtedly corresponds with the Aramaic of II, 1, 4 and therefore most likely it presents a phrase completed as the editors of *IGRR*, III, 1056 and *CIS*, II, 3913 suggest. Based on II, 1, 4 we suggest the following reconstruction of the text: παρ' οὗ [δὲ σώματ]α ουετραν[ὰ πωλεῖ Χ ι']. The word σώματα is preferable to the term ἀνδράποδα because the latter is not compatible with the size of the *lacuna* (as indicated by *CIS*, II, 3913, though it does not suggest any alternative) and by analogy with the previous and following lines.

Lines 7–8

These lines correspond with the Aramaic II, 1, 5 where the discussion is about the export of a slave by a buyer (זבונא). *OGIS*, 629 reads ['Εξ]άγηται ἑκάστου σώμ[ατος πράξει]; *IGRR*, III, 1056 omits the verb πράξει. However, for the Aramaic יתי there would be a Greek parallel in διδότω. In this passage, we suggest, for the Aramaic זבונא there was a probable Greek parallel in [ὑπ]ὸ το[ῦ πριαμένου].

Line 9

ὁ αὐτὸς δημοσιώνη[ς] - the Greek text is identical to Palmyrene II, 1, 6: הו מ[כסא]. Dessau (1884: 515–16) notes here that all tax collecting responsibility was given in Palmyra to one and the same person or group of financial officers. *OGIS*, 629 (note 27) agrees with this.

[ξηροφόρτου] - so *IGRR*, III, 1056 (with a question mark showing the hypothetical character of the restoration) and *CIS*, II, 3913. This restoration is

Commentary

a match for the Palmyrene text II, 1, 6: יבי[שין].

Line 10

γόμο[υ καμηλικοῦ] - de Vogüé 1883b: 152: γόμο[υ καμη]λικ[οῦ]. See in II, 1, 6 [מ]ן טעון גמלא.

Line 11

εἰσκομισ[θέ]ντος - *gen. abs.*; in the parallel Aramaic text למעלנא, also throughout the Greek text of the 'new' law.

Line 12

ἐκκομισθ[έντ]ος - *gen. abs.*; in the parallel Aramaic text there is a certain restoration למ[פקנא], also throughout the Greek text of the 'new' law.

[γόμου καμηλικοῦ] - so de Vogüé (1883b: 152): γό[μου καμηλικοῦ].

Line 14

ὀνικ[οῦ] - Dessau (1884: 506) notes the usage of this word instead of ὀνείου.

[ἑκάστο]υ εἰ[σκομισθέντος] - de Vogüé (1883b: 152).

Line 15

ἐκκομσθέν[τος] - de Vogüé (1883b: 152).

Lines 16–17

πορφύρας μηλωτῆ[ς] - according to Dessau (1884: 506, n. 2) there should be rather πορφύρας, μηλωτῆς ἑκάστης εἰσκομισθείσης κ.τ.λ. As *OGIS*, 629. n. 30 suggests (in fact, this is also in the main text: Dessau 1884: 506), the purple wool in Palmyra should have been called in Greek πορφύρα μηλωτή.

ἑκά[στου δέρμα]τος - de Vogüé (1883b: 152).

[πράξει ἀσσάρια η´] - cf. Dessau (1884: 506). de Vogüé (1883b: 152) thought mistakenly that the tax was 3 *denarii*.

Line 18

ἀσσάρια η´ - *IGRR*, III, 1056.

Lines 19–20

κ[αμηλικοῦ] - de Vogüé (1883b: 152).

μύρου - in the Greek text there is no specification of the type of oil such as would be parallel to the Aramaic בשמא.

[τοῦ ἐν ἀλαβάσ]τροις - de Vogüé (1883b: 152).

ε[ἰσκομισθέντος πράξει] - de Vogüé (1883b: 152).

Line 21

το[ῦ γόμου καμηλικοῦ μύρου τοῦ ἐν ἀλαβάστροις] - *OGIS*, 629 reads κἀπο before this reconstruction, following Dessau (1884: 500). *IGRR*, III, 1056: καὶ τὸ... The subsequent text is reconstructed on the basis of the formula of the previous two lines and the content of the parallel Palmyrene clause II, 1, 14–15.

Line 22

ἐκ[κομισθέντος πράξει] - de Vogüé (1883b: 152): ἐκ[κομισθέντος]. For the word [πράξει] see *OGIS*, 629.

Line 23

γ[όμου καμηλικοῦ μύρου τοῦ ἐν ἀσκοῖς] - de Vogüé (1883b: 154). Cf. II, 1, 16-17.

Line 24

[εἰσκομισθέντος πράξει ✱ ιγ´] - de Vogüé (1883b: 154).

Line 25

[ἐκ]κ[ομισθέντος] - de Vogüé (1883b: 154). *OGIS*, 629: [ἐκκομισθέντος πράξει]; *IGRR*, III, 1056: [ἐκκομισθέντος].

Line 26

[γόμου ὀνικοῦ μύ]ρου - de Vogüé (1883b: 154).

ἐ[ν ἀλαβάστροις] - de Vogüé (1883b: 154). *OGIS*, 629 reads [γόμου ὀνικοῦ μύρου τοῦ ἐν ἀσκ]οῖς [αἰγείοις] κ.τ.λ. This, however, makes no sense in the text; *IGRR*, III, 1056 gives ἐ[ν ἀλαβάσ]τροις.

Line 27

εἰσ[κομισ]θέν[τος] πράξει - de Vogüé (1883b: 154). He reads [πράξει].

Commentary

Line 28

[ἐκκομισ]θέν[τος] - see de Vogüé (1883b: 154).

Line 29

μ[ύρου τοῦ ἐν ἀσκοῖς] - de Vogüé (1883b: 154).

Line 30

εἰσκομ[ισθέντο]ς - de Vogüé (1883b: 154).

πρ[άξει] - de Vogüé (1883b: 154): [πράξει].

Line 31

π[ρ]ά̣ξ[ει] - *OGIS*, 629.

Lines 32–3

γόμου ἐλεηροῦ - *OGIS*, 629 reads ἐλ(αι)ηροῦ, referring to the form ΕΛΕΗΡΟΥ in the inscription.

το[ῦ ἐν ἀσκο]ῖς [τεσσάρ]σι - de Vogüé (1883b: 154).

Lines 33–4

ἐπὶ καμή[λου εἰσκομισθέν]τος - de Vogüé (1883b: 154). He and *OGIS*, 629 reconstruct [πράξει] after it.

Line 35

ἐκκομισθέντο[ς] - *OGIS*, 629 reads ἐκκομισθέντο[ς πράξει]. Cf. de Vogüé (1883b: 154): ἐκκομισθέντος; *IGRR*, III, 1056: ἐκκομισθέντο[ς]; so in *CIS*, II, 3913.

Line 36–7

ἐλαιηροῦ - cf. ἐλεηροῦ in line 32. These different spellings surely show that in the second quarter of the second century AD the diphthong *ai* in the Greek language in Palmyra was pronounced as an *e* (long?) — this change is generally a typical development of koine (Borovskiĭ 1953: 315).

τοῦ ἐ[ν ἀσκοῖς δυσὶ αἰ]γείοις - de Vogüé (1883b: 154) reads [τοῦ ἐν ἀσκο]ῖς δυ[σὶ αἰ]γείοις; *OGIS*, 629: τοῦ ἐ[ν ἀσκο]ῖς δυ[σὶ αἰ]γείοις and also *IGRR*, III, 1056. Our reading agrees with *CIS*, II, 3913.

ἐπὶ καμήλ[ου εἰσκομισθέντος] - de Vogüé (1883b: 154).

Line 39

ἐκκομισθέντο[ς] - de Vogüé (1883b: 154): ἐκκομισθέντος; *OGIS*, 629: ἐκκομισθέντο[ς πράξει]; *IGRR*, III, 1056: ἐκκομισθέντος; *CIS*, II, 3913: ἐκκομισθέντο[ς].

Lines 40–1

γόμου ἐλε[ηροῦ τοῦ ἐπ' ὄνο]υ ε[ἰσκομισθέν]τος π[ράξει] - de Vogüé (1883b: 154): ἐλ[αιηροῦ τοῦ ἐπ' ὄνου εἰσκομισθέν]τος [πράξει]; *OGIS*, 629: γόμου ἐλ(αι)[ηροῦ τοῦ ἐπ' ὄνο]υ ε[ἰσκομισθέν]το[ς πράξει]; *IGRR*, III, 1056: ε[ἰσκομισθέν]τος [πράξει]; *CIS*, II, 3913: π[ράξει].

Line 42

ἐκ[κμομισθέντος] - de Vogüé (1883b: 154).

Line 43

γόμ[ου καύσεως] - de Vogüé (1883b: 154) reads γόμ[ου κ......] by analogy with line 46. The Greek text of III, 1, 43 – III, 2, 4 corresponds with Palmyrene II, 1, 28–32. Therefore, after γόμ[ου] there must be a word that matches the Aramaic דהנא and begins with κ. If דהנא means 'fat, oil' that was used for lamps (cf. Mishnah Menahot, 8, 5; Mishnah Shabbat 2, 2; Mishnah Demai 1, 3), then the Greek probably read γόμ[ου καύσεως]. Cf. Preisigke 1925, I: col. 782: τιμὴ ἐλαίου καύσεως λύχνων, καύσεις λύχνων κ.τ.λ.

Olive oil was commonly also used for lamps (*TA*, I: 69).

[τοῦ ἐν ἀσκοῖς τ]έσσαρσι – de Vogüé (1883b: 154): [τοῦ ἐν ἀσκοῖς τέσσαρσι]; *OGIS*, 629 - [τοῦ ἐν ἀσκοῖς τ]ἐσ[σαρσι]; *IGRR*, III, 1056 and *CIS*, II, 3913 read the the text the same way as we do.

Line 44

[εἰσκομισθέντος πρά]ξει - de Vogüé (1883b: 154): [ἐπι καμήλου εἰσκομισθέντος πρά]ξει (so *IGRR*, III, 1056); *OGIS*, 629: [εἰσκομισθέντος πρά]ξει (so in *CIS*, II, 3913).

Line 45

ἐκκομι[σ]θέ[ντος] - de Vogüé (1883b: 154) saw this word on the *estampage*.

Commentary

Line 46

γόμου κ|αύσεως] - see comments on line 43.

[τοῦ ἐν] ἀ|σ|κοῖς - de Vogüé (1883b: 154).

Line 47

ἐπὶ κ|αμήλου εἰσ|κομισθέντος - de Vogüé (1883b: 154) read κἀπὶ κ[αμήλου εἰσ]κομισθέντος. We accept the reading of *OGIS*, 629.

Column 2

Line 1

[ἐκκομισ|θέντος - de Vogüé (1883b: 154) and *IGRR*, III, 1056: [ἐκκομι]σθέντος. We accept the reading of *CIS*, II, 3913.

Lines 2–3

|γόμου ὀ|ν|ικοῦ καύσεως εἰσκομισθέντος πράξει| - cf. III, 1, 40–1. The same in de Vogüé (1883b: 154) and *IGRR*, III, 1056. On καύσεως see comments on III, 1, 43.

Line 4

|ἐκκομισθ|έν|τος| - de Vogüé (1883b: 154) and *IGRR*, III, 1056: [ἐκκ]ο[μισθέντος]; we accept the reconstruction and reading in *CIS*, II, 3913.

Lines 5–6

By analogy with the Aramaic text we can assume that the discussion is about the import of salted fish. Cf., however, de Vogüé (1883b: 154) and *IGRR*, III, 1056: [γόμου καμηλικοῦ....]ς εἰ[σκομισθέντος πράξει δηνάρια ι´ ἐκκομισθέντος δηνάρια.]; we accept the reading in *CIS*, II, 3913 which is based on the *estampage*, as well its restoration.

Lines 7–20

Impossible to reconstruct; in lines 17, 19 and 20 there are only a few signs surviving; lines 7–16 and 18 are erased completely.

Line 21

|κα]μήλου - *OGIS*, 629; *CIS*, II, 3913.

The Palmyrene Tax Tariff

Line 22

[θ]ρέμματος - Schröder (1884: 427). Cf. *OGIS*, 629.

Line 23

Impossible to reconstruct.

Line 24

[τ]εθυμένη - *CIS*, II, 3913.

Line 25

δ[ημ]οσιώνης - de Vogüé (1883b: 154) read δημοσιώνης.

ἑκάσ[του] μη[νός] - de Vogüé (1883b: 154) read ἑκάστου ...; *OGIS*, 629: ἑκάσ[του μηνός]. The *estampage*, which was used by the editor of *CIS*, II, 3913, confirms the reconstruction by Dittenberger.

Lines 26–7

ἑκ[άστου] - *OGIS*, 629.

τῶ[ν τό] - *OGIS*, 629.

ἔλαιον - cf. in the Aramaic text: משחא בשימא (II, 1, 45–6).

κατα - Dessau (1884: 518; see *OGIS*, 629 and cf. Reckendorf 1888: 376) reads κατα[κομιζόντων], which, according to *CIS*, II, 3913, does not fit into the size of the *lacuna*. The clause of lines 25–7 corresponds with the Aramaic text II, 1, 45–6 where the discussion is about collecting a monthly tax of 2 *assarii* from those who sell perfumed oil: מן די יהוא מזבן משחא בשימא. Since the Aramaic יהוא מזבן corresponds with the restored Greek in line 27, we can assume that the combination [πωλού]ντων introduces some sort of circumstance of the sale in the Greek text which is not discussed in the Aramaic version for some reason. At the same time those circumstances were not essential for the matter itself; perhaps it was so minor that the editor of the Aramaic text decided to drop it. Is it possible that behind the symbols κατα...π.ον......ις is a term which signifies businesses specialized in trading different types of oil and fat or a specific place in Palmyra where they were located?

[πωλού]ντων - reconstructed by Dessau (1884: 518).

[ἀσσάρια β′] - our reconstruction by analogy with II, 1, 46.

Commentary

Lines 28–32

These lines are parallel with Aramaic II, 1, 46–II, 2, 2, where the discussion is about the collecting of tax from prostitutes.

ὁ αὐτ|ὸς δημοσιώνης| - de Vogüé (1883b: 156). *OGIS*, 629 read ὁ αὐ[τὸς δημοσιώνης.........] (π)ρά[ξει]...

πρά|ξει| - de Vogüé (1883b: 156] read πρ[άξει]; *IGRR*, III, 1056: πρά[ξει].

|τῶν ἑταιρ|ῶν - *CIS*, II, 3913.

|λαμβά|νουσιν - *IGRR*, III, 1056.

|ἀ|σσάρια - de Vogüé (1883b: 156).

α η´ (end of line 31) - *CIS*, II, 3913 gives αιη. However] α η´ (*OGIS*, 629) is preferable.

|ἀσ|σάρια - de Vogüé (1883b: 156), however, reads ὀκτώ after it (rather than η´).

ἐλ - *OGIS*, 629 reconstructs ἐ[λ.... in line 32.

Let us contrast the Aramaic text and the extant Greek fragments:

II, 1, 46–2, 2	III, 2, 28–32
אף יגבא מכסא	ὁ αὐτ[ὸς δημοσιώνης] πρά[ξει].......λει
מן זניתא	..[τῶν ἑταιρ]ῶν
מן מן די שקלא דינר	ὅσαι.................[λαμβά]νουσιν π..
[או] יתיר דנרא חד מן אתתא	....
ומן מן די שקלא אסרין תמניא	.......[ἀσ]σάρια ὀκτώ..........α η
יגבא אסרין תמניי	
ומן מן די שקלא [א]סרי[ן ש]תא	.......[ἀσ]σάρια ἕξ ἐλ ...καστ
יגבא אסרין [ש]ת[א]	ἀσσ ς´

From the foregoing it is evident that the reconstruction of the text suggested by V. Dittenberger (*OGIS*, 629) is the most reliable.

Concerning the form ἔλαβον, Dittenberger notes: 'Supplevi; aoristum offensioni esse sane non nego.' Cf. *SDGY*, 295: 'The aorist can signify an action that usually happens ... This aorist ... can be translated in the present, future or non-continuous past.'

Line 33

|ὁ αὐτὸς δημ|οσιώνης - de Vogüé (1883b: 156).

πρ|άξ|ει - *OGIS*, 629. de Vogüé (1883b: 156) reads π[ράξ]ει.

ἐργαστηρίων - de Vogüé (1883b: 156) and *IGRR*, III, 1056 suggest that this word ends the sentence and the clause. The position of *OGIS*, 629 (cf. also *CIS*, II, 3913) is more acceptable and is based on the context of lines 33–6, which are treated as a single unit; between the words ἐργαστηρίων and παντοπωλ[ικ]ῶν there must be another word, similar in meaning (line 34). The Aramaic parallel II, 2, 3–5 also confirms the unity of the text of III, 2, 33–6.

Line 34

[ῥαφιδικῶν] - restored by analogy with σκυτικῶν and the Aramaic parallel II, 2, 4 - א[ט׳]ח. I.F. Fikhman has shown that there must be a form of the adjective ῥαφιδικός here.

παντοπωλ[ικ]ῶν - de Vogüé (1883b: 156) reads παντοπωλειῶν; *OGIS*, 629: παντοπωλ[εί]ων; also the subsequent editions. Reconstructed in accordance with σκυτικῶν (the adjectival form was suggested by Fikhman).

Line 35

[τὸ τέλος] - de Vogüé (1883b: 156) reads at the beginning of the line [πράξει]. Other editions did not try to reconstruct the line. We reconstruct [τὸ τέλος] for the following reasons. These are not references to the specific trades or workshops, since the earlier part of the clause mentions them in the genitive plural. By analogy with I, 9–10 (τό ἐκ συνηθείας τέλος) it is plausible that near the expression ἐκ συνηθείας stood the word [τέλο]ς, as the natural object of the verb πρ[άξ]ει (line 33); and besides this does not contradict the Aramaic text II, 2, 3–5, but clarifies it. See the examples of the use of the term τὸ τέλος in business documents outside the Tariff (Preisigke 1925: III: 250–1).

Lines 37–8

εἰσκομιζόντ[ων ἢ πω]λούντων - de Vogüé (1883b: 156); cf. Dessau 1884: 516.

ἀσσά[ρια β′] - de Vogüé (1883b: 156). Cf. Dessau (1884: 516): ἀσσά[ρια δύο].

Lines 39–40

πωλ[οῦν]τες - de Vogüé (1883b: 156) reads πω[λοῦν]τες; Dessau (1884: 516): πωλ[οῦν]τες.

ποιεῖν - *OGIS*, 629 reads γ[ιν]έσ[θω]. Reckendorf (1888: 376) reconstructs hypothetically τ[ελος?] (also Schröder 1884: 429); *IGRR*, III, 1056: τ[έλ]ος. On the *estampage* made by Ricci and published in *CIS*, II, 3913 there is a clear

Commentary

reading of ποιει. Therefore there is only one possible reading, ποιεῖ[ν] (including an implication of obligation). Cf. in the parallel Aramaic text (II, 2. 7): יהן מוט.

Line 41

χρήσεος - expected χρήσεως.

Line 42

ὁ αὐτὸς - referring to the δημοσιώνης. Cf. III, 2, 28 and 33.

Column 3

Lines 1–22, that contain the title and the beginning clauses of the 'old' law, which correspond with the Aramaic text II, 2, 13–21, are almost completely destroyed. There are only a few letters remaining, including the article τῆς at the beginning of the third line; πορφ[ύρας ?] at the beginning of the eighth line; and εινετω at the end of line 22 (*OGIS*, 629: [λαμβα]νέτω; perhaps more plausibly [γ]εινέτω ?).

Line 23

ἄλα[ς ἔχ]ῃ - Dessau (1884: 518, n. 3): ἄλ[ας] and, after him, *OGIS*, 629: ἄλ[ας...πωλ]ῇ; *CIS*, II, 3913 reads ἄλ[ας ἔχ]ῇ.

This understanding is identical to the parallel Aramaic text in II, 2, 22: מן די יהוא לה מלח.

Παλμύροις - expected Παλμύρᾳ. Probably either the Greek Πάλμυρα could be interpreted sometimes as a neuter plural, or a form Παλμύροι existed alongside the common form. See also *CIS*, II, 3913 and III, 3, 36–7.

[ἐν ὅροις] - *CIS*, II, 3913; in the parallel Aramaic text II, 22 there is a clear reconstruction [בתחא]מא. *OGIS*, 629 reads [ἢ ἐν τῇ χώρᾳ τῇ] Παλμυρηνῶν.

Lines 24–5

Παλμυρη[ν]ῶν - de Vogüé (1883b: 158) reads Παλμυρηνῶν (also *OGIS*, 629; *IGRR*, III, 1056); cf. however, *CIS*, II, 3913.

παραμετρησάτω - de Vogüé (1883b: 158) has, mistakenly, παραμετρησαίτο.

[τῷ δημο]σιώνῇ - de Vogüé (1883b: 158), as well as *OGIS*, 629 read [ὁ δημο]σιώνης. *IGRR*, III, 1056 and then *CIS*, II, 3913 read more precisely [τῷ δημο]σιώνῇ.

ε[ἰς ἕκ]αστον - *IGRR*, III, 1056. *OGIS*, 629: [εἰς ἕκ]αστον.

ἀσσά[ριον] - *OGIS*, 629. de Vogüé (1883b: 158): ἀσσάρια; *IGRR*, III, 1056: ἀσσά[ριον α΄]. Cf. in the Aramaic text (II, 2, 23): באסרא חד.

Lines 26–7

Based on the extant fragments, it seems this clause contained the decision on sanctions against people who did not pay taxes on salt (cf. Dessau 1884: 518, n. 3); the parallel Aramaic text, II, 2, 21 corresponds with this and includes a fine of 2 *sestertii* for a *modius*. Let us compare the two texts:

II, 2, 21	III, 3, 26–7
ו[די] לא י[כל]	ὃς δ' ἂν οὐ ....ν παραμετρήσ[ῇ]......
י[פרע לכל מדא]	ση ἔχων το..... δημο[σιων]....
מן נמ[וס]א דנה	
סוסטרטין [תר]ן	

It is evident that in the extant fragments of the Greek text there is 1) no reference to the law, 2) no unit of measure and 3) no indication of the size of the tax. At the same time, there are some words extant in the Greek that are missing from the Aramaic version: ἔχων, δημο[σιων]....; in other words the Greek text is not identical to the Aramaic, although their general meaning is probably the same. This makes the reconstruction of these two lines impossible.

....ν - *CIS*, II, 3913 thinks that this can be read as [πᾶσα]ν.

παραμετρήσῇ - *OGIS*, 629 and after it *CIS*, II, 3913. de Vogüé (1883b: 158) reads παραμετρή[σαιτο]; *IGRR*, III, 1056 - παραμετρη[σάτω].

ση - cf. Dessau 1884: 501 and Ricci's *estampage* (*CIS*, II, 3913), also *OGIS*, 629. de Vogüé (1883b: 158) and after him *IGRR*, III, 1056 read ον for ση.

ἔχων το - de Vogüé (1883b: 158): ἔχοντες.

δημο[σιων].... - *OGIS*, 629: δημο[σιώνης].

Lines 28–33

This section is not in the Aramaic version of the text (see also lines 38–45); it is about pledges given to the tax farmer for the paying of tax and about paying double the amount to the tax farmer, perhaps as a fine for illegal actions (Dessau 1884: 594).

Commentary

δ[ημοσι]ώνης - de Vogüé (1883b: 158): δημοσιώνης; *OGIS*, 629: δ[ημοσι]ώνης; *IGRR*, III, 1056: δη[μοσι]ώνης. As *IGRR*, III, 1056 suggests, after this word one could add [τὸ τέλος πράξας]. However, we do not have any reason to consider this restoration reliable.

[ἐνέ]χυρα - Dessau (1884: 524).

λά[βῇ] - Dessau (1884: 524).

ἀποδο[θῶ]σιν - *OGIS*, 629 and after it *CIS*, II, 3913.

αβρει - the meaning of these signs in line 30 is difficult to determine.

[δημοσιών]ῇ - *OGIS*, 629.

τοῦ διπ[λοῦ] - *gen. pretii. OGIS*, 629 read οὗ[τος τ]ὸ κ.τ.λ. Both the *estampage* and the text that is preserved on the stone confirm the following reading: τοῦ διπ[λοῦ]; cf. *IGRR*, III, 1056 and *CIS*, II, 3913.

ε[ἰσα]γέσθω - cf. Dessau (1884: 524) although with a question mark.

Lines 34–7

The clause about the resolution of arguments between the tax farmer and other people is missing from the Aramaic text of the Tariff.

δημ[ο]σιώνης - de Vogüé (1883b: 158) reads δημοσιώνης; Dessau (1884: 524): δημ[ο]σιώνης.

δημοσιώ[νης ἀ]πό τινος - de Vogüé (1883b: 158) read these words as completely extant. However Dessau (1884: 524) and *OGIS*, 629 have them as restored.

δικαιοδο[τείσ]θω - Dessau (1884: 524; *OGIS*, 629; *IGRR*, III, 1056). de Vogüé (1883b: 158) read δικαιοδοθήτω.

παρὰ τῷ ἐν Παλμύροις τεταγμένῳ - The discussion is clearly about the Roman official who was appointed in Palmyra by the provincial government to fulfil responsibilities in regard to administration of justice (cf. de Vogüé 1883b: 181; Dessau 1884: 524). Despite some doubts expressed by Dessau (1884: 524, n.2; cf. the very ambiguous position in *OGIS*, 629), we think that that *dikaiodotēs* was meant here (Cagnat 1884: 141; Shifman 1977). The verb δικαιοδο[τείσ]θω is used here because the discussion is about functions of the *dikaiodotēs*. The appeal to the Roman official can be explained on the grounds that tax farmers might deal with people who were outside the domain of Palmyra and therefore not under its jurisdiction. Cf. also *IGRR*, III, 1056.

O. Eissfeldt believes that here we are dealing with the commander of the Roman garrison, who fulfilled the responsibilities of a higher judge in matters of dispute in Palmyra (Eissfeldt 1941: 67). This suggestion does not sound probable to us. As far as we know, the commanders of Roman garrisons in cities like Palmyra did not have judicial responsibilities.

Lines 38–45

These clauses are about the rights of the tax farmers to take pledges from non-payers of taxes and to sell them. They are missing from the Aramaic text of the Tariff.

κύρι[ον] ἔ[σ]τω - *OGIS*, 629. *IGRR*, III, 1056 reads κύριο[ν] ἔ[σ]τω. Cf. *OGIS*, 225: καὶ κυρία ἔ[σ]ται προσφερομένη πρὸς πόλιν ἣν ἂν βούληται.

ἀπολ[υόντων] - *CIS*, II, 3913; this restoration is plausible because at the beginning of line 39 there is a clear letter λ on Ricci's *estampage*. However, Dessau (1884: 523), and after him *OGIS*, 629, as well as *IGRR*, III, 1056, read ἀπ[ο]γρα[φομένων]. This does not correspond with the actual text of the inscription.

[ἐν]έχυρα - Dessau (1884: 523). *OGIS*, 629 read [ἐ]νέχυρα.

[λ]α[μβάνει]ν - Dessau (1884: 523).

[τῶν ὑπη]ρ[ετῶν] - Dessau (1884: 523) reads [τῶν ὑπηρετῶν]; *IGRR*, III, 1056 and *CIS*, II, 3913: [τῶν ὑπη]ρ[ετῶν]; *OGIS*, 629: [δι' ἄλλου τινός], which is not possible because there is a clear ρ surviving.

[κἂν τα]ῦτα - *CIS*, II, 3913. *OGIS*, 629 reads [ἐὰν δὲ τα]ῦτα; *IGRR*, III, 1056: [καὶ τα]ῦτα.

[ἐνέ]χυρα - *OGIS*, 629.

[τρισίν] - *IGRR*, III, 1056 with a reference to Dareste.

[μὴ λυθῇ] - *OGIS*, 629.

[ἐξέστω τῷ δημ]οσιώνῃ - Dessau (1884: 524, n. 1)

[τοιαῦτα ἐνέχυρα] - reconstruction by Dareste: see *IGRR*, III, 1056.

[ἐν τόπῳ δημ]οσίῳ - *IGRR*, III, 1056.

πο[νηροῦ] - *OGIS*, 629, by analogy with the Latin *sine dolo malo*. Dareste (*IGRR*, III, 1056) read πέ[ντε καὶ δέκα ἡμέραις ἀφ' οὗ]. *OGIS*, 629 reads πο[νηροῦ] after [εἰ δέ τι ἐνέχυρον μείονος], assuming that if the pledge is sold for less than the required tax, the payer would have to pay the tax collector the

Commentary

difference; however, this is in contradiction with Ricci's *estampage*, where in the middle of the line there is a clear ωλ. Besides, the verb πράσσω means 'collect'. [Ed.: it appears that Shifman accidentally read ἐπράχθη from πράσσειν at the end of line 43. His Greek text correctly gives ἐπράθη from πιπράσκω/πέρνημι. For the following line it is not easy to see what Shifman had in mind.]

π[ράσσ]ειν - *OGIS*, 629 reads π[ράσ]σειν; *CIS*, II, 3913: π[ράσσ]ειν.

δη[μοσιώνῇ] - *OGIS*, 629.

OGIS, 629 reconstructs line 45 as follows: καὶ [ἔξε]στιν ἐκ τοῦ νόμου [ἐζέ]στω. *CIS*, II, 3913 notes that the two reconstructed forms do not match with the size of the *lacunae*, although they do make good sense. In any case, there was a reference here to the law which confirms the rights of the tax farmer.

Line 46

This is the beginning of the section that will continue in line 47 and further in IV, 1, 1–5, containing a prohibition against a tax farmer giving to someone else his rights to take action with regard to market taxation or taxes for the use of water supplies ('to collect', 'to give', and 'to charge'). This explanation is confirmed by the expression τῷ μισθωτῇ... ἐξέστω, as well as the fact that line IV, 1, 1 does not have an 'outdent', which is normal when the Greek text begins a new clause (cf. *CIS*, II, 3913). Dessau already noted this (1884: 523). However, he thought that the clause starts with IV, 1, 1. He considers the content of III, 3, 46–7 to be unclear and the word λιμένος in combination with the following [πη]γῶν enigmatic (1884: 522). D. Schlumberger (1937: 279) suggests reading Λιμένος Π[αλμύρων καὶ πη]γῶν ὑδάτων Καίσαρος τῷ μισθωτῇ.

Π[αλμύρων] - a restoration that we believe is plausible. Cf. in the general title of the Aramaic part (Panel II): למנא די הדרינא תדמר. The subsequent text: [καὶ πη]γῶν ὑδάτων Καίσαρος — also corresponds with the general Aramaic title: עינתא די מיא [די אי]לס קיסר.

[πη]γῶν - Dessau (1884: 523), de Vogüé (1883b: 160): ...τον.

Line 47

εντος - this combination of signs is probably the ending of a masculine or neuter first aorist passive participle, genitive singular (-θέντος).

παρασχέσ[θαι] - de Vogüé (1883b: 160).

Panel IV

Column 1

Line 1

διδόναι - *OGIS*, 629: διδό[ν]αι. Dessau (1884: 523, n. 3) does not know how to understand the word διδόναι in this context. The meaning is clear, though, if we consider that it is one of the verbs which describe the actions of a tax farmer with regard to imposition of taxes (cf. *CIS*, II, 3913).

λαμ[βάνειν] - de Vogüé (1883b: 160).

Line 2

....νωφο - *OGIS*, 629: ωφε[λ..].

ἀνθρ[ωπ..μή] - *OGIS*, 629.

Line 3

[ὀν]όματι - *OGIS*, 629.

At the end of the line *OGIS*, 629 reads [ὅς δ' ἄν], which is hardly likely according to *CIS*, II, 3913.

Lines 4–5

[πραχθήτω τὸ] διπλοῦν - *OGIS*, 629.

Lines 6–9

There are only a few signs remaining here; line 7 is completely destroyed.

Lines 10–11

At the beginning of line 10 there is an 'outdent' which marks the beginning of a new clause in the Greek; the combination γαιο shows that this is a citation from the rescript of Gaius Licinius Mucianus (see II, 2, 24). Therefore, the most plausible reconstruction is that made by *OGIS*, 629 (specifying the proper name): Γαῖο[ς Λικίνιος Μουκιανὸς πρεσβευτὴς καὶ] ἀντι[στρατηγὸς λέγει] (cf. Seyrig 1941b: 167).

In *CIS*, II, 3913 Chabot doubts this reconstruction, though he does not explain his own view.

The text is reconstructed in *OGIS*, 629 corresponds with the titulature of the Roman governors of Syria.

Line 12

μεταξὺ Παλ[μυρηνῶν] - *IGRR*, III, 1056: μετα[ξ]ὺ Παλ[μυρηνῶν?]. *CIS*, II, 3913 also (but without a question mark), based on Ricci's *estampage*. In the Aramaic text the parallel is ביני תדמריא (II, 2, 25). The discussion in the text is about disputes between the Palmyrenes and tax collectors (II, 2, 25–6: לביני מ[כ]ס[י]ת). The analogous circumstance in the resolution of the Palmyrene council is expressed as follows:

I, 7–8	I, 20
[με]ταξὺ τῶν ἐνπόρων	ביני תגרא לביני
πρὸς τοὺς τελώνας	מכסיא

Based on this, we can suggest the reconstruction of the Greek text of IV, 1, 12: μεταξὺ Παλ[μυρηνῶν πρὸς τοὺς τελώνας]. The readings by de Vogüé (1883b: 160; μετὰ ταῦτα) and *OGIS*, 629 (μετὰ ὑπα[τείαν]) are not confirmed. D. Schlumberger (1937: 290) reconstructed μεταξὺ Παλ[μυρηνῶν καὶ Ἀλκίμου] ... νους, based on the reconstructed parallel Palmyrene text, though this reconstruction is not supported by direct evidence.

Line 13

γνοὺς ἐστι - *CIS*, II, 3913. All the previous editions have ἐστι. Perhaps the γνούς is the masculine singular active aorist participle of γιγνώσκω, here 'reckon, count, enact'? If so, the Aramaic parallel to this (II, 2, 26) would be the word א[ק]י[מ]ת.

Line 14

γείνεσθαι καθ᾽ οι - *CIS*, II, 3913. *OGIS*, 629 reads κα[ὶ] οι; *IGRR*, III, 1056: γείνεσθαι..κα[ὶ].ο.ι.. The Greek γείνεσθαι corresponds with מהוא in the Aramaic text (II, 2, 27); the discussion in this line and in the following is probably about the collecting of taxes according to the norms that were set in the tax farming agreement, the one that was made with Alkimos, and also according to the law (cf. II, 2, 26–8).

Lines 15–17

Reconstruction is impossible. In line 15 *OGIS*, 629 and *IGRR*, III, 1056 read ες instead of εὐ.

The Palmyrene Tax Tariff

Line 18

The reading given is from *CIS*, II, 3913; cf. *OGIS*, 629: ...α εἰς π...; *IGRR*, III, 1056: ...αεισπ...; *CIS*, II, 3913 reconstructs αὐτο[ῖ]ς or αὐτο[ύ]ς. As a parallel to αὐτο[ῖ]ς Chabot suggests (although with a question mark) להן (II, 2, 28). If this is correct, then here and later we have a resolution that sets the rights and obligations of business partners (cf. II, 2, 28–9).

Line 19

OGIS, 629 reads the beginning of the line mistakenly as τῷ α[ὐτῷ δημοσι]ώνῃ. *CIS*, II, 3913 notes: 'this does not correspond with the background and the *estampage*.'

Line 20

Reconstructed according to *OGIS*, 629.

Lines 21–32

Impossible to reconstruct. At the beginning of line 21 *OGIS*, 629 read οἱ δ' ἄνε[υ] and then [ἐ]ξάγ[οντες]. At the beginning of line 24 it read καθ' ἂν λογ...; *IGRR*, III, 1056: καθ' ἀνα.ογ (ἀνα[λ]ογ[ίαν]?). In line 25 *OGIS*, 629 adds τοῦ δὲ ἐξαγω[γὴν ἔχοντος]. We cannot evaluate these reconstructions since we lack data on them. The parallel for the word ἐρίων at the beginning of line 27 (*CIS*, II, 3913) is the Aramaic עמרא (II, 2, 43). We agree with *CIS*, II, 3913 in the reading of lines 31–2.

Lines 33–6

το - de Vogüé (1883b: 162): το[ῦ].

|ἰτ]αλικῶν - S.S. Abamelek-Lazarev (1884) read υαλικων; de Vogüé (1883b: 162): [ἰ]ταλικῶν. *OGIS*, 629: ['Ἰτ]αλικῶν. Based on the parallel Aramaic text (II, 2, 46: [א]איטליקא עמרא), it is plausible that at the end of line 33 there was the word ἐρίων.

ἐξαγ[ομένω]ν - *OGIS*, 629. de Vogüé (1883b: 162) and *IGRR*, III, 1056 read ἐξαγ[όντω]ν.

ὕστ[ερον ὡς συν]εφωνήθη - de Vogüé (1883b: 162): ὕστ[ερον συν]εφωνήθη; also *OGIS*, 629. We accept the reconstruction of *IGRR*, III, 1056 and *CIS*, II, 3913.

μ[ὴ ἀπὸ τ]ούτων - *CIS*, II, 3913. de Vogüé (1883b: 162) and *IGRR*, III, 1056 read μ[ὴ ὑπ]ὸ τῶν.

Commentary

ἐξαγο|μένων τὸ τέλος δί|δοσθαι - *CIS*, II, 3913. de Vogüé (1883b: 162) and *IGRR*, III, 1056 read ἐξαγό[ντων.....δί]δοσθαι; *OGIS*, 629: ἐξαγο[μένων δί]δοσθαι.

Line 37

ἀσκο|ῖς αἰγεί|οις - de Vogüé (1883b: 162).

πρά[ξει ὁ τελώνης] - *IGRR*, III, 1056. *OGIS*, 962: πρά[ξει].

Lines 38–40

ἁμ|άρ|τημα - *CIS*, II, 3913. *IGRR*, III, 1056 reads [ἁμάρ]τημα in accordance with the Aramaic כטו (II, 2, 49).

προτεθέντι - *OGIS*, 962: προτέ[ρῳ ἔτ]ει.

|δ|εῖ - reconstructed according to the context.

κ|αθῶς ἐν τῷ συν|εσφραγισμένῳ - *OGIS*, 962 (with reference to Wilhelm). de Vogüé (1883b: 162) and *IGRR*, III, 1056 read καθὼς ἐν τῷ ἐσφραγισμένῳ. It is notable that [συν]εσφραγισμένῳ is written instead of [συν]εισφραγισμένῳ.

Line 41

τὸ τοῦ σφάκτρου τέλος - cf. the parallel Aramaic text (II, 3, 3–8). Dessau (1884: 519) notes that in the Palmyrene Tax Tariff the discussion is about a tax that is collected on slaughtered livestock without any distinction.

λο[γεύεσθαι] - de Vogüé (1883b: 162) and *IGRR*, III, 1056 read λ[ογεύεσθαι]; *OGIS*, 629 and *CIS*, II, 3913: λο[γεύεσθαι].

εἰς δηνάριον - indirect object introduced by the preposition εἰς = *dat. instr.*

Lines 42–3

τῆς πρὸς Στατείλι|ον ἐπισ|τολῆς - *OGIS*, 629 and the subsequent editions. de Vogüé (1883b: 162) reads τῆς πρὸς Στατείλιον ἐπιστολῆς.

Στατείλι[ος] = Statilius; therefore ει = ι.

πρὸς ἀσσάριον - indirect object introduced by the preposition πρός = *dat. instr.*

ἰτα[λικόν] - de Vogüé (1883b: 162): ἰτα(λικόν); *IGRR*, III, 1056 and *CIS*, II, 3913 read ἰτα[λικόν]. *OGIS*, 629 mistakenly reads πά[ντα].

Line 44

τέλο[ς] - *OGIS*, 629 reads τέλο[ς τῇ]. However, *IGRR*, III, 1056 and *CIS*, II, 3913 confine themselves to the obvious reconstruction τέλο[ς]. Cf. de Vogüé (1883b: 162): τέλος.

Line 45

κέρμα - the name of a local Syrian coin; cf, in the Aramaic text (II, 3, 8): ער[פ]ן.

πρὸς κέρμα - indirect object with πρός = *dat. instr.*

Line 46

ρειπτουμένων - expected would be ῥιπτομένων. Here the writing is ει instead of ι and ου instead of ο.

τέλο[ς οὐκ ὀφείλεται] - *OGIS*, 629; *IGRR*, III, 1056; *CIS*, II, 3913. de Vogüé (1883b: 162) reads τέλο[ς οὐ πράξει].

Line 47

τῶν βρωτῶν - masculine here. Cf. line 49 τοὺς δὲ (i.e. βρώτους).

κα<τὰ> - de Vogüé (1883b: 162). The text has KATON.

δην[άριον] - *OGIS*, 629; *IGRR*, III, 1056; *CIS*, II, 3913. de Vogüé (1883b: 162) reads δηνά[ριον]. Dessau (1884: 511, n. 1) notes 'τοῦ γόμου is to be linked with δηνάριον; in this case, however, we would expect ὑπέρ or παρὰ τοῦ νόμου.' *OGIS*, 629 is more plausible in suggesting that τοῦ γόμου is a typical genitive in this text signifying the object of the taxation.

Line 48

εἴστημι - expected ἵστημι (ει instead of ι). Cf. comments on II, 3, 10.

εἰσά[γηται] - de Vogüé (1883b: 162).

Lines 49–51

[χω]ρίων - *OGIS*, 629; *IGRR*, III, 1056; *CIS*, II, 3913. de Vogüé (1883b: 162) reads χωρίων.

συνεφώνησεν - according to Dessau (1884: 511) the subject of this verb is ὁ νόμος. As *OGIS*, 629 rightly notes, however, this understanding contradicts the meaning of the verb συμφωνέω. According to the *OGIS* view, nothing can prevent us from considering the subject of the action to be the tax farmer (δημοσιώνης, τελώνης). In the parallel Aramaic text (II, 3, 14) the Greek ὡς καὶ συνεφώνησεν αὐτοῖς corresponds with היך די הוו ספון. Therefore, the interpretation of *CIS*, II, 3913 is more plausible. It thinks that the Greek verb should probably mean 'eis accidit esse concordes'. However, we do not think that in this case it means a tax farmer and archons or a tax farmer and traders. The discussion is clearly about the agreement made between different groups of people in Palmyra.

Line 51

κώνου - in the parallel Aramaic text (II, 3, 15): אסטרבילי. Κώνου καὶ τῶν ὁμοίων agree with ὅσα in line 52.

Lines 52–3

ἔδ[ο]ξεν - de Vogüé (1883b: 162) reads ε[ἴδων] ξένος ἃ κ.τ.λ.

ἐμπορείαν - instead of ἐμπορίαν.

τὸ τέλος - *accusat. relat.*

ξηρόφορτον - as shown by Dessau (1884: 513), a compound word from ξηρός and φόρτος.

γείνεται - instead of γίνεται.

Line 54

Καμήλων ἐάν τε κεναὶ ἐάν τε ἔνγομοι - In the parallel Aramaic text we find the masculine: גמליא הן טענין והן סריקין (II, 3, 19). O. Klima thinks that it is possible that the discussion in the Tariff is either about pregnant or non-pregnant camels, or the translator of the Greek version thought that the discussion was about types of camel (Klima 1965: 147–51; for critical comments see Teixidor 1971: 483). We think that the suggestion about pregnant or non-pregnant camels is baseless: it contradicts the Aramaic passage about camels (גמליא) and the corresponding clause of the 'new' law. The material presented by Klima (and he refers particularly to Gen. 32:16; 37:25; 24:63; 1 Kgs 10:2 et al.) shows that in the translation of Semitic texts into Greek the masculine gender ('camels') is usually replaced by the feminine in the translated text ('female camels'). Therefore, the translator of the Greek text of the Tariff does not contradict this translation rule within Near Eastern tradition. This also explains well the seeming contradiction between the Aramaic and the Greek texts. This tradition came from the peculiar usage of the Greek word κάμηλος: it could refer to a group of camels or camel cavalry or be a specific term for 'camels' (so in Herodotus, 1. 80; cf. LS, s.v. κάμηλος). This last usage occurs in the Septuagint and here in the Palmyrene Tax Tariff.

Lines 56–7

Κουρβούλων - cf. Latin Corbulo. In the commentary in *OGIS*, 548 the editor refers to the analogous forms Φουρτουνᾶτος, Κουρνοῦτος, κουρνουκλάριος and Πουστούμιος in inscriptions, identifying them as representing vulgar pronunciation.

ἐσημιώσατο - *OGIS*, 629 reads ἐσημ{ε}ιώσατο. The writing ἐσημιώσατο instead of ἐσημειώσατο is an instance of itacism.

Column 2

Line 3.

ἄγεσ[θαι] - *CIS*, II, 3913.

Lines 6–7

For the reconstruction refer to *IGRR*, III, 1056 and *CIS*, II, 3913.

Lines 9–33

Only a few letters have been preserved; at the end of line 9 a reconstruction [πρ]άσσειν is possible, and at the beginning of line 18 νόμον is the most probable reading. Lines 19–30 are obliterated completely; only random letters and parts of words survive in lines 31–3. *OGIS*, 629 reads τὰς συμφω[νηθείσας] in line 33.

Line 34

τελώ[ν]ην - *OGIS*, 629 thought the following reconstruction of the text is possible: τὰς συμφω[νηθείσας πρὸς τὸν] τελώνην.

γείνεσθαι - instead of γίνεσθαι.

[τό ἐκ τοῦ] - Dessau (1884: 521); *IGRR*, III, 1056. *OGIS*, 629 reads [τὸ κατὰ τὸν] νόμο[ν]. The formulary in the main part of the decree (I, 9–10: τό ἐκ συνηθείας τέλος) argues in favour of the former reconstruction.

Line 35

νόμο[υ] - *IGRR*, III, 1056 in connection with the preceding [τό ἐκ τοῦ].

φ[έρειν] - *OGIS*, 629. Dessau (1884: 591) and *IGRR*, III, 1056 read φ[ημὶ? λογεύσθαι].

Lines 36–8

ἐννόμιον - tax for use of public pastures.

πράσσε|ιν ἐκτὸς τῶν| τελῶν - *CIS*, II, 3913 with reference to Haussoullier. *OGIS*, 629 reads πράσσ[ειν τοὺς ἐγχωρίους, τ]ῶν δὲ ἐπὶ νομὴν μεταγομένων κ.τ.λ., which does not correspond with the actual text.

[εἰς Παλ]μυρηνήν - *CIS*, II, 3913. *OGIS*, 629 reads [ἔξωθε]ν θρεμμάτων and after it ὀφείλεσθαι - ✕ α΄. As Chabot shows, neither is correct.

χαρα|κτη|ρίσασθαι - *CIS*, II, 3913. *OGIS*, 629 reads [χαρακτη]ρίσασθαι; *IGRR*, III, 1056: χαρίσασθαι.

δημο|σιώνης| - *CIS*, II, 3913.

Fragments (*Inv.* X, 143).

Reconstructed by the editor, J. Starcky (*Inv.* X).

Glossaries

References follow the normal scheme of *Panel No., Column No.* (where applicable), *Line No.* (e.g. II, 1, 5 and III, 2,17). The following special *sigla* are used in the numbering of lines which are outside this normal scheme:

D = The Greek Dating Formula at the top of, but outside the frame of, Panel II (p. 97)
T = The Aramaic Title at the top of Panel II, inside the frame (p. 98)
P = The Aramaic "Postscriptum" at the bottom of Panel II (p. 103)
Inv. X, 143 = The Greek fragments included at the end of the edition (p. 110)
Glosses have sometimes been expanded for clarity in English.

Greek Text

A

ἄγω - to conduct, lead, carry out
    I, 4: βουλῆ[ς] νομίμου ἀγομένης
    IV, 2, 3: ....ἄγεσ[θαι]

Ἀδριανός - Roman *cognomen* (Hadrianus)
    D1: [Τραιανοῦ Ἀδριανοῦ Σεβαστοῦ]

αἴγειος - of a goat (adjective)
    III, 1, 24: γ[όμου καμηλικοῦ μύρον τοῦ ἐν τοῦ ἀσκοῖς] αἰγείοις εἰσκομ[ισθέντος πράξει ✕ ιγ´]
    III, 1, 30: γόμου ὀνικοῦ μ[ύρου τοῦ ἐν ἀσκοῖς] αἴγειος εἰσκομ[ισθέντο]ς πρ[άξει ✕ ζ´]
    III, 1, 33: γόμου ἐλαηροῦ το[ῦ ἐν ἀσκο]ῖς [τέσσαρ]σι αἰγείοις ἐπὶ καμήλ[ου εἰσκομισθέν]τος
    III, 1, 36–7: γόμου ἐλαιηροῦ τοῦ ἐ[ν ἀσκοῖς δυσὶ αἰ]γείοις ἐπὶ καμήλ[ου εἰσκομισθέντος] πράξει
    III, 1, 44: γόμ[ου καύσεως τοῦ ἐν ἀσκοῖς τ]έσσ[αρσι] αἰγείοις [εἰσκομισθέντος πρά]ξει
    III, 1, 46: γόμου κ[αύσεως τοῦ ἐν] ἀ[σ]κοῖς δυσὶ αἰγείοις ἐπὶ κ[αμήλου εἰσ]κομισθέντος πράξει

IV, 1, 37: μύρου τοῦ ἐν ἀσκο[ῖς αἰγεί]οις πρά[ξει ὁ τελώνης] κατὰ τὸν νόμο[ν]

Αἴλιος - Roman *nomen* (Aelius)

D2: Λουκίου Αἰλίου Καίσαρος

Αἰράνης - proper name (חירן)

I, 2: ἐπι Βωννέους Βωννέους τοῦ Αἰράνου προέδρου

ἀκολούθως - according to, in accordance with

I, 6: τὴν πρᾶξιν ποιεῖσθαι ἀκολούθ[ω]ς τῷ νόμῳ καὶ τῇ συνηθείᾳ

ἅλας, τό - salt, salt-works

III, 3, 23: ὃς δ᾽ ἂν ἅλα[ς ἔχ]ῃ ἐν Παλμύροις ἢ [ἐν ὅροις] Παλμυρη[ν]ῶν

ἀλάβαστρον, τό - alabaster jar (type of container)

III, 1, 19–20: γόμου κ[αμηλικοῦ] μύρου [τοῦ ἐν ἀλαβάσ]τροις ε[ἰσκομισθέντος πράξει ✳ κε´]

III, 1, 21: καὶ το[ῦ γόμου καμηλικοῦ μύρου τοῦ ἐν ἀλαβάστροις] ἐκ[κομισθέντος πράξει ✳ ιγ´]

III, 1, 26: [γόμου ὀνικοῦ μύ]ρου τοῦ ἐ[ν ἀλαβάστροις] εἰσ[κομισ]θέν[τος] πράξει ✳ ιγ´]

Ἀλέξανδρος - proper name

I, 2: ἐπὶ ... Ἀλεξάνδρου Ἀλεξάνδρου τοῦ Φιλοπάτορος

ἄλλος - other

IV, 1, 1: παρασχές[θαι] ἄλλῳ μηδενὶ πράσσειν διδόναι λαμ[βάνειν] ἐξέστω

ἁμάρτημα, τό - mistake

IV, 1, 38–9: ἁμ[άρ]τημα γέγονεν τῷ προτεθέντι.εῖ

ἄν - in the combination ὃς ἄν: whoever, ὃ ἄν: whatever

III, 3, 23: ὃς δ᾽ ἂν ἅλα[ς ἔχ]ῃ ἐν Παλμύροις

III, 3, 26: ὃς δ᾽ ἂν οὐ ....ν παραμετρήσ[ῃ]

III, 3, 28: παρ᾽ οὗ ἂν ὁ δ[ημοσι]ώνης.........[ἐνέ]χυρα λά[βῃ]

III, 3, 34–5: περὶ οὗ ἂν ὁ δημ[ο]σιώνης τινὰ ἀπαιτῇ, περί τε οὗ ἂν ὁ δημοσιώ[νης ἀ]πό τινος ἀπαιτῆται

IV, 1, 21: οἳ δ᾽ ἂν ε..α...ασω....ἐξα[γ]........

ἀνάγω - to lift up, bring together, equate

IV, 1, 53: κώνου καὶ τῶν ὁμοίων ἔδ[ο]ξεν ὅσα εἰς ἐμπορείαν φέρεται τὸ τέλος εἰς τὸ ξηρόφορτον ἀνάγεσθαι

ἀναλαμβάνω - to inscribe, list, include

I, 5: πλεῖστα τῶν ὑποτελῶν οὐκ ἀνελήμφθη

I, 9: τὰ μὴ ἀνειλημμένα τῷ νόμῳ

Glossaries (Greek and Aramaic)

ἀντιστρατηγός, ὁ - *propraetor*
    IV, 1, 11: Γαῖο[ς Λικίνιος Μουκιανὸς πρεσβευτὴς καὶ] ἀντι[στρατηγὸς λέγει]

ἀντικρύς - opposite
    I, 11: ἀντικρὺς ἱερ[οῦ]

ἀξιόω - to demand
    IV, 1, 33: ἀξιοῦντος το.....νου εἰ καὶ μὴ …

ἀπαιτέω - to demand
    III, 3, 34–5: περὶ οὗ ἂν ὁ δημ[ο]σιώνης τινὰ ἀπαιτῇ, περί τε οὗ ἂν ὁ δημοσιώ[νης ἀ]πό τινος ἀπαιτῆται

ἀπελεύθερος, ὁ - freedman
    III, 2, 46: Κίλιξ Καίσαρος ἀπελεύθερος ἔπραξεν

ἀπό - from, out of
    III, 3, 35: περί τε οὗ ἂν ὁ δημοσιώ[νης ἀ]πό τινος ἀπαιτῆται
    IV, 1, 35: μ[ὴ ἀπὸ τ]ούτων ἐξαγο[μένων τὸ τέλος δί]δοσθαι
    IV, 1, 49: ἀπὸ τῶν [χω]ρίων κατακομίζοντας

ἀποδίδωμι - to sell
    III, 3, 30: ἀποδο[θῶ]σιν ο...

ἀπολύω - to pay, to settle up
    III, 3, 38–9: τῷ δημοσιώνῃ κύρι[ον] ἔ[σ]τω παρὰ τῶν μὴ ἀπολ[υόντων ἐν]έχυρα [λ]α[μβάνει]ν

ἀρχιερεύς, ὁ - high priest (*pontifex maximus*)
    D1: [ἀρχιερέως μεγίστου]

ἄρχων, ὁ - archon
    I, 3–4: ἐπὶ ... Μαλίχου Ὀλαιοῦς καὶ Ζεβείδου Νεσᾶ ἀρχόντων
    I, 8 : τοὺς ἐνεστῶτας ἄρχοντας
    I, 12: τοὺς τυγχάνοντας κατὰ καιρὸν ἄρχοντας

ἀσκός, ὁ - hide, fell
    III, 1, 23: γ[όμου καμηλικοῦ μύρου τοῦ ἐν ἀσκοῖς] αἰγείοις [εἰσκομισθέντος πράξει Χ ιγ΄]
    III, 1, 29: γόμου ὀνικοῦ μ[ύρου τοῦ ἐν ἀσκοῖς] αἰγείοις εἰσκομ[ισθέντο]ς πρ[άξει Χ ζ΄]
    III, 1, 32: γόμου ἐλεηροῦ το[ῦ ἐν ἀσκο]ῖς [τέσσαρ]σι αἰγείοις
    III, 1, 36: γόμου ἐλαιηροῦ τοῦ ἐ[ν ἀσκοῖς δυσὶ αἰ]γείοις
    III, 1, 43: γόμ[ου καύσεως τοῦ ἐν ἀσκοῖς τ]έσσ[αρσι] αἰγείοις [εἰσκομισθέντος πρά]ξει
    III, 1, 46: γόμου κ[αύσεως τοῦ ἐν] ἀ[σ]κοῖς δυσὶ αἰγείοις ἐπι κ[αμήλου

The Palmyrene Tax Tariff

εἰσ]κομισθέντος πράξει

IV, 1. 37: μύρου τοῦ ἐν ἀσκο[ῖς αἰγεί]οις πρά[ξει ὁ τελώνης] κατὰ τὸν νόμο[ν]

ἀσσάριον, τό - *assarius*

III, 1, 17–18: πορφύρας μηλωτῆ[ς], ἑκά[στου δέρμα]τος εἰσκομισθέν[τ]ος [πράξει ἀσσάρια η΄] ἐκκομισθ[έντο]ς [ἀσσάρια η΄]

III, 2, 27: Ὁ αὐτὸς δ[η]μοσιώνης ἑκάσ[του] μη[νὸς] παρ' ἑκ[άστο]υ τῶ[ν τὸ] ἔλαιον κατα... π.ον......ις [πωλού]ντων [ἀσσάρια β΄]

III, 2, 31–2: [ὅσαι δὲ ἔλαβον ἀ]σσάρια ὀκτὼ [πράξει ἀσσαρι]α η΄, [ὅσαι δὲ ἀσ]σάρια ἓξ ἔ[λαβον ἑ]καστ[ης πράξει] ασσ<άρια> ς΄

III, 2, 38: παρὰ τῶν δέρματα εἰσκομιζόντ[ων ἢ πω]λούντων ἑκάστου δέρματος ἀσσά[ρια β΄]

III, 3, 25: παραμετρησάτω [τῷ δημο]σιώνῃ ε[ἰς ἕκ]αστον μόδιον, ἀσσά[ριον]

IV, 1, 43: δεῖ πρὸς ἀσσάριον ἰτα[λικὸν] τὰ τέλη λογεύεσθαι

ἀτελής - free of duty

IV, 1, 49–50: τοὺς δὲ εἰς χωρία ἢ ἀπὸ τῶν [χω]ρίων κατακομίζοντας ἀτελεῖς εἶναι

αὐτοκράτωρ, ὁ - emperor, *imperator*

D1: Ἐπὶ Αὐτοκράτορος Καίσαρος

D2: αὐτοκράτορος τὸ β΄

αὐτός - he, himself, *plur.* them (ὁ αὐτὸς - the same)

III, 1, 9: ὁ αὐτὸς δημοσιώνη[ς ξηροφόρτου] πράξει

III, 2, 25: ὁ αὐτὸς δ[η]μοσιώνης ἑκάσ[του] μη[νὸς] παρ' ἑκ[άστο]υ τῶ[ν τὸ] ἔλαιον κατα... π.ον......ις [πωλού]ντων

III, 2, 28: ὁ αὐτ[ὸς δημοσιώνης] πρά[ξει ἐν τῃ πό]λει [ἐκ τῶν ἑταιρ]ῶν ὅσαι [δηνάριον ἢ πλέον λαμβά]νουσιν π[ράξει δηνάριον]

III, 2, 33: [ὁ αὐτὸς δημ]οσιώνης πρ[άξ]ει ἐργαστηρίων [ῥαφιδικῶν] παντοπωλ[ικ]ῶν σκυτικῶν [τὸ τέλο]ς

III, 2, 42: ὁ αὐτὸς πρά[ξ]ει γόμου πυρικοῦ οἰνικοῦ ἀχύρων καὶ τοιούτου γένους

IV, 1, 18: αὐτο[ῖ]ς ...τα....λεισπ............

IV, 1, 51: ἀτελεῖς εἶναι, ὡς καὶ συνεφώνησεν αὐτοῖς

ἄχυρον, τό - straw

III, 2, 42–3: ὁ αὐτὸς πρά[ξ]ει γόμου πυρικοῦ οἰνικοῦ ἀχύρων καὶ τοιούτου γένους

Β

Βαλβῖνος - Roman *cognomen* (Balbinus)

D2: [Πουβλίου Κοιλίου Βαλβίνου]

Inv. X, 143, 2: [Πουβ]λίου Κοιλίο[υ Βαλβίνου]

Βάρβαρος - proper name (Barbarus)

IV, 1, 57: ἐν τῇ πρὸς Βάρβαρον ἐπιστολῇ

βουλή, ἡ - council

I, 1: δόγμα βουλῆς

I, 3: γραμματέως βουλῆς καὶ δήμου

I, 4: βουλῆ[ς] νομίμου ἀγομένης

βρωτόν, τό - food, food items

IV, 1, 47: τῶν βρωτῶν τὸ κα<τὰ> τὸν νόμον τοῦ γόμου δην[άριον] εἴστημι πράσσεσθαι

Βωννῆς - proper name (בונא)

I, 2: ἐπὶ Βωννέους Βωννέους

Γ

Γαῖος - Roman *praenomen* (Gaius)

IV, 1, 10: Γαῖο[ς Λικίνιος Μουκιανὸς πρεσβευτὴς καὶ] ἀντι[στρατηγὸς λέγει]

γένος, τό - kind, type, sort

I, 25: γόμος καρρικὸς παντὸς γένους

III, 2, 43: γόμου πυρικοῦ οἰνικοῦ ἀχύρων καὶ τοιούτου γένους

Γερμανικός - Roman *cognomen* (Germanicus)

IV, 1, 42: καὶ Γερμανικοῦ Καίσαρος διὰ τῆς πρὸς Στατείλι[ον ἐπισ]τολῆς διασαφήσαντος

γίγνομαι - to take place, happen

I, 7: συνέβαινεν δὲ πλειστάκις περὶ τούτου ζητήσεις γείνεσθ[αι]

III, 3, 22: [γ]εινέτω

IV, 1, 14: γείνεσθαι καθ᾽ οἱ....................

IV, 1, 39: ἁμ[άρ]τημα γέγονεν τῷ προτεθέντι.εῖ

IV, 1, 53: ὡς καὶ ἐν ταῖς λοιπαῖς γείνεται πόλεσι

IV, 2, 34: .... τελώ[ν]ην γείνεσθαι

γιγνώσκω - to know, think, decide, decree

IV, 1, 13: γνούς ἐστι

γόμος, ὁ - load, cargo, shipment

I, 25: γόμος καρρικὸς παντὸς γένους· τεσσάρων γόμων καμηλικῶν τέλος ἐπράχθη

III, 1, 10: ὁ αὐτὸς δημοσιώνη[ς ξηροφόρτου] πράξει ἑκάστου γόμο[υ καμηλικοῦ]

III, 1, 12: ἐκκομισθ[έντ]ος [γόμου καμηλικοῦ] ἑκάστου

III, 1, 14: γόμου ὀνικ[οῦ ἑκάστο]υ εἰ[σκομισθέντος ✗ β΄] ἐκκομισθέν[τος ✗ β΄]

III, 1, 19: γόμου κ[αμηλικοῦ] μύρου [τοῦ ἐν ἀλαβάσ]τροις ε[ἰσκομισθέντος πράξει ✗ κε΄]

III, 1, 21: καὶ το[ῦ γόμου καμηλικοῦ μύρου τοῦ ἐν ἀλαβάστροις] ἐκ[κομισθέντος πράξει ✗ ιγ΄]

III, 1, 23: γ[όμου καμηλικοῦ μύρου τοῦ ἐν ἀσκοις] αἰγείοις [εἰσκομισθέντος πράξει ✗ ιγ΄]

III, 1, 26: [γόμου ὀνικοῦ μύ]ρου τοῦ ἐ[ν ἀλαβάστροις] εἰσ[κομισ]θέν[τος] πράξει ✗ ιγ΄]

III, 1, 29: γόμου ὀνικοῦ μ[ύρου τοῦ ἐν ἀσκοῖς] αἰγείοις εἰσκομ[ισθέντο]ς πρ[άξει ✗ ζ΄]

III, 1, 32: γόμου ἐλεηροῦ το[ῦ ἐν ἀσκο]ῖς [τέσσαρ]σι αἰγείοις ἐπὶ καμήλ[ου εἰσκομισθέν]τος

III, 1, 36: γόμου ἐλαιηροῦ τοῦ ἐ[ν ἀσκοῖς δυσὶ αἰ]γείοις ἐπὶ καμήλ[ου εἰσκομισθέντος]

III, 1, 40: γόμου ἐλε[ηροῦ τοῦ ἐπ' ὄνο]υ ε[ἰσκομισθέν]τος π[ράξει]

III, 1, 43: γόμ[ου καύσεως τοῦ ἐν ἀσκοῖς τ]έσσ[αρσι] αἰγείοις [εἰσκομισθέντος πρά]ξει

III, 1, 46: γόμου κ[αύσεως τοῦ ἐν] ἀ[σ]κοῖς δυσὶ αἰγείοις ἐπὶ κ[αμήλου εἰσ]κομισθέντος πράξει

III, 2, 2: [Γόμου ὀ]ν[ικοῦ καύσεως εἰσκομισθέντος πράξει]

III, 2, 42-3: Ὁ αὐτὸς <δημοσιώνης> πρά[ξ]ει γόμου πυρικοῦ οἰνικοῦ ἀχύρων καὶ τοιούτου γένους ἑκάστου γόμου καμηλικοῦ καθ' ὁδὸν ἑκάστην ✗ α΄

IV, 1, 47: τῶν βρωτῶν τὸ κα<τὰ> τὸν νόμον τοῦ γόμου δην[άριον] εἴστημι πράσσεσθαι

γραμματεύς, ὁ - clerk, secretary, scribe

I, 3: ἐπὶ ... Ἀλεξάνδρου Ἀλεξάνδρου τοῦ Φιλοπάτορος γραμματέως βουλῆς καὶ δήμου

Δ

δέ - and, but

I, 5: ἐπράσ[σετο] δ[ὲ ἐ]κ συνηθείας

I, 7: συνέβαινεν δὲ πλειστάκις περὶ τούτου ζητήσεις γείνεσθ[αι]

Glossaries (Greek and Aramaic)

I, 11: ἐπιμελεῖσθαι δὲ τοὺς τυγχάνοντας κατὰ καιρὸν ἄρχοντας καὶ δεκαπρώτους καὶ συνδίκο[υς]

III, 1, 4: παρ' οὗ δ[ὲ παῖδας ἐν τῇ πόλει πωλεῖ]

III, 1, 6: παρ' οὗ [δὲ σώματ]α οὐετραν[ὰ πωλεῖ]

III, 2, 31: [ὅσαι δὲ ἔλαβον ἀ]σσάρια ὀκτώ

III, 2, 32: [ὅσαι δὲ ἀσ]σάρια ἓξ ἔ[λαβον]

III, 3, 23: ὅς δ' ἂν ἅλα[ς ἔχ]ῃ

III, 3, 26: ὅς δ' ἂν οὐ ....ν παραμετρήσ[ῃ]

IV, 1, 16: ......οσα δὲ ἐξ.......

IV, 1, 21: οἳ δ' ἂν ε..α...ασω....ἐξα[γ]

IV, 1, 25: τοῦ δὲ ἐξαγω....

IV, 1, 32: τοῦ δὲ ....

IV, 1, 44: τὸ δὲ ἐντὸς δηναρίου τέλο[ς] συνηθείᾳ ὁ τελώνης πρὸς κέρμα πράξει

IV, 1, 45: τῶ[ν δὲ] διὰ τὸ νεκριμαῖα εἶναι ῥειπτουμένων τὸ τέλο[ς οὐκ ὀφείλεται]

IV, 1, 49: τοὺς δὲ εἰς χωρία ἢ ἀπὸ τῶν [χω]ρίων κατακομίζοντας ἀτελεῖς εἶναι

IV, 2, 37: [τ]ῶν δὲ ἐπὶ νομὴν μεταγομένων [εἰς Παλ]μυρηνὴν θρεμμάτων ὀφείλεσθαι

δεκάπρωτος, ὁ - *dekaprōtos*, chief municipal official (one of ten)

I, 8: τοὺς ἐνεστῶτας ἄρχοντας καὶ δ[εκα]πρώτους

I, 12: τοὺς τυγχάνοντας κατὰ καιρὸν ἄρχοντας καὶ δεκαπρώτους

δέρμα, τό - fleece, fell

III, 1, 16–17: πορφύρας μηλωτῆ[ς], ἑκά[στου δέρμα]τος εἰσκομισθέν[τ]ος [πράξει ἀσσάρια η´]

III, 2, 37–8: παρὰ τῶν δέρματα εἰσκομιζόντ[ων ἢ πω]λούντων ἑκάστου δέρματος ἀσσά[ρια β´]

δέω - to lack, be due, be necessary

III, 3, 44: δοθῆναι ἔδει

IV, 1, 39: [δ]εῖ κ[αθὼς ἐν τῷ συν]εσφραγισμένῳ νόμῳ τέτακται

IV, 1, 43: ὅτι δεῖ πρὸς ἀσσάριον ἰτα[λικὸν] τὰ τέλη λογεύεσθαι

IV, 2, 36: ἐννόμιον συνεφωνήθη μὴ δεῖν πράσσε[ιν ἐκτὸς τῶν] τελῶν

δημαρχικός - of the tribune, tribunician

D1: [δημαρχικῆς ἐξουσίας τὸ κα´]

δῆμος, ὁ - people, popular assembly

I, 3: γραμματέως βουλῆς καὶ δήμου

δημόσιος - of the people, social, public

III, 3, 42: [ἐξέστω τῷ δημ]οσιώνῃ πωλεῖν [τοιαῦτα τὰ ἐνέχυρα ἐν τόπῳ δημ]οσίῳ

δημοσιώνης, ὁ - tax farmer, *publicanus*

III, 1, 9: ὁ αὐτὸς δημοσιώνη[ς ξηροφόρτου] πράξει

III, 2, 25: ὁ αὐτὸς δ[η]μοσιώνης ἑκάσ[του] μη[νὸς] παρ' ἑκ[άστο]υ τῶ[ν τὸ] ἔλαιον κατα...π.ον......ις [πωλού]ντων [ἀσσάρια β']

III, 2, 28: ὁ αὐτ[ὸς δημοσιώνης] πρά[ξει ἐν τῇ πό]λει [ἐκ τῶν ἑταιρ]ῶν

III, 2, 33: [ὁ αὐτὸς δημ]οσιώνης πρ[άξ]ει ἐργαστηρίων [ῥαφιδικῶν] παντοπωλ[ικ]ῶν σκυτικῶν [τὸ τέλο]ς

III, 2, 40: ὁμοίως ἱματιοπῶλαι μεταβόλοι πωλ[οῦν]τες ἐν τῇ πόλει τῷ δημοσιώνῃ τὸ ἱκανὸν ποιεῖ[ν]

III, 2, 42: ὁ αὐτὸς <δημοσιώνης> πρά[ξ]ει

III, 3, 24–5: παραμετρησάτω [τῷ δημο]σιώνῃ ε[ἰς ἕκ]αστον μόδιον ἀσσά[ριον]

III, 3, 27: ση ἔχων το ..... δημο[σιών]....

III, 3, 28: παρ' οὗ ἂν ὁ δ[ημοσι]ώνης .... [ἐνέ]χυρα λά[βῃ]

III, 3, 31: δημο[σιώνῃ] τοῦ διπ[λοῦ] τὸ ἱκανὸν λαμβανέτω

III, 3, 32: πρὸς τὸν δημοσιώνην τοῦ διπλοῦ ε[ἰσα]γέσθω

III, 3, 34–5: περὶ οὗ ἂν ὁ δημ[ο]σιώνης τινὰ ἀπαιτῇ, περί τε οὗ ἂν ὁ δημοσιώ[νης ἀ]πό τινος ἀπαιτῆται

III, 3, 38: τῷ δημοσιώνῃ κύρι[ον] ἔ[σ]τω

III, 3, 41: [ἐξέστω τῷ δημ]οσιώνῃ πωλεῖν

III, 3, 44: π[ράσσ]ειν τῷ δη[μοσιώνῃ] καθὼς ... [ἐξέσ]τω

IV, 2, 39: χαρα[κτη]ρίσασθαι τὰ θρέμματα ἐὰν θέλῃ ὁ δημο[σιώνης] ἐξέστω

δηνάριον, τό - *denarius*

III, 2, 29–30: [ἐκ τῶν ἑταιρ]ῶν ὅσαι [δηνάριον ἢ πλέον λαμβά]νουσιν π[ράξει δηνάριον]

IV, 1, 41: τὸ τοῦ σφάκτρου τέλος εἰς δηνάριον ὀφείλει λο[γεύεσθαι]

IV, 1, 44: τὸ δὲ ἐντὸς δηναρίου τέλο[ς] συνηθείᾳ ὁ τελώνης πρὸς κέρμα πράξει

IV, 1, 47: τὸ κα<τὰ> τὸν νόμον τοῦ γόμου δην[άριον] εἴστημι πράσσεσθαι

IV, 1, 55: ὀφείλεται δηνάριον ἑκάστης

IV, 2, 6: [παρὰ τῶν] ἑταιρῶ[ν αἳ δηνάριον ἢ πλέον λαμβάνουσιν]

IV, 2, 35: [τὸ ἐκ τοῦ] νόμο[υ] τέλος πρὸς δηνά[ρ]ιον φ[έρειν]

Glossaries (Greek and Aramaic)

διά - through, as a result of, by means of

    III, 3, 39: [ἐν]έχυρα [λ]α[μβάνει]ν δι' ἑαυτοῦ ἢ δι[ὰ τῶν ὑπη]ρ[ετῶν]

    IV, 1, 42: καὶ Γερμανικοῦ Καίσαρος διὰ τῆς πρὸς Στατείλι[ον ἐπισ]τολῆς διασαφήσαντος

    IV, 1, 46: τῶ[ν δὲ] διὰ τὸ νεκριμαῖα εἶναι ῥειπτουμένων

διακρείνω - to think over, consider, examine

    I, 8: διακρείνοντας τὰ μὴ ἀνειλημμένα τῷ νόμῳ

διασαφέω - to explain

    IV, 1, 43: καὶ Γερμανικοῦ Καίσαρος διὰ τῆς πρὸς Στατείλι[ον ἐπισ]τολῆς διασαφήσαντος

δίδωμι - to give, give away

    III, 1, 8: ἑκάστου σώμα[τος διδότω Χ ιβ´]

    III, 3, 44: δοθῆναι ἔδει

    IV, 1, 1: παρασχέσ[θαι] ἄλλῳ μηδενὶ πράσσειν διδόναι λαμ[βάνειν] ἐξέστω

    IV, 1, 20: τῷ τελών[ῃ διδόσ]θω

    IV, 1, 35–6: μ[ὴ ἀπὸ τ]ούτων ἐξαγο[μένων τὸ τέλος δί]δοσθαι

δικαιοδοτέω - to administer justice, conduct a trial (as a *dikaiodotēs*, legate)

    III, 3, 36: περὶ τούτου δικαιοδο[τείσ]θω παρὰ τῷ ἐν Παλμύροις τεταγμένῳ

διπλοῦν, τό - double

    III, 3, 31: δημο[σιώνῃ] τοῦ διπ[λοῦ] τὸ ἱκανὸν λαμβανέτω

    III, 3, 33: πρὸς τὸν δημοσιώνην τοῦ διπλοῦ ε[ἰσα]γέσθω

    IV, 1, 5: [πραχθήτω τὸ] διπλοῦν

δόγμα, τό - decree, enactment

    I, 1: δόγμα βουλῆς

δοκέω - to have an opinion, think, suppose, seem (good) to

    I, 8: δεδόχθαι τοὺς ἐνεστῶτας ἄρχοντας καὶ δ[εκα]πρώτους διακρείνοντας τὰ μὴ ἀνειλημμένα τῷ νόμῳ ἐνγράψαι τῇ ἔνγιστα μισθώσει καὶ ὑποτ[ά]ξαι ἑκάστῳ εἴδει τὸ ἐκ συνηθείας τέλος

    IV, 1, 51–2: κώνου καὶ τῶν ὁμοίων ἔδ[ο]ξεν ὅσα εἰς ἐμπορείαν φέρεται τὸ τέλος εἰς τὸ ξηρόφορτον ἀνάγεσθαι

δόλος, ὁ - intention

    III, 3, 43: πωλεῖν [τοιαῦτα τὰ ἐνέχυρα ἐν τόπῳ δημ]οσίῳ χωρὶς δόλου πο[νηροῦ]

δύο - two

    III, 1, 36: γόμου ἐλαιηροῦ τοῦ ἐ[ν ἀσκοῖς δυσὶ αἰ]γείοις

    III, 1, 46: γόμου κ[αύσεως τοῦ ἐν] ἀ[σ]κοῖς δυσὶ αἰγείοις

E

ἐάν - if

    III, 1, 7: κἂν τὰ σώμα[τα ὑπ]ὸ το[ῦ πριαμένου ἐξ]άγηται

    III, 3, 40: [κἂν τα]ῦτα τὰ [ἐνέ]χυρα ἡμέραις [τρισίν μὴ λυθῇ]

    IV, 1, 54: καμήλων ἐάν τε κεναὶ ἐάν τε ἔνγομοι εἰσάγωνται

    IV, 2, 39: χαρα[κτη]ρίσασθαι τὰ θρέμματα ἐὰν θέλῃ ὁ δημο[σιώνης] ἐξέστω

ἑαυτοῦ - him/her/itself (relexive pronoun)

    III, 3, 39: [ἐν]έχυρα [λ]α[μβάνει]ν δι᾽ ἑαυτοῦ ἢ δι[ὰ τῶν ὑπη]ρ[ετῶν

εἰ - if

    IV, 1, 4: εἰ ποιήσῃ

    IV, 1, 33: εἰ καὶ μὴ ...

εἶδος, τό - kind, sort

    I, 9: ὑποτ[ά]ξαι ἑκάστῳ εἴδει τὸ ἐκ συνηθείας τέλος

εἰμί - to be, be situated

    I, 11: στήλῃ λιθίνῃ τῇ οὔσῃ ἀντικρὺς ἱερ[οῦ]

    III, 3, 38: τῷ δημοσιώνῃ κύρι[ον] ἔ[σ]τω

    IV, 1, 13: γνούς ἐστι

    IV, 1, 46: τῶ[ν δὲ] διὰ τὸ νεκριμαῖα εἶναι ῥειπτουμένων

    IV, 1, 50: τοὺς δὲ εἰς χωρία ἢ ἀπὸ τῶν [χω]ρίων κατακομίζοντας ἀτελεῖς εἶναι

εἰς - to, in, into, for

    III, 1, 1–2: παρὰ τ[ῶν παῖδας εἰς Παλμύρους] ἢ εἰς τὰ ὅ[ρια Παλμυρηνῶν εἰσ]αγόντω[ν]

    III, 3, 25: παραμετρησάτω [τῷ δημο]σιώνῃ ε[ἰς ἕκ]αστον μόδιον ἀσσά[ριον]

    IV, 1, 41: τὸ τοῦ σφάκτρου τέλος εἰς δηνάριον ὀφείλει λο[γεύεσθαι]

    IV, 1, 49: τοὺς δὲ εἰς χωρία ἢ ἀπὸ τῶν [χω]ρίων κατακομίζοντας

    IV, 1, 52: ὅσα εἰς ἐμπορείαν φέρεται τὸ τέλος εἰς τὸ ξηρόφορτον ἀνάγεσθαι

    IV, 2, 37: [τ]ῶν δὲ ἐπὶ νομὴν μεταγομένων [εἰς Παλ]μυρηνὴν θρεμμάτων

εἰσάγω - to bring in, carry in, import

    III, 1, 2–3: [εἰς Παλμύρους] ἢ εἰς τὰ ὅ[ρια Παλμυρηνῶν εἰσ]αγόντω[ν]

    III, 2, 45: καμήλου ὃς κενὸς εἰσαχθῇ

    III, 3, 33: πρὸς τὸν δημοσιώνην τοῦ διπλοῦ ε[ἰσα]γέσθω

    IV, 1, 48: ὅταν ἔξωθεν τῶν ὅρων εἰσά[γηται] ἢ ἐξάγηται

    IV, 1, 54: καμήλων ἐάν τε κεναὶ ἐάν τε ἔνγομοι εἰσάγωνται

εἰσκομίζω - to deliver, import

    III, 1, 11: πράξει ἑκάστου γόμο[υ καμηλικοῦ] εἰσκομισ[θέ]ντος

    III, 1, 14: γόμου ὀνικ[οῦ ἑκάστο]υ εἰ[σκομισθέντος]

Glossaries (Greek and Aramaic)

III, 1, 17: πορφύρας μηλωτῆ[ς], ἑκά[στου δέρμα]τος εἰσκομισθέν[τ]ος

III, 1, 20: γόμου κ[αμηλικοῦ] μύρου [τοῦ ἐν ἀλαβάσ]τροις ε[ἰσκομισθέντος]

III, 1, 24: γ[όμου καμηλικοῦ μύρου τοῦ ἐν ἀσκοις] αἰγείοις [εἰσκομισθέντος]

III, 1, 27: [γόμου ὀνικοῦ μύ]ρου τοῦ ἐ[ν ἀλαβάστροις] εἰσ[κομισ]θέν[τος]

III, 1, 30: γόμου ὀνικοῦ μ[ύρου τοῦ ἐν ἀσκοῖς] αἰγείοις εἰσκομ[ισθέντο]ς

III, 1, 33–4: γόμου ἐλεηροῦ το[ῦ ἐν ἀσκο]ῖς [τέσσαρ]σι αἰγείοις ἐπὶ καμήλ[ου εἰσκομισθέν]τος

III, 1, 37: γόμου ἐλαιηροῦ τοῦ ἐ[ν ἀσκοῖς δυσὶ αἰ]γείοις ἐπὶ καμήλ[ου εἰσκομισθέντος]

III, 1, 40–1: γόμου ἐλε[ηροῦ τοῦ ἐπ᾽ ὄνο]υ ε[ἰσκομισθέν]τος

III, 1, 44: γόμ[ου καύσεως τοῦ ἐν ἀσκοῖς τ]έσσ[αρσι] αἰγείοις [εἰσκομισθέντος]

III, 1, 47: γόμου κ[αύσεως τοῦ ἐν] ἀ[σ]κοῖς δυσὶ αἰγείοις ἐπι κ[αμήλου εἰσ]κομισθέντος

III, 2, 2–3: [γόμου ὀ]ν[ικοῦ καύσεως εἰσκομισθέντος]

III, 2, 37: παρὰ τῶν δέρματα εἰσκομιζόντ[ων]

ἐκ - from, out of, in compliance with

I, 5: ἐπράσ[σετο] δ[ὲ ἐ]κ συνηθείας

I, 10: τὸ ἐκ συνηθείας τέλος

III, 2, 29: πρά[ξει ἐν τῇ πό]λει [ἐκ τῶν ἑταιρ]ῶν

IV, 2, 34: [τὸ ἐκ τοῦ] νόμο[υ] τέλος

ἕκαστος - each, every

I, 9: ἑκάστῳ εἴδει

III, 1, 3: [πράξει ἑκάστου σώματος]

III, 1, 5: [ἑκάστ]ου σ[ώματος Χ ιβ´]

III, 1, 8: ἑκάστου σώμα[τος διδώτο]

III, 1, 10: πράξει ἑκάστου γόμο[υ καμηλικοῦ]

III, 1, 13: ἐκκομισθ[έντ]ος [γόμου καμηλικοῦ] ἑκάστου

III, 1, 14: γόμου ὀνικ[οῦ ἑκάστο]υ

III, 1, 16: πορφύρας μηλωτῆ[ς] ἑκά[στου δέρμα]τος

III, 2, 25–6: ἑκάσ[του] μη[νὸς] παρ᾽ ἑκ[άστο]υ τῶ[ν τὸ] ἔλαιον κατα...π.ον......ις [πωλού]ντων

III, 2, 32: [ἑ]καστ[ης πράξει]

III, 2, 35–6: [τὸ τέλο]ς ἐκ συνηθείας ἑκάστου μηνὸς καὶ ἐργαστηρίου ἑκάστου

III, 2, 38: ἑκάστου δέρματος ἀσσά[ρια β´]

III, 2, 41: ἑκάστου ἔτους Ж ω´

III, 2, 43–4: ἑκάστου γόμου καμηλικοῦ καθ᾿ ὁδὸν ἑκάστην Ж α´

III, 3, 25: παραμετρησάτω [τῷ δημο]σιώνῃ ε[ἰς ἕκ]αστον μόδιον ἀσσά[ριον]

IV, 1, 55: ὀφείλεται δηνάριον ἑκάστης

IV, 2, 7: [παρὰ τῶν] ἑταιρῶ[ν αἳ δηνάριον ἢ πλέον λαμβάνουσιν ..ἑ]κάστης

ἐκκομίζω - to export

III, 1, 12: ἐκκομισθ[έντ]ος [γόμου καμηλικοῦ] ἑκάστου

III, 1, 15: ἐκκομισθέν[τος Ж β´]

III, 1, 18: ἐκκομισθ[έντο]ς [ἀσσάρια η´]

III, 1, 22: καὶ το[ῦ γόμου καμηλικοῦ μυρον τοῦ ἐν ἀλαβάστροις] ἐκ[κομισθέντος πράξει Ж ιγ´]

III, 1, 25: [ἐκ]κ[ομισθέντος Ж ζ´]

III, 1, 28: [ἐκκομισ]θέν[τος Ж ζ´]

III, 1, 31: ἐκκομισθέντος π[ρ]άξ[ει Ж δ´]

III, 1, 35: ἐκκομισθέντο[ς Ж ιγ´]

III, 1, 39: ἐκκομισθέντο[ς Ж ζ´]

III, 1, 42: ἐκ[κομισθέντος Ж ζ´]

III, 1, 45: ἐκκομι[σ]θέ[ντος] Ж ιγ´

III, 2, 1: [ἐκκομισ]θέντος [Ж ζ´]

III, 2, 4: ἐκκομισθ]έν[τος Ж ζ´]

III, 2, 6: [ἐκκ]ο[μισθέντ]ο[ς πράξ]ει [Ж ι´]

ἐκτός - byond, beside, over

IV, 2, 36: ἐννόμιον συνεφωνήθη μὴ δεῖν πράσσε[ιν ἐκτὸς τῶν] τελῶν

ἐλαιηρός - of olive oil (adjective)

III, 1, 32: γόμου ἐλεηροῦ το[ῦ ἐν ἀσκο]ῖς [τέσσαρ]σι αἰγείοις ἐπὶ καμήλ[ου εἰσκομισθέν]τος

III, 1, 36: γόμου ἐλαιηροῦ τοῦ ἐ[ν ἀσκοῖς δυσὶ αἰ]γείοις ἐπὶ καμήλ[ου εἰσκομισθέντος] πράξει

III, 1, 40: γόμου ἐλε[ηροῦ τοῦ ἐπ᾿ ὄνο]υ ε[ἰσκομισθέν]τος π[ράξει]

ἔλαιον, τό - oil, olive oil

III, 2, 26: παρ᾿ ἑκ[άστο]υ τῶ[ν τὸ] ἔλαιον κατα...π.ον......ις [πωλού]ντων [ἀσσάρια β´]

ἐμπορεία, ἡ - trade

IV, 1, 52: ὅσα εἰς ἐμπορείαν φέρεται

ἐν - in

I, 4: [ἐν το]ῖς πάλαι χρόνοις

Glossaries (Greek and Aramaic)

I, 5: ἐν τῷ τε[λω]νικῷ νόμῳ

III, 1, 4: [παῖδας ἐν τῇ πόλει πωλεῖ]

III, 1, 19: μύρου [τοῦ ἐν ἀλαβάσ]τροις

III, 1, 21: [μύρου τοῦ ἐν ἀλαβάστροις]

III, 1, 23: [μῦρου τοῦ ἐν ἄσκοις] αἰγείοις

III, 1, 26: [μύ]ρου τοῦ ἐ[ν ἀλαβάστροις]

III, 1, 29: μ[ύρου τοῦ ἐν ἀσκοῖς] αἰγείοις

III, 1, 32: γόμου ἐλεηροῦ το[ῦ ἐν ἀσκο]ῖς [τέσσαρ]σι αἰγείοις

III, 1, 36: γόμου ἐλαιηροῦ τοῦ ἐ[ν ἀσκοῖς δυσὶ αἰ]γείοις

III, 1, 43: γόμ[ου καύσεως τοῦ ἐν ἀσκοῖς τ]έσσ[αρσι] αἰγείοις

III, 1, 46: γόμου κ[αύσεως τοῦ ἐν] ἀ[σ]κοῖς δυσὶ αἰγείοις

III, 2, 28: ὁ αὐτ[ὸς δημοσιώνης] πρά[ξει ἐν τη πό]λει

III, 2, 40: ἱματιοπῶλαι μεταβόλοι πωλ[οῦν]τες ἐν τῇ πόλει

III, 3, 23: ἐν Παλμύροις ἢ [ἐν ὅροις] Παλμυρη[ν]ῶν

III, 3, 36: παρὰ τῷ ἐν Παλμύροις τεταγμένῳ

III, 3, 42: πωλεῖν [τοιαῦτα τὰ ἐνέχυρα ἐν τόπῳ δημ]οσίῳ

IV, 1, 37: μύρου τοῦ ἐν ἀσκο[ῖς αἰγεί]οις

IV, 1, 39: κ[αθώς ἐν τῷ συν]εσφραγισμένῳ νόμῳ τέτακται

IV, 1, 53: ὡς καὶ ἐν ταῖς λοιπαῖς γείνεται πόλεσι

IV, 1, 57: ἐσημιώσατο ἐν τῇ πρὸς Βάρβαρον ἐπιστολῇ

ἔγγιστα - next

I, 9: τῇ ἔγγιστα μισθώσει

ἔγγομος - loaded, laden

IV, 1, 54: καμήλων ἐάν τε κεναὶ ἐάν τε ἔγγομοι εἰσάγωνται

ἐγγράφω - to write down

I, 5–6: ἐγγραφομέ[νου] τῇ μισθώσει τὸν τελωνοῦντα τὴν πρᾶξιν ποιεῖσθει

I, 9: ἐγγράψαι τῇ ἔγγιστα μισθώσει

I, 10: ἐγγραφῆναι μετὰ τοῦ πρώτου νόμου στήλῃ λιθίνῃ

ἐνεστώς - in residence, stationed (participle < ἐνίστημι)

I, 8: τοὺς ἐνεστῶτας ἄρχοντας καὶ δ[εκα]πρώτους

ἐνέχυρον, τό - deposit, pledge

III, 3, 28–9: [ἐνέ]χυρα λά[βῃ]

III, 3, 39: παρὰ τῶν μὴ ἀπολ[υόντων ἐν]έχυρα [λ]α[μβάνει]ν

III, 3, 40: [κἂν τα]ῦτα τὰ [ἐνέ]χυρα ἡμέραις [τρισίν μὴ λυθῇ]

III, 3, 42: πωλεῖν [τοιαῦτα τὰ ἐνέχυρα]

ἐννόμιον, τό - tax for pasturage
  IV, 2, 36: ἐννόμιον συνεφωνήθη μὴ δεῖν πράσσε[ιν ἐκτὸς τῶν] τελῶν
ἔνπορος, ὁ - merchant
  I, 7: [με]ταξὺ τῶν ἐνπόρων πρὸς τοὺς τελώνας
ἐντός - inside, within, less than
  IV, 1, 44: τὸ δὲ ἐντὸς δηναρίου τέλο[ς]
ἕξ - six
  III, 2, 32: [ὅσαι δὲ ἀσ]σάρια ἓξ ἔ[λαβον ἑ]καστ[ης πράξει] ασσ<άρια> ϛ´
ἐξάγω - to take out, export
  III, 1, 5: παρ᾽ οὗ δ[ὲ παῖδας ἐν τῇ πόλει πωλεῖ ἢ] μι[... ἐξάγει]
  III, 1,7–8: κἂν τὰ σώμα[τα ὑπ]ὸ το[ῦ πριαμένου ἐξ]άγηται
  IV, 1, 34: [ἐρίων ἰτ]αλικῶν ἐξαγ[ομένω]ν πράσσειν
  IV, 1, 35: μ[ὴ ἀπὸ τ]ούτων ἐξαγο[μένων τὸ τέλος δί]δοσθαι
  IV, 1, 49: ὅταν ἔξωθεν τῶν ὅρων εἰσά[γηται] ἢ ἐξάγηται
ἔξειμι - to be permitted, allowed, authorized
  III, 3, 41: [ἐξέστω τῷ δημ]οσιώνη πωλεῖν
  III, 3, 45: π[ράσσ]ειν τῷ δη[μοσιώνη] καθὼς καὶ.....στιν......τοῦ νόμου [ἐξέσ]τω
  IV, 1, 2: παρασχέσ[θαι] ἄλλῳ μηδενὶ πράσσειν διδόναι λαμ[βάνειν] ἐξέστω
  IV, 2, 40: χαρα[κτη]ρίσασθαι τὰ θρέμματα ἐὰν θέλῃ ὁ δημο[σιώνης] ἐξέστω
ἐξουσία, ἡ - power
  D1: [δημαρχικῆς ἐξουσίας τὸ κα´]
ἔξωθεν - from outside
  IV, 1, 48: ὅταν ἔξωθεν τῶν ὅρων εἰσά[γηται] ἢ ἐξάγηται
  IV, 1, 54: εἰσάγωνται ἔξωθεν τῶν ὅρων
ἐπειδή - because
  I, 4: ἐπειδὴ [ἐν το]ῖς πάλαι χρόνοις ... οὐκ ἀνελήμφθη
ἐπειδάν - after (conjunction)
  I, 10: καὶ ἐπειδὰν κυρωθῇ τῷ μισθουμένῳ
ἐπί - at, on, for, in the time of
  D1: [ἐπὶ αὐτοκράτορος]
  I, 2: ἐπὶ Βωννέους Βωννέους τοῦ Αἰράνου
  III, 1, 33: ἐπὶ καμήλ[ου εἰσκομισθέν]τος
  III, 1, 37: ἐπὶ καμήλ[ου εἰσκομισθέντος]
  III, 1, 40: [ἐπ᾽ ὄνο]υ ε[ἰσκομισθέν]τος

III, 1, 47: ἐπι κ[αμήλου εἰσ]κομισθέντος

IV, 2, 37: [τ]ῶν δὲ ἐπὶ νομὴν μεταγομένων

ἐπιμελέομαι - to take care of, have charge of (*or* that)

I, 11: ἐπιμελεῖσθαι δὲ ... [τοῦ] μηδὲν παραπράσσειν τὸν μισθούμενον

ἐπιστολή, ἡ - letter

IV, 1, 42–3: καὶ Γερμανικοῦ Καίσαρος διὰ τῆς πρὸς Στατείλι[ον ἐπισ]τολῆς διασαφήσαντος

IV, 1, 57: ὡς καὶ Κουρβούλων ὁ κράτιστος ἐσημιώσατο ἐν τῇ πρὸς Βάρβαρον ἐπιστολῇ

ἐργαστήριον, τό - shop

III, 2, 33: [ὁ αὐτὸς δημ]οσιώνης πρ[άξ]ει ἐργαστηρίων...[τὸ τέλο]ς ἐκ συνηθείας ἑκάστου μηνὸς καὶ ἐγαστηρίου ἑκάστου

ἔριον, τό - wool

IV, 1, 27: ἐρίων......

IV, 1, 33: [ἐρίων ἰτ]αλικῶν ἐξαγ[ομένω]ν πράσσειν

ἑταίρα, ἡ - *hetaera*, prostitute

III, 2, 29: ὁ αὐτ[ὸς δημοσιώνης] πρά[ξει ἐν τη πό]λει [ἐκ τῶν ἑταιρ]ῶν

IV, 2, 6: [παρὰ τῶν] ἑταιρῶ[ν αἲ δηνάριον ἢ πλέον λαμβάνουσιν]

ἔτος, τό - year

I, 1: [ἔτ]ους ημυ´ μηνὸς Ξανδικοῦ ιη´

III, 2, 41: ἑκάστου ἔτους Χ ω´

ἔχω - to have

III, 3, 23: ὅς δ᾽ ἂν ἄλα[ς ἔχ]ῃ

III, 3, 26: ση ἔχων το.....

Z

Ζεβεῖδας - proper name (זבידא)

I, 3: ἐπὶ ... Μαλίχου Ὀλαιοῦς καὶ Ζεβείδου Νεσᾶ ἀρχόντων

ζήτησις, ἡ - dispute, lawsuit

I, 7: συνέβαινεν δὲ πλειστάκις περὶ τούτου ζητήσεις γείνεσθ[αι]

H

ἡ - feminine definite article (*passim*)

ἥ - this

IV, 1, 24: καθ᾽ ἣν ἀναλο.........

ἤ - or

III, 1, 2: [εἰς Παλμύρους] ἢ εἰς τὰ ὅ[ρια Παλμυρηνῶν]

III, 1, 4: ἐν τῇ πόλει πωλεῖ ἤ] μι[... ἐξάγει]

III, 2, 29: ὅσαι [δηνάριον ἢ πλέον λαμβά]νουσιν
III, 2, 37: παρὰ τῶν δέρματα εἰσκομιζόντ[ων ἢ πω]λούντων
II, 3, 23: ἐν Παλμύροις ἢ [ἐν ὅροις] Παλμυρη[ν]ῶν
III, 3, 39: [ἐν]έχυρα [λ]α[μβάνει]ν δι᾽ ἑαυτοῦ ἢ δι[ὰ τῶν ὑπη]ρ[ετῶν
III, 3, 44: ..... ἐπράθη ἢ δοθῆναι ἔδει
IV, 1, 4: τούτων εἰ ποιήσῃ ἢ ε.......
IV, 1, 49: εἰσά[γηται] ἢ ἐξάγηται
IV, 1, 49: εἰς χωρία ἢ ἀπὸ τῶν [χω]ρίων
IV, 2, 6: [αἳ δηνάριον ἢ πλέον λαμβάνουσιν]

ἡμέρα, ἡ - day
III, 3, 40: [κἂν τα]ῦτα τὰ [ἐνέ]χυρα ἡμέραις [τρισίν μὴ λυθῇ]

Θ

θέλω - to wish
IV, 2, 39: ἐὰν θέλῃ ὁ δημο[σιώνης]

θεός, ὁ - god
D1: [θεοῦ Τραιανοῦ Παρθι]κοῦ υἱο[ῦ]
D1: [θε]ο[ῦ Νέρουα υἱωνοῦ]

θρέμμα, τό - sheep
III, 2, 22: [θ]ρέμματος .εσ...ενου
IV, 2, 38: [τ]ῶν δὲ ἐπὶ νομὴν μεταγομένων [εἰς Παλ]μυρηνὴν θρεμμάτων
IV, 2, 39: χαρα[κτη]ρίσασθαι τὰ θρέμματα

Ι

ἱερόν, τό - temple
I, 11: ἀντικρὺς ἱερ[οῦ] λεγομένου Ῥαβασείρη

ἱκανόν, τό - sufficient, appropriate (thing, payment) (< ἱκάνος)
III, 2, 40: τῷ δημοσιώνῃ τὸ ἱκανὸν ποιεῖ[ν]
III, 3, 31: τὸ ἱκανὸν λαμβανέτω

ἱματιοπώλης, ὁ - clothing vendor
III, 2, 39: ἱματιοπῶλαι μεταβόλοι πωλ[οῦν]τες ἐν τῇ πόλει

ἵστημι - to establish, make stand
IV, 1, 47: τῶν βρωτῶν τὸ κα<τὰ> τὸν νόμον τοῦ γόμου δην[άριον] εἴστημι πράσσεσθαι

ἰταλικός - Italian, from Italy, Italic
IV, 1, 34: [ἐρίων ἰτ]αλικῶν ἐξαγ[ομένω]ν
IV, 1, 43: δεῖ πρὸς ἀσσάριον ἰτα[λικὸν] τὰ τέλη λογεύεσθαι

Glossaries (Greek and Aramaic)

Κ

καθώς - just as, accordingly

III, 2, 46: καθὼς Κίλιξ Καίσαρος ἀπελεύθερος ἔπραξεν

III, 3, 44: καθὼς καὶ.....στιν......τοῦ νόμου

IV, 1, 39: κ[αθώς ἐν τῷ συν]εσφραγισμένῳ νόμῳ τέτακται

καί - and, also

I, 3: βουλῆς καὶ δήμου

I, 3–4: Μαλίχου Ὀλαιοῦς καὶ Ζεβείδου Νεσᾶ ἀρχόντων

I, 6: ἀκολούθ[ω]ς τῷ νόμῳ καὶ τῇ συνηθείᾳ

I, 8: ἄρχοντας καὶ δ[εκα]πρώτους

I, 9–10: ἐνγράψαι...καὶ ὑποτ[ά]ξαι..καὶ...ἐνγραφῆναι

I, 12: ἄρχοντας καὶ δεκαπρώτους καὶ συνδίκο[υς]

III, 1, 7: κἂν τὰ σώμα[τα ὑπ]ὸ το[ῦ πριαμένου ἐξ]άγηται

III, 1, 21: καὶ το[ῦ γόμου καμηλικοῦ μυρου

III, 2, 36: ἑκάστου μηνὸς καὶ ἐγαστηρίου ἑκάστου

III, 2, 43: ἀχύρων καὶ τοιούτου γένους

III, 3, 40: [κἂν τα]ῦτα τὰ [ἐνέ]χυρα ἡμέραις [τρισίν μὴ λυθῇ]

III, 3, 45: καθὼς καὶ ....

III, 3, 46: λιμένος Π[αλμύρων καὶ πη]γῶν ὑδάτων

IV, 1, 10: [πρεσβευτὴς καὶ] ἀντι[στρατηγὸς]

IV, 1, 33: εἰ καὶ μὴ ...

IV, 1, 42: καὶ Γερμανικοῦ Καίσαρος ... διασαφήσαντος

IV, 1, 50: ὡς καὶ συνεφώνησεν αὐτοῖς

IV, 1, 51: κώνου καὶ τῶν ὁμοίων

IV, 1, 53: ὡς καὶ ἐν ταῖς λοιπαῖς γείνεται πόλεσι

IV, 1, 56: ὡς καὶ Κουρβούλων ὁ κράτιστος ἐσημιώσατο

καιρός, ὁ - time

I, 12: τοὺς τυγχάνοντας κατὰ καιρὸν ἄρχοντας

Καῖσαρ - Roman *cognomen* (Caesar) (imperial title)

D1: [ἐπὶ Αὐτοκράτορος Καίσαρος]

D2: [Λουκίου Αἰλίου Καίσαρος]

III, 2, 46: Κίλιξ Καίσαρος ἀπελεύθερος

III, 3, 46: [πη]γῶν ὑδάτων Καίσαρος

IV, 1, 42: καὶ Γερμανικοῦ Καίσαρος

Inv. X, 143, 2: [Καί]σαρος

The Palmyrene Tax Tariff

κάμηλος, ὁ, ἡ - camel (male/female)

    III, 1, 33: ἐπὶ καμήλ[ου εἰσκομισθέν]τος

    III, 1, 37: ἐπὶ καμήλ[ου εἰσκομισθέντος]

    III, 1, 47: ἐπι κ[αμήλου εἰσ]κομισθέντος

    III, 2, 21: ... [κα]μήλου το ...

    III, 2, 45: καμήλου ὃς κενὸς εἰσαχθῇ πράξει

    IV, 1, 54: καμήλων ἐάν τε κεναὶ ἐάν τε ἔνγομοι εἰσάγωνται

καμηλικός - of a camel (adjective)

    I, 25: τεσσάρων γόμων καμηλικῶν τέλος

    III, 1, 10: πράξει ἑκάστου γόμο[υ καμηλικοῦ]

    III, 1, 12: [γόμου καμηλικοῦ] ἑκάστου

    III, 1, 19: γόμου κ[αμηλικοῦ] μύρου [τοῦ ἐν ἀλαβάσ]τροις

    III, 1, 21: το[ῦ γόμου καμηλικοῦ μύρου τοῦ ἐν ἀλαβάστροις]

    III, 1, 23: γ[όμου καμηλικοῦ μύρου τοῦ ἐν ἀσκοις] αἰγείοις

    III, 2, 44: ἑκάστου γόμου καμηλικοῦ καθ᾿ ὁδὸν ἑκάστην

καρρικός - of a cart (adjective)

    I, 25: γόμος καρρικὸς

κατά - during, in, according to

    I, 12: κατὰ καιρὸν

    III, 2, 44: καθ᾿ ὁδὸν ἑκάστην

    IV, 1, 14: γείνεσθαι καθ᾿ οἱ.....

    IV, 1, 24: καθ᾿ ἣν ἀναλο.....

    IV, 1, 38: κατὰ τὸν νόμο[ν]......

    IV, 1, 47: τὸ κα<τὰ> τὸν νόμον τοῦ γόμου δην[άριον]

    IV, 1, 55: δηνάριον ἑκάστης κατὰ τὸν νόμον

κατακομίζω - to deliver, bring

    IV, 1, 50: τοὺς δὲ εἰς χωρία ἢ ἀπὸ τῶν [χω]ρίων κατακομίζοντας

καῦσις, ἡ - fuel (oil)

    III, 1, 43: γόμ[ου καύσεως τοῦ ἐν ἀσκοῖς τ]έσσ[αρσι] αἰγείοις

    III, 1, 46: γόμου κ[αύσεως τοῦ ἐν] ἀ[σ]κοῖς δυσὶ αἰγείοις

    III, 2, 2: [Γόμου ὀ]ν[ικοῦ καύσεως]

κενός - empty

    III, 2, 45: καμήλου ὃς κενὸς εἰσαχθῇ

    IV, 1, 54: καμήλων ἐάν τε κεναὶ ἐάν τε ἔνγομοι εἰσάγωνται

κέρμα, τό - *kerma* (Syrian bronze coin)

    IV, 1, 45: τὸ δὲ ἐντὸς δηναρίου τέλο[ς] συνηθείᾳ ὁ τελώνης πρὸς κέρμα πράξει

Κίλιξ - proper name

  III, 2, 46: Κίλιξ Καίσαρος ἀπελεύθερος

Κοίλιος - Roman *nomen* (Caelius)

  D2: [Πουβλίου Κοιλίου Βαλβίνου]

  Inv. X, 143, 2: [Πουβ]λίου Κοιλίο[υ Βαλβίνου]

Κουρβούλων - Roman *cognomen* (Corbulo)

  IV, 1, 56: ὡς καὶ Κουρβούλων ὁ κράτιστος ἐσημιώσατο

κράτιστος - most excellent (in rank) (< κρατύς)

  IV, 1, 56: ὡς καὶ Κουρβούλων ὁ κράτιστος ἐσημιώσατο

κύριον, τό - power, right

  III, 3, 38: τῷ δημοσιώνῃ κύρι[ον] ἔ[σ]τω παρὰ τῶν μὴ ἀπολ[υόντων ἐν]έχυρα [λ]α[μβάνει]ν

κυρόω - to confirm, assert, ratify

  I, 10: κυρωθῇ τῷ μισθουμένῳ

κῶνος, ὁ - (pine *or* cedar) cones, nuts

  IV, 1, 51: κώνου καὶ τῶν ὁμοίων ἔδ[ο]ξεν ὅσα εἰς ἐμπορείαν φέρεται τὸ τέλος εἰς τὸ ξηρόφορτον ἀνάγεσθαι

Λ

λαμβάνω - to take

  III, 2, 30–2: [ἐκ τῶν ἑταιρ]ῶν ὅσαι [δηνάριον ἢ πλέον λαμβά]νουσιν π[ράξει δηνάριον, ὅσαι δὲ ἔλαβον ἀ]σσάρια ὀκτὼ [πράξει ἀσσαρι]α η´, [ὅσαι δὲ ἀσ]σάρια ἓξ ἔ[λαβον ἑ]καστ[ης πράξει] ασσ<άρια> ς´

  III, 3, 29: [ἐνέ]χυρα λά[βῃ]

  III, 3, 31–2: τὸ ἱκανὸν λαμβανέτω

  III, 3, 39: [ἐν]έχυρα [λ]α[μβάνει]ν

  IV, 1, 1: ἄλλῳ μηδενὶ πράσσειν διδόναι λαμ[βάνειν] ἐξέστω

  IV, 2, 6–7: [αἳ δηνάριον ἢ πλέον λαμβάνουσιν]

λέγω - to say, name

  I, 11: ἱερ[οῦ] λεγομένου Ῥαβασείρῃ

  IV, 1, 11: Γαῖο[ς Λικίνιος Μουκιανὸς πρεσβευτὴς καὶ] ἀντι[στρατηγὸς λέγει]

λιθίνος - of stone (adjective)

  I, 11: ἐνγραφῆναι ... στήλῃ λιθίνῃ

Λικίνιος - Roman *nomen* (Licinius)

  IV, 1, 10: Γαῖο[ς Λικίνιος Μουκιανός]

The Palmyrene Tax Tariff

λιμήν, ὁ - market, port
  III, 3, 46: λιμένος Π[αλμύρων]
λογεύω - to calculate, reckon
  IV, 1, 41: εἰς δηνάριον ὀφείλει λο[γεύεσθαι]
  IV, 1, 44: πρὸς ἀσσάριον ἰτα[λικὸν] τὰ τέλη λογεύεσθαι
λοιπή, ἡ - remainder, rest
  IV, 1, 53: ὡς καὶ ἐν ταῖς λοιπαῖς γείνεται πόλεσι
Λούκιος - Roman *praenomen* (Lucius)
  D2: [Λουκίου Αἰλίου Καίσαρος]
λύω - to buy back, redeem
  III, 3, 41: [κἂν τα]ῦτα τὰ [ἐνέ]χυρα ἡμέραις [τρισίν μὴ λυθῇ]

Μ

Μαλῖχος - proper name (מלכו)
  I, 3: ἐπὶ ... Μαλίχου Ὀλαιοῦς
μέγας - great
  D1: [ἀρχιερέως μεγίστου]
μετά - together, with
  I, 10: μετὰ τοῦ πρώτου νόμου
μετάβολος, ὁ - vagrant
  III, 2, 39: ἱματιοπῶλαι μεταβόλοι πωλ[οῦν]τες ἐν τῇ πόλει
μετάγω - to drive (from one place to antoher)
  IV, 2, 37: [τ]ῶν δὲ ἐπὶ νομὴν μεταγομένων [εἰς Παλ]μυρηνὴν θρεμμάτων
μεταξύ - between
  I, 7: [με]ταξὺ τῶν ἐνπόρων πρὸς τοὺς τελώνας
  IV, 1, 12: μεταξὺ Παλ[μυρηνῶν πρὸς τοὺς τελώνας]
μή - not
  I, 9: τὰ μὴ ἀνειλημμένα
  III, 3, 38: παρὰ τῶν μὴ ἀπολ[υόντων]
  III, 3, 41: [μὴ λυθῇ]
  IV, 1, 2: ἐξέστω μήτε τι..ε.... [μή]τε τινὶ [ὀν]όματι
  IV, 1, 33: εἰ καὶ μὴ ...
  IV, 1, 35: μ[ὴ ἀπὸ τ]ούτων ἐξαγο[μένων τὸ τέλος δί]δοσθαι
  IV, 2, 36: μὴ δεῖν πράσσε[ιν ἐκτὸς τῶν] τελῶν
μηδείς, μηδεμία, μηδέν - nobody, nothing
  I, 12: [τοῦ] μηδὲν παραπράσσειν
  IV, 1, 1: ἄλλῳ μηδενί

μηλωτή, ἡ - wool

III, 1, 16: πορφύρας μηλωτῆ[ς] ἑκά[στου δέρμα]τος

μήν, ὁ - month

I, 1: [Ἔτ]ουσ ημυ´ μηνὸς Ξανδικοῦ ιη´

III, 2, 25: ἑκάσ[του] μη[νὸς] παρ᾿ ἑκ[άστο]υ τῶ[ν τὸ] ἔλαιον κατα...π.ον......ις [πωλού]ντων

III, 2, 35: ἑκάστου μηνὸς καὶ ἐργαστηρίου ἑκάστου

μισθόω - to hire

I, 10: ἐπειδὰν κυρωθῇ τῷ μισθουμένῳ

I, 13: [τοῦ] μηδὲν παραπράσσειν τὸν μισθούμενον

μίσθωσις, ἡ - hire, contract

I, 6: ἐνγραφομέ[νου] τῇ μισθώσει

I, 9: ἐνγράψαι τῇ ἔνγιστα μισθώσει

μισθωτής, ὁ - tax collector

III, 3, 47: τῷ μισθωτῇ ... ἐξέστω

μόδιος, ὁ - *modius*

III, 3, 25: παραμετρησάτω [τῷ δημο]σιώνῃ ε[ἰς ἕκ]αστον μόδιον, ἀσσά[ριον]

Μουκιανός - Roman *cognomen* (Mucianus)

IV, 1, 10: Γαῖο[ς Λικίνιος Μουκιανὸς πρεσβευτὴς καὶ] ἀντι[στρατηγὸς λέγει]

μύρον, τό - perfumed oil

III, 1, 19: γόμου κ[αμηλικοῦ] μύρου [τοῦ ἐν ἀλαβάσ]τροις

III, 1, 21: το[ῦ γόμου καμηλικοῦ μύρου τοῦ ἐν ἀλαβάστροις]

III, 1, 23: γ[όμου καμηλικοῦ μύρου τοῦ ἐν ἀσκοις] αἰγείοις

III, 1, 26: [γόμου ὀνικοῦ μύ]ρου τοῦ ἐ[ν ἀλαβάστροις]

III, 1, 29: γόμου ὀνικοῦ μ[ύρου τοῦ ἐν ἀσκοῖς] αἰγείοις

IV, 1, 37: μύρου τοῦ ἐν ἀσκο[ῖς αἰγεί]οις

N

νεκριμαῖος - related to bodies of animals, carrion (adjective)

IV, 1, 46: τῶ[ν δὲ] διὰ τὸ νεκριμαῖα εἶναι ῥειπτουμένων

Νέρουα - Roman *cognomen* (Nerva)

D1: [θε]ο[ῦ Νέρουα υἱωνοῦ]

Νέσα - proper name (נשא)

I, 3: Ζεβείδου Νεσᾶ

νομή, ἡ - pasturage

    IV, 2, 37: [τ]ῶν δὲ ἐπὶ νομὴν μεταγομένων [εἰς Παλ]μυρηνὴν θρεμμάτων

νομίμος - lawful (adjective)

    I, 4: βουλῆ[ς] νομίμου ἀγομένης

νόμος, ὁ - law

    I, 5: ἐν τῷ τε[λω]νικῷ νόμῳ

    I, 6: ἀκολούθ[ω]ς τῷ νόμῳ

    I, 9: τὰ μὴ ἀνειλημμένα τῷ νόμῳ

    I, 10–11: μετὰ τοῦ πρώτου νόμου

    III, 3, 45: ......τοῦ νόμου [ἐξέσ]τω

    IV, 1, 38: πρά[ξει ὁ τελώνης] κατὰ τὸν νόμο[ν]

    IV, 1, 40: κ[αθὼς ἐν τῷ συν]εσφραγισμένῳ νόμῳ τέτακται

    IV, 1, 47: τὸ κα<τὰ> τὸν νόμον τοῦ γόμου δην[άριον]

    IV, 1, 56: ὀφείλεται δηνάριον ἑκάστης κατὰ τὸν νόμον

    IV, 2, 18: .....νόμον .τ....

    IV, 2, 35: [τὸ ἐκ τοῦ] νόμο[υ] τέλος

Ξ

Ξανδικός - month name

    I, 1: μηνὸς Ξανδικοῦ

ξηρόφορτον, τό - dry cargo, goods

    III, 1, 9: [ξηροφόρτου] πράξει

    IV, 1, 52–3: τὸ τέλος εἰς τὸ ξηρόφορτον ἀνάγεσθαι

Ο

ὁ - masculine definite article (*passim*)

ὁδός, ἡ - road, trip

    III, 2, 44: ἑκάστου γόμου καμηλικοῦ καθ' ὁδὸν ἑκάστην

οἰνικός - of wine (adjective)

    III, 2, 42: γόμου πυρικοῦ οἰνικου ἀχύρων καὶ τοιούτου γένους

ὀκτώ - eight

    III, 2, 31: [ἔλαβον ἀ]σσάρια ὀκτώ

Ὀλαῖος - proper name (עליי)

    I, 3: Μαλίχου Ὀλαιοῦς

ὅμοιος - similar

    IV, 1, 51: κώνου καὶ τῶν ὁμοίων

ὁμοίως - similarly

    III, 2, 39: ὁμοίως ἱματιοπῶλαι μεταβόλοι πωλ[οῦν]τες ἐν τῇ πόλει τῷ δημοσιώνῃ τὸ ἱκανὸν ποιεῖ[ν]

ὀνικός - of a donkey (adjective)

    III, 1, 14: γόμου ὀνικ[οῦ ἑκάστο]υ

    III, 1, 26: [γόμου ὀνικοῦ μύ]ρου τοῦ ἐ[ν ἀλαβάστροις]

    III, 1, 29: γόμου ὀνικοῦ μ[ύρου τοῦ ἐν ἀσκοῖς] αἰγείοις

    III, 2, 2: [γόμου ὀ]ν[ικοῦ καύσεως]

ὄνομα, τό - name

    IV, 1, 3: [μή]τε τινὶ [ὀν]όματι

ὄνος, ὁ - donkey

    III, 1, 40: γόμου ἐλε[ηροῦ τοῦ ἐπ᾿ ὄνο]υ ε[ἰσκομισθέν]τος

ὅριον, τό - border

    III, 1, 2: εἰς τὰ ὅ[ρια Παλμυρηνῶν εἰσ]αγόντω[ν]

ὅρος, ὁ - border, limit

    III, 3, 23: ἐν Παλμύροις ἢ [ἐν ὅροις] Παλμυρη[ν]ῶν

    IV, 1, 48: ἔξωθεν τῶν ὅρων

    IV, 1, 55: ἔξωθεν τῶν ὅρων

ὅς, ἥ, ὅ - who, which, that which (relative pronoun)

    III, 1, 4: παρ᾿ οὗ δ[ὲ παῖδας ἐν τῇ πόλει πωλεῖ]

    III, 1, 6: παρ᾿ οὗ [δὲ σώματ]α οὐετραν[ὰ πωλεῖ]

    III, 2, 45: καμήλου ὃς κενὸς εἰσαχθῇ πράξει

    III, 3, 23: ὅς δ᾿ ἂν ἅλα[ς ἔχ]ῃ

    III, 3, 26: ὅς δ᾿ ἂν οὐ ....ν παραμετρήσ[ῃ] ......

    III, 3, 28: παρ᾿ οὗ ἂν ὁ δ[ημοσι]ώνης .... [ἐνέ]χυρα λά[βῃ]

    III, 3, 34–5: περὶ οὗ ἂν ὁ δημ[ο]σιώνης τινὰ ἀπαιτῇ, περί τε οὗ ἂν ὁ δημοσιώ[νης ἀ]πό τινος ἀπαιτῆται, περὶ τούτου δικαιοδο[τείσ]θω παρὰ τῷ ἐν Παλμύροις τεταγμένῳ

    IV, 1, 21: οἳ δ᾿ ἂν ε..α...ασω....

    IV, 2, 6: [παρὰ τῶν] ἑταιρῶ[ν αἳ δηνάριον ἢ πλέον λαμβάνουσιν]

ὅσος, -η, -ον - all who, which, as great/much/many as

    III, 2, 29–32: [ἐκ τῶν ἑταιρ]ῶν ὅσαι [δηνάριον ἢ πλέον λαμβά]νουσιν π[ράξει δηνάριον, ὅσαι δὲ ἔλαβον ἀ]σσάρια ὀκτὼ [πράξει ἀσσαρι]α η´, [ὅσαι δὲ ἀσ]σάρια ἓξ ἔ[λαβον ἑ]καστ[ης πράξει] ασσ<άρια> ς´

    IV, 1, 52: κώνου καὶ τῶν ὁμοίων ἔδ[ο]ξεν ὅσα εἰς ἐμπορείαν φέρεται τὸ τέλος εἰς τὸ ξηρόφορτον ἀνάγεσθαι

ὅταν - when

    IV, 1, 48: ὅταν ἔξωθεν τῶν ὅρων εἰσά[γηται] ἢ ἐξάγηται

ὅτι - that (subordinating conjuction)

IV, 1, 43: διασαφήσαντος ὅτι δεῖ πρὸς ἀσσάριον ἰτα[λικὸν] τὰ τέλη λογεύεσθαι

οὐ, οὐκ- not

I, 5: οὐκ ἀνελήμφθη

III, 3, 26: οὐ ....ν παραμετρήσ[ῃ]......

IV, 1, 38: ....οὔτε...........

IV, 1, 46: τὸ τέλο[ς οὐκ ὀφείλεται]

οὐετρανός, ὁ - veteran

III, 1, 6: παρ' οὗ [δὲ σώματ]α οὐετραν[ὰ πωλεῖ]

οὗτος - this

I, 7: περὶ τούτου

III, 3, 32: περὶ τ[ο]ύτου

III, 3, 36: περὶ τούτου

III, 3, 40: [τα]ῦτα τὰ [ἐνέ]χυρα

IV, 1, 4: τούτων εἰ ποιήσῃ

IV, 1, 35: [ἀπὸ τ]ούτων ἐξαγο[μένων]

ὀφείλω - to be due, owe, follow, ought

IV, 1, 41: εἰς δηνάριον ὀφείλει λο[γεύεσθαι]

IV, 1, 46: τὸ τέλο[ς οὐκ ὀφείλεται]

IV, 1, 55: ὀφείλεται δηνάριον ἑκάστης

IV, 2, 38: [τ]ῶν δὲ ἐπὶ νομὴν μεταγομένων [εἰς Παλ]μυρηνὴν θρεμμάτων ὀφείλεσθαι

Π

παῖς, ὁ - boy, slave

III, 1, 1: παρὰ τ[ῶν παῖδας εἰς Παλμύρους] ἢ εἰς τὰ ὅ[ρια Παλμυρηνῶν εἰσ]αγόντω[ν]

III, 1, 4: παρ' οὗ δ[ὲ παῖδας ἐν τῇ πόλει πωλεῖ]

πάλαι - formerly, earlier, long ago

I, 4: [ἐν το]ῖς πάλαι χρόνοις

Παλμυρηνή - Palmyrena

IV, 2, 37-8: μεταγομένων [εἰς Παλ]μυρηνήν

Παλμυρηνός, ὁ - Palmyrene citizen

III, 1, 2: εἰς τὰ ὅ[ρια Παλμυρηνῶν]

III, 3, 24: ἐν Παλμύροις ἢ [ἐν ὅροις] Παλμυρη[ν]ῶν

IV, 1, 12: μεταξὺ Παλ[μυρηνῶν πρὸς τοὺς τελώνας]

Glossaries (Greek and Aramaic)

Παλμύροι - Palmyra
    III, 1, 1: [εἰς Παλμύρους] ἢ εἰς τὰ ὅ[ρια Παλμυρηνῶν]
    III, 3, 23: ἐν Παλμύροις ἢ [ἐν ὅροις] Παλμυρη[ν]ῶν
    III, 3, 36–7: παρὰ τῷ ἐν Παλμύροις τεταγμένῳ
    III, 3, 46: λιμένος Π[αλμύρων καὶ πη]γῶν ὑδάτων Καίσαρος

παντοπωλικόν, τό - general shop, stall (adjective used nominally)
    III, 2, 34: ἐργαστηρίων [ῥαφιδικῶν] παντοπωλ[ικ]ῶν σκυτικῶν

παρά - with, from, at
    III, 1, 1: παρὰ τ[ῶν παῖδας] … [εἰς]αγόντω[ν]
    III, 1, 4: παρ' οὗ δ[ὲ παῖδας … πωλεῖ]
    III, 1, 6: παρ' οὗ [δὲ σώματ]α οὐετραν[ὰ πωλεῖ]
    III, 2, 26: παρ' ἑκ[άστο]υ τῶ[ν τὸ] ἔλαιον … [πωλού]ντων
    III, 2, 37: παρὰ τῶν δέρματα εἰσκομιζόντ[ων ἢ πω]λούντων
    III, 3, 28: παρ' οὗ ἂν ὁ δ[ημοσι]ώνης………[ἐνέ]χυρα λά[βῃ]
    III, 3, 36: παρὰ τῷ ἐν Παλμύροις τεταγμένῳ
    III, 3, 38: παρὰ τῶν μὴ ἀπολ[υόντων ἐν]έχυρα [λ]α[μβάνει]ν
    IV, 2, 6: [παρὰ τῶν] ἑταιρῶ[ν]

παραμετρέω - to measure out, count out
    III, 3, 24: ὅς δ' ἂν ἅλα[ς ἔχ]ῃ … παραμετρησάτω [τῷ δημο]σιώνῃ
    III, 3, 26: ὅς δ' ἂν οὐ ....ν παραμετρήσ[ῃ]

παραπράσσω - to exact excessively
    I, 12: [τοῦ] μηδὲν παραπράσσειν τὸν μισθούμενον

παρέχω - to give, grant
    III, 3, 47: ………παρασχέσ[θαι] ἄλλῳ μηδενὶ πράσσειν διδόναι λαμ[βάνειν] ἐξέστω

Παρθικός - Parthian, of Parthia
    D1: [ἐπὶ Αὐτοκράτορος Καίσαρος θεοῦ Τραιανοῦ Παρθι]κοῦ υἱο[ῦ]

πᾶς - all, every
    I, 25: γόμος καρρικὸς παντὸς γένους

πατήρ, ὁ - father
    D2: π[ατ]ρὸς πατρίδος

πατρίς, ἡ - fatherland
    D2: π[ατ]ρὸς πατρίδος

περί - because of, for
    I, 7: περὶ τούτου
    III, 3, 32: περὶ τ[ο]ύτου

The Palmyrene Tax Tariff

    III, 3, 34: περὶ οὗ

    III, 3, 34–5: περί τε οὗ

    III, 3, 35–6: περὶ τούτου

πέρνημι - to sell

    III, 3, 43: ..... ἐπράθη

πηγή, ἡ - spring

    III, 2, 41: χρήσεος πηγῶν β΄

    III, 3, 46: [καὶ πη]γῶν ὑδάτων Καίσαρος

πλειστάκις - often

    I, 7: συνέβαινεν δὲ πλειστάκις περὶ τούτου ζητήσεις γείνεσθ[αι]

ποιέω - to do, carry out

    I, 6: τὸν τελωνοῦντα τὴν πρᾶξιν ποιεῖσθει

    III, 2, 40: τῷ δημοσιώνῃ τὸ ἱκανὸν ποιεῖ[ν]

    IV, 1, 4: τούτων εἰ ποιήσῃ ἢ ε..........

πόλις, ἡ - city

    III, 1, 4: [ἐν τῇ πόλει πωλεῖ]

    III, 2, 28: πρά[ξει ἐν τῃ πό]λει

    III, 2, 40: πωλ[οῦν]τες ἐν τῇ πόλει

    IV, 1, 53: ὡς καὶ ἐν ταῖς λοιπαῖς γείνεται πόλεσι

πολύς - many, much (comparative πλείων, πλέων, πλέον; superlative πλεῖστα)

    I, 5: πλεῖστα τῶν ὑποτελῶν

    III, 2, 29–30: ὅσαι [δηνάριον ἢ πλέον λαμβά]νουσιν

    IV, 2, 6: [αἳ δηνάριον ἢ πλέον λαμβάνουσιν]

πονηρός - evil, mean

    III, 3, 43: χωρὶς δόλου πο[νηροῦ]

πορφύρα, ἡ - purple (noun)

    III, 1, 16: πορφύρας μηλωτῆ[ς], ἑκά[στου δέρμα]τος

Πούβλιος - Roman *praenomen* (Publius)

    D2: [Πουβλίου Κοιλίου Βαλβίνου]

    Inv. X, 143, 2: [Πουβ]λίου Κοιλίο[υ Βαλβίνου]

πρᾶξις, ἡ - exaction, retribution

    I, 6: τὴν πρᾶξιν ποιεῖσθει

πράσσω - to exact

    I, 5: ἐπράσ[σετο] δ[ὲ ἐ]κ συνηθείας

    I, 26: τέλος ἐπράχθη

    III, 1, 3: [πράξει ἑκάστου σώματος]

III, 1, 10: πράξει ἑκάστου γόμο[υ καμηλικοῦ]

III, 1, 17: [πράξει ἀσσάρια η΄]

III, 1, 20: [πράξει Χ κε΄]

III, 1, 22: [πράξει Χ ιγ΄]

III, 1, 24: [πράξει Χ ιγ΄]

III, 1, 27: πρά[ξει Χ ιγ΄]

III, 1, 30–1: εἰσκομ[ισθέντο]ς πρ[άξει Χ ζ΄] ἐκκομισθέντος π[ρ]άξ[ει Χ δ΄]

III, 1, 38: [εἰσκομισθέντος] πράξει

III, 1, 41: ε[ἰσκομισθέν]τος π[ράξει]

III, 1, 44: [εἰσκομισθέντος πρά]ξει

III, 1, 47: [εἰσ]κομισθέντος πράξει

III, 2, 3: [εἰσκομισθέντος πράξει]

III, 2, 6: [ἐκκ]ο[μισθέντ]ο[ς πράξ]ει

III, 2, 28: πρά[ξει ἐν τῃ πό]λει [ἐκ τῶν ἑταιρ]ῶν

III, 2, 30: π[ράξει δηνάριον]

III, 2, 31: [πράξει ἀσσαρι]α η΄

III, 2, 32: [πράξει] ασσ<άρια> ς΄

III, 2, 33: πρ[άξ]ει ἐργαστηρίων [ῥαφιδικῶν] παντοπωλ[ικ]ῶν σκυτικῶν [τὸ τέλο]ς

III, 2, 42: πρά[ξ]ει γόμου πυρικοῦ ... Χ α΄

III, 2, 45–6: καμήλου ὃς κενὸς εἰσαχθη πράξει Χ α΄ καθὼς Κίλιξ Καίσαρος ἀπελεύθερος ἔπραξεν

III, 3, 44: ἐπράθη ἢ δοθῆναι ἔδει π[ράσσ]ειν

IV, 1, 1: ἄλλῳ μηδενὶ πράσσειν διδόναι λαμ[βάνειν] ἐξέστω

IV, 1, 4–5: [πραχθήτω τὸ] διπλοῦν

IV, 1, 34: ἐξαγ[ομένω]ν πράσσειν

IV, 1, 37: πρά[ξει ὁ τελώνης] κατὰ τὸν νόμο[ν]

IV, 1, 45: ὁ τελώνης πρὸς κέρμα πράξει

IV, 1, 48: δην[άριον] εἴστημι πράσσεσθαι

IV, 2, 9: ....[πρ]άσσειν

IV, 2, 36: μὴ δεῖν πράσσε[ιν ἐκτὸς τῶν] τελῶν

πρεσβευτής, ὁ - legate

IV, 1, 10: Γαῖο[ς Λικίνιος Μουκιανὸς πρεσβευτὴς καὶ] ἀντι[στρατηγὸς λέγει]

πρίαμαι - to buy

III, 1, 7: κἂν τὰ σώμα[τα ὑπ]ὸ το[ῦ πριαμένου ἐξ]άγηται

πρόεδρος, ὁ - *proedros*, president

I, 2: ἐπὶ Βωννέους Βωννέους τοῦ Αἰράνου προέδρου

πρός - to, against, opposite, up to, in

I , 8: πρὸς τοὺς τελώνας

III, 3, 32: πρὸς τὸν δημοσιώνην τοῦ διπλοῦ ε[ἰσα]γέσθω

IV, 1, 12: μεταξὺ Παλ[μυρηνῶν πρὸς τοὺς τελώνας]

IV, 1, 42: διὰ τῆς πρὸς Στατείλι[ον ἐπισ]τολῆς

IV, 1, 43: δεῖ πρὸς ἀσσάριον ἰτα[λικόν] τὰ τέλη λογεύεσθαι

IV, 1, 45: ὁ τελώνης πρὸς κέρμα πράξει

IV, 1, 57: ἐν τῇ πρὸς Βάρβαρον ἐπιστολῇ

IV, 2, 35: τέλος πρὸς δηνά[ρ]ιον φ[έρειν]

προτίθημι - set forth, establish, put down in writing earlier

IV, 1, 39: ἁμ[άρ]τημα γέγονεν τῷ προτεθέντι [δ]εῖ

πρῶτος - first

I, 10: μετὰ τοῦ πρώτου νόμου

πυρικός - of wheat (adjective)

III, 2, 42: γόμου πυρικοῦ οἰνικοῦ ἀχύρων καὶ τοιούτου γένους

πωλέω - to sell

III, 1, 4: [παῖδας ἐν τῇ πόλει πωλεῖ]

III, 1, 6: [σώματ]α οὐετραν[ὰ πωλεῖ]

III, 2, 27: τῶ[ν τὸ] ἔλαιον κατα...π.ον......ις [πωλού]ντων

III, 2, 37–8: παρὰ τῶν δέρματα εἰσκομιζόντ[ων ἢ πω]λούντων

III, 2, 39–40: ἱματιοπῶλαι μεταβόλοι πωλ[οῦν]τες ἐν τῇ πόλει

III, 3, 41: [ἐξέστω τῷ δημ]οσιώνῃ πωλεῖν

Ρ

Ῥαβασείρη - name of a god (רבאסירא)

I, 11: ἱερ[οῦ] λεγομένου Ῥαβασείρη

ῥαφιδικόν, τό - tailor's shop (adj. < ῥαφιδᾶς, "embroiderer", used nominally)

III, 2, 34: ἐργαστηρίων [ῥαφιδικῶν] παντοπωλ[ικ]ῶν σκυτικῶν

ῥείπτω - to throw away

IV, 1, 46: τῶ[ν δὲ] διὰ τὸ νεκριμαῖα εἶναι ῥειπτουμένων

Σ

Σεβαστός - *Augustus*

D1: [Τραιανοῦ Ἁδριανοῦ Σεβαστοῦ]

σημειόω - to point out, indicate, signal, interpret

IV, 1, 56–7: ὡς καὶ Κουρβούλων ὁ κράτιστος ἐσημιώσατο

σκυτίκον, τό - shoemaker's shop (adjective used nominally)

III, 2, 34: ἐργαστηρίων [ῥαφιδικῶν] παντοπωλ[ικ]ῶν σκυτικῶν

Στατείλιος - Roman *cognomen* (Statilius)

IV, 1, 42: διὰ τῆς πρὸς Στατείλι[ον ἐπισ]τολῆς

στήλη, ἡ - stele, panel, block, (inscribed) stone

I, 11: ἐνγραφῆναι ... στήλη λιθίνη

συμβαίνω - to happen, take place

I, 7: συνέβαινεν δὲ πλειστάκις περὶ τούτου ζητήσεις γείνεσθ[αι]

συμφωνέω - to come to an agreement, negotiate

IV, 1, 34–5: ὕστ[ερον ὡς συν]εφωνήθη μ[ὴ ἀπὸ τ]ούτων ... δί]δοσθαι

IV, 1, 50–1: ἀτελεῖς εἶναι, ὡς καὶ συνεφώνησεν αὐτοῖς

IV, 2, 36: ἐννόμιον συνεφωνήθη μὴ δεῖν πράσσε[ιν ἐκτὸς τῶν] τελῶν

συνδίκος, ὁ - syndic

I, 12: τοὺς τυγχάνοντας κατὰ καιρὸν ἄρχοντας καὶ δεκαπρώτους καὶ συνδίκο[υς]

συνήθεια, ἡ - custom

I, 5: ἐπράσ[σετο] δ[ὲ ἐ]κ συνηθείας

I, 7: ἀκολούθ[ω]ς τῷ νόμῳ καὶ τῇ συνηθείᾳ

I, 10: τὸ ἐκ συνηθείας τέλος

III, 2, 35: [τὸ τέλο]ς ἐκ συνηθείας

IV, 1, 45: τὸ δὲ ἐντὸς δηναρίου τέλο[ς] συνηθείᾳ ὁ τελώνης πρὸς κέρμα πράξει

συσφραγίζω - to seal jointly

IV, 1, 39–40: κ[αθὼς ἐν τῷ συν]εσφραγισμένῳ νόμῳ τέτακται

σφάκτρον, τό - butchering

IV, 1, 41: τὸ τοῦ σφάκτρου τέλος

σῶμα, τό - body, individual, slave

III, 1, 3: [πράξει ἑκάστου σώματος]

III, 1, 5: [ἐξάγει ἑκάστ]ου σ[ώματος]

III, 1, 6: παρ' οὗ [δὲ σώματ]α οὐετραν[ὰ πωλεῖ]

III, 1, 7–8: κἂν τὰ σώμα[τα ὑπ]ὸ το[ῦ πριαμένου ἐξ]άγηται

III, 1, 8: ἑκάστου σώμα[τος διδώτο ✕ ιβ΄]

Τ

τάσσω - to set, establish

III, 3, 37: παρὰ τῷ ἐν Παλμύροις τεταγμένῳ

IV, 1, 40: κ[αθὼς ἐν τῷ συν]εσφραγισμένῳ νόμῳ τέτακται

The Palmyrene Tax Tariff

τε – and, both ... and

    III, 3, 34: περὶ οὗ ἂν ... περί τε οὗ ἂν

    IV, 1, 2–3: μήτε τι ... [μή]τε τινὶ [ὀν]όματι

    IV, 1, 38: ... οὔτε ...

    IV, 1, 54: ἐάν τε κεναὶ ἐάν τε ἔνγομοι εἰσάγωνται

τέλος, τό - tax

    I, 10: τὸ ἐκ συνηθείας τέλος

    I, 25–6: τέλος ἐπράχθη

    III, 2, 35: [τὸ τέλο]ς ἐκ συνηθείας

    IV, 1, 35: [τὸ τέλος δί]δοσθαι

    IV, 1, 41: τὸ τοῦ σφάκτρου τέλος

    IV, 1, 44: ὅτι δεῖ πρὸς ἀσσάριον ἰτα[λικὸν] τὰ τέλη λογεύεσθαι· τὸ δὲ ἐντὸς δηναρίου τέλο[ς] συνηθείᾳ ὁ τελώνης πρὸς κέρμα πράξει

    IV, 1, 46: τὸ τέλο[ς οὐκ ὀφείλεται]

    IV, 1, 52: τὸ τέλος εἰς τὸ ξηρόφορτον ἀνάγεσθαι

    IV, 2, 35: [τὸ ἐκ τοῦ] νόμο[υ] τέλος

    IV, 2, 37: μὴ δεῖν πράσσε[ιν ἐκτὸς τῶν] τελῶν

τελώνεω - to collect tax, act as *telōnēs*

    I, 6: τὸν τελωνοῦντα τὴν πρᾶξιν ποιεῖσθει

τελώνης, ὁ - tax collector

    I, 8: [με]ταξὺ τῶν ἐνπόρων πρὸς τοὺς τελώνας

    IV, 1, 12: μεταξὺ Παλ[μυρηνῶν πρὸς τοὺς τελώνας]

    IV, 1, 20: τῷ τελών[ῃ διδόσ]θω

    IV, 1, 37: πρά[ξει ὁ τελώνης] κατὰ τὸν νόμο[ν]

    IV, 1, 45: ὁ τελώνης πρὸς κέρμα πράξει

    IV, 2, 34: .....τελώ[ν]ην γείνεσθαι

τελωνικός - of tax (adjective)

    I, 5: ἐν τῷ τε[λω]νικῷ νόμῳ

τέσσαρες - four

    I, 25: τεσσάρων γόμων καμηλικῶν τέλος

    III, 1, 32–3: γόμου ἐλεηροῦ το[ῦ ἐν ἀσκο]ῖς [τέσσαρ]σι αἰγείοις

    III, 1, 43: γόμ[ου καύσεως τοῦ ἐν ἀσκοῖς τ]έσσ[αρσι] αἰγείοις

τίς, τί - anybody, anything, some sort of

    III, 3, 34–5: περὶ οὗ ἂν ὁ δημ[ο]σιώνης τινὰ ἀπαιτῇ περί τε οὗ ἂν ὁ δημοσιώ[νης ἀ]πό τινος ἀπαιτῆται

    IV, 1, 3: [μή]τε τινὶ [ὀν]όματι

Glossaries (Greek and Aramaic)

τό - neuter definite article (*passim*)

τοιοῦτος - such

 III, 2, 42: γόμου πυρικοῦ οἰνικου ἀχύρων καὶ τοιούτου γένους

 III, 3, 42: πωλεῖν [τοιαῦτα τὰ ἐνέχυρα]

τόπος, ὁ - place

 III, 3, 42: [ἐν τόπῳ δημ]οσίῳ

Τραιανός - Roman *cognomen* (Traianus)

 D1: [θεοῦ Τραιανοῦ Παρθι]κοῦ υἱο[ῦ]

 D1: [Τραιανοῦ Ἀδριανοῦ Σεβαστοῦ]

 Inv. X, 143, 1: ... [Τρ]αιανο[ῦ] ...

τρεῖς - three

 III, 3, 41: [κἂν τα]ῦτα τὰ [ἐνέ]χυρα ἡμέραις [τρισίν μὴ λυθῇ]

τυγχάνω - to happen, come about

 I, 11–12: τοὺς τυγχάνοντας κατὰ καιρὸν ἄρχοντας καὶ δεκαπρώτους καὶ συνδίκο[υς]

Υ

ὕδωρ, τό - water

 III, 3, 46: λιμένος Π[αλμύρων καὶ πη]γῶν ὑδάτων Καίσαρος

υἱός, ὁ - son

 D1, 1: [θεοῦ Τραιανοῦ Παρθι]κοῦ υἱο[ῦ]

υἱωνός, ὁ - grandson

 D1: [θε]ο[ῦ Νέρουα υἱωνοῦ]

ὕπατος, ὁ - consul

 D2: [ὑπ]άτου τὸ γ´

 D2: ὑπάτ[ων Λουκίου Αἰλίου Καίσαρος τὸ β´ Πουβλίου Κοιλίου Βαλβίνου]

ὑπηρέτης, ὁ - clerk, civil servant, assistant (to a high official)

 III, 3, 40: δι᾽ ἑαυτοῦ ἢ δι[ὰ τῶν ὑπη]ρ[ετῶν]

ὑπό - by, through, by means of

 III, 1, 7: κἂν τὰ σώμα[τα ὑπ]ὸ το[ῦ πριαμένου ἐξ]άγηται

ὑποτάσσω - to set in order, determine, establish below (referring to subjoined item)

 I, 4: ἐψηφίσθη τὰ ὑποτεταγμένα

 I, 9: ὑποτ[ά]ξαι ἑκάστῳ εἴδει τὸ ἐκ συνηθείας τέλος

ὑποτελές, τό - something subject to tax

 I, 5: πλεῖστα τῶν ὑποτελῶν

The Palmyrene Tax Tariff

ὕστερος - later

    IV, 1, 34: ὑστ[ερον] ... μ[ὴ] ... [τὸ τέλος δί]δοσθαι

Φ

φέρω - to bring, deliver

    IV, 1, 52: ὅσα εἰς ἐμπορείαν φέρεται

    IV, 2, 35: [τὸ ἐκ τοῦ] νόμο[υ] τέλος πρὸς δηνά[ρ]ιον φ[έρειν]

Φιλοπάτωρ - proper name

    I, 2–3: Ἀλεξάνδρου Ἀλεξάνδρου τοῦ Φιλοπάτορος

Χ

χαρακτηρίζω - to stamp, brand

    IV, 2, 38–9: χαρα[κτη]ρίσασθαι τὰ θρέμματα

χρῆσις, ἡ - usage

    III, 2, 41: χρήσεος πηγῶν β΄

χρόνος, ὁ - time

    I, 4: [ἐν το]ῖς πάλαι χρόνοις

χωρίον, τό - settlement

    IV, 1, 49–50: τοὺς δὲ εἰς χωρία ἢ ἀπὸ τῶν [χω]ρίων κατακομίζοντας

χωρίς - besides, apart from

    III, 3, 42: χωρὶς δόλου πο[νηροῦ]

Ψ

ψηφίζω - to enact, decree

    I, 4: ἐψηφίσθη τὰ ὑποτεταγμένα

Ω

ὡς - thus

    IV, 1, 34: [ὡς συν]εφωνήθη

    IV, 1, 50: ὡς καὶ συνεφώνησεν αὐτοῖς

    IV, 1, 53: ὡς καὶ ἐν ταῖς λοιπαῖς γείνεται πόλεσι

    IV, 1, 56: ὡς καὶ Κουρβούλων ὁ κράτιστος ἐσημιώσατο

Glossaries (Greek and Aramaic)

Aramaic Text

Nouns are generally given here in their absolute form (feminines with א- ending).

א

אגור - tax farmer
I, 22: ומדי אשר לאגורא
I, 24: לא יהוא גבא אגורא

אגוריא - tax agreement
I, 18: הוא מתכתב באגוריא
I, 21: בשטר אגריא חדתא
II, 2, 15: היך א[גור]יא] ד[י א[ת]אגר קדם מרינס היגמונא

אגר - to farm, enter into a tax agreement
II, 2, 15: א[גור]יא] ד[י א[ת]אגר קדם מרינס היגמונא
II, 2, 27: [מכ]סא [די] אגר בה אלקמס

אגרא - letter, rescript
II, 3, 5: אף גרמנקוס קיסר באגרתא די כתב לסטטילס

אדרט - statue
II, 3, 29: [על] צלמי נחשא אדרטיא אתחזי

או - or
II, 1, 2: מתאעלין לתדמר או לתחומיה
II, 1, 3: ב]מדי[ת]א או י]פק
II, 1, 47: מן די שקלא דינר [או] יתיר
II, 2, 6: משך די [י]תאעל או יזבן
II, 2, 22: בתד]מר או בתחו[מא ד[י] ת[דמרי]א
II, 2, 31: לתדמר [א[ו לתח[ו]מ]יה
II, 3, 12: מדי יהוא מת[אע]ל בר מן תחומא או מאפק
II, 3, 13: מן די מפק ל[קרי]א[או מ]אעל מן קריא
II, 3, 28: עלימתא די שקלן דנר או יתיר

אחרן - other
II, 3, 18: היך ליביש היך די הוא אף במדינתא אחרניתא

איטליא - Italy
II, 2, 45: עמרא די איט]ליא[

איטליק - Italic, Italian

253

II, 2, 46: עמרא איטליק[א]
II, 3, 6: אסר איטלק[ן]
II, 3, 34: אסר איטלק[ן]
אילס - Roman *nomen* (Aelius)
T: עינתא די מיא [די אי]לס קיסר
אית - there is
II, 3, 25: אית בהון תגרתא
אלא - except, however, but
P: אלא לענ>א< די תהוא מאעלא ל[גו מן תחום] תדמר
אלכסדרס - proper name (Ἀλέξανδρος)
I, 15: אלכסדרס בר אלכסדרס בר פלפטר
אלן - these
I, 19: על צבותא אלן
I, 20: ארכוניא אלן
II, 3, 23: אף אלן כפרו די מכס לא גבן
אלקמס - proper name (Ἄλκιμος)
II, 2, 28: [מכ]סא [די] אגר בה אלקמס
אמר - sheep
II, 1, 39: א.....[מ]רי[א..
II, 1, 41: מ[ן גדיא די] אמריא
אן - if
P: אן יצבא מכסא <למחתם> יהוא [שביק]א לה
אנש - person, man
I, 24: לא יהוא גבא אגורא מן אנש מדעם יתיר
אסטרביל - pine/cedar nut/cone
II, 3, 15: אסטרביליא ומדי דמא להון
אסר - *assarius*
II, 1, 11: אסרין 8
II, 1, 40: ..... [אס]רין 2
II, 1, 41: לרשא חד אסרא חד
II, 1, 42: מן [ח/בו/כר]א גמלא א[סרי]ן 3
II, 1, 43: [י]גבא מכסא א[סרין 2
II, 1, 44: [מ]ַ[כ]סא אסר[א חד
II, 1, 45: מן די יהוא מזבן משחא בשימא אסרין 2
II, 1, 48–2, 2: ומן מן די שקלא אסרין תמניא יגבא אסרין תמניא ומן מן די שקל[א]אסרי[ן ש[תא יגבא אסרין [ש[ת[א]

254

Glossaries (Greek and Aramaic)

II, 2, 6: למשכא אסרין 2

II, 2, 19: [ית]ג[ב]א אסרא חד למדיא

II, 2, 23: יכילנה ל[מסכ]א [א]פי מדיא באסרא חד

II, 3, 6: [יה]ן מכסיא אפי אסר איטלק[ן] גבן

II, 3, 34: יהוא יהב למדיא אסר איטלק[ן]

II, 3, 36: אפי אסר יהוא מתקבל

II, 3, 44: למעלן שלחא אסרין 2

אף - also, and

II, 1, 45: אף [י]ג[ב]א מכ[סא]

II, 1, 46: אף יגבא מכסא מן זניתא

II, 2, 3: אף יגבא מכ[סא מן ארגסטר[י]ן]

II, 2, 18: אף יגבא [מכס]א מן גנסיא כלהון

II, 2, 43: ... די אף ...

II, 3, 4: אף גרמנקוס קיסר באגרתא די כתב לסטטילס פשק

II, 3, 14: היך די אף הוו ספון

II, 3, 17: היך ליביש היך די הוא אף במדינתא אחרניתא

II, 3, 23: על גלדיא די גמלי[א] אף אלן כפרו

II, 3, 35: ואף מכסא [מ]לחא די הוא בתדמר

II, 3, 45: [היך די א]ף הוו ספון

II, 3, 46: אף הן [למגז תהוא מת]אעלא

P: [אף] מן...מ[די] פרע מכסא לא יהוא מתגבא

אפי - for, in, before

II, 3, 22: יכילנה ל[מסכ]א [א]פי מדיא באסרא חד

II, 3, 3: מכסא די קצבא אפי דנר חיב למתחשבו

II, 3, 6: [יה]ן מכסיא אפי אסר איטלק[ן] גבן

II, 3, 36: אפי אסר יהוא מתקבל

ארבע - four

I, 26: ארבעא טעונין

II, 1,22: [מש]הא די בזק[ין] ארבע די עז

II, 1, 28: דהנא די בזקין א[רבע] די עז

II, 3, 39: ארבעא ופלג ...

ארגון - purple

II, 1, 10: מן א[רג]ונא מלטא

II, 2, 17: מ[ן א[ר]גונא] מלטא לכל משך

II, 3, 38: [מכ]סא די ארגונא

255

ארגסטתיון - workshop, shop

II, 2, 3: אף יגבא מכ[סא מן ארגסטר[יו[ן] ופטפלי

ארח - journey, trip

II, 2, 10: לארח חדא

ארכון - archon

I, 20: ארכוניא אלן

I, 23: ויהוא מבטל לארכוניא

ארכוניא - post of archon, archonate

I, 15: וארכוניא מלכו בר עליי בר מקימו וזבידא בר נשא

אשכיף - shoemaker

II, 2, 4: אף יגבא מכ[סא מן ארגסטר[יו[ן] ופטפלי [ואשכ]יפא [ומן] ח[יט]א היך עדתא

אשל - *ashal* (unit of measurement, surface area)

II, 3, 44: למעלן שלחא אסרין 2 אשל[א יהוא] מתגבא

אתר - place

II, 3, 32–3: באתר די דמס תהוא מתזבנא באתר די מתכנשין

אתתא - woman

II, 1, 47: דנרא חד מן אתתא

II, 3, 28: לאת[תא דנ[ר

ב - for, in

I, 14: ניסן יום

I, 14: בפלהדרותא

I, 17: בזבניא קדמיא

I, 17: בנמוסא די מכסא

I, 18: הוא מתכתב באגוריא

I, 19: בנמוסא ובעידא

I, 21: לא מסק בנמוסא

I, 21: ויכתב בשטר אגריא חדתא

I, 22: וכתב עם נמוסא קדמיא בגללא

I, 23: ארכוניא די הון בזבן

II, 1, 3: י[זב]ן ב[מדי[נ]ת[א]

II, 1, 4: יזבן [במדיתא]

II, 1, 13: מתאעל [ב[ש]טיפי]א

II, 1,17: [יתאעל] בזקי[ן די] ע[ז ל]

II, 1, 19: יתאעל ב[שטיפ]יא

II, 1, 21: יתאעל בזקי[ן די ע[ז

II, 1, 22: מש]חא די בזק[ין ארבע די עז

256

Glossaries (Greek and Aramaic)

II, 1, 25: מש[הא] די בזקין תרתן די עז

II, 1, 28: דהנא די בזקין א[רבע] די עז

II, 1, 30: דהנא די בזקין תרת[ן די] עז

II, 2, 7: הפכין במדיתא

II, 2, 8: עינן תרתן די מ[י] די במדיתא

II, 2, 14: עינתא די מיא ומל[הא ד]י ב[מ]דיתא ותחומיה

II, 2, 22: מן די יהוא לה מלח בתד[מר או בתחו]מא ד[י] ת[ד]מרי[א

II, 2, 23: [א]פי מדיא באסרא חד

II, 2, 27: [מכ]סא [די] אגר בה אלקמס

II, 2, 37: [היך די] כתיב בנמוסא

II, 2, 48: משחא ב[שימא די] בזקין די עז

II, 2, 49: בטעון די כתב די טעא מכס[א]

II, 3, 2: בנמוסא רציף

II, 3, 5: באגרתא די כתב לסטטילס

II, 3, 10: הי<ך> בנמ[ו]ס[א

II, 3, 17: היך די הוא אף במדינתא אחרניתא

II, 3, 21: היך בנמוסא

II, 3, 22: באגרתא די כתב לברברס

II, 3, 25: אית בהון תגרתא

II, 3, 31: ויהוא פרע צלם בפלגות [טעו]ן

II, 3, 32–3: באתר די דמס תהוא מתזבנא באתר די מתכנשין

II, 3, 35: היך בנמוסא

II, 3, 36: מכסא [מ]ל[ח]א די הויא בתדמר

II, 3, 36: היך בה[ו] נמוס[א

II, 3, 40: מ[ה]לכין ב[מ]ד[ת]א>

P: היך בנמוסא

בדיל די - just as, since, in accordance with the fact that, because

I, 17: בדיל די ... לא אסקו

II, 2, 39: ...... לא כתיב בדיל [די] מדעם לא ...

II, 2, 49: בדיל די בטעון די כתב די טעא מכס[א]

II, 3, 25: בדיל די אית בהון תגרתא

II, 3, 38: [מכ]סא די ארגונא בדיל די ...

בולא - council

I, 14: דגמא די בולא

I, 15: גרמטוס די בולא ודמס

I, 16: כד הות בולא כנישא מן נמוסא

בונא - proper name: אתחזי לבולא :I, 20
I, 14: בונא בר בונא בר חירן
בטל - to forbid
I, 23: ויהוא מבטל לארכוני
בין - to consider, study, think over
I, 21: אתחזי לבולא די ארכוניא אלן ו{}ל{די} עשרתא ו{די} יבנ[ו]ן מדעם די לא מסק בנמוסא
ביני - between
I, 20: ביני תגרא לביני מכסיא
II, 2, 25: ביני תדמריא ל[ביני] [ס[ק[ו]ת מכסי[א]
בכר - young camel
II, 1, 42: מן [ה/בו/כר]א גמלא
במדען די - because, as
I, 18: במדען די הוא מתכתב
בעא - to look for, search for
II, 2, 20: [ו]מא די יתבעא יתן [לה]ן לתשמישא
בר - son
I, 14–15: בונא בר בונא בר חירן
I, 15: אלכסדרס בר אלכסדרס בר פלפטר
I, 16: מלכו בר עליי בר מקימו וזבידא בר נשא
בר חרי - freedman
II, 2, 12: קלקיס בר חרי קיסר
בר מן - from outside
II, 3 12: מת[אע]ל בר מן תחומא
II, 3, 20: מתאעלין בר מן תחומא
II, 3, 46: [מ[תאאלא מ[ן בר] מן תחומא
ברברס - proper name (Barbarus)
II, 1, 12: באגרתא די כתב לברברס
בשים - fragrant, sweet, pefumed
II, 3, 28: משחא בשימא
II, 1, 16: [מ[שחא בשימא
II, 1, 18: משחא [בשימא]
II, 1, 46: משחא בשימא
II, 2, 48: משחא ב[שימא]
בתר - after
II, 2, 45: ... מכסא למפקנא בתר כות הוו ספו[ן]

258

Glossaries (Greek and Aramaic)

ג

גבא (= גבי ג) - to collect (taxes)

I, 18: והוו מתגבין מן עידא

I, 19: מכסא {ו}[ה]וא גבא היך בנמוסא ובעידא

I, 24: לא יהוא גבא אגורא

I, 27: מכסא גבי

II, 1, 2: [י]גבא מכס[א] לכל רגל

II, 1, 6: הו מ[כסא יג]בא [מ]ן טעון גמלא

II, 1, 34: ומן מפק מנהון [יגבא מכסא]

II, 1, 37: יגבא מכסא ד 3

II, 1, 43: [י]גבא מכסא א[סרין 2

II, 1, 45: אף [י]ג[ב]א מכ[ס]א לכל יר[ה

II, 1, 46: אף יגבא מכסא מן זניתא

II, 1, 48–II, 2, 2: ומן מן די שקלא אסרין תמניא יגבא אסרין תמניא ומן מן די שקל[א אסרין] ש[תא יגבא אסרין ש]ת[א]

II, 2, 3: אף יגבא מכ[סא] ... היך עדתא

II, 2, 9: [י]גבא מכסא לטעונא די חטא

II, 2, 11–12: לגמלא כדי יתאיעל סריק יגבא ד 1 היך [די] גב[א]קלקיס

II, 2, 18: אף יגבא [מכס]א מן גנסיא כלהון

II, 2, 19: [יתג]בא אסרא חד למדיא

II, 2, 49: יהוא מכסא מת[גבא היך נמוס[א

II, 3, 7: [יה]ן מכסיא אפי אסר איטלק[ן] גבן

II, 3, 8: מכסא היך עדתא ע[ר]פן יהוא גבא

II, 3, 11: יהוא מתג[ב]א דנר

II, 3, 24: אף אלן כפרו די מכס לא גבן

II, 3, 27: ה[ן] מכסא יג[ב]א מכ[ס]א מן עלימתא

II, 3, 29: מדי הי שקלא [יגבא]

II, 3, 30: יתגב[ו]ן היך [נח]שא

II, 3, 42: יהוא מתגבא מכסא

II, 3, 44–5: למעלן שלחא אסרין 2 אשל[א יהוא] מתגבא ול{מ}מפקנא לטעונ[א יגב]א [היך די א]ף הוו ספון

P: מכסא ... [יתגב]א ... דנה מתגבא [אף] מן ... מכסא לא יהוא מתגבא

גדי - lamb

II, 1, 41: מ[ן] גדיא די [א]מריא

גו מן - (from) within, less than

II, 3, 7: ומדי גו מן דנר חיב

גזז - to shear (cut)

47 ,3 ,II: והן לגו מן [תחומא תהוא] מתאעלא
P: תהוא מאעלא ל[גו מן תחום] תדמר

47 ,3 ,II: אף הן [למגז תהוא מת]אעלא
48 ,3 ,II: מתאעלא למדיתא למגז מכס לא חיב

גיס לקניס מקינס - proper name (Gaius Licinius Mucianus)

24 ,2 ,II: מ[ן די אקם] גיס [לקניס מ]קינ[ס] היגמונא

גלד - skin

23 ,3 ,II: על גלדיא די גמלי[א]

גלל - stone slab

22 ,I: וכתב עם נמוסא קדמיא בגללא

גמל - camel

26 ,I: טעונין די גמלין
6 1 ,II: טעון גמלא די יבי[שין]
7 ,1 ,II: [לכלמא] די טעון גמלא
8 ,1 ,II: מן [טעון גמלא] למ[פקנא]
12 ,1 ,II: מן טע[ון ג]מל[א] די משחא בשימא
15 ,1 ,II: למפקנ[א מן טעון] גמל לטעונא
16 ,1 ,II: מן טעון גמלא די [מ]שחא בשימא
23 ,1 ,II: למעלן טעון ג[מ]לא
26 ,1 ,II: למעל[ן ט]ע[ונ]א די גמלא
29 ,1 ,II: מן טעון דהנא ... די טעון גמל
31 ,1 ,II: מן טעון דהנא ... לטעון גמל
33 ,1 ,II: לטעונא די [גמלא]
35 ,1 ,II: לטעונא די גמלא
42 ,1 ,II: מן [ח/בו/כר]א גמלא
10 ,2 ,II: [לכ]ל גמל לארח חדא
11 ,2 ,II: לגמלא כדי יתאיעל סריק
16 ,2 ,II: לכ[ל] טעון די גמל
21–19 3 ,II: גמליא הן טעינין והן סריקין יהן מתאעלין בר מן תחומא חיב כל גמל דנר
23 ,3 ,II: על גלדיא די גמלי[א]

גנס - sort, kind, variety

26 ,I: טעון קרס די כלמא גנס כלה
18 ,2 ,II: מן גנסיא כלהון

גרמטוס - scribe, *grammateus*

15 ,I: גרמטוס די בולא ודמס

Glossaries (Greek and Aramaic)

גרמטיא - period of office as *grammateus*, *grammateus*-ship

I, 15: גרמטיא די אלכסדרס

גרמנקוס - Roman *cognomen* (Germanicus)

II, 3, 4: אף גרמנקוס קיסר באגרתא די כתב לסטטילס פשק

ד

דגם - decree, decision

I, 14: דגמא די בולא

דהן - (fuel) oil

II, 1, 28: מן טעון דהנא

II, 1, 30: מן טעון דהנא

II, 1, 32: מן טעון [דה]נא

די - *nota genitivi*

I, 14: דגמא די בולא ... בפלהדדרותא די בונא

I, 15: גרמטוס די בולא ודמס

I, 17: נמוסא די מכסא

I, 23: היכלא די רבאסירא

I, 26: טעון קרס די כלמא גנס כלה לארבעא טעונין די גמלין

T: נמוסא די מכסא די למנא די הדרינא תדמר ...

II, 1, 6: טעון גמלא די יבי[שין]

II, 1, 7: [לכלמא] די טעון גמלא

II, 1, 12: טע[ון ג]מל[א] די משחא בשימא

II, 1, 16–17: טעון גמלא די [מ]שחא בשימא [די יתאעל]

II, 1, 18: ט[עון חמר די] משחא [בשימא]

II, 1, 21: בזקי[ן די ע]ז

II, 1, 22–3: טעון די מש[ח]א די בזק]ין ארבע די עז

II,1, 25: טעון די מש[הא] די בזקין תרתן די עז

II, 1, 26: ט[עונ]א די גמלא

II, 1, 27: טעו[ן] חמר די משח

II, 1, 28: דהנא די בזקין א[רבע] די עז

II, 1, 30: דהנא די בזקין תרת]ן די] עז

II, 1, 32: טעון [דה]נא די חמר

II, 1, 33: לטעונא די [גמלא]

II, 1, 35: לטעונא די גמלא

II, 1, 41: [גדיא די] אמריא

II, 2, 8: עינן תרתן די מ[י']

II, 2, 9: לטעונא די חטא וחמרא ותבנא

II, 2, 13: נמ[וסא די מכ]סא די תדמר ועינתא די מיא ומל[חא]
II, 2, 16: לכ[ל] טעון די גמל
II, 2, 22: [בתחו]מא ד[י] ת[דמרי]א
II, 2, 45: עמרא די איט[לי]א
II, 2, 48: משחא ב[שימא די] בזקין די עז
II, 3, 3: מכסא די קצבא
II, 3, 23: גלדיא די גמלי[א]
II, 3, 26: מכסא די עלימתא
II, 3, 32: באתר די דמס
II, 3, 38: [מכ]סא די ארגונא

די - that, so that

I, 18: במדען די הוא מתכתב באגוריא די מכסא {ו}הוא גבא היך בנמוסא ובעידא
I, 20: אתחזי לבולא די ארכוניא וג'
I, 24: ויהוא מבטל ... די לא יהוא גבא
II, 2, 26: [א]קי[מ]ת די ... [מ]כסא חיב למהוא [היך מכ]סא
II, 3, 5–6: פשק די הא כשר די [יה]ן מכסיא אפי אסר איטלק[ן] גבן
II, 3, 11: אקימת די יהוא מתג[ב]א דנר
II, 3, 15: אתחזי די לכל די עלל לחשבן תגרא יהוא מכסא היך ליביש
II, 3, 24: אתחזי די להון יהבין מכ[סא]
II, 3, 30: אתחזי די יתגב[ון] היך [נח]שא
II, 3, 32: [א]תחזי לי באתר די דמס תהוא מתזבנא

די - just as, because

II, 3, 23: כפרו די מכס לא גבן

די - that which, which

I, 21: מדעם די לא מסק בנמוסא
I, 22: מכסה די מן עידא
I, 23: בגללא די לקבל היכלא די רבאסירא
I, 23: ויהוא מבטל לארכוניא די הון בזבן
II, 1, 1: עלימיא די מתאעלין לתדמר
II, 1, 3: עלם די י[זב]ן ב[מדי]ת[א]
II, 1, 4: עלם וטר[ן] די יוזבן [במדיתא]
II, 1, 12: משחא בשימא [די] מתאעל [ב]ש[טיפי]א
II, 1, 16: [מ]שחא בשימא [די יתאעל] בזקי[ן די] ע[ז]
II, 1, 18: משחא [בשימא ד]י יתאעל ב[שטיפ]יא
II, 1, 20: משחא ב[שי]מא די יתאעל בזקי[ן די ע]ז
II, 1, 22: מש[חא] די בזק[י]ן ארבע די עז

Glossaries (Greek and Aramaic)

II, 1, 25 [די בזקין תרתן די עז משׁ[חא]
II, 1, 28–9: מן טעון דהבנא די בזקין א[רבע] די עז די טעון גמל
II, 1, 30 [עז [דהבנא די בזקין תרתן די
II, 1, 36: [מן טעון]..א די טעון חמרא
II, 1, 45: מן די יהוא מזבן משחא בשימא
II, 2, 6: משך די [י]תאעל או יזבן
II, 2, 7: [מזבנ]י נחתיא די הפכין במדיתא
II, 2, 8: עינן תרתן די מ[י] די במדיתא
II, 2, 14: עינתא די מיא ומל[חא ד[י] ב[מ]דיתא ותחומיה
II, 2, 15: א[גור[י]א [ד]י א[ת]אגר קדם מרינס היגמונא
II, 2, 19: מדיא די קסטון עשר ו[ש]ת
II, 2, 21: ו[די] לא י[כל]
II, 2, 24: מ[ן] די אקם]
II, 2, 27: [מכ[סא [די] אגר בה אלקממס
II, 2, 29: א..... די ...
II, 2, 35: ו[ד[י] מעל..
II, 2, 39: ו[די מ[פק..
II, 2. 43: ודי עמרא. .. די אף
II, 2, 48: משחא ב[שימא די] בזקין די עז
II, 2, 49–3, 1: בטעון די כתב די טעא מכס[א]
II, 3, 5: באגרתא די כתב לסטטילס
II, 3, 9: פגרין די משתדן מכס לא חיבין
II, 3, 16: כל די עלל לחשבן תגרא
II, 3, 22: באגרתא די כתב לברברס
II, 3, 27: עלימתא די שקלן דנר או יתיר
II, 3, 33: באתר די מתכנשין
II, 3, 35: מכסא [מ]לחא די הויא בתדמר
II, 3, 40: [מזבני נחתיא די] מ[ה]לכין ב[ה]ית[מד]א>
II, 3, 41: ד ... די יהוא
II, 3, 49: ומן די <> היך <ד>י הון הון [ס]פון
P: אלא לענ<א> די תהוא מאעלא ל[גו מן תחום תדמר

דמא - to be similar

II, 2, 10: לטעונא די חטא וחמרא ותבנא ו[כ]ל מדי דמא [להון]
II, 2, 41: לא דמיא
II, 3,15: אסטרביליא ומדי דמא להון

דמס - people
I, 15: בולא ודמס
2, 3, 32: באתר די דמס

דנה - this
II, 1, 14: [משח]א דנה
II, 2, 21: מן נמ[וס]א דנה
II, 2, 34: לכל [רגל על]מיא דנה

דנר, דינר - denarius
II, 1, 47: מן מן די שקלא דינר [או] יתיר דנרא חד
II, 3, 3: מכסא די קצבא אפי דנר חיב למתחשבו
II, 3, 7: ומדי גו מן דנר
II, 3, 11: יהוא מתג[ב]א דנר
II, 3, 21: חיב כל גמל דנר
II, 3, 27–8: עלימתא די שקלן דנר או יתיר לאת[תא דנ]ר
P: [יתגב]א היך בנמוסא דנה מתגבא

ה - 3rd singular suffixed pronoun
II, 2, 22: מן די יהוא לה
II, 2, 23: יכילנה
II, 2, 28: [ח]ב[רה]
P: יהוא [שביק]א לה

הא - here, indeed
II, 3, 6: הא כשר

הדרינא - Hadriana (adj.)
T: נמוסא די מכסא די למנא די הדרינא תדמר

הו - he (independent pronoun)
II, 2, 35: [יפרע] הו ד 10

הו - that (demonstrative)
II, 1, 6: הו מ[כסא יג]בא
II, 3, 36: היך בה]ו נמוס[א

הוא - to be
I, 16: כד הות בולא כנישא
I, 18: והוו מתגבין מן עידא ... הוא מתכתב באגוריא
I, 19: מכסא {ו}הוא גבא היך בנמוסא ובעידא
I, 20: סרבנין הוו
I, 23: ויהוא מבטל לארכוניא די הון בזבן
I, 24: לא יהוא גבא

Glossaries (Greek and Aramaic)

II, 1, 45: מן די יהוא מזבן משחא בשימא
II, 2, 7: [מזבנ]י נחתיא די הפכין במדיתא יהן מוט מכסא
II, 2, 22: מן די יהוא לה מלח
II, 2, 25: [סרבן הוא] ביני תדמריא ל[ביני] [ס]ק[ו]ת מכסי[א]
II, 2, 27: [מ]כסא חיב למהוא [היך מכ]סא [די] אגר בה
II, 2, 29: יהוא פרע למכסא מן די מעל רגלין
II, 2, 44: פרעא תהוא
II, 2, 46: כות הוו ספונ[ן]
II, 2, 47: לא עמרא איטליק[א ת]הוא פרעא [מכ]ס[א]
II, 2, 48: יהוא מכסא מת[א]גבא היך נמוס[א]
II, 3, 6: [יה]ן מכסיא אפי אסר איטלק[ן] גבן
II, 3, 8: ע[ר]פן יהוא גבא
II, 3, 11: יהוא מתג[ב]א דנר
II, 3, 12: מדי יהוא מת[א]ע[ל] בר מן תחומא או מאפק
II, 3, 14: היך די אף הוו ספון
II, 3, 16–17: יהוא מכסא היך ליביש היך די הוא אף במדיתא אחרניתא
II, 3, 19: גמליא הן טעינין והן סריקין יהן מתאעלין בר מן תחומא
II, 3, 24: יהון יהבין מכ[סא]
II, 3, 28: והן חסיר תהוה שקלא
II, 3, 30: ויהוא פרע צלם
II, 3, 32: באתר די דמס תהוא מתזבנא
II, 3, 34: יהוא יהב למדיא אסר איטלק[ן]
II, 3, 35: [מ]לחא די הויא בתדמר
II, 3, 36: אפי אסר יהוא מתקבל
II, 3, 37: יהוא מזבן היך עידא
II, 3, 41: די יהוא
II, 3, 42: יהוא מתגבא מכסא
II, 3, 44: למעלן שלחא אסרין 2 אשל[א יהוא] מתגבא
II, 3, 45: [היך די א]ף הוו ספון
II, 3, 46: ענא ת[ה]ו[א מ]תאעלא מ[ן בר]
II, 3, 47: הן [למגז תהוא מת[א]עלא
II, 3, 48: והן לגו מן [תחומא תהוא] מתאעלא למדיתא למגז
II, 3, 49: היך >ד<י ... הון [ס]פ[ון]
P: לא יהוא מתגבא ... לענ>א< די תהוא מאעלא ... יהוא [שביק]א לה

הון - they (independent pronoun)

II, 3, 49: היך >ד<י הון הון [ס]פון

The Palmyrene Tax Tariff

הן, הון - 3rd masculine plural suffixed pronoun
II, 2, 10: מדי דמא [להון]
II, 2, 18: מן גנסיא כלהון
II, 2, 20: יתן [לה]ן לתשמישא
II, 2, 29: מדעם להן משתתף
II, 3, 15: מדי דמא להון
II, 3, 25: אית בהון תגרתא

הי - she (independent pronoun)
II, 3, 29: מדי הי שקלא

היגמון - Roman governor, prefect
II, 2, 15: קדם מרינס היגמונא
II, 2, 24: מ[ן די אקם] גיס [לקניס מ[קינ]ס] היגמונא

היך - like, as, in accordance with
I, 19: היך בנמוסא ובעידא
II, 2, 4: היך עדתא
II, 2, 14: היך א[גור]יא
II, 2, 27: [היך מכ[סא [די] אגר בה אלקמס
II, 2, 28: [היך] נמוסא
II, 2, 49: [היך נמוס[א
II, 3, 7: היך עדתא
II, 3, 10: הי>ך<בנמ[ו]ס[א
II, 3, 17: יהוא מכסא היך ליביש
II, 3, 21: היך בנמוסא
II, 3, 30: יתגב[ו]ן היך [נח]שא
II, 3, 35: היך בנמוסא
II, 3, 36: היך בה]ו נמוס[א
II, 3, 37: היך עידא
P: היך בנמוסא

היך די - as, since
II, 2, 12: היך [די] גב[א] קלקיס בר חרי קיסר
II, 2, 18: היך די כתיב מן למעל
II, 2, 37: [היך די] כתיב בנמוסא
II, 3, 4: היך די אף גרמנקוס קיסר באגרתא די כתב לסטטילס פשק
II, 3, 14: היך די אף הוו ספון
II, 3, 17: היך די הוא אף במדינתא אחרניתא
II, 3, 21: היך די אשר קרבלון כשירא

Glossaries (Greek and Aramaic)

II, 3, 26: היך די נמוסא מוחא פשקת

II, 3, 43: היך די כ[תיב מן ל]על

II, 3, 45: [היך די א]ף הוו ספון

II, 3, 49: היך>ד<י הון הון [ס]פון

היכל - temple

I, 23: בגללא די לקבל היכלא די רבאסירא

הלך - to go, walk

II, 3, 40: [מזבני נחתיא די] מ[ה]לכין ב[ה]ל[מד]ית>א<

הן - if

II, 1, 5: והן זבונא יפק עלי[מ]י

II, 3, 19: גמליא הן טעינין והן סריקין יהן מתאעלין בר מן תחומא

II, 3, 27: ה[ן] מכסא יג[בא מכ]סא מן עלימתא

II, 3, 28: והן חסיר תהוה שקלא

II, 3, 46: אף הן [למגז תהוא מת]אעלא

II, 3, 47: והן לגו מן [תחומא תהוא] מתאעלא

הפך - to return, wander

II, 2, 7: [מזבנ]י נחתיא די הפכין במדיתא

ו

ו - and (*passim*)

וחא - to indicate

II, 3, 26: היך די נמוסא מוחא

וטרן - veteran

II, 1, 4: מן עלם וטר[ן] די יזבן [במדיתא]

II, 2, 33: ו[מן] די י[זבן על]ם וטרן

II, 2, 36: מן די מפק עלם וטרן

ז

זבון - buyer

II, 1, 5: והן זבונא יפק עלי[מ]ין

זבידא - proper name

I, 16: זבידא בר נשא

זבן - time, moment

I, 17: זבניא קדמיא

I, 19: זבנין שגין

I, 23: ארכוניא די הון בזבן

זבן - to sell, buy

II, 1, 3: מן עלם די י[זב]ן ב[מדי]ב[ת]א[ב]

267

II, 1, 4: מן עלם וטר[ן] די יזבן [במדיתא]
II, 1, 45: מן די יהוא מזבן משחא בשימא
II, 2, 6: [מן כ]ל משך די [י]תאעל או יזבן
II, 2, 7: [מזבנ]י נחתיא די הפכין במדיתא
II, 2, 32: ו[מן] די [מזבן רגלין ומ]פק
II, 2, 33: ו[מן] די י]זבן על[ם וטרן
II, 2, 38: [מן] די יז]בן] ....
II, 3, 33: באתר די דמס תהוא מתזבנא
II, 3, 34: ומן מן תדמריא יזבן לחש[ת]ה
II, 3, 37: ול[תדמרי]א יהוא מזבן
II, 3, 40: [מזבני נחתיא די] מ[ה]לכין ב[מד]ית>א

זניא - *hetaera*, prostitute

II, 1, 46: אף יגבא מכסא מן זניתא

זק - skin (container for liquid)

II, 1, 17: [מ]שחא בשימא [די יתאעל] בזקי[ן די] ע[ז]
II, 1, 21: משחא ב[שי]מא די יתאעל בזקי[ן די ע]ז
II, 1, 22: מש[חא די בזק]ין ארבע די עז
II, 1, 25: מש[חא] די בזקין תרתן די עז
II, 1, 28: דהנא די בזקין א[רבע] די עז
II, 1, 30: דהנא די בזקין תרת[ן די] עז
II, 2, 48: משחא ב[שימא די] בזקין די עז

ח

חבר - associate, companion

II, 2, 28: אגר בה אלקמס וח[ברה היך] נמוסא

חד - one

II, 1, 41: לרשא חד אסרא חד
II, 1, 44: [מ]כ[סא אסר]א חד
II, 1, 47: דנרא חד
II, 2, 10: לארח חדא
II, 2, 19: אסרא חד
II, 2, 23: אסרא חד

חדת - new

I, 21: בשטר אגריא חדתא

חוב - to be liable, owing

I, 17: עבידן שגין חיבן מכסא
II, 2, 27: [מ]כסא חיב למהוא

Glossaries (Greek and Aramaic)

II, 3, 3: אפי דנר חיב למתחשבו

II, 3, 7: ומדי גו מן דנר חיב

II, 3, 9: פגרין די משתדן מכס לֹא חיבין

II, 3, 14: מכס לא חיב

II, 2, 20: חיב כל גמל דנר

II, 3, 47: מכסא חיבא

II, 3, 48: מכס לא חיב[א]

חור - calf

II, 1, 42: מן [חור]א גמל[א

חזי - to see, perceive, regard, decide

I, 20: אתחזי לבולא

II, 3, 15: אתחזי די ... יהוא מכסא היך ליביש

II, 3, 24: אתחזי די יהון יהבין מכ[סא]

II, 3, 30: אתחזי די יתגב[ון] היך [נח]שא

II, 3, 32: [א]תחזי לי באתר די דמס תהוא מתזבנא

חט - wheat

II, 2, 9: [י]גבא מכסא לטעונא די חטא

חיט - tailor

II, 2, 4: אף יגבא מכ[סא]יו[ן] ...[ומן] ח[י]ט[א] היך עדתא

II, 3, 40: [מ]זבני נחתיא די מ[ה]לכין ב[מד]ית[א] וחיטא

חירן - proper name

I, 15: בונא בר בונא בר חירן

חמר - donkey

II, 1, 9: מן ט[עון] חמרא

II, 1, 18: מן ט[עון חמר די] משחא [בשימא]

II, 1, 20: מן טעון חמר [ד]י משחא ב[שי]מא

II, 1, 27: מן טעו[ן] חמר די משח

II, 1, 32: מן טעון [דה]נא די חמר

II, 1, 36: [מן טעון].. א די טעון חמרא

חמר - wine

II, 2, 9: לטעונא די חטא וחמרא ותבנא

חנות - shop

II, 2, 5: היך עדתא [לכל] יר[ח] מן חנותא

חסיר - less

II, 3, 28: והן חסיר תהוה שקלא

269

חשב - to reckon
II, 3, 4: מכסא די קצבא אפי דנר חיב למתחשבו
חשב - calculation
II, 3, 37: חשב.....
חשחא - benefit, advantage, need
II, 3, 34: ומן מן תדמריא יזבן לחש[חת]ה
חתם - to stamp, seal
P: אן יצבא מכסא <למחתם>

ט

טב - good
II, 2, 19: [מל]ח טב [יתג]בא אסרא חד
טעא - to err
II, 3, 1: בדיל די בטעון די כתב די טעא מכס[א]
טעון - error
II, 2, 49: בדיל די בטעון די כתב די טעא מכס[א]
טעון - load, burden
I, 26: טעון קרס ... טעונין די גמלין
II, 1, 6: [מ]ן טעון גמלא
II, 1, 7: [לכלמא] די טעון גמלא
II, 1, 8: מן [טעון גמלא] למ[פקנא]
II, 1, 9: מן ט[עון] חמרא
II, 1, 12: מן טע[ון ג]מל[א] די משחא בשימא
II, 1, 15: [מן טעון] גמל לטעונא
II, 1, 16: מן טעון גמלא די [מ]שחא בשימא
II, 1, 18: מן ט[עון חמר די] משחא [בשימא]
II, 1, 20: מן טעון חמר [ד]י משחא ב[שי]מא
II, 1, 22: מן טעון די מש[חא]
II, 1, 23: למעלן טעון ג[מ]לא
II, 1, 25: מן טעון די מש[חא]
II, 1, 26: למעל[ן] ט[עון]א די גמלא
II, 1, 27: מן טעו[ן] חמר די משח
II, 1, 28: מן טעון דהנא
II, 1, 29: טעון גמל
II, 1, 30: מן טעון דהנא
II, 1, 31: לטעון גמל
II, 1, 32: מן טעון [דה]נא די חמר

Glossaries (Greek and Aramaic)

33 ,1 ,II: מן טעון נ[ונ]י א[מליחיא לטעונא די [גמלא]

35 ,1 ,II: [מן טעון]..א לטעונא די גמלא

36 ,1 ,II: [מן טעון] .. א די טעון חמרא

9 ,2 ,II: [י]גבא מכסא לטעונא די חטא

16 ,2 ,II: מ[ן יבישין] לכ[ל] טעון די גמל

10 ,3 ,II: לטעונא אקימת די יהוא מתג[ב]א דנר

31 ,3 ,II: ויהוא פרע צלם בפלגות [טעו]ן וצלמין תרן טעון

45 ,3 ,II: לטעונ[א יגב]א

טעמא - food

10 ,3 ,II: לטעמתא הי<ד>בנמ[ו]סא

טען - to load

19 ,3 ,II: גמליא הן טעינין

י

י - 1st singular suffixed pronoun

32 ,3 ,II: [א]תחזי לי

יביש - dry

6 ,1 ,II: טעון גמלא די יבי[שי]ן

16 ,2 ,II: מ[ן יבישין] לכ[ל] טעון די גמל

17 ,3 ,II: יהוא מכסא היך ליביש

יהב - to give

25 ,3 ,II: אתחזי די יהון יהבין מכ[סא]

34 ,3 ,II: יהוא יהב למדיא אסר איטלק[ן]

יום - day

14 ,I: בירח ניסן יום 18

ירח - month

14 ,I: בירח ניסן

45 ,1 ,II: אף [י]ג[ב]א מכ[סא לכל יר]ח מן די יהוא מזבן משחא בשימא

5 ,2 ,II: אף יגבא מכ[סא] ... [לכל ירח] מן חנותא

יתיר - more

24 ,I: לא יהוא גבא אגורא מן אנש מדעם יתיר

47 ,1 ,II: מן מן די שקלא דינר [או] יתיר

28 ,3 ,II: עלימתא די שקלן דנר או יתיר

כ

כד, כדי - when

16 ,I: כד הות בולא כנישא מן נמוסא

11 ,2 ,II: לגמלא כדי יתאיעל סריק יגבא ד 1

271

The Palmyrene Tax Tariff

כדון - mule
II, 1, 38: ולכודנ[א ד] 10
כול - to count, measure out
II, 2, 21: ו[די] לא י[כל י]פרע
II, 2, 23: יכילנה ל[מסכ]א [א]פי מדי באסרא חד
כות - similarly, as
II, 2, 46: כות הוו ספונ[ן]
כל - all, every, any
I, 26: כלמא גנס כלה
II, 1, 2: [י]גבא מכס[א] לכל רגל
II, 1, 5: יתן לכל רגלי
II, 1, 10: מן א[ר]ג[ו]נא מלטא לכל מ[שך]
II, 1, 45: אף [י]ג[ב]א מכ[ס]א לכל יר[ח]
II, 2, 5: אף יגבא מכ[סא] ... [לכל] יר[ח] מן חנותא
II, 2, 6: [מן כ]ל משך
II, 2, 10: [י]גבא מכסא לטעונא די חטא וחמרא ותבנא ו[כ]ל מדי דמא [להון לכ]ל גמל
II, 2, 16: לכ[ל] טעון די גמל
II, 2, 17: מ[ן א]ר[ג]ונא מלטא לכל משך
II, 2, 18: אף יגבא [מכס]א מן גנסיא כלהון
II, 2, 21: [י]פרע לכל מדא מן נמ[וס]א
II, 2, 31: יהוא פרע ... לכל רגלי
II, 2, 34: לכל [רגל על]מיא
II, 3, 16: לכל די עלל לחשבן תגרא
II, 3, 20: חיב כל גמל דנר
כלמא - every, any
I, 26: טעון קרס די כלמא גנס כלה
II, 1, 7: [לכלמא] די טעון גמלא
כנש - to gather together, summon
I, 16: כד הות בולא כנישא מן נמוסא
II, 3, 33: באתר די מתכנשין
כפר - to free, exempt
II, 3, 23: כפרו די מכס לא גבן
כשיר - magnificent, excellent
II, 3, 22: היך די אשר קרבלון כשירא
כשר - to be acceptable, appropriate, just
II, 3, 6: הא כשר די [יה]ן מכסיא אפי אסר איטלק[ן] גבן

272

Glossaries (Greek and Aramaic)

כתב - to write

I, 17: מדי כתיב מן לתחת

I, 18: הוא מתכתב באגוריא

I, 21: ויכתב בשטר אגריא חדתא ויכתב למדעמא מדעמא מכסה

I, 22: ו<י>כתב עם נמוסא קדמיא

II, 2, 18: היך די כתיב מן למעל

II, 2, 37: [היך די] כתיב בנמוסא

II, 2, 39: ......לא כתיב בדיל [די] מדעם לא ...

II, 3, 5: אף גרמנקוס קיסר באגרתא די כתב לסטטילס פשק

II, 3, 22: באגרתא די כתב לברברס

II, 3, 43: היך די כ]תיב מן ל[על

כתב - record

II, 3, 1: בדיל די בטעון די כתב די טעא די מכס[א]

ל

ל - nota dativi, accusativi, distributivi

I, 20: אתחזי לבולא

I, 21: ויכתב למדעמא מדעמא

I, 22: ומדי אשר לאגורא

I, 23: ויהוא מבטל לארכוניא

I, 26: לארבעא טעונין די גמלין מכסא גבי

II, 1, 1–2: מתאעלין לתדמר או לתחומיה

II, 1, 2: [יגבא מכס]א לכל רגל

II, 1, 5: יתן לכל רגלי

II, 1, 7: למעלנא [לכלמא] די טעון גמלא

II, 1, 8: מן [טעון גמלא] למ[פקנא]

II, 1, 9: מן ט[עון] חמרא למעלנא ו[למפקנא]

II, 1, 10: מן א[ר]ג[ו]נא מלטא לכל מ[שך למעלנא] ולמ[פ]קנא

II, 1, 14: ולמא ד[י] יפק משח[א דנה

II, 1, 15: למפקנ[א] מן טעון] גמל לטעונא

II, 1, 17: [ל[מ]על[נא ד 13 ולמפק[נא ד 7]

II, 1, 19: ולמפקנא ד 7

II, 1, 21: [ולמ]פקנא ד 4

II, 1, 23–4: למעלן טעון ג[מ]ל[א ד 13 ולמפקנב

II, 1, 26: למעל[ן] ט[עונ]א די גמלא ד [7] ולמפקנא ד [7]

II, 1, 27: למע[לנא] ד 7 ול<מ>פקנא [ד 7]

II, 1, 29: <ל>מעלנא ד 13 ול[מפק[נא ד 13

273

The Palmyrene Tax Tariff

II, 1, 31: לטעון גמל למעלנא ד 7 ולמ[פקנא ד] 7

II, 3, 32: למעלנא [ד 7 ולמפקנא ד] 7

II, 1, 33–4: לטעונא די [גמלא למע]לנ[א ד] 10

II, 1, 35: לטעונא די גמלא למ[עלנא ולמפקנא ד]

II, 1, 36–7: למעלנ[א] ד] ... ולמפק]נא יגבא מכסא ד 3

II, 1, 38: מן [מעלי סוס]יא ד 10 ולכודנ[א ד] 10

II, 1, 41: למע]לן ולמפקן] לרשא חד אסרא חד

II, 1, 45: [י]ג[ב]א מכ[סא לכל יר]ח

II, 2, 5: יגבא ... [לכל] יר[ח] מן חנותא

II, 2, 6: למשכא אסרין 2

II, 2, 8: [לתש]מיש עינן תרתן די מ[י] די במדיתא

II, 2, 9: [י]גבא מכסא לטעונא די חטא

II, 2, 10: [להון לכ]ל גמל לארח חדא

II, 2, 11: לגמלא כדי יתאיעל סריק

II, 2, 16: לכ]ל] טעון די גמל מעלן ד 4 ולמפקן ד 4

II, 2, 17: לכל משך למעלנא ד 4 ולמפקנא ד 4

II, 2, 19: [יתג]בא אסרא חד למדיא

II, 2, 20: יתן [לה]ן לתשמישא

II, 2, 21: [י]פרע לכל מדא

II, 2, 22: מן די יהוא לה מלח

II, 2, 23: יכילנה ל[מסכ]א

II, 2, 27: חיב למהוא

II, 2, 29: מדעם להן משתתף

II, 2, 30–1: יהוא פרע למכסא מן די מעל רגלין לתדמר [א]ו לתח[ו]מ[י]ה ומפק לכל רגלי ד 22

II, 2, 32: יפרע למכ[סא]

II, 2, 3: ..... לכל [רגל על]מיא דנה

II, 2, 45: ... מכסא למפקנא

II, 2, 47: [ת]הוא פרעא [מכ[ס]א] למפק<נ>א

II, 3, 4: מכסא די קצבא אפי דנר חיב למתחשבו

II, 3, 5: באגרתא די כתב לסטטילס

II, 3, 10: לטעמתא הי<ד> בנמ[ו]סא לטעונא

II, 3, 13: מן די מפק ל[קרי]א

II, 3, 15: מדי דמא להון

II, 3, 16–17: לכל די עלל לחשבן תגרא יהוא מכסא היך ליביש

II, 3, 22: באגרתא די כתב לברברס

II, 3, 28: מן עלימתא די שקלן דנר או יתיר לאת[תא דנ]ר

Glossaries (Greek and Aramaic)

II, 3, 32: [א]תחזי לי

II, 3, 34: יזבן לחש[חת]ה יהוה יהב למדיא אסר איטלק[ן]

II, 3, 37: ול[תדמרי]א יהוה מזבן

II, 3, 43–5: למעלן שלחא אסרין 2 אשל[א יהוא] מתגבא ול{מ}מפקנא לטעונ[א יגב]א

II, 3, 47: הן [למגז תהוא מת[אעלא

II, 3, 47–8: והן לגו מן [תחומא תהוא] מתאעלא למדיתא למגז

P: אלא לענ<א> די תהוא מאעלא ל[גו מן תחום] תדמר אן יצבא מכסא <לחתם> יהוא [שביק]א לה

לא - not

I, 18: לא אסקו

I, 21: לא מסק בנמוסא

I, 24: לא יהוא גבא

III, 2, 21: ו[די] לא י[כל]

II, 2, 39–40: לא כתיב בדיל [די] מדעם לא ...

II, 2, 41: לא דמיא

II, 2, 44: ל[א מ]כס........

II, 2, 46: לא עמרא איטליק[א ת]הוא פרעא

II, 3, 9: מכס לא חיבין

II, 3, 14: מכס לא חיב

II, 3, 24: מכס לא גבן

II, 3, 48: מכס לא חיב[א]

P: לא יהוא מתגבא

לחשבן - for, for the sake of

II, 3, 16: כל די עלל לחשבן תגרא

למן - market, *portus*

T: נמוסא די מכסא די למנא די הדרינא תדמר

לקבל - opposite, facing

I, 23: בגללא די לקבל היכלא די רבאסירא

מ

מדי, מא די - that which

I, 17: אשרת מדי כתיב מן לתחת

II, 1, 14: ולמא ד[י] יפק משח[א] דנה

II, 2, 10: [כ]ל מדי דמא [להון]

II, 2, 20: [ו]מא די יתבעא

II, 3, 7: ומדי גו מן דנר

II, 3, 15: ומדי דמא להון

The Palmyrene Tax Tariff

מדי - when, after

II, 3, 29 :מדי הי שקלא
I, 22 :ומדי אשר לאגורא
II, 3, 12 :יהוא מתג[ב]א דנר מדי יהוא מת[אע]ל בר מן תחומא או מאפק
P: מ[די] פרע מכסא לא יהוא מתגבא

מדיא, מדא - modius

II, 2, 19 :[יתג]בא אסרא חד למדיא
II, 2, 21 :[י]פרע לכל מדא
II, 2, 23 :[א]פי מדיא באסרא חד
II, 3, 34 :יהוא יהב למדיא אסר איטלק[ן]

מדינא - city, polis, state

II, 1, 3 :י[זב]ן ב[מדי]ת[א]
II, 1, 4 :יזבן [במדיתא]
II, 2, 7 :[מזבנ]י נחתיא די הפכין במדיתא
II, 2, 8 :עינן תרתן די מ[י]ן די במדיתא
II, 2, 14 :עינתא די מיא ומל[חא ד]י ב[מ]דיתא
II, 3, 17 :היך די הוא אף במדינתא אחרניתא
II, 3, 40 :[מזבני נחתיא די] מ[ה]לכין ב[מד]ית<א>
II, 3, 48 :[תהוא] מתאעלא למדיתא

מדעם - that which, whatever, anything

I, 21 :מדעם די לא מסק בנמוסא
I, 22–3 :ויכתב למדעמא מדעמא
I, 24 :לא יהוא גבא אגורא מן אנש מדעם יתיר
II, 2, 29 :מדעם להן משתתף
II, 2, 40 :בדיל [די] מדעם לא ...

מוט - to be sufficient, satisfy

II, 2, 7 :יהן מוט מכסא

מטלכות - therefore

I, 19 :ומטלכות זבנין שגין על צבותא אלן סרבנין הוו

מי - water

T : עינתא די מיא
II, 2, 8 :עינן תרתן די מ[י]
II, 2, 13 :עינתא די מיא ומל[חא]

מכס - tax collector, tax farmer

I, 19 :מכסא {ו}הוא גבא היך בנמוסא ובעידא
I, 20 :סרבנין הוו ביני תגרא לביני מכסיא

Glossaries (Greek and Aramaic)

II, 1, 2: מכס[א לכל רגל יגבא
II, 1, 6: הו מ[כסא יג[בא מ]עון גמלא
II, 1, 34: ומן מפק מנהון [יגבא מכסא]
II, 1, 37: יגבא מכסא ד 3
II, 1, 43: יגבא מכסא[סרין 2
II, 1, 45: ף [י]ג[ב]א מכ[סא לכל יר[ח
II, 1, 46: אף יגבא מכסא מן זניתא
II, 2, 3: אף יגבא מכ]סא מן ארגסטר[יו]ן]
II, 2, 7: יהן מוט מכסא
II, 2, 9: [י]גבא מכסא לטעונא די חטא
II, 2, 18: אף יגבא [מכס]א מן גנסיא כלהון
II, 2, 23: יכילנה ל[מ]סכ[א
II, 2, 30: יהוא פרע למכסא
II, 2, 32: יפרע למכ[סא ד 12
II, 3, 27: ה[ז] מכסא יג[ב]א מכ[סא מן עלימתא
P: אן יצבא מכסא

מכס - tax

I, 17: בנמוסא די מכסא
I, 18: עבידן שגין חיבן מכסא
I, 22: מכסה די מן עידא
I, 27: לארבעא טעונין די גמלין מכסא גבי
T: נמוסא די מכסא
II, 1, 44: מן [עת]וד[א מ]כ[סא אסר]א חד
II, 2, 13: נמ[ו]סא די מכ[סס
II, 2, 25–6: [על] חשבן מכ[ס סרבן הוא] ביני תדמריא ל[ביני ס[ק]ו]ת מכסי[א]
II, 2, 26–7: [מ]כסא חיב למהוא [היך מכ]סא [די] אגר בה אלקמס
II, 2, 44: ל[א מ]כס........פרעא
II, 2, 45: מכסא למפקנא בתר כות הוו ספו[ן]
II, 2, 47: לא עמרא איטליק[א ת]הוא פרעא [מכ]ס[א]
II, 2, 48–3: יהוא מכסא מת[ג]בא היך נמוס[א בדיל די בטעון די כתב די טעא מכס[א]
II, 3, 3: מכסא די קצבא
II, 3, 6: [יה]ן מכסיא אפי אסר איטלק[ן] גבן
II, 3, 7: מכסא היך עדתא ע[ר]פן יהוא גבא
II, 3, 9: פגרין די משתדן מכס לא חיבין
II, 3, 14: מכס לא חיב
II, 3, 16: יהוא מכסא היך ליביש

The Palmyrene Tax Tariff

II, 3, 23: מכס לא גבן
II, 3, 25: יהון יהבין מכ[סא]
II, 3, 26: מכסא די עלימתא
II, 3, 35: ואף מכסא [מ]לחא די הויא בתדמר
II, 3, 38: [מכ]סא די ארגונא
II, 3, 43: יהוא מתגבא מכסא
II, 3, 47: מכסא חיבא
II, 3, 48: מכס לא חיב[א]
P: מכסא .. [יתגב]א היך בנמוסא דנה מתגבא ב[שי]מא

מלח - salt

II, 2, 14: עינתא די מיא ומל[חא]
II, 2, 19: [מל]ח טב [יתג]בא אסרא חד
II, 2, 22: מן די יהוא לה מלח
II, 3, 31: על מלחא קשט[א א]תחזי לי

מלח - related to salt (adj.)

II, 3, 35: ואף מכסא [מ]לחא די הויא בתדמר

מלט - sheep's wool

I, 1,10: מן א[רג]ונא מלטא
II, 2, 17: מ[ן א]ר[גונא] מלטא

מליח - salted

II, 1, 33: מן טעון נ[וני]א מליחיא

מלכו - proper name

I, 16: מלכו בר עליי בר מקימו

מן - from, away from, in accordance with

I, 16: כד הות בולא כנישא מן נמוסא
I, 18: והוו מתגבין מן עידא
I, 22: מכסה די מן עידא
I, 24: לא יהוא גבא אגורא מן אנש
II, 1, 1: מן מעלי עלימיא
II, 1, 3: מן עלם די י[זב]ן ב[מדי]ת[א] או י[פק
II, 1, 4: מן עלם וטר[ן] די יזבן [במדיתא]
II, 1, 6: הו מ[כסא יג]בא [מ]ן טעון גמלא
II, 1, 8: מן [טעון גמלא]
II, 1, 9: מן ט[עון] חמרא
II, 1, 10: מן א[רג]ונא מלטא
II, 1, 12: מן טע[ון ג]מל[א] די משחא בשימא

278

Glossaries (Greek and Aramaic)

II, 1, 15: [מן טעון] גמל לטעונא
II, 1, 16: מן טעון גמלא די [מ]שחא בשימא
II, 1, 18: מן ט[עון חמר די] משחא [בשימא]
II, 1, 20: מן טעון חמר [ד]י משחא ב[שי]מא
II, 1, 22: מן טעון די מש[חא די בזק]ין ארבע די עז
II, 1, 25: מן טעון די מש[חא] די בזקין תרתן די עז
II, 1, 27: מן טעון [ן] חמר די משח
II, 1, 28: מן טעון דהנא
II, 1, 30: מן טעון דהנא
II, 1, 32: מן טעון [דה]נא די חמר
II, 1, 33: מן טעון נ[וני]א מליחיא
II, 1, 34: ומן מפק מנהון ...
II, 1, 35: [מן טעון] ..א לטעונא די גמלא
II, 1, 36: [מן טעון]..א די טעון חמרא
II, 1, 38: מן [מעלי סוס]יא
II, 1, 39: מן......אמ]רי[א..
II, 1, 41: מ[ן גדיא די] אמריא
II, 1, 42: מן [ח/בו/כר]א גמלא
II, 1, 43: מן..[עז]א רבא [יגבא מכסא]
II, 1, 44: מן [עת]וד[א מ]כ[סא אסר]א חד
II, 1, 45: אף [י]ג[ב]א[מכ]סא לכל יר[ח] מן די יהוא מזבן משחא בשימא
II, 46–2, 2: אף יגבא מכסא מן זניתא מן מן די שקלא דינר [או] יתיר דנרא חד מן אתתא ומן מן די שקלא אסרין תמניא יגבא אסרין תמניא ומן מן די שקל[א] אסרי[ן ש]תא יגבא אסרין [ש]ת[א]
II, 3, 3–5: אף יגבא מכ[סא מן ארגסטר]יו[ן] ופטפלי [ואשכ]יפא [ומן ח]ט[י]א היך עדתא [לכל יר[ח] מן חנותא
II, 2, 6: [מן כ]ל משך
II, 2, 16: מ[ן יבישין]
II, 2, 17: מ[ן א]ר[גונא] מלטא
II, 2, 18: אף יגבא [מכס]א מן גנסיא כלהון
II, 2, 21: [י]פרע לכל מדא מן נמ[וס]א דנה
II, 2, 24: מ[ן די אקם] גיס [לקניס מ[קינ]ס] היגמונא
II, 3, 13: מן די מפק ל[קרי]א [או מ]אעל מן קריא
II, 3, 27: [מכ]סא מן עלימתא
II, 3, 33: ומן מן תדמריא יזבן
II, 3, 46: ענא ת[ה]ו[א מ]תאעלא מ[ן] בר [מן] תחומא

279

The Palmyrene Tax Tariff

II, 3, 49: ומן די ◇

P: [אף] מן ...

מן - who

II, 1, 34: ומן מפק מנהון

II, 3, 33: ומן מן תדמריא יזבן

מן די - the one who

II, 1, 47: מן מן די שקלא דינר [או] יתיר

II, 1, 48: ומן מן די שקלא אסרין תמניא

II, 2, 1: ומן מן די שקל[א] אסרי[ן ש]תא

II, 2, 22: מן די יהוא לה מלח

II, 2, 30: יהוא פרע למכסא מן די מעל רגלין

II, 2, 32: ו[מן] די [מזבן רגלין]

II, 2, 33: ו[מן] די י[זבן על]ם וטרן יפרע

II, 2, 36: מן די מפק עלם וטרן

II, 2, 38: [מן] די יז[בן]

II, 3, 13: מן די מפק ל[קרי]א

מן לעל - above

II, 2, 18: היך די כתיב מן לעל

II, 3, 43: היך די כ[תיב מן ל]על

מן לתחת - below

I, 17: מדי כתיב מן לתחת

מעלן - importation, bringing in

II, 1, 7: למעלנא [לכלמא] די טעון גמלא

II, 1, 9: מן ט[עון] חמרא למעלנא ו[למפקנא]

II, 1, 10: לכל מ[שך למעלנא] ולמ[פ]קנא

II, 1, 17: [ל]מ[על]נא ד 13 ולמפק[נא ד 7]

II, 1, 23: למעלן טעון ג[מ]לא

II, 1, 26: למעל[ן] ט[עונ]א די גמלא

II, 1, 27: מן טעו[ן] חמר די משח למע[לנא] ד7

II, 1, 29: >ל<מעלנא ד 13 ול[מפק]נא ד 13

II, 1, 31: למעלנא ד 7 ולמ[פקנא ד] 7

II, 1, 32: למעלנא [ד 7 ולמפקנא ד] 7

II, 1, 34: [למע]לנ[א ד] 10

II, 1, 35: למ[עלנא ולמפקנא ד]

II, 1, 36: למעלנ[א] ד

II, 1, 41: למע[לן ולמפקן]

Glossaries (Greek and Aramaic)

II, 2, 16: מעלן ד 4 ולמפקן ד4
II, 2, 17: למעלנא ד 4 ולמפקנא ד4
II, 2, 42: ומעלן מכ..
II, 3, 43: למעלן שלחא

מפקן - exportation, taking out

II, 1, 8: מן [טעון גמלא] למ[פקנא]
II, 1, 9: למעלנא ו[למפקנא]
II, 1, 11: [למעלנא] ולמ[פ]קנא
II, 1, 15: למפקנ[א מן טעון] גמל
II, 1, 17: [ל]מ[על]נא ד 13 ולמפק[נא ד 7]
II, 1, 19: ולמפקנא ד 7
II, 1, 21: [ולמ]פקנא ד 4
II, 1, 26: ולמפקנא ד [7]
II, 1, 27: ול<מ>פקנא [ד 7]
II, 1, 29: ול[מ]פקנא ד 13
II, 1, 31: ול[מ]פקנא ד 7
II, 1, 32: [ולמפקנא ד] 7
II, 1, 35: [ולמפקנא ד]
II, 1, 37: [ולמפק]נא יגבא מכסא ד 3
II, 1, 41: [ולמפקן]
II, 2, 16: ולמפקן ד 4
II, 2, 17: ולמפקנא ד 4
II, 2, 45: מכסא למפקנא בתר כות הוו ספו[ן]
II, 2, 47: [ת]הוא פרעא [מכ]ס[א] למפק<נ>א
II, 3, 44: ול{מ}מפקנא לטעונ[א יגב]א

מקימו - proper name

I, 16: מלכו בר עליי בר מקימו

מקינס - Roman *cognomen* (Mucianus)

II, 2, 24: גיס [לקניס מ]קינ[ס] היגמונא

מרינס - Roman *cognomen* (Marinus)

II, 2, 15: א[גור[יא [ד]י א[ת]אגר קדם מרינס היגמונא

משח - oil, perfumed oil, myrrh

II, 1, 12: מן טע[ון ג]מל[א] די משחא בשימא
II, 1, 14: ולמא ד[י] יפק משח[א] דנה
II, 1, 16: מן טעון גמלא די [מ]שחא בשימא
II, 1, 18: ט[עון חמר די] משחא [בשימא]

II, 1, 20: טעון חמר [ד]י משחא ב[שי]מא

II, 1, 22: טעון די מש[חא די בזק]ין ארבע די עז

II, 1, 25: טעון די מש[חא] די בזקין תרתן די עז

II, 1, 27: טעו[ן] חמר די משח

II, 1, 45: מן די יהוא מזבן משחא בשימא

II, 2, 48: משחא ב[שימא די] בזקין די עז

משך - hide, fleece

II, 1, 10: מן א[רג]ונא מלטא לכל מ[שך]

II, 2, 6: [מן כ]ל משך די [י]תאעל או יזבן למשכא אסרין 2

II, 2, 17: מ[ן א]ר[גונא] מלטא לכל משך

נ

נון - fish

II, 1, 33: מן טעון נ[וני]א מליחיא

נחש - bronze, copper

II, 3, 30: [על] צלמי נחשא אדרטיא אתחזי די יתגב[ון]

נחת - garment

II, 2, 7: [מזבנ]י נחתיא די הפכין במדיתא

II, 3, 40: [מזבני נחתיא די] מ[ה]לכין ב[מ]ד>ית<א

ניסן - month name (Nīsān)

I, 14: בירח ניסן

נמוס - law

I, 16: כד הות בולא כנישא מן נמוסא

I, 17: בנמוסא די מכסא

I, 19: בנמוסא ובעידא

I, 21: לא מסק בנמוסא

I, 22: ו>י<כתב עם נמוסא קדמיא

T: נמוסא די מכסא די למנא די הדרינא תדמר

II, 2, 13: נמ[ו]סא די מכ[סא די תדמר

II, 2, 21: [י]פרע לכל מדא מן נמ[וס]א דנה סטרטין [תר]ן

II, 2, 28: [היך] נמוסא

II, 2, 37: [היך די] כתיב בנמוסא

II, 2, 49: יהוא מכסא מת[גבא היך נמוס]א

II, 3, 2: ובנמוסא רציף

II, 3, 10: הי>ך< בנמ[ו]סא

II, 3, 21: היך בנמוסא

II, 3, 26: היך די נמוסא מוחא פשקת

282

Glossaries (Greek and Aramaic)

II, 3, 35: היך בנמוסא
II, 3, 36: היך בה[ו] נמוס[א
P: היך בנמוסא

נפק - to take out, drive out (Af'el)

II, 1, 3: יפ[ק י או א]ת[מדי ב]זב[ן י]
II, 1, 5: והן זבונא יפק עלי]מ[ן
II, 1, 14: הנה ד]י יפק משח[א ולמא
II, 2, 34: ומן מפק מנהון
II, 2, 31: מן די מעל רגלין לתדמר [א]ו לתח[ן ומ]פק ומ[יה
II, 2, 32: ו]מ[ן] די [מזבן רגלין ומ]פק
II, 2, 35: ומפק [ד] 12
II, 2, 36: מן די מפק עלם וטרן
II, 2, 39: ו]די מ[פ]ק.....
II, 3, 12: מדי יהוא מת[א]ל[ע בר מן תחומא או מאפק
II, 3, 13: מן די מפק ל[קרי]א

נש - proper name

I, 16: זבידא בר נשא

נתן - to give, give back

II, 1, 5: יתן לכל רגלי
II, 2, 20: ו]מ[א די יתבעא יתן [לה]ן לתשמישא

נתירא - windfall fruits

II, 3, 24: עשב[י]א ו]נת[ירתא אתחזי די יהון יהבין

ס

סדק - syndic

I, 24: ארכוניא ... ועשרתא וסדקיא

סוס - horse

II, 1, 38: מן [מעלי סוס[י]א ד 10

סטטילס - Roman nomen (Statilius)

II, 3, 5: באגרתא די כתב לסטטילס

סלק - to inscribe, enter in writing (Af'el)

I, 18: לא אסקו
I, 21: לא מסק בנמוסא

סטרט - sestertius

II, 2, 21: י]פ[רע לכל מדא מן נמ]ו[ס]א דנה ססטרטין [תר]ן

ספן - in agreement (with הוה)

II, 2, 46: כות הוו ספנ[ן

II, 3, 14: היך די אף הוו ספון
II, 3, 45: [היך די א]ף הוו ספון
P: היך ‹ד›י הון הון [ס]פון

סקות - tax collector
II, 2, 26: [סרבן הוא] ביני תדמריא ל[ביני ס]ק[ו]ת מכסי[א]

סרבן - dispute, lawsuit
I, 20: סרבנין הוו ביני תגרא לביני מכסיא
II, 2, 25: [סרבן הוא] ביני תדמריא ל[ביני ס]ק[ו]ת

סריק - empty, unladen, unloaded
II, 2, 11: לגמלא כדי יתאיעל סריק
II, 3, 19: גמליא הן טעינין והן סריקין יהן מתאעלין

ע

עבידא - object, product
I, 17: עבידן שגין חיבן מכסא לא אסקו

עדא - custom
II, 2, 4, 2: היך עדתא
II, 3, 8: מכסא היך עדתא

עז - goat
II, 1, 17: בזקי[ן] די [ע]ז
II, 1, 23: [בזק]ין ארבע די עז
II, 1, 25: בזקין תרתן די עז
II, 1, 28: בזקין א[ר]בע[] די עז
II, 1, 30: בזקין תרת[ן] די עז
II, 1, 43: מן .. [עז]א רבא
II, 2, 48: בזקין די עז

עיד - custom
I, 18: והוו מתגבין מן עידא
I, 19: היך בנמוסא ובעידא
I, 22: מכסה די מן עידא
II, 3, 37: היך עידא

עינא - spring
T: עינתא די מיא
II, 2, 8: עינן תרתן די מ[י] די במדיתא
II, 2, 13: עינתא די מיא ומל[חא]

על - upon, above, for the sake of, concerning
I, 1, 9: על צבותא אלן

Glossaries (Greek and Aramaic)

II, 3, 23 :על גלדיא די גמלי[א] אף אלן כפרו
II, 3, 29 :[על] צלמי נחשא אדרטיא אתחזי
II, 3, 31 :על מלחא קשט[א א]תחזי לי

על חשבן - because of, on the subject of

II, 2, 25 :[על] חשבן מכ]ס סרבן הוא]

עליי - proper name

I, 16 :מלכו בר עליי בר מקימו

עלימא - prostitute, *hetaera*

II, 3, 26–7 :מכסא די עלימתא היך די נמוסא מוחא פשקת ה[ן] מכסא יג[בא מכ]סא מן עלימתא די שקלן דנר או יתיר לאת[נא דנ]ר

עלל - import, deliver (Af'el)

II, 1, 1 :מן מעלי עלימיא די מתאעלין לתדמר
II, 1, 13 :מן טע[ו]ן ג[מל[א] די משחא בשימא [די] מתאעל [ב]ש[טיפ]א
II, 1, 16 :[מ]שחא בשימא [די יתאעל] בזקי[ן די] ע[ז]
II, 1, 18 :משחא [בשימא ד]י יתאעל ב[שטיפ]יא
II, 1, 21 :משחא ב[ש]י[מ]א די יתאעל בזקי[ן] די ע[ז]
II, 1, 38 :מן [מעלי סוס]יא
II, 2, 6 :[מן כ]ל משך די י[תאעל או יזבן]
II, 2, 11 :לגמלא כדי יתאיעל סריק
II, 2, 30 :מן די מעל רגלין לתדמר
II, 2, 35 :ו[ד]י מעל..
II, 3, 12 :מדי יהוא מת[אע]ל בר מן תחומא
II, 3, 13 :[מ]אעל מן קריא
II, 3, 16 :לכל די עלל לחשבן תגרא
II, 3, 20 :יהן מתאעלין בר מן תחומא
II, 3, 46–8 :ענא ת[ה]ו[א מ[תאעלא מ[ן בר] מן תחומא אף הן [למגז תהוא מת[אעלא מכסא חיבא והן לגו מן [תחומא תהוא] מתאעלא למדיתא למגז מכס לא חיב[א]
P: ענ<א> די תהוא מאעלא ל[גו מן תחום] תדמר

עלם, עלים - slave, boy

II, 1, 1 :מן מעלי עלימיא
II, 1, 3 :מן עלם די י[זב]ן ב[מדי]ת[א]
II, 1, 4 :מן עלם וטר[ן] די יזבן [במדיתא]
II, 1, 5 :והן זבונא יפק עלי[מ]ן
II, 2, 33 :ו[מן] די י[זבן על]ם וטרן
II, 2, 34 :לכל [רגל על]מיא דנה...
II, 2, 36 :מן די מפק עלם וטרן

285

עם - with

I, 22: וכתב עם נמוסא קדמיא

עמרא - wool

II, 2, 43: ודי עמרא

II, 2, 44: ל[א מ]כס.......פרעא תהוא עמרא די איט[לי]א

II, 2, 46: לא עמרא איטליק[א ת]הוא פרעא [מכ]ס[א]

ען - sheep, small cattle

II, 3, 46: ענא ת[ה]ו[א מ]תאעלא

P: ענ<א> די תהוא מאעלא

ערפן - monetary unit (Greek κέρμα)

II, 3, 8: מכסא היך עדתא ע[ר]פן יהוא גבא

עשב - greens, grass, vegetables

II, 3, 24: עשב[י]א ו[נת]ירתא אתחזי די יהון יהבין מכ[סא]

עשר - ten

II, 2, 20: מדיא די קסטון עשר ו[ש]ת

עשרתא - group of ten (*dekaprōtoi*)

I, 20: ארכוניא אלן ועשרתא

I, 23: ארכוניא ... ועשרתא וסדקיא

עתוד - kid, young goat

II, 1, 44: מן [עת]וד[א מ]כ[סא אסר]א חד

פ

פטפלי - small shop

II, 2, 3: אף יגבא מכ[סא מן ארגסטר]יו[ן] פטפלי [ואשכ]יפא [ומן] ח[ט]א היך עדתא

פלגות - half

II, 3, 31: ויהוא פרע צלם בפלגות [טעו]ן

II, 3, 39: ארבעא ופלג ...

פלהדרו - *proedria*

I, 14: בפלהדרותא די בונא בר בונא בר חירן

פלפטר - proper name (Φιλοπάτωρ)

I, 15: אלכסדרס בר אלכסדרס בר פלפטר

פגר - corpse, carrion

II, 3, 9: פגרין די משתדן מכס לא חיבין

פרע - pay

II, 2, 21: [י]פרע לכל מדא מן נמ[וס]א דנה סטטרטין [תר]ן

II, 2, 30: יהוא פרע למכסא מן די מעל רגלין לתדמר

II, 2, 32: ו[מן] די [מזבן רגלין ומ]פק יפרע למכ[סא ד] 12

Glossaries (Greek and Aramaic)

II, 2, 33: ו[מן] די י[זבן על[ם וטרן יפרע ד [10]

II, 2, 35: ו[ד]י מעל ..[יפרע] הו ד 10

II, 2, 38: [מן] די יז[בן].....יפרע ד 9

II, 2, 44: פרעא תהוא

II, 2, 47: לֹא עמרא איטליק[א ת]הוא פרעא [מכ[ס]א]

II, 3, 30: ויהוא פרע צלם בפלגות [טעו]ן

P: מ[די] פרע מכסא לא יהוא מתגבא

פשק - to decide, state, enact

II, 3, 5: אף גרמנקוס קיסר ... פשק

II, 3, 26: היך די נמוסא מוחא פשקת

צ

צבא - to wish

P: אן יצבא מכסא <למחתם>

צבו - matter, subject, thing

I, 19: על צבותא אלן

צלם - image, statue

II, 3, 29–31: [על] צלמי נחשא אדרטיא אתחזי די יתגב[ון] היך [נה]שא ויהוא פרע צלם בפלגות [טעו]ן וצלמין תרן טעון

ק

קבל - to accept, receive

II, 3, 37: אפי אסר יהוא מתקבל

קדם - before

II, 2, 15: א[ג]ור[י]א [ד]י א[ת]אגר קדם מרינס היגמונא

קדמי - first, prior, previous

I, 17: בזבניא קדמיא

I, 22: נמוסא קדמיא

קום - to establish (Af'el)

II, 2, 24: מ[ן] די אקם[] גיס [לקניס מ[קין[ס] היגמונא

II, 2, 26: [א]קי[מ]ת די

II, 3, 10: אקימת די יהוא מתג[ב]א דנר

קיסר - Roman *cognomen* (Caesar), imperial title

T: [אי]לס קיסר

II, 2, 12: קלקיס בר חרי קיסר

II, 3, 4: גרמנקוס קיסר

קלקיס - *cognomen* of a freedman (Cilicius)

II, 2, 12: גב[א] קלקיס בר חרי קיסר

287

קסטון - *sextarius*
II, 2, 19: מדיא די קסטון עשר ו[ש]ת

קצב - butcher
II, 3, 3: מכסא די קצבא אפי דנר חיב למתחשבו

קריא - village, settlement
II, 3, 13: מן די מפק ל[קרי]א [או מ]אעל מן קריא מכס לא חיב

קרס - cart, wagon
I, 26: טעון קרס

קרבלון - Roman *cognomen* (Corbulo)
II, 3, 22: היך די אשר קרבלון כשירא

קשט - right, just
II, 3, 32: קשט[א א]תחזי לי

ר

רב - big
II, 1, 43: [עז]א רבא

רבאסירא - divine name
I, 23: היכלא די רבאסירא

רגל - person, individual, human being
II, 1, 2: [יגבא מכס]א לכל רגל
II, 1, 5: יתן לכל רגלי
II, 2, 30–1: מן די מעל רגלין לתדמר [א]ו לתח[ום]יה ומפק לכל רגלי
II, 2, 32: ו[מן] די [מזבן רגלין ומ]פק
II, 2, 34: לכל [רגל על]מיא דנה

רצף - to fix, stipulate
II, 3, 2: ובנמוסא רציף

רש - head
II, 1, 41: לרשא חד אסרא חד

ש

שבק - to let, allow
P: יהוא [שביק]א לה

שגי - many
I, 17: עבידן שגין חיבן מכסא
I, 19: זבנין שגין

שדא - to throw away, discard
II, 3, 9: פגרין די משתדן מכס לא חיבין

Glossaries (Greek and Aramaic)

שטיף - alabaster (jar)

II, 1, 13: משחא בשימא [די] מתאעל [ב]ש[טיפ]א

II, 1, 19: משחא [בשימא ד]י יתאעל ב[שטיפ]יא

שטר - document

I, 21: ויכתב בשטר אגריא חדתא

שלח - skin, hide

II, 3, 43: למעלן שלחא אסרין 2

שנא - year

I, 14: שנת 448

שקל - to take

II, 1, 47–2, 2: מן מן די שקלא דינר [או] יתיר דנרא חד מן אתתא ומן מן די שקלא אסרין תמניא יגבא אסרין תמניא ומן מן די שקל[א] אסרי[ן ש]תא יגבא אסרין [ש]ת[א]

II, 3, 27: עלימתא די שקלן דנר או יתיר

II, 3, 28–9: והן חסיר תהוה שקלא מדי הי שקלא [יגבא]

שרר - to decree, affirm

I, 16: אשרת מדי כתיב מן לתחת

I, 22: ומדי אשר לאגורא

II, 3, 21: היך די אשר קרבלון כשירא

שת - six

II, 2, 1–2: ומן מן די שקל[א] אסרי[ן ש]תא יגבא אסרין [ש]ת[א]

II, 2, 20: מדיא די קסטון עשר ו[ש]ת

שתף - to agree mutually

II, 2, 29: מדעם להן משתתף

ת

תבנא - straw

II, 2, 9: [י]גבא מכסא לטעונא די חטא וחמרא ותבנא

תגר - merchant

I, 20: ביני תגרא לביני מכסיא

תגרא - trade

II, 3, 16: כל די עלל לחשבן תגרא

תגרא - value, price

II, 3, 25: אית בהון תגרתא

תדמר - Palmyra

T: הדרינא תדמר

II, 1, 1: עלימיא די מתאעלין לתדמר

II, 2, 13: נמ[ו]סא די מכ[סא די תדמר

289

The Palmyrene Tax Tariff

II, 2, 22: מן די יהוא לה מלח בתד[מר]
II, 2, 30: מן די מעל רגלין לתדמר
II, 2, 44: תדמ[ר] ל[א מ]כס
II, 3, 36: מכסא [מ]לחא די הויא בתדמר
P: ענ‹א› די תהוא מאעלא ל[גו מן תחום] תדמר

תדמרי - Palmyrene

II, 2, 23: בתד[מר או בתחו]מא ד[י] ת[דמרי]א
II, 2, 25: ביני תדמריא ל[ביני] [ס][ק][ו]ת מכסי[א]
II, 3, 33: ומן מן תדמריא יזבן לחש[חת]ה
II, 3, 37: ול[תדמרי]א יהוא מזבן היך עידא

תחום - border, boundary

II, 1, 2: לתדמר או לתחומיה
II, 2, 14: [ד]י ב[מ]דיתא ותחומיה
II, 2, 22: בתד[מר או בתחו]מא ד[י] ת[דמרי]א
II, 2, 31: מן די מעל רגלין לתדמ[ר] א[ו לתח]ומ[י]ה
II, 3, 12: מדי יהוא מת[אע]ל בר מן תחומא
II, 3, 20: יהן מתאעלין בר מן תחומא
II, 3, 48: והן לגו מן [תחומא תהוא] מתאעלא למדיתא
P: תהוא מאעלא ל[גו מן תחום] תדמר

תמניא - eight

II, 1 48–9: ומן מן די שקלא אסרין תמניא יגבא אסרין תמניא

תרן, תרתן - two

II, 1, 25: מש[חא] די בזקין תרתן די עז
II, 1, 30: דהנא די בזקין תרת[ן די] עז
II, 2, 8: עינן תרתן די מ[י] די במדיתא
II, 2, 21: [י]פרע לכל מדא מן נמ[וס]א דנה סטטרטין [תר]ן
II, 3, 31: ויהוא פרע צלם בפלגות [טעו]ן וצלמין תרן טעון

תשמיש - usage

II, 2, 8: [לתש]מיש עינן תרתן די מ[י] די במדיתא
II, 2, 20: [ו]מא די יתבעא יתן [לה]ן לתשמישא

Abbreviations and Bibliography

Note: Shifman's abbreviations have been retained where convenient, though some abbreviations which appeared in his Bibliography have been moved to the Abbreviations list. Pagination omitted by Shifman has been supplied. Items of bibliography written in Russian are listed separately first, as in the original.

Abbreviations

AAAS	*Les annales archéologiques arabes syriennes* (Damascus)
Ael.Spart., *Vita Hadr.*	Aelius Spartianus, *Vita Hadriani*
AfO	*Archiv für Orientforschung* (Berlin)
AJA	*American Journal of Archaeology* (Princeton)
Ant.	Flavius Josephus, *Antiquitates Iudaicae*
App., *BC*	Appian, *Bella civilia*
ARAB	D.D. Luckenbill, *Ancient Records of Assyria and Babylonia* (Chicago, 1926–7)
ARM	*Archives Royales de Mari* (Paris)
Arch. AS	Archive of the Academy of Sciences of the USSR (fond [f.], inventory [inv.], number [no.] and page/sheet [p., pp.])
Arch. LO IA	Archive of the Leningrad Branch of the Institute of Archaeology (fond [f.], number [no.] and page/sheet [p., pp.])
Bauer, Leander	Bauer and Leander 1927
BCH	*Bulletin de correspondence Hellénique* (Paris)
BiOr	*Bibliotheca Orientalis* (Leiden)
BLS	Brockelmann 1928
BSG	Brockelmann 1955
CAD	*The Assyrian Dictionary of the Oriental Institute of the University of Chicago*
Caes., *B. Gall.*	Caesar, *Bellum Gallicum*
Cass. Dio.	Cassius Dio, *Historia Romana*
CIG	*Corpus Inscriptionum Graecarum* (Berlin)
CIL	*Corpus Inscriptionum Latinarum* (Berlin)
CIS	*Corpus Inscriptionum Semiticarum* (Paris)
CRAIBL	*Comptes-rendus de l'Académie des Inscriptions et Belles-Lettres* (Paris)
DAN	Dalman 1922
DEPP	Dura-Europos Papyri and Parchments
Dig.	*Digesta*
Ephr.	Ephrem the Syrian
Evagrius, *Hist. eccl.*	Evagrius, *Historia ecclesiae*
Eutrop.	Eutropius, *Historia Romana*

The Palmyrene Tax Tariff

Fl.Vop., *Aurel.*	Flavius Vopiscus, *Vita Aureliani*
FHG	*Fragmenta historicorum Graecorum* (Paris)
Gesenius-Buhl	Gesenius 1910
IFZh	*Istoriko-filologicheskiĭ Zhurnal* (Erevan)
IGLS	*Inscriptions grecques et latines de la Syrie*, 1–7 (Paris, 1929–70)
IGRR, III	R. Cagnat, *Inscriptiones Graecae ad res Romanas pertinentes*, Vol. III (Paris, 1902–6)
ILS	H. Dessau, *Inscriptiones Latinae Selectae*, Vols 1–3 (Berlin, 1902–16)
Inv.	*Inventaire des inscriptions de Palmyre*, Fascicles I–XI (Beirut-Damascus, 1930–65)
IOSPE	*Inscriptiones Antiquae Orae Septentrionalis Ponti Euxini Graecae et Latinae*, ed. B. Latyshev (St Petersburg, 1916)
IRAIK	*Izvestiia Imp. Rossiĭskogo Arkheologicheskogo Instituta v Konstantinopole* (St Petersburg)
JA	*Journal Asiatique* (Paris)
JAOS	*Journal of the American Oriental Society* (New York-New Haven)
JH	Jean and Hoftijzer 1965
JNES	*Journal of Near Eastern Studies* (Chicago)
KAH	O. Schroeder, *Keilschrifttexte aus Assur historischen Inhalts*, Bd 2 (Leipzig, 1922)
KAI	H. Donner, W. Röllig, *Kanaanäische und aramäische Inschriften*, Bd 1–3 (Wiesbaden, 1964)
KBN	*Korpus Bosporskikh Nadpiseĭ* (Moscow/Leningrad, 1965)
KGLL	Krauss 1898–9
Luc., *Het. dial.*	Lucian, *Hetaerarum dialogi*
Luc. *Phars.*	Lucan, *Pharsalia*
LS	Liddel and Scott 1961
LW	Levy 1924
Malal., *Chronogr.*	Malalas *Chronographia* (book no. and page in Dindorf ed.)
MVAG	*Mitteilungen der Vorderasiatisch-Aegyptischen Gesellschaft* (Berlin)
OGIS	G. Dittenberger, *Orientis Graeci Inscriptiones Selectae*, Vol.1-2. (Leipzig, 1903–5)
Onom. sacr.	Eusebius, *Onomastica sacra.*
Oros., *Hist. adv. pag.*	Orosius, *Historiae adversum paganos*
PEQ	*Palestine Exploration Quarterly* (London)
Per. mar. Er.	*Periplus maris Erythraei*
Petr. Patr.	Petrus Patricius
Plin., *NH*	Pliny, *Naturalis Historia*
Polyb.	Polybius, *Historia*
PS	*Palestinskiĭ Sbornik* (Moscow/Leningrad)
P.-W.RE	Pauly's *Realenzyklopädie der klassischen Altertumswissenschaft*, bearb. von G. Wissowa, W. Kroll (Stuttgart)
RAss.	*Revue d'assyriologie et d'archéologie orientale* (Paris)
RB	*Revue biblique* (Paris)
RPh	*Revue philologique* (Paris)
RTP	H. Ingholt, H. Seyrig, J. Starcky, *Receuil des tessères de Palmyre* (Paris, 1955)
SA	*Sovetskaia Arkheologiia* (Moscow)

Abbreviations and Bibliography

SBKPAWB	*Sitzungsberichte der Königlichen Preussischen Akademie der Wissenschaften zu Berlin* (Berlin)
SDGY	Sobolevskiĭ 1948 (Russian bibliography below).
SIG	G. Dittenberger, *Sylloge inscriptionum Graecarum* 1–4 (Leipzig, 1915–24)
St. Byz.	Stephanus of Byzantium
Strabo	Strabo, *Geographica*
Suet., *Calig.*	Suetonius, *Caligula*
Syncellus, *Chronog.*	Syncellus, *Chronographia* (page in Dindorf ed.)
TA	S. Krauss, *Talmudische Archäologie*, Vols 1–2 (Leipzig, 1910–11)
Tot. orb. descr.	*Totius orbis descriptio*
TOVÉ	*Trudy Otdela Vostoka Gosudarstvennogo Érmitazha / Travaux du Département Oriental, Musée de l'Ermitage* (Leningrad)
Treb. Poll. *Gall. duo*	Trebellius Pollio, *Gallieni duo*
Treb. Poll., *Tyr. trig.*	Trebellius Pollio, *Tyranni triginta*
TS	*Thesaurus Syriacus*, ed. R. Payne Smith, Vols 1–2 (Oxford, 1879–1901)
V.	Vinnikov 1958–65 (Russian bibliography below)
VDI	*Vestnik Drevneĭ Istorii* (Moscow)
Wadd.	Le Bas and Waddington 1870
WZKM	*Wiener Zeitschrift für die Kunde des Morgenländes* (Vienna)
ZDMG	*Zeitschrift der Deutschen Morgenländischen Gesellschaft* (Leipzig)
Zosim.	Zosimus

Bibliography

Russian Bibliography

Abamelek-Lazarev, S.S. 1884. Пальмира (Palmyra) (St Petersburg)

Amusin, I. D. 1952. 'Термины, обозначавшие рабов в эллинистическом Египте, по данным Септуагинты' (The Terms for Slave in Hellenistic Egypt according to the Data of the Septuagint), *VDI* 1952 (3), 46–67

Baziiants, A.P. 1978. 'Неопубликованные письма академика П.К. Коковцова С.С. Абамелек-Лазареву (К истории Пальмирского таможенного тарифа)' (Unpublished Letters from Academician P.K. Kokovtsov to S.S. Abamelek-Lazarev [On the history of the Palmyra Customs Tariff]), *IFZh* 1978 (1), 171–5

Borisov, A.Ĩa. 1937. 'Пальмирские тессеры Института истории Академии Наук СССР' (Palmyrene Tesserae of the History Institute of the Russian Academy of Science USSR), in A.S. Orlov (ed.), Вспомогательные исторические дисциплины (The Auxiliary Historical Disciplines) (Moscow/Leningrad), 415–18

—— 1939. 'Пальмирские тессеры Эрмитажа' (Palmyrene Tesserae of the Hermitage), TOVÉ 1, 221–7 (+ plates)

Borovskiĭ, Y.M. 1953. 'Краткий очерк греческой фонетики' (A Short Essay on Greek Phonetics), in P. Chantraine, Историческая морфология греческого языка (Historical Morphology of the Greek Language). (Moscow), 277–318

D'iakonov, I.M., M.A. Dandamaev and V.A. Livshits. 1975. 'Месяцы в древней Передней Азии' (The Months in the Ancient Near East), in E.J. Bickerman (ed.), Хронология древнего мира (Chronology of the Ancient World) (Moscow), 300–4

Dovatur, A.I. 1957. 'История изучения Scriptores historiae Augustae' (History of Research on "Scriptores historiae Augustae"), *VDI* 1957 (1), 245–56

Farmakovskiĭ, B.V. 1903. 'Живопись в Пальмире' (Art in Palmyra), *IRAIK* 8, 172–98

Kokovtsov, P.K. 1900. Открытый в Пальмире князем С.С. Абамелек-Лазаревым камень с таможенным тарифом 137 г. по Р. Хр. и необходимость приобретения его для Росии (The Trade Tariff of AD 137. Found by S.S. Abamelek-Lazarev and the Necessity of Purchasing it for Russia) (St Petersburg)

—— 1903. 'Новые арамейские надписи из Пальмиры' (New Aramaic Inscriptions from Palmyra), *IRAIK* 8, 302–29

Lipets, R.S. 1969. Эпос и древняя Русь (Epos and Ancient Rus) (Moscow)

Mashkin, N.A., 1949. Принципат Августа (Augustus' Principate) (Moscow/Leningrad)

Orbeli, R.R. 1956. 'Академик П.К. Коковцов и его рукописное наследство' (Academician P. K. Kokovtsov and his Manuscript Legacy), in Очерки по истории русского востоковедения (Studies in the History of Russian Oriental Studies 2, Moscow), 341–59

Perikhanian, A.G. 1966. 'К вопросу о происхождении армянской письменности' (On the Question on the Origin of Armenian Writing), *Peredneaziatskiĭ Sbornik* 2, 103–33

Petrov, M.I. 1857. Германик (Germanicus) (St Petersburg)

Piotrovskiĭ, M.B. 1970. 'Арабская версия истории царицы Зенобии (аз-Заббы)' (The Arabic Version of the History of Queen Zenobia [Az-Zabba]), *PS* 21, 170–84

—— 1977. Предание о химиаритском царе Ас'аде ал-Камиле (The Legend about the Himyarite King As'ad al-Kamil) (Moscow)

Ranovich, A.B. 1949. Восточные провинции Римской империи в I–III вв. (The Eastern Provinces of the Roman Empire in the 1st–3rd centuries) (Moscow/Leningrad)

Rostovtzeff, M. I. 1899. История государственного откупа в Римской империи (A History of Tax-Farming in the Roman Empire). (Memoirs of the Historical-Philological Faculty, University of St Petersburg 51) (St Petersburg)

—— 1916. 'Дело о взимании проституционной подати в Херсонесе' (On Taxes on Prostitutes in Chersonesos), *Izvestiia Imperatorskoĭ Arkheologicheskoĭ Komissii* 60, 63–9

Saverkina, I.I. 1965a. Скульптурный портрет Пальмиры II–III вв. н.э. (A Sculptural Portrait of Palmyra [2nd–3rd centuries AD]) (Leningrad)

—— 1965b. 'Портретная скульптура Пальмиры (II–III вв.)' (Portrait Sculpture of Palmyra [2nd–3rd centuries]), *SA* 1965 (1), 168–79

—— 1971. Древняя Пальмира (Ancient Palmyra) (Leningrad)

Shifman, I.S. 1965a. 'Социальная терминология в языке пальмирских надписей' (Social Terminology in Palmyrene Inscriptions), in Семитские Языки (2, i), Материалы Первой Конференции по Семитским Языкам, 26–28 Октября 1964 г. (Semitic Languages [2, i]: Papers for the First Conference on Semitic Languages, 26–28 October 1964) (2nd ed.) (ed. S. Sh. Sharbatov), 177–86

—— 'Имущественные и земельные отношения в Пальмире в I–III вв. н.э. по эпиграфическим данным' (Property and Agrarian Relationships in Palmyra in the 1st–3rd centuries A.D. according to the Epigraphic Data), *PS* 13, 100–13

—— 1966. 'Североарабское государство Лихьян' (The Northern Arabian Kingdom of Lihyan), *Epigrafika Vostoka* 17, 38–44

—— 1974. 'Заметки по эпиграфике пальмиры' (Miscellanea Epigraphica Palmyrena), *PS* 25, 87–94

—— 1977. Сирийское общество эпохи принципата (I–III вв. н. э.) (Syrian Society in the Time of the Principate) (Moscow)

Shtaerman, E.M. 1957. 'Scriptores historiae Augustae как исторический источник' (Scriptores historiae Augustae as a historical source.), *VDI* 1957 (1), 233–45

Shtaerman E.M. and M.K. Trofimova 1971. Рабовладельческие отношения в ранней Римской империи (Италия) (Slavery relationship in the early Roman Empire [Italy]) (Moscow)

Sobolevskiĭ, S.I. 1948. Древнегреческий язык (The Ancient Greek Language) (Moscow)

Vinnikov, I.N. 1958–65. 'Словарь арамейских надписей' (A Dictionary of Aramaic Inscriptions), *PS* 3–13 [series of articles] (3 [66] [1958], 171–216; 4 [67] [1959], 196–240; 7 [70] [1962], 192–237; 9 [72] [1962], 141–58; 11 [74] [1963], 189–232; 13 [76] [1965], 217–62)

I͡ankovskaia, N.B. 1968. Клинописные тексты из Кюль-Тепе в собраниях СССР (Cuneiform Texts from Kültepe in the USSR Collections) (Moscow)

Non-Russian Bibliography

Aistleitner, J. 1963. *Wörterbuch der ugaritischen Sprache* (Berlin)

Arnaud, D. 1975. 'Catalogue des textes cunéiformes trouvés au cours des trois premières campagnes à Meskéné Qadimé Ouest', *AAAS* 25, 87–93

Barthélemy, J.-J. 1759. *Réflexions sur l'alphabet et sur la langue dont on se servoit autrefois à Palmyre* (Mémoires de l'Académie des Inscriptions 26) (Paris)

—— 1789. *Voyage du jeune Anacharsis en Grèce* (Paris)

Bauer, H. and P. Leander. 1927. *Grammatik des Biblisch-Aramäischen* (Halle)

Biberstein Kazimirski, A. de. 1846. *Dictionnaire arabe-français*, I–II (Paris)

Bilgiç, E. 1945–51. 'Die Ortsnamen der "kappodokischen" Urkunden im Rahmen der alten Sprachen Anatoliens', *AfO* 15, 1–37

Birnbaum, S.A., 1952. 'The Qumran (Dead Sea) Scrolls and Paleography', *BASOR Suppl. studies* 13–14 (Chicago)

Borger, A. 1969. 'Weitere ugaritologische Kleinigkeiten (III–V)', *Ugarit-Forschungen* 1, 1–4

Bounni, A. 1967. 'En mission à Palmyre: Bilan de dix années de fouilles', *Archeologia* 16, 40–9

Bounni, A. and N. Saliby. 1968. 'Fouilles de l'annexe de l'Agora à Palmyre. Rapport préliminaire', *AAAS* 18, 93–102 (+ plates in Arabic section, 124)

Brockelmann, C. 1928. *Lexicon syriacum* (Halle)

—— 1955. *Syrische Grammatik* (Leipzig)

Cagnat, R. 1884. 'Remarques sur un tarif récemment découvert à Palmyre', *RPh* 8, 135–44

Cantineau, J. 1930a. 'Inscriptions palmyréniennes', *RAss* 27, 27–51

—— 1930b. 'Textes funéraires palmyréniens', *RB* 39, 520–51

—— 1933a. 'Tadmorea', *Syria* 14, 169–202

—— 1933b. 'Un *restitutor orientis* dans les inscriptions de Palmyre', *JA* 222, 217–33

—— 1935. *Grammaire du Palmyrénien épigraphique* (Cairo)

—— 1936. 'Tadmorea (suite)', *Syria* 17, 267–82

Capelle, A.G. van. 1817. *Dissertatio inauguralis de Zenobia Palmyrenorum Augusta* (Utrecht)

Caskel, W. 1954. *Lihyan und Lihyanisch* (Cologne)

Cellarius, Ch. 1693. *Dissertatio historica de Imperio Palmyreno* (Halle)

Chabot, J.-B. 1922. *Choix des inscriptions de Palmyre* (Paris)

Champdor, A. 1953. *Les ruines de Palmyre* (Paris)

Chantraine, H. 1967. *Freigelassene und Sklaven im Dienst der Römischen Kaiser* (Wiesbaden)

Clermont-Ganneau, Ch. 1920. 'Odeinat et Vaballat, rois de Palmyre, et leur titre Romain de corrector', *RB* 29, 382–419

Collart, P. 1961. 'Le rôle de Palmyre à l'époque hellénistique et romaine d'après les découvertes récentes', in P. Romanelli (ed.) *Atti del settimo congresso internazionale di archeologia classica* I (Rome), 427–35

Costaz, L. 1955. *Grammaire syriaque* (Beirut)

Cross, F.M. 1961. 'The development of the Jewish Scripts', in G.E. Wright (ed.), *The Bible and the Ancient Near East: Essays in Honor of William Foxwell Albright* (Garden City, NY), 133–202

Cumont, F. 1926. *Fouilles de Doura-Europos* (Paris)

—— 1928. 'L'autel palmyrénien du Musée du Capitole', *Syria* 9, 101–9

Dalman, G. 1922. *Aramäisch-neuhebräisches Handwörterbuch* (Frankfurt)

Dessau, H. 1884. 'Der Steuertarif von Palmyra', *Hermes* 19, 486–533

Dhorme, P. 1924. 'Palmyre dans les textes assyriens', *RB* 33, 106–8

Dobiáš, J. 1928. 'Cisař Hadrian v Palmyře', *Listy filologické (Folia Philologica)* (Prague) 55, 190–9

Dossin, G. 1951. 'Quelques textes inédits de Mari', in *Comptes rendus de la première rencontre assyriologique internationale* (Leiden), 19–21

Double, L. 1877. *Les Césars de Palmyre* (Paris)

Drijvers, H.J.W. 1971. *Ba'al Shamîn, de Heer de Hemel* (Assen)

Dupont-Sommer, A. 1949. *Les Araméens* (Paris)

Duval, R. 1881. *Traité de grammaire Syriaque* (Paris)

—— 1884. 'Le passif dans l'araméen biblique et le palmyrénien', *Revue des études juives* 8, 57–63

Eissfeldt, O. 1941. *Tempel und Kulte syrischer Städte in hellenistisch-römischer Zeitalter* (Leipzig)

Février, J.G. 1931a. *Essai sur l'histoire politique et économique de Palmyre* (Paris)

—— 1931b. *La religion des palmyréniens* (Paris)

Foucart, P.-F. 1882. 'Inscription de Palmyre', *BCH* 6, 439–42

Gawlikowski, M. 1970. *Monuments funéraires de Palmyre* (Warsaw)

—— 1973. *Palmyre VI. Le temple palmyrénien. Étude d'épigraphie et de topographie historique* (Warsaw)

Gesenius, W. 1910. *W. Gesenius' Hebräisches und Aramäisches Handwörterbuch über das Alte Testament*, bearbeitet von F. Buhl (Leipzig)

Gichon, M. 1963. 'The Defence of the Solomonic Kingdom', *PEQ* 95, 113–26

Goldmann, W. (= Z. Ben-Hayyim) 1935. *Die palmyrenischen Personennamen* (Leipzig)

Groag, E. 1917. 'Iulius (Marinus), nos 341–342', P.-W.*RE* 1st ser., X.1, Halbband 19, cols 670–72

Gruter, J. 1616. *Inscriptionum Romanarum corpus absolutissimus* (Heidelberg)

Guarducci, M. 1967. *Epigrafica greca* I (Rome)

Harrer, G.A. 1915. *Studies in the History of the Roman Province of Syria* (Princeton)

al-Hassani, Dj., Starcky, J. 1957. 'Autels palmyréniens découverts près de la source Efca (suite)', *AAAS* 7, 95–122 (+ plates)

Heeren, A.H.L. 1831. *Commercia urbis Palmyrae vicinarumque urbium ex monumentis et inscriptionibus illustrate* (Göttingen)

Hoftijzer, J. 1968. *Religio aramaica: Godsdienstige Verschijnselen in Aramese Teksten* (Leiden)

Hommel, F. 1879. *Die Name der Säugethiere bei den südsemitischen Völkern* (Leipzig)

Honigmann, E. 1932. 'Syria, no. 3' in P.-W.*RE* 2nd ser., IVA.2, Halbband 8, cols 1549–1727

Ingholt, H. 1928. *Studier over palmyrensk skulptur* (Copenhagen)

—— 1935. 'Five Dated Tombs from Palmyra', *Berytus* 2, 57–120

—— 1954. *Palmyrene and Gandharan Sculpture. An Exhibition Illustrating the Cultural Interrelations between the Parthian Empire and its Neighbours West and East, Palmyra and Gandhara* (New Haven)

—— 1962. 'Palmyrene inscriptions from the Tomb of Malkū', *Mélanges de l'Université St-Joseph* 38, 99–119

Abbreviations and Bibliography

Jamme, A. 1965. *À propos des rois Hadramoutiques de al-'Uqlah* (Washington)
Jean, Ch.-F. and J. Hoftijzer. 1965. *Dictionnaire des inscriptions sémitiques de l'Ouest* (Leiden)
Kappelmacher, A. 1926. 'Licinius (Mucianus), no. 116a', P.-W.*RE* XIII.1, Halbband 25, cols 436–43
Kautzsch, E. 1884. *Grammatik des Biblisch-Aramäischen* (Leipzig)
Klima, O. 1965. 'Zum Palmyrenischen Zolltarif', in *Studia semitica philologica necnon philosophica Ioanni Bakoš dicata* (Bratislava), 147–51
Kodama, S. 1961. 'A. D. 137 Nén-no 'parumira kanzeihou' ni tsuite [Japanese]' (Remarks on the Tariff of Palmyra of A.D. 137), *Shirin (Journal of History)* [Kyoto] 44: 6, 96–125
Krauss, S. 1898–9. *Griechische und lateinische Lehnwörter im Talmud, Midrasch und Targum*, vols 1–2 (Berlin)
Laet, J. de. 1949. *Portorium* (Bruges)
Leander, P. 1966. *Laut- und Formlehre des Ägyptisch-Aramäischen* (Hildesheim)
Le Bas, Ph. and H. Waddington. 1870. *Voyage archéologique en Grèce et en Asie Mineure*, Vol. 3 (Paris)
Ledrain, E. 1885. 'Quelques inscriptions palmyréniennes', *RAss* 1:ii, 73–6
—— 1888. 'Inscriptions palmyréniennes inédites', *RAss* 2:i, 23–8
—— 1889. 'Inscriptions palmyréniennes inédites', *RAss* 2:ii, 68–72
—— 1891. 'Quelques inscriptions inédites entrées au Musée du Louvre', *RAss* 2:iii, 93–5
—— 1892. 'Quelques inscriptions sémitiques du Louvre', *RAss* 2:iv, 143–5
—— 1893. 'Inscriptions sémitiques inédites', *RAss* 3:i, 27–30
Levy, J. 1924. *Wörterbuch über die Talmudim und Midraschim*, Vols 1–4 (Berlin)
Liddel, H.G. and R.A. Scott. 1961. *A Greek-English Lexicon* (Oxford)
Lidzbarski, M. 1898. *Handbuch der nordsemitischen Epigraphik*, Vols 1–2 (Weimar)
—— 1902–15. *Ephemeris für semitische Epigraphik*, Vols 1–3 (Giessen)
Littmann, E. 1905. *Semitic Inscriptions* (New York)
Löw, I. 1881. *Aramaeische Pflanzennamen* (Leipzig)
Malamat, A. 1963. 'Aspects of the Foreign Policies of David and Solomon', *JNES* 22, 1–17
Mau, A. 1899. 'Carrus', P.-W.*RE* 1st ser., III.2, Halbband 6, col. 1615.
Mesnil du Buisson, R. du. 1939. *Inventaire des inscriptions palmyréniennes de Doura Europos (32 avant J.-C. à 256 après J.-C.* (Paris)
—— 1962. *Les tessères et les monnaies de Palmyre* (Paris)
—— 1964. 'Les origines du panthéon palmyrénien', *Mélanges de l'Université Saint-Joseph* 39: 3, 167–95
—— 1966. 'Première campagne des fouilles à Palmyre', *CRAIBL* 158–90
—— 1967. 'Découverte de la plus ancienne Palmyre, ville amorite de la fin du IIIe millénaire', *Archeologia* 16, 50–1
Michałowski, K. 1966. *Palmyra* (Warsaw)
Michelini Tocci, F. 1960. *La Siria nell'età di Mari* (Rome)
Montgomery, J.A. 1913. *Aramaic Incantation Texts from Nippur* (Philadelphia)
Mordtmann, A.D. 1875. *Neue Beiträge zur Kunde Palmyras* (Sitzungsberichte der philosophisch-philologischen Classe der Bayerischen Akademie der Wissenschaften Bd. II, (Supplement-Heft III) (Munich)
Müller, D.H. 1884. 'Vier palmyrenische Grabinschriften im Besitze des Ministerial-Concipisten Herrn Dr. J. C. Samson', *Sitzungsberichte der Wiener Akademie der Wissenschaften, phil.-hist. Klasse* 108, 973–7
—— 1892. 'Palmyrenica aus dem British Museum', *WZKM* 6, 317–26
—— 1894. 'Palmyrenica aus dem British Museum II', *WZKM* 8, 11–16

―― 1898. Palmyrenische Inschriften nach Abklatschen des Herrn dr. Alois Musil (*Denkschriften der kaiserlichen Akademie der Wissenschaften zu Wien, phil.-hist. Classe* 46 [3]) (Vienna)

Müller, F. 1902. *Studien über Zenobia und Palmyra nach orientalischen Quellen* (Kirchhain)

Naveh, J. 5734 (Jewish calendar). *Hitpatḥut haktav ha'arami*. (Jerusalem) [see 1970. *The Development of the Aramaic Script*, Jerusalem.]

Nestle, E. 1883. *Syrische Grammatik* (Berlin)

Nöldeke, Th. 1875. *Mandäische Grammatik* (Halle)

Payne Smith, J. 1903. *A Compendious Syriac Dictionary* (Oxford)

Pirenne, J. 1963. 'Aux origines de la graphie Syriaque', *Syria* 40, 101–37

Pognon, H. 1907. *Inscriptions sémitiques de la Syrie, de Mésopotamie et de la région de Mossoul*. (Paris)

Preisigke, F. 1925. *Wörterbuch der griechischen Papyruskunden* (Berlin)

Reckendorf, S. 1888. 'Der aramäische Theil des palmyrenischen Zoll- und Steuertarifs', *ZDMG* 42, 370–415

Reinach, S. 1885. *Traité d'épigraphie grecque* (Paris)

Rosenthal, F. 1936. *Die Sprache der palmyrenischen Inschriften und ihre Stellung innerhalb des Aramäischen* (Leipzig)

―― 1963. *A Grammar of Biblical Aramaic* (Wiesbaden)

―― 1964. *Die aramaistische Forschung seit Th. Nöldeke's Veröffentlichungen*. (Leiden)

Rostovtzeff, M.I. 1932a. *Caravan Cities* (Oxford)

―― 1932b. 'Seleucid Babylonia', *Yale Classical Studies* 3, 1–114

―― 1932c. 'Les inscriptions caravanières de Palmyre', in *Mélanges Gustave Glotz* 2 (Paris), 793–811

―― 1933. 'Hadad and Atargatis at Palmyra', *AJA* 37, 58–63

―― 1935. 'Une nouvelle inscription caravanière de Palmyre', *Berytus* 2, 143–8

Ryckmans, J. 1964. 'Les rois de Ḥaḍramawt mentionnés à 'Uqla', *BiOr* 21, 277–89

Sachau, E. 1882. 'Edessenische Inschriften', *ZDMG* 36, 142–67

―― 1883. 'Über den palmyrenischen νόμος τελωνικός', *ZDMG* 37, 562–71

Sallet, A. von. 1866. *Die Fürsten von Palmyra unter Gallienus, Claudius und Aurelian* (Berlin)

Schlumberger, D. 1937. 'Réflexions sur la loi fiscale de Palmyre', *Syria* 18, 271–97

―― 1939. 'Bornes frontières de la Palmyrène', *Syria* 20, 43–73

―― 1951. *La Palmyrène du Nord-Ouest* (Paris)

Schröder, P. 1884. 'Neue palmyrenische Inschriften', *SBKPAWB*, 417–36

Seller, A. 1696. *The Antiquities of Palmyra Containing History of the City and Its Emperors from Its Foundation to the Present Time* (London)

Seyrig, H. 1933. 'Antiquités syriennes, 13. Le culte de Bêl et de Baalshamîn', *Syria* 14, 238–52 (whole article 238–82)

―― 1937. 'Antiquités syriennes, 20. Armes et costumes iraniens de Palmyre', *Syria* 18, 20–31 (whole article 1–53)

―― 1941a. 'Antiquités syriennes, 35. Les inscriptions de Bostra', *Syria* 22, 35–48 (whole article 31–48)

―― 1941b. 'Antiquités syriennes, 36. Le statut de Palmyre', *Syria* 22, 155–75

―― 1971. 'Antiquités syriennes, 93. Bêl de Palmyre', *Syria* 48, 85–114

Sobernheim, M. 1905. 'Palmyrenische Inschriften II', *MVAG*, 17–73

Soden, W. von. 1966. *Akkadisches Handwörterbuch* (Wiesbaden)

Spoer, H.H. 1904. 'Palmyrene Inscriptions found at Palmyra in April, 1904', *JAOS* 25, 314–19

Starcky, J. 1952. *Palmyre* (Paris)

―― 1967. 'Les grands heures de l'histoire de Palmyre', *Archeologia* 16, 30–9

Starcky, J. and C.-M. Bennett. 1968. 'Découvertes récentes au sanctuiare du Qasr à Pétra: III. Les inscriptions du téménos', *Syria* 45, 41–66
Stark, J. K. 1971. *Personal Names in Palmyrene Inscriptions* (Oxford)
Stein, A. 1929. 'Statilius, no. 3' P.-W.*RE* 2nd ser., IIIA.2, Halbband 6, col. 2185
Stein, E. 1918. 'Domitius (Corbulo), no. 50', P.-W.*RE* Supplementband III, cols 394–410
Strzygowski, J. 1901. *Orient oder Rom* (Leipzig)
Swinton, J. 1754. 'An Explication of All the Inscriptions in the Palmyrene Language and Character Hitherto Published', *Philosophical Transactions* 48:2, 690–756
Szilágyi, J. 1966. 'Zu den Statuenpreisen in der römischen Kaiserzeit', in *Corolla memoriae Erich Swoboda dedicata* (Römische Forschungen in Niederösterreich 5) (Graz-Cologne), 214–24
Tchalenko, G. 1953–8. *Villages antiques de la Syrie du Nord*. Vols 1–3 (Paris)
Teixidor, J. 1971. 'Bulletin d'épigraphie sémitique 1971', *Syria* 48, 453–93
—— 1972. 'Bulletin d'épigraphie sémitique 1972', *Syria* 49, 413–49
Thumb, A. 1901. *Die griechische Sprache im Zeitalter des Hellenismus* (Strassbourg)
Turner, E.G. 1936. 'Egypt and the Roman Empire, the δεκάπρωτοι', *Journal of Egyptian Archaeology* 22, 7–19
Vogüé, M. de. 1868–77. *Syrie centrale. Inscriptions sémitiques* (Paris)
——1883a. 'Inscriptions palmyréniennes inédites', *JA* 8th ser. 1, 231–45
—— 1883b. 'Inscriptions palmyréniennes inédites (suite)', *JA* 8th ser. 2, 149–83
Volney, C.-F. 1787. *Voyage en Syrie et en Égypte*. (Paris)
Wallace, Sh. 1938. *Taxation in Egypt from Augustus to Diocletian*. (Princeton)
Will, E. 1949. 'La tour funéraire de Palmyre', *Syria* 26, 87–116
—— 1957. 'Marchands et chefs des caravanes à Palmyre', *Syria* 34, 262–77
Wood, R. 1819. *Les ruines de Palmyre, autrement dite Tedmor au désert* (Paris)

Plates

Photographs taken by I͡a. Khouri reproduced by courtesy of the State Hermitage Museum, St Petersburg, with the generous cooperation of Elena Obukhov and Alexander Nikitin (State Hermitage Museum).

Images for two plates missing from the photgraphic archives were provided by Professor J.-B. Yon (photothèque UMR 5189 Histoire et Sources des Mondes Antiques/HiSoMA).

An attempt has been made to reproduce the best plates available corresponding to those which appeared in the Russian original. In one case (the fifth plate) it was not possible to locate the original of the picture used in Shifman's book.

Palmyrene Tariff. Panel I
(courtesy of the State Hermitage Museum, St Petersburg)

Palmyrene Tariff. Panel II
(photothèque UMR 5189 HiSoMA)

Palmyrene Tariff. Panel III
(photothèque UMR 5189 HiSoMA)

Palmyrene Tariff. Panel IV
(courtesy of the State Hermitage Museum, St Petersburg)

Palmyrene Tariff (*in situ*) before the Separation of the Panels
(courtesy of the State Hermitage Museum, St Petersburg)

Palmyrene Tariff (*in situ*, after cutting of the stone)
(courtesy of the State Hermitage Museum, St Petersburg)